Construction Law

Books are to be returned on or before
the last date below.

**7—DAY
LOAN**

LIBREX–

WITHDRAWN

D1380396

Construction Law
Liability for the Construction of Defective Buildings

Michael F. James, B.Sc. (Econ.), LL.B. (Wales), M.Sc. (London)

Lecturer in Law, University of Wales Swansea

Second Edition

palgrave

First published 2002 by
PALGRAVE
Houndmills, Basingstoke, Hampshire RG21 6XS and
175 Fifth Avenue, New York, N.Y. 10010
Companies and representatives throughout the world

PALGRAVE is the new global academic imprint of
St. Martin's Press LLC Scholarly and Reference Division and
Palgrave Publishers Ltd (formerly Macmillan Press Ltd).

ISBN 0–333–79306–4

This book is printed on paper suitable for recycling and
made from fully managed and sustained forest sources.

A catalogue record for this book is available
from the British Library.

10   9   8   7   6   5   4   3   2   1
11   10   09   08   07   06   05   04   03   02

Printed and bound in Great Britain by
Creative Print & Design (Wales)
Ebbw Vale

Contents

Preface to the First Edition

The term 'Construction Law' is used in three senses:
  (i) the principles which govern the duties and liabilities of the parties involved in the construction process and which arise out of that process;
  (ii) the law which affects the construction industry; and
  (iii) the rules governing the administration of a construction contract.

It is only the first of these senses which is Construction Law proper. Under this definition, Construction Law is that body of law which governs civil liability for the construction of defective buildings. The second two senses are not Construction Law properly defined. Thus, (ii) above would cover a range of subjects going beyond the scope of Construction Law in the first sense; it would, for example, include torts affecting the use of land, employment law and health and safety law. (iii) above is concerned with the application of the standard form contracts, such as the JCT and the ICE, to the running of a construction project and the resolution of disputes which may arise out of the project. This, in my view, is more properly referred to as 'construction contract administration' and is essentially a matter for quantity surveyors rather than lawyers.

This book is concerned with Construction Law in the first of the senses defined above. Essentially it examines three questions:

(1) Who can be sued if a building is defectively constructed?
(2) Who can sue – building owner, tenant, subsequent owner, etc.?
(3) What damages are recoverable?

This book is not, therefore, concerned with liability for matters which may arise *in the course* of building works. Rather it examines the position *after* the work is complete, and the building has been taken over.

There are, I think, three reasons why Construction Law thus defined is worthy of study as a separate branch of the law. In the first place, construction and building cases have been, and continue to be, a source of important developments in the common law. The famous (or infamous) advance and retreat of the tort of negligence and economic loss have involved largely this category of case. Secondly, liability for buildings is an important matter for the individual consumer. For the most part, buildings liability is looked on as of import for construction companies or their professional advisers. Indeed it is, but it is too often forgotten that the victim of defective building works or of unsound advice in relation thereto is an individual. To this extent, Construction Law is an aspect of consumer law. Thus, the recent retreat in the law of negligence has had particularly serious effects for the consumer; it is contract which is now the major source of liability for defective buildings, but in many cases concerning domestic buildings the purchaser will not have a contract with the builder or designer. Thirdly, many recent and forthcoming developments in Construction Law now emanate from the EC. These developments have as their aims the promotion of competition throughout the Community and the protection of the consumer.

The major sources of the general law of construction are common law, statute, private law (i.e., the provisions of any of the standard form building and engineering contracts which may apply to a particular contractual relationship) and, as mentioned in the previous paragraph, EC law. There is no shortage of books on the standard form building and engineering contracts and no independent chapters are devoted to that aspect of Construction Law. Instead, attention is devoted to the relationship between contract and tort and the effect of changes in that relationship upon liabilities in the construction industry and its related professions. Thus, a separate chapter is devoted to collateral warranties and buildings insurance as a result of the impact of the decision in *Murphy* v. *Brentwood DC*. Throughout the book the need for the law to find a balance between professional and consumer interests in the area of civil liability for defective buildings is kept uppermost in mind.

The parameters to Construction Law, as in other areas of law, are set by the appellate courts in the landmark cases. But how those parameters are applied falls usually to the judges at first instance. In the field of Construction Law these judges are known as Official Referees. They are High Court judges with a specialist knowledge of this subject, and it is one of the purposes of this book to examine carefully their most important decisions.

One final point by way of introduction needs to be made. This is not intended to be a book for a beginner. It is intended principally for use by students reading Construction Law as a specialist subject in the later stages of their degree. As such, it assumes a knowledge of the principles of contract and tort. (It is worth stressing at this point the importance of mastering these subjects, without which more specialist areas of law cannot hope to be understood. Not for nothing are contract and tort among the 'core' legal subjects demanded by the Law Society and the Bar Council!) Nor is this intended to be a practitioner's work, though it is hoped that some practitioners will find in it stimulation to debate further the problematical issues raised by this subject.

The law is as stated at 1 March 1994.

M.F.J.   *Swansea/University of Surrey*

Preface to the Second Edition

My aim in writing this second edition is the same as in writing the first: it is to set out the principles which govern the duties and liabilities of the parties involved in the construction process and which arise out of that process. It is, in essence, a work on liability for the construction of defective building works *after* their completion and as such it is an applied work on the law of obligations.

It is now seven years since the first edition of this book was published. During that time a number of developments have occurred in the general law of contract and tort which have an important bearing on Construction Law. In addition, several reports have been published proposing reforms which would affect key areas of this subject.

In the first place, the appeal courts in Canada, New Zealand and Australia have declined to follow the exclusionary rule governing negligence and economic loss laid down by the House of Lords in *D & F Estates* v. *Church Commissioners for England* [1988] 2 All ER 992 and *Murphy* v. *Brentwood District Council* [1990] 2 All ER 908. These Commonwealth decisions highlight the problematical nature of this area and the importance of the policy considerations which underly it. The New Zealand case in point, *Invercargill City Council* v. *Hamlin* [1994] 3 NZLR 513 went to the Privy Council, who refused to overturn the decision of the New Zealand Court of Appeal.

In the UK, there have been a number of decisions of the House of Lords governing professional negligence and concurrent liability in contract and tort. The decisions in *Henderson* v. *Merrett Syndicates* [1995] 2 AC 145, *Spring* v. *Guardian Assurance* [1995] 2 AC 296, and *White* v. *Jones* [1995] 2 AC 267 have given a new lease of life to *Hedley Byrne* v. *Heller* liability, and they have important implications for the liability of construction professionals, though they leave intact the exclusionary rule in relation to third party liability in negligence.

In the area of contract law, further decisions on the reasonableness test in the Unfair Contract Terms Act 1977 and the decision of the House of Lords in *Ruxley Electronics* v. *Forsyth* [1995] 3 All ER 268 on the extent of the damages recoverable by a building owner for defective building have meant an expanded discussion of the contractual obligations of the building contractor.

The advent of the Unfair Terms in Consumer Contracts Regulations 1994/99, based on the EU Directive of this name, has led me to introduce a new chapter into this work. These Regulations affect standard form contracts made between businesses and consumers. The novel concepts of unfairness and good faith introduced into our law by these Regulations are so radical that I believe they merit their own chapter. They cannot be dismissed as outside the realm of Construction Law.

Since publication of the first edition, the Law Commission has produced its report on privity of contract (*Privity of Contract: Contracts for the Benefit of Third Parties*, Law Com. No. 242, Cmd. 3329, 1996). The proposals contained in this report have now been incorporated into law by the Contracts (Rights of Third Parties) Act 1999. No area of law more than Construction Law has been so dramatically affected by this reform and I have remodelled and renamed the chapter on collateral warranties as a consequence. As well as statutory reform, there have been several reported cases on the issue of whether the employer can recover substantial damages from the contractor for loss sustained by a third party, most notably *Alfred McAlpine Construction Ltd* v. *Panatown Ltd* [2000] 4 All ER 97.

In the field of professional negligence, there have been a number of reported decisions on the *Bolam* standard. However, the most important decision for valuers is that of the House of Lords in *Banque Bruxelles Lambert SA* v. *Eagle Star Insurance Co. Ltd* AC 191 [1997], which determines the extent of liability of negligent valuers acting for lenders. Construction professionals frequently act as adjudicators or arbitrators in the resolution of disputes in the construction industry. Their role in this respect is likely to be much affected by the Human Rights Act 1998. In incorporating these developments I have taken the opportunity to expand the chapters on design professionals and surveyors.

The steady, if not relentless, flow of judicial authority and legislation since publication of the first edition has not stayed pressure for reform. The report of Sir Michael Latham (*Constructing the Team*, HMSO, 1994) contains proposals for reform of joint liability, limitation of action and latent defects insurance. The Law Commission has produced a recent consultation paper on limitations of actions (Law Commission Consultation Paper No. 151, 1998) and in 1996 the DTI published an investigation of joint and several liability by the Common Law Team of the Law Commission. These proposals, together with the passing of the Contracts (Rights of Third Parties) Act 1999, have meant a major overhaul of the chapter on reform.

There has been little progress of late on the proposals emanating from the European Union for the harmonisation of construction liability and the proposal for a Directive on the liability of suppliers of services has been dropped. As a consequence, there is no longer a separate section of the book devoted to European Construction Law. Instead, the harmonisation proposals have been incorporated into the chapter on reform and there is a separate chapter on construction products liability.

The one aspect of Construction Law to remain unchanged since publication of the first edition is the exclusionary rule in relation to third party liability for economic loss resulting from negligence. Essentially, this area of law rests upon policy rather than legal rationale, a point recognised by the commentary on the Canadian decision of *Winnipeg Condominium Corporation No. 36* v. *Bird Construction Co. Ltd.* in the Building Law Reports:

> Most developed societies are mobile. Therefore a purely contractual liability for defective work is always likely to be of limited utility. Most societies identify a community. Therefore the interest of the community in a well-constructed housing stock is a legitimate policy aim. Most societies value prevention of danger. Therefore the costs of rectifying a dangerous defect which has not yet caused harm should be recoverable.
> (1995) 74 BLR 5

As with the first edition, special thanks are due to Roy and Valerie Anthony for their word processing. Their patience and skill with a chaotic manuscript have not declined with the years and Roy's attention to detail (including footnote numbering!) has been invaluable.

This edition is dedicated to the memory of our cat, Toby (1982–2000).

The law is stated on the basis of materials available to me on 31 January 2001.

M.F.J.   *Swansea*

Acknowledgements

Extracts from *The Law Reports* and *The Weekly Law Reports* are reproduced by permission of the Incorporated Council of Law Reporting for England and Wales.

Extracts from *The All England Reports* and *Emden's Construction Law* are reproduced by permission of The Butterworths Division of Reed Elsevier (UK) Limited.

Extracts from the *Building Law Reports* are reproduced by permission of Pearson Education Limited.

Extracts from the *Construction Law Reports* are reproduced by permission of Professor M.P. Furmston (ed.).

Extracts from the *Lloyd's Reports* are reproduced by permission of LLP Professional Publishing.

Extracts from the *Estates Gazette Law Reports* are reproduced by permission of egi.co.uk.

Extracts from the JCT 98 Standard Form of Building Contract are reproduced by permission of the copyright holders,© JCT Ltd.

The extract from J.R. Spencer, *The Defective Premises Act 1972 – Defective Law and Defective Law Reform* [1974] CLJ 307 is reproduced by permission of the author and M.J Prichard, editor of the *Cambridge Law Journal*.

The extract from Jon Holyoak and David Allen, *Civil Liability for Defective Premises* is reproduced by permission of David Allen and The Butterworths Division of Reed Elsevier (UK) Limited.

Crown copyright material is reproduced with the permission of the Controller of Her Majesty's Stationery Office.

Material in the author's articles in *Professional Negligence* is used by permission of Tolley.

Abbreviations

AC	Law Reports, Appeal Cases
ACE	Association of Civil Engineers
All ER	All England Reports
ALR	Australian Law Reports
Bing.	Bingham's Court of Common Pleas Reports, 1822–34
BLM	Building Law Monthly
BLR	Building Law Reports
CBNS	Common Bench Reports, New Series, 20 vols, 1856–65
Ch.	The Law Reports, Chancery Division
CILL	Construction Industry Law Letter
Cl&F	Clark and Finnelly's Reports, House of Lords, 12 vols, 1831–46
CLJ	Cambridge Law Journal
CLY	Current Law Year Book
Cmnd/Cmd	Command Paper
Co Litt	Coke on Littleton (1 Inst)
Con. LR	Construction Law Reports
Const. LJ	Construction Law Journal
DC	District Council
DoE	Department of the Environment
DTI	Department of Trade and Industry
EC	European Community (sometimes referred to as the EEC – European Economic Community)
EG	Estates Gazette
EGCS	Estates Gazette Case Summaries
EGLR	Estates Gazette Law Reports
EU	European Union (formerly European Community)
ICE	Institution of Civil Engineers
J	Justice
JCT	Joint Contracts Tribunal
KB	The Law Reports, King's Bench Division
Law Com.	Law Commission Report
LBC	London Borough Council
LJ & LJJ	Lord Justice, Lord Justices
LQR	Law Quarterly Review
LR Ex	Law Reports, Exchequer Division, 5 vols, 1875–80
MBC	Metropolitan Borough Council
MLR	Modern Law Review

MR	Master of the Rolls
M&W	Meeson and Welsby's Reports, Exchequer, 16 vols, 1836–47
NLJ	New Law Journal
NZLJ	New Zealand Law Journal
OJ	Official Journal of the European Communities
OJC	Official Journal of the European Communities: Information and Notices
OJL	Official Journal of the European Communities: Legislation
PII	Professional Indemnity Insurance
PN	Professional Negligence
QB	The Law Reports, Queen's Bench Division, 1952–
RIBA	Royal Institute of British Architects
RICS	Royal Institution of Chartered Surveyors
SI	Statutory Instrument
SLT	Scots Law Times
Stark	Starkie's Reports, Nisi Prius, 3 vols, 1814–23
Term Rep.	Term Reports, King's Bench, 1785–1800
UDC	Urban District Council
US	United States Reports
WLR	The Weekly Law Reports

Table of Cases

Table of Statutes and Statutory Instruments

UK and Commonwealth legislation

EU legislation

Other legislation

1

Builders' Liability in Contract

INTRODUCTION

Before examining in detail the potential liability of a builder for defective premises, two things must be made clear: the complexity of many building projects and the nature of the contract entered into by the builder.

A building project, especially a large one, involves a number of parties and, consequently, a network of contractual relationships. The person who commissions the work, usually on land over which he has rights of occupation or ownership, and who acquires the building when it is completed, is referred to as the building owner or the employer, or sometimes the client. The person who undertakes the work is referred to as the builder or the contractor, or the building contractor. In a large building project the legal relationship between the building owner and the contractor is known as the main contract. If a builder builds on land which he owns and then sells the building, he is known as a vendor/builder. In addition, it is usual for a number of other parties to be involved in a large project. Firstly, an architect or engineer will be employed by the building owner to design the project. The important point to note here is that such architect or engineer is in a contractual relationship with the building owner, not the contractor. In some cases the contractor will design as well as build the works or subcontract the design to an architect or engineer. The legal relationship between the building owner and contractor is then known as a design and build contract. Secondly, it is usual for the contractor to subcontract parts of the work to specialist firms. These subcontractors each have a contract with the main contractor; they do not have a contract with the building owner unless they provide him with a warranty, e.g. as to the quality of the works. Thirdly, there are suppliers, who supply the contractor with materials and components. The relationship between the contractor and each of his suppliers is that of a contract for the sale of goods. In order to retain control over the cost and quality of the works, the building owner may retain the power under the main contract to direct the contractor to employ particular subcontractors and use particular suppliers. In these circumstances the subcontractors and suppliers are referred to as nominated subcontractors and suppliers.

The above network of relationships is that which obtains in a traditional building project. However, an increasingly common feature of the building

1

industry is the use of what is known as a management contract. The main feature of this kind of contract is that there is a management contractor who carries out little or no construction work himself but subcontracts it, and organises and co-ordinates the work of the subcontractors. Architects or engineers will be engaged by the employer as in the conventional procedure.[1] A variation on this form of contract is the construction management contract. The management contractor in a construction management contract does not enter into contracts with subcontractors. The construction work is carried out under a series of contracts made between the employer and specialist contractors. It is the role of the management contractor under this form of contract to supply management and other professional services to the employer.

It is important to note that the first purchaser or lessee of a building may not be in contract with the builder, e.g. where a developer has employed a building contractor to develop a particular site and then leased the completed building. In these circumstances it is the builder who is in contract with the developer. Where a person buys land and a building from a vendor/builder, he will have a contract with the builder. Such a contract is known as a contract for the sale of land and it is based on the principle of *caveat emptor*. That is, there is no warranty as to quality implied on the part of the builder and the purchaser must satisfy himself as to the condition of the building through a surveyor's inspection.[2]

This chapter, however, is not principally concerned with contracts for the sale of completed buildings; rather it is concerned with contracts for the erection of works, e.g. a contract for the erection of a supermarket or a house on land already owned by the employer. The essence of this sort of contract is that the contractor agrees to supply work and materials for the erection of a building or other works for the benefit of the employer. It is an example of a type of contract known as a contract for work and materials.

Building contracts impose a wide range of obligations on the contractor. It must be emphasised that this chapter is concerned only with contractual liabilities for defects in the building; other aspects of construction contracts such as delay, frustration, etc. are outside its scope.[3] In other words, the subject matter of this chapter is the contractual obligations of the builder for the quality and safety of the works he constructs. We shall also be concerned with the remedies available to the employer in the event of the contractor being in breach of those obligations and whether or not the contractor can effectively exclude or limit his liability for such breach.

One final point needs to be made by way of introduction. The discussion so far has concerned commercial building contracts where both employer and contractor are contracting by way of trade or business. However, many building contracts are of a domestic nature; i.e. the employer is not a business such as a public company but a private individual employing a building contractor, and possibly an architect and subcontractors, to erect a domestic dwelling on his land or, more probably, to carry out repairs or improvements to an existing dwelling. There is no distinct set of common law or statutory rules concerning quality and safety which apply to such domestic building contracts; the principles governing these matters are the same whether or not the employer or building owner is a business. Two important legal differences between commercial building works and domestic building works must, however, be pointed out. In the first place, commercial building works are likely to be conducted under written standard forms of contracts which set out fully the rights and obligations of the parties to such contracts. In the case of domestic building works the construction industry does not usually employ pre-formulated contracts and a domestic building contract may frequently be wholly or partly oral. The result is that the parties' obligations under a domestic building contract are contained largely in common law or statute, rather than in the express terms of the contract. The second important difference relates to the fact that a domestic building contract is a form of consumer contract. As a consequence any clauses in a domestic building contract excluding or restricting the liability of the contractor under the contract are subject to a more rigorous degree of statutory control, in the form of the Unfair Contract Terms Act 1977, than such clauses in a commercial construction contract. In addition, if a domestic building contract consists of the contractor's standard form terms which are not negotiated with the employer/building owner, then any unfair terms in the contract are subject to the control of the Unfair Terms in Consumer Contracts Regulations 1999.[4]

THE CONTRACTOR'S OBLIGATIONS

The essence of a construction or building contract is that the building contractor supplies work and materials to the building owner or employer. So goods and services are supplied under such a contract, but its main purpose or substance is the provision of services and the supply of goods is of secondary importance. This contrasts with a contract of sale, where the substance of the contract is the production of something to be sold.

The core obligation imposed upon the building contractor is that he must ensure that the quality and safety of the building work meet the required standard. This standard is defined by reference to: (1) the express terms of the contract; and (2) the implied terms.

(1)   Express terms

Express terms are the terms agreed upon by the parties to the contract. Such terms may be oral, written or partly oral and partly written. Contracts in the construction industry generally involve complex arrangements with many difficult points of procedure which have to be provided for. As a result the contractual terms will invariably all be set down in writing. Indeed the industry has gone one stage further and has evolved standard forms of contract for use in large projects. The one most frequently used for building projects is the standard form of building contract published by the Joint Contracts Tribunal (the JCT).[5] The standard form of contract most frequently used for engineering projects is the one published by the Institution of Civil Engineers (the ICE).[6] Essentially, these contracts are bodies of private law governing the relationships of the parties to them. They are enforceable in the courts in that it is a basic principle of English contract law that, subject to certain exceptions, the parties to a commercial project may make any arrangement they wish governing that project, without regard to fairness or equity.

The provisions of the JCT and ICE relating to the contractor's obligations for quality and safety are to be found in the clauses on workmanship and materials and the statutory obligations of the contractor in relation to design.

Workmanship and materials

The contractor's express obligations with regard to workmanship and materials are contained in clauses 2 and 8 of the 1998 JCT form. The essence of these obligations is that the contractor must erect the building as specified in the contract and subject to the approval of the architect and carry out the work in a proper and workmanlike manner. Thus, clause 2.1 provides as follows:

> The Contractor shall upon and subject to the Conditions carry out and complete the Works in compliance with the Contract Documents, using materials and workmanship of the quality and standards therein specified, provided that where and to the extent that approval of the quality of materials or of the standards of workmanship is a matter for the opinion of the Architect/Contract Administrator such quality and standards shall be to the reasonable satisfaction of the Architect/Contract Administrator.

Clause 8.1 states:

> 8.1.1   All materials and goods shall, so far as procurable, be of the kinds and standards described in the Contract Bills, ... provided that [they] shall be to the reasonable satisfaction of the Architect/the Contract Administrator where and to the extent that this is required in accordance with clause 2.1.
>
> 8.1.2   All workmanship shall be of the standards described in the Contract Bills, ... or, to the extent that no such standards are described in the Contract Bills, ... shall be of a standard appropriate to the Works, provided that workmanship shall be to the reasonable satisfaction of the Architect/the Contract Administrator where and to the extent that this is required in accordance with clause 2.1.
>
> 8.1.3   All work shall be carried out in a proper and workmanlike manner and in accordance with the Health and Safety Plan.

Clause 8 goes on to provide that the contractor may be called upon by the architect to vouch that these obligations have been complied with; however, clause 8.2.2 requires the architect to express any dissatisfaction with any materials, goods or workmanship comprised in the work within a reasonable time. The architect can demand that completed work be uncovered and inspected or that tests be carried out on the materials used in the works to assess their quality. If the work or materials are below the standard required by the contract then the contractor will have to pay for them; in other cases the cost is added to the contract price. In the event of default the architect can order removal of work or materials that fail to meet contractual specifications and at any time he may reasonably order the dismissal of any person or firm employed on the site.[7]

The provisions of the ICE relating to workmanship and materials are contained in clauses 36–39. Under the provisions of clause 36(1) all materials and workmanship must be of the kind described in the contract and in accordance with the engineer's instructions. The engineer has the power to order that tests be carried out, either at the place of manufacture or on site. Clause 38(1) states that no work may be covered up without the consent of the engineer and the contractor must allow the engineer to examine and measure any work which is about to be covered up.

Clause 38(2) permits the engineer to order uncovering of work and provides for apportioning the cost. Under the provisions of clause 39(1), if the materials used are not in accordance with the contract, the engineer has the power to order their removal from the site and he can require the contractor to substitute materials which are in accordance with the contract. If the contractor defaults on the obligations, then under the provisions of clause 39(2) the employer is entitled to employ other persons to carry them out and recover the cost of so doing from the contractor.

Design

The liability of the builder under the general law for defects in the design is still not entirely clear, though it is probable that he has a duty to bring to the attention of the architect or engineer any obvious errors in the design of which he has actual knowledge.[8] The duties of the builder under the JCT form in this regard are somewhat clearer.[9] Firstly, under the provisions of clause 2.3 he has an express duty to give the architect written notice of any discrepancy or divergence between the Contract Drawings, the Contract Bills and other documents issued by the architect. Secondly, under the provisions of clause 6.1 he must comply with the Building Regulations.[10] This imposes a heavy onus on him, but it is alleviated by saving provisions in clause 6.1. Under these provisions, if the builder does find any divergence between the Building Regulations and the contractual specifications then he must give written notice to the architect.[11] The architect then has seven days from receipt of this notice to issue instructions regarding the works to be varied accordingly.[12] Clause 6.1 goes on to state that provided that the contractor has complied with its provisions he is not liable if the works do not comply with the Building Regulations.[13]

(2)   Implied terms

The common law has always implied a number of terms into a contract for building works:

(1)   that the contractor will carry out this work in a good and workmanlike manner;
(2)   that any materials supplied by him will be of good quality and reasonably fit for their purpose; and
(3)   that in the case of a dwelling house, it will be fit for human habitation.[14]

These terms are imposed on the parties by law, regardless of whether they intend them to be included in the contract. The implied terms relating to work and materials are now in statutory form, and are contained in the Supply of Goods and Services Act 1982. It should be noted that this Act does not replace the common law obligations, and the case law on this subject is therefore still of great importance.

Workmanship

As a general rule, there is an implied duty of care and skill imposed on the contractor requiring him to exercise the skill and competence required of an ordinarily competent building contractor. One of the earliest authorities for this rule is *Harmer* v. *Cornelius*,[15] where it was held that an employee owed an obligation to his employer to carry out his duties under his contract of employment with a reasonable degree of skill. This implied duty is now contained in section 13 of the Supply of Goods and Services Act 1982, which provides that in a contract for the supply of a service where the supplier is acting in the course of a business, there is an implied term that the supplier will carry out the service with reasonable care and skill.

In addition, it appears that there is an implied term that the completed building will be reasonably fit for any purpose for which the contractor knew it would be required. Fitness for purpose is a greater obligation than the duty of reasonable care and skill; it is an obligation of strict liability.

Authority for an implied term of fitness for purpose is to be found in two cases, *Greaves & Co. (Contractors) Ltd* v. *Baynham Meikle and Partners*[16] and *Independent Broadcasting Authority* v. *EMI Electronics Ltd and BICC Construction Ltd*.[17]

In *Greaves*, contractors agreed to design and construct a warehouse and office for a company who intended to use the warehouse as a store for oil drums. The oil drums were to be kept on the first floor and moved into position by fork-lift trucks. The contractors engaged structural engineers to design the structure of the warehouse and they told the design engineers the purpose for which it was required. The engineers in their design did not take into account the effect of the vibrations from the fork-lift trucks. The result was that, when the warehouse was completed, the floor cracked under the weight of the oil drums and the trucks. The building contractors sued the engineers for breach of an implied warranty that the floor would be fit for the purpose for which they knew it was required. The Court of Appeal held that the engineers were liable. In the course of his judgement Lord Denning discussed the obligations of the building contractors. He said:

> The owners made known to the contractors the purpose for which the building was required, so as to show that they relied on the contractor's skill and judgement. It was therefore the duty of the contractors to see that the finished work was reasonably fit for the purpose for which the building was required. It was not merely an obligation to use reasonable care.[18]

IBA v. *EMI & BICC* concerned a contract to erect a TV mast. *EMI* was the main contractor; *BICC* were subcontractors responsible for the design of the mast. In bad, though not exceptional, weather conditions the mast collapsed, after just three years in service. The Court of Appeal held that there was an implied term in the contract that the mast should be fit for its intended purpose, i.e. that it should be able to withstand likely weather conditions in the area where it was built. The House of Lords upheld this finding on the ground that EMI's obligations to IBA extended to the design of the mast. The fact that BICC had been negligent in the design of the mast was no defence.

These two cases have attracted a great deal of comment and a word of caution about their effect is necessary. Both cases arose on particular facts and they did not involve the commonly found relationship between designers, contractors and employers. In *Greaves*, the contract was a design and build contract; in *IBA* v. *EMI & BICC*, it was the subcontractor who carried out the design. Neither case can be taken as authority for the general imposition of an implied term as to fitness for purpose into contracts for work and materials. In other words, such a term arises only in fact, not in law.[19] This view of the law was confirmed by the Court of Appeal in *George Hawkins* v. *Chrysler (UK) Ltd and Burne Associates*.[20] Further, the Law Commission has concluded that no immediate reform in this area of the law is necessary.[21]

Materials

As we have seen, the building contractor must ensure the materials which he uses for the building work and which he thereby supplies to the building owner must meet the express requirements of the contract in terms of description, quality and fitness. In the absence of any express specification as to these matters, the materials must meet the standards set by the implied terms. These terms are contained in sections 3–5 of the Supply of Goods and

Services Act 1982 and they are modelled on the terms implied in contracts of sale by the Sale of Goods Act 1979. The origin of the implied terms, in contracts of sale and contracts for work and materials, however, lies in the common law. Neither the 1979 Act nor the 1982 Act displaces the common law in this area and the common law may still be instructive in ascertaining the exact nature of the standards set by the implied terms.

The common law

At common law, a person contracting on the basis of work and materials impliedly warrants that the materials will be of good quality and reasonably fit for their purpose, unless he can show that the purchaser did not rely on his skill and judgement. Authority for the implication of these warranties in building contracts is provided by the cases of *Young & Marten Ltd* v. *McManus Childs Ltd*[22] and *Gloucestershire County Council* v. *Richardson*.[23]

In *Young & Marten*, building contractors subcontracted roofing work and specified that the subcontractors were to use a particular kind of tile known as 'Somerset 13'. The tiles had a latent defect which caused them to disintegrate within a few years. The House of Lords held that the subcontractors were liable in damages for breach of the implied warranty that the materials supplied be of good quality, even though the person to whom they had supplied them had nominated the source of supply. There was, however, no implied warranty as to fitness in this case because the materials were chosen by the main contractors and therefore they did not rely on the skill and judgement of the subcontractors in that respect.

In *Gloucestershire County Council* v. *Richardson* under a contract to build an extension to a college, the contractors were obliged to obtain concrete columns from suppliers nominated by the employer. The columns suffered from latent defects. The House of Lords held that the contractors were not liable for these defects. There were two particular factors which influenced their Lordships in coming to that decision. Firstly, very detailed specifications were laid down by the employer. Secondly, the contractor was obliged by his contract with the employer to purchase materials on terms which excluded certain of the manufacturer's normal liabilities. This decision does appear to be an exception to the general rule that the contractor will be held liable in most instances for defects in the materials which he supplies, even when they are not of his choosing. The opening statement of Lord Pearce's speech can be taken as authority for this view:

> ... the contractor in any particular field of business, when he engages to do certain work and supply materials, impliedly warrants that the materials will be of good quality, unless the particular circumstances of the case show that the parties intended otherwise.[24]

Liability for breach of the warranties as to quality and fitness is strict; it is no defence for the builder to say that he took all reasonable care. This point is well illustrated by *Hancock* v. *B.W. Brazier (Anerley) Ltd.* In that case the defendant developed an estate of houses. Within four years of completion three of the houses developed serious cracking of the walls and floor. This was found to be due to the presence of sodium sulphate in the hardcore. When exposed to moisture, this expands, causing the concrete to crack. At first instance, it was held that although this characteristic of sodium sulphate was known at the time when the estate was developed, it was not thought as likely to happen in the ordinary course of building a house. The builder was therefore not negligent. None the less, he was held to be in breach of the implied terms of quality and fitness.

The imposition of these implied terms may seem rather harsh on the builder. The House of Lords explained their rationale in *Young & Marten* by saying that the subcontractor could sue his supplier under what is now section 14(2) of the Sale of Goods Act 1979 for breach of the implied term as to merchantable quality under their contract of sale. That supplier could then sue his supplier under this provision. He was probably the manufacturer of the tiles, so that by this chain of contractual litigation liability would ultimately come to rest upon the party at fault.[25] This is the classic contractual model of product liability. It may be thought that it would be more efficient to allow the party at the end of the chain to sue the manufacturer direct. That is possible, following the decision of the House of Lords in *Donoghue* v. *Stevenson,* [26] where the defect in the product has led to personal injury or damage to other property. But where the loss suffered is simply to have acquired a poor quality product, one whose actual value is less than the price paid for it, the courts have clung rigidly to the classic model of litigation, saying that to allow otherwise would be to circumvent the doctrine of privity of contract. In practice, the chain of product liability may break down because of insolvency or the existence of a valid exclusion clause in one of the contracts.[27]

Supply of Goods and Services Act 1982

The implied obligations of the contractor in relation to the materials used are now contained in Part I of the Supply of Goods and Services Act 1982 ('the 1982 Act'). The common law obligations in this respect are very similar to, if not identical with, the obligations imposed upon the seller in a contract for the sale of goods.[28] However, it was felt that from the point of clarity of the law and in order to put the matter beyond doubt, the obligations should be cast in statutory form to conform as near as possible to those in a contract of sale.[29] It is the purpose of Part I of the 1982 Act to do that. Part I does not merely apply to contracts for work and materials; it extends to a whole range of contracts where goods are supplied but which are not contracts of sale in the strict meaning of that term.[30] It is based on the concept of a contract for the transfer of property in goods. These are defined by the 1982 Act as contracts under which one person transfers or agrees to transfer to another the property in goods (section 1(1)). Contracts for the sale of goods, hire-purchase agreements and contracts for the sale of land are excluded from this definition (section 1(2)). A normal building contract is clearly within the scope of this definition because the builder transfers the property (i.e. ownership) of the materials he uses to the building owner.

The obligations imposed upon the supplier are contained in sections 2–5 of the 1982 Act. They are paralleled on the obligations imposed on the seller in a contract of sale by the Sale of Goods Act and are as follows:

(a) *An implied condition relating to title*
     The transferor has the right to transfer the property in the goods (section 2(1)), and he impliedly warrants that the goods are free from charges or encumbrances not disclosed or known to the transferee before the contract is made and that the transferee will enjoy quiet possession of the goods (section 2(2)).

(b) *An implied condition relating to description*
     The goods transferred must correspond with their description (section 3(2)). If the transferor transfers or agrees to transfer the property in the goods by sample as well as by description, it is not sufficient that the bulk of the goods correspond with the sample if the goods do not also correspond with the description (section 3(3)). There is still a transfer by description if the goods are selected by the transferee (section 3(4)).

(c) An *implied condition relating to quality*
     By section 4(2) where the transferor transfers the property in goods in the course of a business, there is an implied condition that the goods supplied under the contract are of satisfactory quality. Section 4(3) states that there is no such implied condition
     (i)   as regards defects specifically drawn to the transferee's attention before the contract is made; or
     (ii) if the transferee examines the goods before the contract is made, as regards defects which that examination ought to reveal.

Thus, in a contract for work and materials there are two circumstances where the implied term as to satisfactory quality does not apply. The first is where a defect is specifically drawn to the building owner's attention before the contract is made. The second is where the building owner, or more realistically the architect which he employs, examines the materials before the contract is made and that examination ought to have revealed the defect which makes the materials of unsatisfactory quality.

The key question in this area of law concerns the precise scope and meaning of satisfactory quality. This has always been, and remains, a matter of some uncertainty. The implied term as to quality was first given statutory form by the Sale of Goods Act 1893. That Act (which is now the Sale of Goods Act 1979) applies only to contracts for the sale of goods. The implied term as to quality in that Act referred originally to merchantable quality. Essentially, this was a term of commerce; under the common law goods were of merchantable quality if they were resaleable and fit for their purpose. In 1973 a statutory definition of merchantable quality was introduced which said that goods were of merchantable quality if they were fit for the purpose or purposes for which goods of that kind were commonly supplied as it is reasonable to expect having regard to any description applied to them, the price (if relevant) and all the other relevant circumstances.[31]

This definition was felt by many, particularly consumer organisations, not to be detailed enough and in 1987 the Law Commission recommended that the implied term of merchantable quality be replaced by one of satisfactory quality.[32] Their recommendation was put into effect by the Sale and Supply of Goods Act 1994 which amended both the Sale of Goods Act 1979 and the Supply of Goods and Services Act 1982 in respect of the implied term as to quality.

In contracts for the transfer of property in goods the definition of satisfactory quality is contained in section 4(2)(A) of the 1982 Act. This section provides that goods are of satisfactory quality if they meet the standard that a reasonable person would regard as satisfactory, taking account of any description of the goods, the price (if relevant) and all the other relevant circumstances.[33]

This statutory definition does not replace the considerable body of common law which has grown up on the subject over the last century. Indeed recourse to this body of law is essential for a full understanding of the many facets of this implied term. The common law in question concerns contracts of sale. A detailed analysis of the scope of satisfactory quality is a subject for a text on commercial or consumer law, not one on construction law.[34] But the main principles governing this subject, derived from common law and the new statutory definition introduced in 1994, may be summarised as follows. The fundamental principle is that goods are of satisfactory quality if they meet the standard that a reasonable person would regard as satisfactory. It is clear that this principle includes the standard of a reasonable consumer buyer as well as the standard of non-consumer buyer who intends to resell the goods. The fact that the contractor may supply building materials which are fit for their purpose may not be sufficient to satisfy this standard. The building owner can legitimately expect the materials to be of satisfactory finish, appearance, etc. as well as functionable. This has been made clear by the Court of Appeal in *Rogers* v. *Parish (Scarborough) Ltd*[35] in the context of the sale of a new Range Rover. The Court of Appeal stressed that it was incorrect to conclude that because a vehicle was capable of starting and being driven in safety from one point to another it must necessarily be of merchantable quality. Mustill LJ said:

> one would include in respect of any passenger vehicle not merely the
> buyer's purpose of driving the car from one place to another but of doing

so with the appropriate degree of comfort, ease of handling and reliabil-
ity and, one might add, of pride in the vehicle's outward and interior
appearance.[36]

Applying this dictum to a construction contract, the contractor in supplying
bricks, for example, would be under an obligation to ensure that the bricks
were not only satisfactory in ensuring that they were of sufficient thickness,
damp-proof etc., but were also of the appearance appropriate to the building.

The statutory definition of satisfactory quality makes it clear that this
concept cannot be divorced from description, price and all the other relevant
circumstances. Thus, the exact assessment of what the building owner may
expect in terms of satisfactory quality must depend on any description of the
building or the materials contained in the contract. Thus the building owner
cannot reasonably expect brick which is to be covered up by rendering or
plaster to be of the same standard as brick described as, say, 'facing brick'.

In terms of price, the general rule is that the higher the price of the materials the higher the standard to be expected of them. The relationshhip of price
and description to satisfactory quality was emphasised by the Court of Appeal
in *Rogers* v. *Parish (Scarborough) Ltd*, where Mustill LJ stated:

> In the present case the vehicle was sold as new. Deficiencies which might
> be acceptable for a secondhand car were not to be expected in one pur-
> chased as new. Next, the description 'Range Rover' would conjure up a
> particular set of expectations, not the same as those relating to an ordi-
> nary saloon car, as to the balance between performance, handling,
> comfort and resilience. The factor of price was also significant. At more
> than £14,000 this vehicle was, if not at the top end of the scale, well
> above the level of an ordinary family saloon. The buyer was entitled to
> expect value for his money.[37]

'All other relevant circumstances' is a provision which makes it clear that
the concept of satisfactory quality is a relative and not an absolute one. In particular, it is closely linked to the contract specification; the higher the standard of the materials expressly required by the contract the more that can be
expected of them in terms of the implied obligation of satisfactory quality.

The statutory definition of satisfactory quality in Part I of the Supply of
Goods and Services Act 1982 makes no reference to the issues of safety and
durability. The common law, however, lays down that in a contract of sale
safety is an important aspect of quality. Thus in *Lee* v. *York Coach &
Marine*,[38] the Court of Appeal held that a second-hand car was not of merchantable quality because it was unsafe to drive. A contractor, therefore, is
under an obligation to ensure that the materials he supplies are safe.

Durability is a more problematical issue. In contracts of sale, particularly
consumer contracts of sale, the relationship between quality and durability
has never been satisfactorily determined. For the purposes of sale, the Sale of

Goods Act now requires goods to be durable before they can be of satisfactory quality. This provision has not been extended to contracts for the transfer of property in goods, but the common law is not silent on this matter. In *Lambert* v. *Lewis*, Lord Diplock stated:

> I do not doubt that [quality] is a continuing warranty that the goods will be fit for their purpose for a reasonable time after delivery, so long as they remain in the same apparent state as that in which they were delivered, apart from normal wear and tear. What is a reasonable time will depend upon the nature of the goods.[39]   [p. 276]

The essential feature of this dictum is that durability is seen as an aspect of quality, not as a separate obligation.

An interesting illustration of the continuing nature of the obligations as to quality and fitness in the context of builders' materials is provided by *Lee* v. *West*.[40] In that case a builder contracted to provide an electronically operated up-and-over door for the plaintiff's garage. For this purpose the builder selected a lintel from a manufacturer's brochure. Some two and a half years after the contract was completed the lintel deflected, damaging the brickwork. Remedial work had to be carried out, and the plaintiff sought the cost of this work from the builder. The Court of Appeal held that even though the builder had not been negligent in selecting the lintel or in attaching it to the garage door, he was liable for breach of the implied terms as to quality and fitness contained in section 4 of the 1982 Act. Thus far the case is unremarkable. The interesting point raised by it is that the Court of Appeal accepted the fact that the lintel had failed *after two and a half years* as evidence that it was unfit *at the time of sale*. So it seems clear that durability, although not part of the definition of satisfactory quality contained in the 1982 Act, is an aspect of quality in building contracts.[41]

(d) *An implied condition of fitness for purpose*
Where the transferor transfers the property in goods in the course of a business and the transferee, expressly or by implication, makes known to the transferor any particular purpose for which the goods are being acquired, there is an implied condition that the goods supplied under the contract are reasonably fit for that purpose, whether or not that is a purpose for which such goods are commonly supplied (sections 4(4) and (5)). There is no obligation of fitness for purpose where there was no reliance upon the skill and judgement of the contractor in the choice of those materials (section 4(6)).

There are thus three provisos to the obligation of fitness for purpose in a construction contract:

(1) the building owner must make known to the contractor the particular purpose for which the materials are supplied;

(2) the building owner must rely on the contractor's skill and judgement in the choice of materials;[42] and

(3) it must be reasonable for the building owner to rely on the contractor's skill and judgement in this matter.

It is often the case in a construction contract that the materials used are specified by the employer, after he has sought the advice of his architect. As a consequence it has frequently been a matter of doubt as to whether the necessary requirement of reliance can be found in a construction contract in order for this implied duty to apply. This issue came before the Court of Appeal in *Rotherham Metropolitan Borough Council* v. *Frank Haslam Milan & Co. Ltd and M.J. Gleeson (Northern) Ltd.*[43]

In 1979, Rotherham as employer engaged Haslam as contractors to carry out Phase I of the site preparation and construction of a new five storey office building, known as Norfolk House to be used by Rotherham. Phase I involved site preparation and some foundation work. Gleeson were employed as contractors to construct Phase II of the development, that is, the remaining foundations of the superstructure. Both contracts were governed by the JCT standard form of building contract (1977 edition) under which the materials used were specified in the Bill of Quantities and were subject to the approval of the Architect. These were, therefore, traditional tripartite forms of construction contract. The contractors were employed to prepare the site and the foundations according to the contract specifications. The quality of the work and of the materials used was subject to the approval of an architect, who was engaged by Rotherham, the employer.

The contracts with Haslam and Gleeson specified that hardcore used for the foundations 'shall be graded or uncrushed gravel, stone, rock fill, crushed concrete or slag or natural sand or a combination of any of these.' The hardcore used by the contractors contained steel slag. This material was approved by Rotherham's staff. Unknown to any of the parties, it proved an expansive, rather than an inert, material and this resulted in cracking in the reinforced concrete slabs of the office block. In February 1979 the Building Research Establishment published a digest pointing out that steel slag possessed expansionary properties and that it was not suitable for fill or hardcore purposes. The evidence established that neither the architect nor the staff of Rotherham were aware of this research.

The major issue in the Court of Appeal was whether the contractors were liable to Rotherham for failing to supply hardcore which was fit for its purpose. The Court of Appeal held that they were not. All the judgements emphasise that the crucial question in this matter was whether the wording of the contract and the surrounding circumstances showed that the employer relied on the contractors' skill and judgement. The Court of Appeal held that the circumstances showed that Rotherham did not rely on the contractors' skill and judgement so that the implied duty of fitness did not apply. The judgement of Ward LJ Identifies the following factors which were considered to be relevant in this respect.

1. There was no express requirement that the materials to be placed around the foundations should be inert because the employer believed, albeit erroneously, that all slag was inert.
2. In deciding the question of reliance the comparative experience and knowledge of the contracting parties, the architects and engineers, the suppliers of the material and the producers of the material, are all relevant. Neither Rotherham nor Rotherham's architects were aware in 1979 of the expansive properties of steel slag, but, said Ward LJ, the opportunity for them to acquire that knowledge was there and was not beyond their competence.
3. The factor which justifies the imposition of liability on the contractor is his ability to pass on that responsibility down the chain of liability so that ultimate responsibility comes to rest with the producer. However, in this case the chain of liability had obviously weak links. There was no nominated supplier and at the time when the contract was made the employer would not have known from whom the contractor would obtain the hardcore. Ward LJ thought it unrealistic to expect the contractors to rely on the skill and knowledge of the supplier to point out the little known property of steel slag to expand and so be unfit for its purpose because in a steel town like Rotherham that supplier might be a demolition constructor.
4. The reality in this case was that the architects and engineers assumed the responsibility for the whole design and specification of the work. They specified hardcore to include steel slag because they thought that such slag was suitable for the purpose. They trusted to their own knowledge rather than relying on the contractor.

The decision in *Rotherham* applies the reasoning of the House of Lords in *Young & Marten* and, to that extent, it does not break new ground. In so far as the implied warranty of fitness in a construction contract depends on reliance by the employer on the contractor's skill and judgement, whether or not such reliance exists, is as much a question of fact as of law. The significance of the Court of Appeal's decision lies in its detailed consideration of the tripartite JCT contractual nexus which existed in this case. It seems that if the employer wishes to ensure that the implied warranty of fitness is not excluded in these circumstances then he must lay down a very detailed contractual specification for the materials to be used. *Rotherham* also highlights the difference between the implied duties of fitness and quality. Goods or materials may be unfit for a particular purpose but still be of merchantable quality. The steel slag could not be used as an *inert* hardcore, but it could still command a good price as hardcore.

(e) *An implied condition relating to sample*
     By section 5 where the transferor transfers or agrees to transfer the prop-
     erty in the goods by reference to a sample there is an implied condition –
     (a) that the bulk will correspond with the sample in quality;
          and
     (b) that the transferee will have a reasonable opportunity of comparing
          the bulk with the sample; and
     (c) that the goods will be free from any defect, rendering them unmer-
          chantable, which would not be apparent on reasonable examination
          of the sample.

Before leaving the subject of the implied statutory terms, two points concerning their general nature must be made. In the first place, the implied obligations in sections 2–5 of the 1982 Act are, with the exception of the obligation
contained in section 2(2), *conditions.* This has an important implication: in
the event of the supplier being in breach of one or more of these obligations,
however minor the breach, the transferee can elect either to reject the goods
and claim damages or accept the goods and claim damages. The remedies for
breach of statutory condition in non-consumer cases, however, are modified
by section 5A. This section provides as follows:

'(1) Where in the case of a contract for the transfer of goods –
     (a) the transferee would, apart from this sub section, have the right to
          treat the contract as repudiated by reason of a breach on the part of
          the transferor of a term implied by section 3, 4 and 5(2) (a) or (c)
          above, but
     (b) the breach is so slight that it would be unreasonable for him to do so,
          then, if the transferee does not deal as consumer, the breach is not to be
          treated as a breach of condition but may be treated as a breach of warranty.
(2) This section applies unless a contrary intention appears in, or is to be
     implied from, the contract.
(3) It is for the transferor to show that a breach fell within subsection (1) (b)
     above.'[44]

    Section 5A means that an important difference exists between consumer
and non-consumer building contracts in terms of the remedies available to the
building owner in the event of the builder being in breach of the implied
statutory obligations. In the case of a consumer building contract, the builder
owner may reject the materials supplied, however slight the breach. In the
case of non-consumer building contracts, where the builder can establish that
the breach is so slight that it would be unreasonable for the building owner to
reject the materials supplied, the building owner's only remedy is damages.
This provision, in effect, imports the common law innominate term approach
to express terms into the area of implied terms. This means that the question
of whether or not a breach of these obligations would enable a (non-con-

sumer) transferee to terminate the contract would depend on whether the breach deprived him of substantially the whole benefit which it was intended he should obtain under the contract.[45] There is a policy reason for this importation: namely to prevent non-consumer transferees from using a technical breach of an implied condition as an excuse to escape from what turns out to be a commercially bad bargain.[46] It must be emphasised that in the case of building contracts the effect of section 5A may be of little practical relevance where the breach of an implied obligation does not become apparent until after the materials have become incorporated into the building structure. In that eventuality, rejection is a purely theoretical remedy and the building owner's only recourse will be to claim damages, whether or not he acts as a consumer.

By contrast to the implied obligations in sections 2–5, the implied obligation in section 13 of the 1982 Act is a *term*; i.e. it is not classified as a condition or as a warranty. This means that the courts are free to treat this implied obligation as innominate.

The second aspect of the general nature of the implied terms which must be examined is the standard of liability which pertains to them. Here again there is a marked contrast between sections 2–5 and section 13. Liability for breach of sections 2–5 is strict; i.e. it is not dependent on the transferor failing to exercise reasonable care and skill.[47] However, the standard of liability which applies to section 13 is a negligence standard; the supplier of a service is liability of breach of the implied term in section 13 only if it can be shown by the recipient that he failed to exercise the standard of care which could reasonably be expected of a competent supplier in the business or profession concerned. These variable standards of liability can mean considerable uncertainty in defective building works where it is unclear as to whether the cause of the defect is defective materials or defective workmanship or both.

As previously stated, the implied obligations in sections 2–5 of the 1982 Act are modelled on sections 12–15 of the Sale of Goods Act. However, no attempt has been made to reproduce the provisions of sections 34 and 35 of the Sale of Goods Act, which set out the circumstance in which the buyer is deemed to have accepted the goods, thereby converting all conditions to warranties and depriving him of his right to reject the goods. Arguably, in the absence of these provisions the common law doctrine of affirmation applies to contracts for the transfer of property in goods. However, there is no authority on this point and this does create uncertainty concerning the remedies of the building owner.

The contractor's duty to warn[48]
We have seen that in a design and build contract the builder is under a duty to see that the building is fit for any purpose made known to him. We have

also seen that, under the conventional JCT form of building contract, where the builder is aware that the design does not comply with the Building Regulations he is under an express duty to bring that fact to the attention of the architect. The question for consideration in this section of the chapter is whether in the conventional tripartite form of building contract there is a duty under the general law on the builder to warn the employer of any defects in the design which he has reason to believe may exist. The cases appear to be in conflict on this matter.

In *Duncan* v. *Blundell,*[49] the plaintiff erected a stove in the defendant's shop and laid a tube under the floor to carry off smoke, but the plan failed entirely. Bayley J said:

> Where a person is employed in a work of skill, the employer buys both his labour and his judgement; he ought not to undertake the work if he cannot succeed, and he should know whether it will or not; of course it is otherwise if the party employing him choose to supersede the workman's judgement by using his own.

In *Lynch* v. *Thorne*[50] a builder constructed, as specified, a solid brick wall of a house without rendering. This allowed rain to enter the house. The Court of Appeal held that there was no implied term that the walls would be water-proof and that the builder was not liable for the defect. The rationale of this decision was expressed by Lord Evershed in the following terms:

> if two parties elect to make a bargain which specifies in precise detail what one of them will do, then, in the absence of some other express pro-vision, it would appear to me to follow that the bargain is that which they have made; and as long as the party doing the work does that which he has contracted to do that is the extent of his obligation.[51]

The *Lynch* v. *Thorne* approach to the duty to warn issue was not followed in the Canadian case of *Brunswick Construction Ltd* v. *Nowlan.*[52] In 1962 Brunswick Corporation entered into a contract with Dr *Nowlan*, for the con-struction of a house in accordance with drawings and a specification prepared for Dr Nowlan by a firm of architects. The contract contemplated the appoint-ment of an engineer to supervise the execution of the work but no one was appointed to perform that function. After the house had been built and occu-pied, leaks developed in the roof which required extensive major repairs. The cause of the problem was the design, which did not contain sufficient provi-sion for ventilation of the roof space and timbers, with the result that the house became seriously affected by rot. Ritchie J, giving the majority judge-ment of the Supreme Court of Canada, held that a company of the experience of Brunswick Corporation should have detected that the design of the house was bad. As the house owner did not appoint an architect or engineer to supervise the works then he must be taken to have relied entirely on the skill of the contractors. The contractors must have known of this reliance and they were therefore under a duty to warn the house-owner of the defects in the architect's design. Ritchie J then went to say that the contractors' obligation was to carry out work which would perform the intended duty or function, and that obligation overrode the obligation to comply with the plans and specifications. Dickson J, in his dissenting judgement, said that the building contractor could not be expected to have detected the design errors. He thought that there was no warranty implied in the contract that the house be reasonably fit for the purpose for which it was required: namely, human habitation.

With one exception, recent English decisions at first instance have followed the reasoning in *Brunswick* rather than that in *Lynch* v. *Thorne*. In *Equitable Debenture Assets Corporation Ltd (EDAC)* v. *William Moss Corp. Ltd*,[53] Judge Newey held that there was an implied term in a contract requiring contractors to inform their employer's architect of any defects in the design of which they knew. In *Victoria University of Manchester* v. *Hugh Wilson*,[54] it was held that this duty extended to defects which the builders believed to exist.

In *University of Glasgow* v. *William Whitfield & John Laing (Construction) Ltd*,[55] however, Judge Bowsher followed the reasoning in *Lynch* v. *Thorne*. He said that where there is a detailed contract, together with plans produced by an architect, there is no room for the implication of a duty to warn about possible defects in design. He suggested that there are two circumstances in which a term may be implied requiring a contractor to warn a building owner of defects in the design: firstly, where there is a special relationship between the parties so that the contractor knows that the building owner is relying upon him; and secondly, where the builder undertakes to achieve a particular purpose or a function.

In *Lindenberg* v. *Canning*,[56] Judge Newey held that a builder was in breach of his duty of reasonable care and skill in circumstances where he simply obeyed his employer's instructions, which proved defective. The judge, however, reduced the damages awarded to the employer by 75 per cent on the ground of his contributory negligence.

Judge Newey's approach to the duty to warn issue seems, to the author, to be more satisfactory than that of Judge Bowsher. If the employer does give exact specifications to the builder, that surely does not mean that he would not rely on the builder to warn him of any defects in those specifications. Indeed in *Department of National Heritage* v. *Stienson Varming Mulcahy*,[57] the Official Referee explicitly recognised a duty to warn on the part of the builder. He said that contractors have a duty to warn the design team immediately it becomes apparent that elements of the design indicate a lack of buildability.

In *Plant Construction plc* v. *Clive Adams Associates*,[58] the duty of contractors to warn their employers of dangers in the construction works was considered by the Court of Appeal. The court held that the contractor usually owes an obligation to the employer to exercise the skill and care expected from an ordinarily competent contractor. The factual extent of this duty depends on all relevant circumstances. In the case of a dangerous defect of which the contractor was aware, this duty extended to giving the employer proper warnings about the risk. The court did not disapprove of the decisions in *Lindenberg* v. *Canning* and *Brunswick Construction* v. *Nowlan*, but they did not say whether the duty to warn extended to circumstances where the contractor did not know, but should have known, that the design was dangerous or defective.

EXCLUSION OF LIABILITY[59]

It is common to find a clause in a contract whereby one party who would otherwise be under a certain liability in relation to that contract seeks to exclude or limit that liability. These clauses are frequently found in standard form contracts, though there is no such clause in the JCT or ICE forms. However, it is always open to a contractor to vary those forms to include an exclusion or limitation clause. In a domestic building contract the contractor may well seek to exclude or limit his liability under the contract.

Exclusion and limitation clauses are controlled both by the common law and by statute in the form of the Unfair Contract Terms Act 1977 (UCTA) and the Unfair Terms in Consumer Contracts Regulations 1994, which are discussed in Chapter 2.

The common law controls these clauses and notices by requiring that to be effective they must meet certain conditions. In the first place, it must be shown that they have been incorporated into the contract, or in the case of a non-contractual notice, that they have been brought to the attention of the other party. Secondly, assuming that the clause has been incorporated into the contract (or the notice brought to the other party's attention), it must adequately cover the breach of contract or tort in question. The Act does not replace these rules and they continue to be of importance, for two reasons: firstly, because some very important classes of contract are outside the scope of the Act altogether; and secondly, because where the Act provides that an exclusion clause is valid if reasonable, the recipient of the clause may argue:

(a) that it has not been incorporated into the contract; or
(b) that, on its true construction, the clause does not cover the breach in question, in which case it is ineffective even if reasonable.

However, it is UCTA which is now the most important form of control and it is to that Act which most attention must be devoted.

The scope of the Act

The title of the Act is misleading in two respects. Firstly, it is not confined to contractual terms; it imposes limits on the extent to which civil liability for breach of contract and for negligence can be excluded or limited by contract terms or notices. Secondly, it is not concerned with contract terms that may be thought 'unfair', but only with clauses that exclude or restrict liability and indemnity clauses.

The concept of an exclusion clause is given an extended definition by section 13(1) of the Act, and the following types of terms are caught by the Act:

(a) a term making the liability or its enforcement subject to restrictive or onerous conditions;

(b) a term excluding or restricting any right or remedy in respect of the liability, or subjecting a person to any prejudice in consequence of his pursuing any such right or remedy; and

(c) a term excluding or restricting rules of evidence or procedure.

Section 13(1) also prevents the restriction or exclusion of liability by the exclusion or restriction of the relevant obligation or duty. Thus, a disclaimer to the effect that no responsibility is undertaken for, say, the contents of a report would be caught by the Act.[60] The courts, in general, look to the substance and effect of a clause rather than its form in order to determine whether it is an exclusion clause.[61]

The Act covers only business liability, i.e. liability for things done by a person in the course of a business or which arise from his use of premises for business purposes. There is no definition of 'business' in the Act but section 14 provides that 'business' includes a profession and the activities of any government department or local or public authority.

The provisions of the Act

The provisions of the Act are of immense importance for business and for the professions because it imposes severe restrictions on the effective use of exclusion clauses. Under the basic scheme of the Act these clauses can be divided into three categories:

(a) clauses which are not allowed to operate at all;

(b) clauses which, in order to be legally effective, must satisfy a statutory test of reasonableness; and

(c) clauses not covered by the Act.

The detailed provisions of the Act are best examined in relation to the areas of liability which they concern.

Negligence liability

Negligence is defined by section 1 of the Act as the breach not only of a duty of care imposed by the law of tort, but also of one arising out of contract. It also includes the breach of the duty owed by the occupier of premises to his lawful visitors under the Occupiers' Liability Act 1957. Under the provisions of section 2(1) any attempt to exclude liability for death or personal injury is rendered ineffective. Under the provisions of section 2(2) any attempt to exclude liability for 'other loss or damage' is also ineffective, except where the term or notice satisfies the requirement of reasonableness. 'Other loss or damage' includes damage to property and financial loss. It should be noted that if a contractor does seek to rely on a clause or term excluding his liability for negligence, he will not be permitted to argue the doctrine of *volenti non fit injuria*. This is because, under the provisions of section 2(3), a person's agreement to or awareness of such a term cannot of itself be taken as indicating his voluntary acceptance of any risk.

Liability arising in contract

Under the provisions of section 3 of the Act, where a person deals as a consumer or on the other's written standard terms of business, the other cannot by reference to any contract term:

(a)   when himself in breach of contract, exclude or restrict any liability of his in respect of the breach; or
(b)   claim to be entitled
  (i)   to render a contractual performance substantially different from that which was reasonably expected of him, or
  (ii) in respect of the whole or any part of his contractual obligation, to render no performance at all,

except in so far as the contract term satisfies the requirement of reasonableness in these respects.

There is no definition of 'written standard terms of business' in section 3, or in any other part of UCTA. Further, there is no English appellate authority on the meaning of this concept, though it has been considered by the Scottish Outer House in *McCrone* v. *Boots Farm Sales Ltd*,[62] and by the High Court (Official Referee's Business) in *The Chester Grosvenor Hotel Company Ltd* v. *Alfred McAlpine Management Ltd*.[63]

In *McCrone,* Lord Dunpark said that although he did not attempt to formulate a comprehensive definition of a standard form contract, its meaning was not difficult to comprehend. In relation to section 17 of the Act, which applies in Scotland, he said:

> the section is designed to prevent one party to a contract from having his contractual rights, against a party who is in breach of contract, excluded or restricted by a term or condition which is one of a number of fixed terms or conditions invariably incorporated in contracts of the kind in question by the party in breach, and which have been incorporated in the particular contract in circumstances in which it would be unfair and unreasonable for the other party to have his rights so excluded or

restricted. If the section is to achieve its purpose, the phrase 'standard form contract' cannot be confined to written contracts in which both parties use standard forms. It is, in my opinion, wide enough to include any contract, whether wholly written or partly oral, which includes a set of fixed terms or conditions which the proponer applies, without material variation, to contracts of the kind in question.[64]

In *The Chester Grosvenor Hotel* the plaintiffs, Grosvenor, were the owners of the Chester Grosvenor Hotel, a luxury hotel. They engaged the defendants, McAlpine, as management contractors on two refurbishment contracts in 1984 and 1985. The form of these contracts was devised by McAlpine. One of the questions for consideration was whether McAlpine's management contract fell within the meaning of 'written standard terms of business'. In considering this matter Judge Stannard relied on Lord Dunpark's dictum. He said:

What is required for terms to be standard is that they should be regarded by the party which advances them as its standard terms and that it should habitually contract in those terms. If it contracts also in other terms, it must be determined in any given case, and as a matter of fact, whether this has occurred so frequently that the terms in question cannot be regarded as standard, and if on any occasion a party has substantially modified its prepared terms, it is a question of fact whether those terms have been so altered that they must be regarded as not having been employed on that occasion.[65]

The judge concluded that the two management contracts in question were entered into on McAlpine's written standard terms of business.

The interesting question for the construction industry is whether the JCT and ICE forms come within the scope of section 3. There is no binding authority on this question and the two leading academic works on Construction Law appear to differ on it. In the view of the editor of *Keating on Building Contracts* the use of a JCT or ICE form would not fall into the category of written standard terms because they are 'compromise' contracts drawn up by bodies representative of all branches of the construction industry, including employers.[66] However, the editors of *Emden's Construction Law* take the view that the provisions of section 3 do not prevent a set of standard terms from coming within their scope merely because they are the standard terms of the other party.[67] The author inclines to the view of *Keating*, for two reasons. Firstly, it is consistent with the general philosophy of UCTA, which is to protect contracting parties from having exclusion clauses imposed upon them; the JCT and ICE forms are freely negotiated contracts. Secondly, it accords with the approach to standard form contracts adopted by the EC Directive on unfair terms in consumer contracts:

A term shall always be regarded as not having been individually negotiated where it has been drafted in advance and the consumer has therefore not been able to influence the substance of the term.[68]

The supply of goods

Where the possession or ownership of goods passes under a contract which is not a contract of sale, then under the provisions of section 7(2), as against a person dealing as consumer, liability in respect of the implied terms of description, quality, fitness and sample cannot be excluded. However, where the supplier deals with a person who is not a consumer, then under the provisions of section 7(3) that liability can be excluded if the requirement of reasonableness is satisfied. Clearly, contracts for the transfer of property in goods as defined in Part I of the Supply of Goods and Services Act 1982, such as a contract for work and materials, are within the scope of section 7. Thus, a builder engaged by a consumer would not be able to exclude his liability for the quality, fitness, etc. of the materials he uses. On the other hand, a builder engaged by another business may exclude such liability if reasonable.

The concept of 'dealing as consumer' is defined in section 12 of UCTA. This section states that a party to a contract 'deals as a consumer' in relation to another party if:

(a) he neither makes the contract in the course of a business nor holds himself out as doing so; and
(b) the other party does make the contract in the course of a business; and
(c) in the case of a contract for the sale of goods or hire purchase, or a contract for the supply of goods, the goods passing under the contract are of a type ordinarily supplied for private use or consumption.

This definition has not proved entirely satisfactory, as it is not clear from the wording whether or not it covers the case of the business person who buys an article for use in his business but whose business does not deal in that article. The test adopted by the courts for deciding this question is whether the purchase is an integral part of the buyer's business; if so, then the buyer does not deal as a consumer within the meaning of UCTA. Thus, in *R & B Customs Brokers Co. Ltd* v. *United Dominions Trust Ltd*,[69] the Court of Appeal held that the acquisition of a car for the use of a director of a shipping brokerage did not require the company to be treated as a consumer within the meaning of UCTA. This approach was adopted in *The Chester Grosvenor Hotel*, where the judge had to decide whether Grosvenor had 'dealt as a consumer'. He held that they had entered into the management contracts as an essential part of its business of providing luxury hotel facilities. Therefore, these contracts were an integral part of Grosvenor's business and in entering them it did not 'deal as a consumer'.

The requirement of reasonableness

The one area of doubt in this area of the law is the precise meaning of the requirement of reasonableness. The Act itself provides only limited guidance on this point. Thus, section 11(1) provides that a term will satisfy the require-ment of reasonableness if it is a fair and reasonable one to be included in the contract having regard to the circumstances which arose, or ought reasonably to have been known to or in the contemplation of the parties when the con-tract was made. In the case of a non-contractual notice, section 11(3) states that it should be fair and reasonable to allow reliance on it having regard to all the circumstances obtaining when the liability arose or (but for the notice) would have arisen. Under the provisions of section 11(5) the burden of proving that a contract term satisfies the requirement of reasonableness rests upon the party who claims that it is reasonable.

In relation to contracts for the sale and supply of goods, Schedule 2 to UCTA provides the courts with a (non-exhaustive) list of guidelines to follow when assessing reasonableness. They are:

(a) the strength of the bargaining positions of the parties relative to each other, taking into account (among other things) alternative means by which the customer's requirements could have been met;

(b) whether the customer received an inducement to agree to the term, or in accepting it, had an opportunity of entering into a similar contract with other persons, but without having to accept a similar term;

(c) whether the customer knew or ought reasonably to have known of the existence and extent of the term (having regard, among other things, to any custom of the trade and any previous course of dealing between the parties);

(d) where the term excludes or restricts any relevant liability if some condition is not complied with, whether it was reasonable at the time of the contract to expect that compliance with that condition would be practicable;

(e) whether the goods were manufactured, processed or adapted to the special order of the customer.

The exact meaning of reasonableness in relation to sections 2(2) and (3) of UCTA has been left to the courts to work out. Gradually, a number of guide-lines emerged as cases on this issue have come before the courts.

One of the first of these cases is *Photo Production Ltd* v. *Securicor Ltd.*[70] The plaintiffs, who were factory owners, entered into a contract with the defendants under which the defendants contracted to guard the plaintiffs' factory at night. The defendants' employee who was guarding the factory lit a fire which burnt down the factory. The plaintiffs sought to recover from the defendants damages of £648,000. The defendants in defence sought to rely on an exemption clause in the contract which stated that, 'under no circum-stances' were they 'to be responsible for any injurious act or default by any employee ... unless such act or default could have been foreseen and avoided by the exercise of due diligence on the part of the defendant'. The House of Lords held that this clause must be given its ordinary plain meaning.

Although the defendants were in fundamental breach of contract, the exemption clause on its plain wording was wide enough to cover the breach that had occurred and the defendants were not liable, therefore, for the damage.

In general terms, the House of Lords in this case took a non-interventionist approach to the operation of exemption clauses. This approach is set out in the following passage in the speech of Lord Wilberforce:

> After this Act, in commercial matters generally, when the parties are not of unequal bargaining power, and when risks are normally borne by insurance, not only is the case for judicial intervention undemonstrated, but there is everything to be said, and this seems to have been Parliament's intention, for leaving the parties free to apportion the risk as they think fit and for respecting their decisions.[71]

In *George Mitchell (Chesterhall) Ltd* v. *Finney Lock Seeds Ltd*,[72] the fairness and reasonableness of an exemption clause in a contract for the supply of cabbage seed was considered. The appellants, seed merchants, supplied the respondents, farmers, with Dutch winter cabbage seed for £201.60. The contract was concluded on the basis of the suppliers' standard terms which contained a clause limiting their liability in the event of the seed proving to be defective to the cost of replacing the seed or repaying the price. The seed supplied was of an inferior variety with the result that the crop failed. The farmers were awarded £61,513.78 damages by the trial judge. The Court of Appeal dismissed the suppliers' appeal and their decision was upheld by the House of Lords.

In his judgement, Lord Denning said that it would not be fair and reasonable to allow the seed merchants to rely on their limitation clause. His judgement sets out three reasons for reaching this conclusion:

(a) The clause was not negotiated between persons of equal bargaining power. It was inserted by the seed merchants in their invoices without any negotiation with the farmers.
(b) The seed merchants rarely, if ever, invoked the clause.
(c) The buyers had no opportunity at all of knowing or discovering that the seed was not cabbage seed, whereas the suppliers could and should have known that it was the wrong seed. The buyers were not insured against the risk. Nor could they insure. By contrast, the suppliers could have obtained insurance without any substantial rise in the price of seeds.

Lord Denning's judgement was upheld by the House of Lords.

In the consolidated appeals of *Smith* v. *Bush* and *Harris* v. *Wyre Forest District Council*, Lord Griffiths identified a range of factors which would be relevant to assessing the reasonableness or otherwise of terms and notices seeking to exclude or limit liability for damage to property or economic loss resulting from negligence. Strictly speaking, these guidelines are concerned with the reasonableness or otherwise of disclaimers in mortgage valuation reports, but there seems to be no reason why they will not be capable of a wider application.

The guidelines are as follows:

(a) the relative bargaining strengths of the parties;
(b) the availability of alternative sources of advice;
(c) the difficulty of the professional task involved; and
(d) the practical consequences of the decision, in particular the effect on insurance.

(a) *Relative bargaining strengths*

Where the parties are of unequal bargaining strengths, as in *Smith* v. *Bush* and *Harris*, this will point to an exclusion clause or notice disclaiming liability as being unreasonable. Conversely, where the recipient of such a clause or notice is a business, and the parties are deemed to be of equal bargaining power, the courts are much more likely to uphold the clause or notice as reasonable.

(b) *The availability of alternative sources of advice*

In *Smith* v. *Bush* and *Harris,* the House of Lords thought that it would not be fair to require a purchaser of a domestic property at the lower end of the market to pay twice for the same advice, by his having to commission his own independent survey of the property in question. On the other hand, in the case of commercial properties and very expensive houses with very large sums of money at stake, the House of Lords thought that prudence would require a purchaser to obtain his own structural survey and, in such circumstances, it may be reasonable for the surveyors valuing on behalf of a building society or finance company to include or limit their liability to the purchaser. The wider corollary from this would seem to be that where advice is given to a firm or company with a disclaimer attached, reliance on the disclaimer by the adviser may well be reasonable.

(c) *The difficulty of the professional task*

Lord Griffiths said that the task of mortgage valuation was not a difficult one, since only defects which are observable by a careful visual examination have to be taken into account. Obviously, therefore, where a professional person undertakes a complex task in the course of his profession, this may be a factor pointing to the reasonableness of any exclusion or limitation of liability in his report.

(d) *The availability of insurance*

Lord Griffiths recognised that holding the disclaimers in the mortgage valuation reports concerned to be unreasonable was likely to lead to an increase in surveyors' insurance premiums which would be passed on to the public. However, he felt that it was better to distribute the risk of negligence among all house purchasers through an increase in fees rather than to allow the whole of the risk to fall upon a few unfortunate purchasers.

The upshot of these judicial developments would seem to point to the conclusion that in a non-negotiated contract between a business organisation and a consumer, an exclusion clause will not pass the reasonableness test. However, the application of the reasonableness test in a business to business contract is never beyond doubt, a point illustrated by *Edmund Murray Ltd* v. *BSP International Foundations Ltd*.[73] A small firm of piling contractors, EML, ordered a drilling rig from BSP. The rig was manufactured according to EML's special orders and the contract contained express terms that the rig would comply with its specification. The contract also contained clauses excluding the seller's liability if the rig proved 'defective by reason solely of faulty materials or workmanship', limiting the seller's liability to the cost of repairing or replacing the defective rig in the event of faulty workmanship or materials, and prohibiting outright the recovery of damages for consequential loss. The rig proved unsuitable for the specific function for which it was required and which the seller promised he would perform. The seller argued that he was protected by the above exemption clauses. The Court of Appeal held that these clauses did not satisfy the statutory test of reasonableness, for the following reasons:

(a) the rig was specially ordered;
(b) the specification contained precise details of required technical standards;
(c) EML made known to BSP the purpose for which they required the rig; and
(d) the guarantee was restricted to faulty workmanship or materials.

The Court of Appeal said that in such circumstances it was not fair or reasonable to allow BSP to deprive EML of all redress for breach of the express terms.

The contract in *Edmund Murray* was a one-off contract. In standard form contracts concluded between businesses of equal bargaining strength the courts are much more likely to uphold as fair and reasonable an exemption clause. Thus, in *Monarch Airlines Ltd* v. *London Luton Airport Ltd*[74] the defendant, London Luton Airport Ltd, owned and operated Luton Airport, and the plaintiff, Monarch Airlines Ltd, owned and operated aircraft at Luton Airport. Luton Airport Ltd's standard conditions of use contained the following clause:

> 10. Neither the Airport Company nor its respective servants/agents shall be liable for loss or damage to the aircraft ... occurring while the aircraft is in the course of taking off at the Airport ..., arising or resulting directly or indirectly from any act, omission or neglect or default on the part of the Airport Company or its servants or agents.

One of the issues in the case was whether this clause satisifed the reasonableness test in UCTA and, therefore, operated to exclude the defendant's duty of care to the plaintiff under s.2 of the Occupiers' Liability Act 1957. Clarke J held that clause 10 was a fair and reasonable term to include in the contract. The following passage in his judgment sets out the rationale underlying that decision:

> [the clause] was generally accepted in the market, including the insurance market. Indeed, so far as I am aware, there has been no suggestion in the market (whether it be from the airlines, the airports or the insurers) that the clause be amended in any way. It was accepted by the plaintiff without demur. It has a clear meaning and the insurance arrangements of both parties could be made on the basis that the contract was governed by standard terms which had already been held to be reasonable in principle.[75]

In *Schenkers Ltd* v. *Overland Shoes Ltd*,[76] the plaintiffs were English members of a worldwide network of freight forwarding companies and the defendants were substantial operators in the shoe trade. The parties contracted under the standard conditions of the British International Freight Association (BIFA) which provided *inter alia*:

> 23 (A) The Customer shall pay the Company in cash or as otherwise agreed all sums immediately when due, without reduction or deferment on account of any claim, counterclaim or set-off.

The defendants alleged that the plaintiffs had failed to repay VAT due to them and that that sum could be set off against the plaintiffs' freight-charges. The issue was whether the 'no set-off' clause satisfied the requirement of reasonableness. The Court of Appeal held that it did. The rationale of the decision is set out in the following passage in the judgment of Pill LJ:

> The clause was in common use and well known in the trade following comprehensive discussions between reputable and representative bodies mindful of the consideration involved. It reflects a general view as to what is reasonable in the trade concerned. It was sufficiently well known that any failure by the defendant's officers, in the course of long and substantial dealings, to put their minds to the clause cannot be relied on to establish that it was unfair or unreasonable to include it in the contract. In a situation in which there was no significant inequality of bargaining power, the customs of the trade were an important factor. The parties were well aware of the circumstances in which business was conducted, the heads of expenditure to be incurred and the risks involved.[77]

Finally, in this section reference must be made to s.11(4) of UCTA. This section provides that where a person seeks to limit his liability to a specified party, in assessing the reasonableness of such limitation regard must be had in particular to:

- the resources which he could expect to be available to him for the purpose of meeting the liability should it arise; and
- how far it was open to him to cover himself by insurance.

The purpose of this provision is to protect small firms with limited resources and able to obtain only limited insurance cover. In *St Albans City and District Council* v. *International Computers Ltd*[78] however, a clause in a computer contract which limited liability to £100,000 was held by the trial judge and by the Court of Appeal to be unreasonable. The defendant had not justified the limit of £100,000. Any limitation should be justified in terms of the turnover of the party relying on it and the insurance cover available to him. The defendant was a large company with annual profits of several million pounds.

Although the reasonableness or otherwise of a clause exempting or restricting one party's liability under the contract can never be predicted with certainty, since this statutory test leaves the trial judge with a great deal of discretion, the following broad principles can be said with reasonable confidence to have emerged from the case law on this topic:

(a)   Any clause which is not negotiated and which is the product of a disproportionate inequality of bargaining power is likely to fail the reasonableness test.
(b)   A clause in a standard form contract made between business organisations of equal bargaining strengths is likely to be found reasonable.
(c)   Where two businesses conclude a one-off contract under which one of the parties exempts or restricts his liability the reasonableness or otherwise of such exemption or restriction is difficult to determine. The court, in deciding this question, will need to examine the nature of the contract and the surrounding circumstances, including the relative bargaining strengths of the parties.

The key concepts which underly these principles are knowledge, choice and inequality of bargaining power. An exclusion clause is more likely to satisfy the test of reasonableness where the customer has knowledge of the existence and scope of the clause, where the customer has a choice of contracting with other suppliers (or with the same supplier) without a similar term, or where the parties are of roughly equal bargaining power. It must be stressed that despite the large number of appellate decisions in this area the law has yet to work out a fully developed rationale of reasonableness. In particular, the concept of inequality of bargaining power as applied by the courts is a somewhat rudimentary one, though the courts do seem to recognise that the fact of the customer contracting on the supplier's standard terms does not necessarily denote inequality of bargaining power.

REMEDIES

If a contractor is in breach of his contractual obligations, then the relevant remedy for the employer to seek is damages. A claim for damages may be made either under the common law (unliquidated damages) or under the contract itself (liquidated damages). The contractor may have a defence to a claim for damages where the contract has been frustrated. He may also have a claim in *quantum meruit*, subject to a set-off or counterclaim by the employer.

(1)   Unliquidated damages

(a)   The rules as to remoteness

Unliquidated damages are monetary compensation to put the plaintiff in the position he would have been in had the wrong against him not been committed. In contract this means a sum of money to put the plaintiff in the position he would have been in had the contract been performed.[79]

The innocent party will not always be awarded all the loss resulting from a breach of contract; he will only be awarded those damages which are not too remote from the breach. The test for determining which damages are too remote and which damages are not too remote was laid down by Alderson B in *Hadley* v. *Baxendale*:

> Where two parties have made a contract which one of them has broken, the damages which the other party ought to receive in respect of such breach of contract should be such as may fairly and reasonably be considered either arising naturally, i.e. according to the usual course of things, from such breach of contract itself, or such as may reasonably be supposed to have been in the contemplation of both parties, at the time they made the contract, as the probable result of the breach of it.[80]

This rule was reformulated by Asquith LJ in *Victoria Laundry (Windsor) Ltd* v. *Newman Industries Ltd*.[81] In the course of his judgement he laid down the following three propositions:

(1) In cases of breach of contract, the aggrieved party is only entitled to recover such part of the loss actually resulting as was at the time of the contract reasonably foreseeable as likely to result from the breach.
(2) What is reasonably foreseeable depends on the knowledge then possessed by the parties or, at all events, by the party in breach.
(3) For this purpose, knowledge possessed is of two kinds:
    (i) imputed knowledge, i.e. everyone is taken to know the ordinary course of things and what loss is liable to result from a breach of contract in that ordinary course, and
    (ii) actual knowledge of special circumstances outside the 'ordinary course of things'.

In *Czarnikow Ltd* v. *Koufos, The Heron II*,[82] the House of Lords approved the rule in *Hadley* v. *Baxendale*, but they disapproved of Asquith LJ's criterion of reasonable foreseeability to determine remoteness. They said that the question of whether damages in contract are too remote should be determined by the criterion of whether the probability of their occurrence should have been within the reasonable contemplation of both parties at the time when the contract was made, having regard to their knowledge at that time.

The introduction of different tests for remoteness in contract and tort has led to problems in this area of law. This is illustrated by *H. Parsons (Liverstock) Ltd* v. *Uttley Ingham & Co. Ltd.*[83] The defendants supplied the plaintiffs, who were pig farmers, with a hopper in which to store nuts. The hopper was not properly ventilated, with the result that the nuts became mouldy. The plaintiff's pigs suffered a rare intestinal disease and 254 of them died. The Court of Appeal awarded them damages for this loss on the ground that the type of loss which occurred (physical loss) was within the parties' reasonable contemplation, even if the full extent of that loss was not.

(b)   The measure of damages for defective building work

The actual losses for which damages may be awarded can be divided into three categories:

  (i)   damages for expectation loss; and
 (ii)   damages for consequential losses.
(iii)   damages for mental distress.

Expectation loss

In the case of defective building work, there are two possible ways of assessing damages for expectation loss:

(a) the cost of reinstatement, i.e. putting the plaintiff in the position which he would have been in had the contract been performed; or
(b) the difference in value between the work the plaintiff received and the work he expected to receive.

As a general rule, the owner of a building is entitled to recover such damages as will put him in a position to have the building for which he contracted, and wherever it is reasonable the courts will treat the cost of reinstatement as the measure of general damage.[84] The cost is to be assessed at the earliest date when, having regard to all the circumstances, the repairs could reasonably be undertaken, rather than the date when the damage occurred.[85]

The cost of reinstatement measure was applied by the Court of Appeal in *Minscombe Properties* v. *Sir Alfred McAlpine & Sons.*[86] In 1976 the parties agreed that the defendants should have the right to dump spoil on the plaintiffs' land during construction of the A34. In breach of contract the defendants overdumped and dumped where they were not entitled to. The defendants contended that the measure of the damage was the diminution in the value of the land (about £800), while the plaintiffs contended that they were entitled to removing the cost of the spoil in order for planning permission to be obtained (about £78,000). The judge held that, as the plaintiffs had a good chance of obtaining planning permission, the measure of damages was the cost of removing the spoil. The Court of Appeal upheld the judge's decision.

There are, however, some exceptions to this general rule. In *Applegate* v. *Moss,*[87] the Court of Appeal said that where a building is so defective as to be incapable of repair the appropriate measure of damages is the value of the building less its value as it stands, i.e. the diminution in the value of the property. In *G.W. Atkins Limited* v. *Scott,*[88] the Court of Appeal said that diminution in value is more appropriate where the proportion of defective work is small in relation to the whole property, where the sale of the property is not in prospect, and where the damage only affects the 'amenity value' of the property.

Normally, the cost of reinstatement measure and the difference in value measure will produce the same result. But it can be the case that the two measures can produce dramatically different results and that neither measure provides an adequate basis for assessing damages. This occurred in *Ruxley Electronics and Construction Ltd* v. *Forsyth.*[89] The defendant, the building owner, contracted with the plaintiffs, building contractors, to build a swimming pool in his garden for a price of £70,178. The contract specified that the maximum depth of the pool should be 7ft 6in. After the work had been completed, the owner discovered that the maximum depth of the pool was only 6ft. 9in. And at the point where people would dive into the pool the depth was 6 ft. The owner had paid various sums on account and the builders claimed the balance of the contract price. The owner counterclaimed for breach of contract.

The trial judge held that the shortfall in depth was clearly a breach of contract but it had not decreased the value of the pool. He found that it would be unreasonable to incur the cost of demolishing the existing pool and building a new and deeper one. However, he awarded the owner £2500 general damages for loss of amenity. The *ratio* of his decision, subsequently approved by the House of Lords, was stated in the following terms:

> ... where a contract is for the provision of a pleasurable amenity, such as a swimming pool, it is entirely proper to award a general sum for the loss of amenity. I accept that there has been a loss of amenity brought about by the shortfall in depth and I award damages for loss of that amenity in the sum of £2500.[90]

The Court of Appeal held,[91] by a majority, that it was not unreasonable to award as damages the cost of replacing the swimming pool in order to make good the breach of contract. Accordingly, they set aside the judge's award of £2500 general damages for loss of amenity and awarded the full cost of reinstatement. The rationale underlying this decision was expressed in the following terms in the judgement of Staughton LJ:

> It is unreasonable of a plaintiff to claim an expensive remedy if there is some cheaper alternative which would make good his loss. Thus he cannot claim the cost of reinstatement if the difference in value would make good his loss by enabling him to purchase the building or chattel

that he requires elsewhere. But if there is no alternative course which will provide what he requires, or none which will cost less, he is entitled to the cost of repair or reinstatement even if that is very expensive.[92]

The House of Lords unanimously reversed the decision of the Court of Appeal and restored the trial judge's award. Their Lordships held that in assessing damages for breach of contract for defective building works, if the court took the view that it would be unreasonable for the plaintiff to insist on reinstatement because the expense of the work involved would be out of all proportion to the benefit to be obtained, then the difference in value was the proper measure of damage. However, where the breach of contract did not cause a diminution in value, it was not correct to award the cost of reinstatement as an alternative measure. Where the breach led to loss of expectation of a personal preference or a pleasurable amenity, but no diminution in value, the court should award modest damages.

The Law Lords were at pains to emphasise that the cost of reinstatement and the diminution in value were not the only available measures of damage. Thus, Lord Mustill, in his speech, said:

> These are not two alternative measures of damage, at opposite poles, but only one: namely the loss truly suffered by the promisee. In some cases the loss cannot be fairly measured except by reference to the full cost of repairing the deficiency in performance. In others, and in particular those where the contract is designed to fulfil a purely commercial purpose, the loss will very often consist only of the monetary detriment brought about by the breach of contract. *But these remedies are not exhaustive, for the law must cater for those occasions where the value of the promise to the promisee exceeds the financial enhancement of his position which full performance will secure.* [author's italics][93]

Lord Jauncey, in his speech, distinguished between a case where the contract breaker has entirely failed to achieve the contractual objective and one where the contractual objective has been achieved to a substantial degree. If a building is constructed so defectively that it is of no use for its designed purpose the cost of reinstatement is the true measure of the plaintiff's loss. However, to award the cost of reinstatement where the contract was substantially, though defectively, performed would be to give to the plaintiff a substantial gratuitous benefit. Lord Jauncey illustrated this point by the following example. A man employs a builder to build a house and specifies that the builder use blue bricks. The builder uses yellow bricks instead, but in other respects the house is adequate for its design purpose. It would be unreasonable to award the owner the cost of reconstruction of the house, because his loss was simply the aesthetic pleasure he would have derived from the sight of the blue bricks.

By far by the most interesting aspect of the decision in *Ruxley Electronics* is the reference in Lord Mustill's speech to the work of Harris, Ogus and Phillips on the relationship between contract remedies and the economist's concept of consumer surplus.[94] The concept of consumer surplus is derived from the works of the neo-classical school of economists and their marginal utility theory of consumer demand.[95] The central proposition of this theory is that the price of any commodity, on the demand side, is determined by its marginal utility, i.e. its utility to the consumer at the margin of its consumption. Consider, by way of example, the demand of an individual consumer for lemonade. He may be very thirsty and therefore he may consume his first glass with great satisfaction. In economist's terms, the utility he derives from that first glass is very great. However, as his thirst lessens the utility he derives from subsequent glasses diminishes, or, as an economist would express it, the greater the number of glasses of lemonade he consumes the less is the marginal utility of each glass. This is the idea of diminishing marginal utility. However, there will not be a different value, or price, for each glass of lemonade consumed; that would be hopelessly impracticable. Instead, there will be one price and our consumer will continue to consume glasses of lemonade until the price equals his marginal utility, i.e. the satisfaction gained from the last glass of lemonade consumed.

The work of Harris, Ogus and Phillips has shown that consumer surplus can be a powerful concept in the area of remedies for breach of contract. In their article on this subject they discuss the application of this concept to breach of consumer contracts. They identify three types of contract where, in the event of a breach, damages could be awarded for loss of consumer surplus:

(1) Breach of a contract where the promiser must contemplate that the promisee expects a consumer surplus which could not be obtained through a substitute contract, e.g. the sale of a unique good such as an original painting.

(2) Breach of a contract in circumstances which give the promisee no opportunity to mitigate his loss, e.g. the non-appearance of the photographer at a wedding.

(3) Breach of a contract where the promisee is concerned to acquire exactly what is undertaken, e.g. a contract for the sale of a plot of land.[96]

The contract for the construction of the swimming pool in *Ruxley Electronics* is clearly an example of the first type of contract. The building owner expected a pool whose maximum depth would be 7ft 6in. The fact that the pool was built to a maximum depth of 6ft 9in. meant that he received less than he expected. In economic terms, the utility that he derived from this pool was less than that for which he had contracted. This reduction in utility is the diminution in his consumer surplus as a result of the defective performance of the contract. The award of £2500 for loss of amenity by the trial judge was, in effect, the court's attempt to evaluate this loss of consumer surplus. In short, Mr Forsyth laid down certain specifications for his pool, he expected to gain certain benefits (or consumer surplus) from those specifications and no alternative specifications could meet those expectations (or consumer surplus).

Lord Mustill based his speech on the concept of consumer surplus as set out in the article of Ogus, Harris and Phillips. After recognising that consumer surplus is incapable of precise monetary valuation because of its subjective nature, he stated:

> Nevertheless, where it exists the law should recognise it and compensate the promisee if the misperformance takes it away.[97]

One final point must be made in this section. It is essential to bear in mind that the fact that Mr Forsyth's pool may have been fit for its purpose and have satisfied an ordinary or a reasonable person is irrelevant; consumer surplus is a subjective, not an objective, notion. However, this is not to deny that if consumer surplus is to be reflected in an award of damages (or, for that matter, in any public policy decision) its *assessment* must be made on some objective basis. This means asking the question: what value would the reasonable man put on the consumer surplus? So far as an award of damages is concerned, the judge is of course the reasonable man. His judgement will be informed, if necessary by expert evidence.

Following the decision of the House of Lords in *Ruxley Electronics,* it is suggested that the principles governing the measure of contractual damages for expectation loss resulting from defective building work may be stated as follows:

(1) Where the cost of reinstatement is less than the diminution in value of the work performed, the cost of reinstatement is the correct measure of damages for defective performance of a building contract.

(2) If the court takes the view that it would be unreasonable for the building owner to insist on reinstatement because the expense of the work involved would be out of all proportion to the benefit to be obtained, then the correct measure of damage is the diminution in value of the works, i.e. the difference between the value of the work as performed and its value had the contract been performed.

(3) Where the diminution in value is nil it is not correct to award the cost of reinstatement as an alternative.

(4) The cost of reinstatement and diminution in value are not the only available measures of damages for breach of contract. If the breach of contract has resulted in a loss of amenity or personal preference (but no diminution in value), then the court may award a modest sum in damages.

Damages for consequential loss

This expression refers to further harm, such as personal injury or damage to property, suffered as a result of the breach. Thus, if a garage collapses because of inadequate foundations and causes damage to a car left inside, the builder will be liable not only for the cost of repairing the garage but also for the cost of repairing or replacing the car.

Damages for mental distress[98]

Defective building work involves the building owner, particularly the owner of a dwelling, in much anxiety, and undoubtedly much inconvenience and distress is suffered by such a person while remedial works are carried out. At one time it looked as though the law might award general damages for this inconvenience and distress, but the Court of Appeal in *Watts* v. *Morrow*[99] firmly rejected this development. This section briefly traces the history of this development.

As a matter of contract law in general, the law traditionally denied recovery from mental distress. In *Addis* v. *Gramophone Company Limited*,[100] the House of Lords held that where a servant is wrongfully dismissed from his employment the damages for the dismissal cannot include compensation for the manner of the dismissal, for his injured feelings, or for the loss he may sustain because of the fact that the dismissal of itself makes it more difficult for him to obtain fresh employment. This reasoning was applied by the Court of Appeal in *Bliss* v. *South East Thames Regional Health Authority*.[101] There the regional health authority was held to be in repudiatory breach of contract when it asked one of its consultant surgeons to undergo a psychiatric test after he had written a number of angry and offensive letters to his colleagues. However, Dillon LJ stated an important exception to this general rule:

> There are exceptions now recognised where the contract which has been broken was itself a contract to provide peace of mind or freedom from distress.[102]

The question for present purposes is whether such exception applies to a building contract. In *Perry* v. *Sidney Phillips & Son*,[103] the Court of Appeal awarded damages for the distress, worry, inconvenience and trouble which the plaintiff had suffered while living in the house he bought, due to the defects which his surveyor had overlooked. Lord Denning said that these consequences were reasonably foreseeable, but Kerr LJ stated a narrower test:

> [The deputy judge] awarded these damages *because of the physical consequences of the breach, which were all foreseeable at the time.* [author's italics][104]

In *Hayes* v. *James & Charles Dodd*,[105] however, the Court of Appeal rejected this approach and said that damages for anguish and vexation arising out of a breach of contract were not recoverable unless the object of the contract was to provide peace of mind or freedom from distress. Staughton LJ said:

> It seems to me that damages for mental distress in contract are, as a matter of policy, limited to certain classes of case. I would broadly follow the

classification adopted by Dillon LJ in *Bliss* v. *South East Thames Regional Health Authority.*[106]

He concluded that damages for distress should not be awarded in any case where the object of the contract was not comfort or pleasure, or the relief of discomfort, but simply carrying on a commercial activity with a view to profit.

The rule concerning damages for mental distress laid down in *Hayes* v. *Dodd* was applied by the Official Referee in *Victor Jack Michael* v. *Ensoncraft Limited.*[107] In that case builders negligently caused fire damage to a house. The judge held that the owner was not able to recover damages for inconvenience and annoyance because at the time of the fire the house was let to tenants and he did not live in it.

In *Syrett* v. *Carr & Neave,*[108] the Official Referee, Judge Bowsher, QC, said that the plaintiff who suffered a great deal of disruption after buying a defective property in reliance on a negligent surveyor's report was entitled to damages for inconvenience and distress on a scale which is not excessive, but modest.

In *Watts* v. *Morrow*, however, the Court of Appeal firmly rejected the notion that a house-buyer's contract with a surveyor is a contract to provide peace of mind or freedom from distress as 'an impossible view of the ordinary surveyor's contract'. It said that *Perry* v. *Sidney Phillips* was authority for the proposition that a plaintiff is entitled to damages for the discomfort suffered through having to live for a lengthy period in a defective house which was not repaired between the time the plaintiff acquired it and the date of the trial. The court was at pains to stress that these damages were limited to distress caused by the physical consequences of the breach. Bingham LJ stated the position as follows:

> A contract-breaker is not in general liable for any distress, frustration, anxiety, displeasure, vexation, tension or aggravation which his breach of contract may cause to the innocent party … . But the rule is not absolute. Where the very object of a contract is to provide pleasure, relaxation, peace of mind or freedom from molestation damages will be awarded if the fruit of the contract is not provided … . A contract to survey the condition of a house for a prospective purchase does not, however, fall within this exceptional category.[109]

Bingham LJ did not say whether or not a contract for the carrying out of building works fell outside the above exception, but presumably it does.

The law on damages for mental distress may be summed up as follows:

(1)   As a general rule, damages for mental distress resulting from a breach of contract are not awarded.

(2)   As an exception to this general rule, damages for mental distress resulting from breach of contract will be awarded where the object of the contract is to provide peace of mind or freedom from distress.

(3) Commercial contracts fall outside this exception. Thus, damages for mental distress will not be awarded in the case of a contract to repair or survey a house used as an income-producing asset.
(4) Contracts to survey a house, and presumably contracts to carry out building work on a house, do not have as their object the provision of peace of mind. However, damages are recoverable for any physical discomfort resulting from breach of this kind of contract, together with any mental distress associated with that discomfort.

(2) *Liquidated damages*

The parties may agree that a liquidated (i.e. a fixed) sum shall be paid as damages for breach of contract. Such a term of the contract is known as a liquidated damages clause. It is common for a construction contract to contain a clause making the contractor liable for a liquidated sum (based on a rate of £x per day or per week) by way of damages if he fails to complete the work by the contract completion date.

Liquidated damages and penalty clauses

The contractor may have a defence to a claim for liquidated damages if he can show that the agreed sum is a penalty. The essence of a penalty is that the sum agreed is not a genuine pre-estimate of any loss likely to be sustained by the plaintiff and is substantially in excess of that sum. If such a defence is established the employer will still have a right to a claim for unliquidated damages.

The principles governing the distinction between liquidated damages and penalty clauses are set out in the speech of Lord Dunedin in *Dunlop Pneumatic Tyre Co. Ltd* v. *New Garage and Motor Co. Ltd*.[110] Those principles are as follows:

1. The use of the words 'penalty' or 'liquidated damages' in the contract is not conclusive. The court must find out whether the payment stipulated is in truth a penalty or liquidated damages.
2. The essence of a penalty is a payment of money stipulated as *in terrorem* of the offending party; the essence of liquidated damages is that it is a genuine pre-estimate of the loss likely to be suffered as a consequence of the breach.
3. The question of whether a stipulated sum is a penalty or liquidated damages is one of construction. This question must be decided on the basis of the terms and inherent circumstances of each particular contract, judged at the time when the contract was made, not at the time of the breach.
4. There are various tests to assist the task of construction:
    (a) It will be held to be a penalty if the sum stipulated for is extravagant and unconscionable in amount in comparison with the greatest loss that could conceivably be proved to have followed from the breach.

(b) It will be held to be a penalty if the breach consists only in not paying a sum of money, and the sum stipulated is a sum greater than the sum which ought to have been paid.

(c) There is a presumption (but no more) that it is a penalty when a single lump sum is made payable by way of compensation on the occurrence of one or more or all of several events, some of which may occasion serious and others trifling damage.

(d) The fact that precise pre-estimation of the loss is impossible does not prevent the sum stipulated as being a genuine pre-estimate of damage. On the contrary, that is just the situation when it is probable that pre-estimated damage was the true bargain between the parties.

Liquidated damages and common law damages

Where the employer loses the right to claim liquidated damages (e.g. if he himself causes or contributes to the delay) he may still have a claim for common law damages. Such a claim will not be limited to the amount he could have claimed by way of liquidated damages. If, however, the parties specify '£nil' as the figure for liquidated damages then this precludes both a claim for liquidated damages and a claim for common law damages.[111]

(3) *Frustration of the contract*

A contractor may have a defence to a claim for damages if he can establish that the contract was frustrated. The test for determining whether a contract has been frustrated was set out by Lord Radcliffe in *Davis Contractors Ltd* v. *Fareham UDC* in the following terms:

> Frustration occurs whenever the law recognises that without default of either party a contractual obligation has become incapable of being performed because the circumstances in which performance is called for would render it a thing radically different from that which was undertaken by the contract.[112]

It is important to realise that the doctrine of frustration as expressed in Lord Radcliffe's dictum is a narrow one, a point well illustrated by the facts of the case. The plaintiffs were contractors who entered into a contract with Fareham UDC to build 78 houses for the sum of £92,425. The work was scheduled to last for a period of eight months. However, owing to unexpected circumstances and without the fault of either party, there was a serious shortage of skilled labour and of building materials and the work took 22 months to complete. As a consequence, the contractors incurred additional expense amounting to £17,651. They argued that the contract was frustrated by reason of the delay and that they were entitled to a sum in excess of the contract price on a *quantum meruit* basis. The House of Lords, affirming the decision of the Court of Appeal, held that the contract was not frustrated. Their Lordships emphasised that a contract is frustrated only where the supervening event changes the nature of performance so that the task undertaken would, if performed, be a different thing from that contracted for. The doctrine of frustration could not be invoked by hardship or inconvenience or material loss. The contract in question was for a fixed price and clearly, in the event, the contractor had entered into a bad bargain. Lord Radcliffe emphasised in his speech that this consideration did not establish frustration.

The doctrine of frustration does not apply where the frustration is self-induced, i.e. where performance of the contract has become impossible because of the actions of the party alleging frustration. Nor is a contract frustrated where the parties have made provision for the frustrating event in the contract.

Where a contract is frustrated, the rights of the parties are governed by the Law Reform (Frustrated Contracts) Act 1943. Essentially, the Act makes two provisions. First, under the provisions of section 1(2) all sums paid or payable to any party under the contract shall be recoverable or cease to be payable. Section 1(2) goes on to state that if the party to whom the sums were paid or payable incurred expenses before the time of frustration in the performance of the contract, the court may, if it considers it just to do so, deduct any part of the sums so paid or payable up to the limit of the expenses incurred. Secondly, section 1(3) provides that where one party has conferred a valuable benefit on the other party before the contract is frustrated he shall be entitled to a just sum not exceeding the value of the benefit from the other party.[113]

(4)   *Quantum Meruit*

The expression *quantum meruit* means 'the amount he deserves' and it is essentially a restitutionary claim for a reasonable sum. It 'arises where goods are supplied or services rendered by one person to another in circumstances which entitle the former to be recompensed by the latter by receiving a reasonable price or remuneration'.[114]

A *quantum meruit* claim may be made either by the innocent party or by the guilty party. Where a contract has been broken in such a way as to entitle the innocent party to be regarded as discharged from it then he may sue on *quantum meruit* for the value of the work he has carried out under the contract.[115] The claim is a restitutionary one in the sense that its purpose is to recompense the plaintiff; as such it is an alternative to a claim in damages for breach of contract. Thus, where the employer is in breach of contract by preventing the contractor from completing the works the contractor can claim a *quantum meruit* for the work done.

A *quantum meruit* claim is available also to the party in breach where the contract is divisible or severable in the sense that the right to payment accrues incrementally as various stages of the contract are completed. If the contract is entire, in the sense that one party's performance is made conditional on complete performance by the other party, then no *quantum meruit* claim is possible.[116] The principle of an entire contract is a harsh one and the courts are reluctant to construe contracts as entire. Construction contracts are generally divisible, rather than entire, and as such a contractor in breach of contract may have a right to a *quantum meruit* claim for work done and material supplied, subject to a counterclaim for damages by the employer for loss suffered as a result of the breach. The claim is for a reasonable sum, and is available *only where no price is fixed by the contract*. Its purpose is to prevent the employer unjustly enriching himself by receiving the benefit of work done under the contract without compensating the contractor.

As a restitutionary claim, a *quantum meruit* may also be available in the following circumstances:

(a) where there is a *quasi-contract*; i.e. where a contractor has carried out work in the expectation of a contract which fails to materialise;
(b) where the contractor carries out work outside the contract at the employer's request;[117] and
(c) where the contract has been frustrated, under section 1(3) of the Law Reform (Frustrated Contracts) Act 1943.[118]

(5)   Set-off

Where the contractor substantially performs the contract the employer is not discharged from the obligation to pay the contract price. However, he may counterclaim or set-off against the price any loss resulting from the incomplete or defective performance.[119]

SUMMARY

The contractor's obligations

1.   The contractor's obligations for the safety and quality of the building works are to be found in the express and implied terms of the contract.
2.   The contractor must construct the building works with reasonable care and skill.
3.   The materials used by the contractor must correspond with their description, be of satisfactory quality and be fit for any particular purpose made known to the contractor by the building owner.
4.   The contractor must warn the building owner of any dangerous defects in the design of the building works which come to his (the contractor's) attention.

Exclusion of liability

5. Attempts by the contractor to exclude his liability under his contract with the building owner are strictly controlled, principally by the Unfair Contract Terms Act 1977.
6. Attempts by reference to a contract term or notice to exclude liability for death or personal injury are void. Such attempts to exclude liability for other loss or damage are valid only if they satisfy the statutory requirement of reasonableness.
7. Where the building owner deals as consumer or on the contractor's written standard terms of business, the contractor cannot exclude or restrict liability for his own breach or claim to be entitled to render a contractual performance substantially different from that which was reasonably expected of him or render no performance at all, except in so far as the contract term satisfies the requirement of reasonableness. There is no definition in the 1977 Act of 'written standard terms of business' and there is uncertainty as to whether the JCT and ICE forms fall within the scope of this concept.
8. Where the building owner deals as consumer, any attempt by the contractor to exclude or restrict his liability for breach of his obligations concerning the description, quality and fitness of the materials supplied is void. Where the building owner does not deal as a consumer any attempt to exclude or restrict such liability is valid only if it satisfies the statutory requirement of reasonableness.

Remedies

9. The aim of an award of damages for defective building work is to put the building owner in the position he would have been in had the contract been performed.
10. This award is generally calculated by reference to the cost of reinstatement.
11. If the cost of reinstatement is out of all proportion to the benefit to be obtained by the building owner from the remedial works then the correct measure is the diminution in value.
12. Where, in such circumstances, there is no diminution in value, damages will be awarded for any loss in amenity suffered by the building owner.
13. Damages may be awarded for consequential loss suffered by the building owner.
14. The general rule is that damages cannot be recovered for mental distress resulting from breach of contract except where the object of the contract is to provide peace of mind or freedom from distress.
15. Damages can be awarded only where the loss suffered by the building owner is not too remote a consequence of the contractor's breach of contract.

16.   The parties may agree that a liquidated (i.e. a fixed) sum shall be paid as damages.

17.   To be enforceable, a liquidated damages clause must be a genuine pre-estimation of the loss likely to result from breach of the contract.

18.   A contractor may have a defence to a claim for damages if the contract has been frustrated.

19.   If the contract is frustrated the contractor may have a claim for a just sum for any valuable benefit conferred on the employer before the frustrating event.

20.   A contractor in breach of contract may have a right to a *quantum meruit* claim for work done and materials supplied, subject to a counterclaim by the employer for loss suffered as a result of the breach.

21.   Where the contractor substantially performs the contract, the employer must pay the contract price less a sum for the cost of rectifying the defective or incomplete performance.

NOTES

1.   The Joint Contracts Tribunal has produced a standard form of management contract, JCT Management Contract 1987 Edition. This is published in *Emden's Construction Law*, 8th edn, Butterworths, 1990, Binder 3, Division F.

2.   See *Hancock* v. *B.W. Brazier (Anerley) Ltd* [1966], 1 WLR 1317, p.1324.

3.   For an exposition of these aspects of contractual liability see Sir Anthony May, *Keating on Building Contracts*, 7th edn, Sweet & Maxwell, 2001, *passim*, and *Emden's Construction Law*, Binder 1, *passim*.

4.   The scope and content of these Regulations and their importance for Construction Law are discussed in Chapter 2.

5.   The latest edition of this form was issued in 1998 and is known as the 'JCT '98'. There are various versions of this form and they are published in *Emden's Construction Law*, Binder 2, Divisions A and B.

6.   7th edn, 1999.

7.   The powers of the architect in administering a construction project are discussed in Chapter 7.

8.   Post, pp.19–22.

9.   The Joint Contracts Tribunal uses the term 'contractor', but in this text the terms 'builder' and 'contractor' are used interchangeably.

10.   Now the Building Regulations 1991, SI 1991/2768. The liability issues arising out of breach of these Regulations are explored in Chapter 5.

11.   Subclause 6.1.2.

12.   Subclause 6.1.3.

13.   Subclause 6.1.5.

14.   See *Hancock* v. *B.W. Brazier (Anerley) Ltd, supra*, n.2.

15.   (1858) 5 CBNS 236.

16.   [1975] 3 All ER 99.

17.   (1980) 14 BLR 1.

18.   *Supra*, n. 16, p.102

19. (1986) 38 BLR 36. The implication of these cases for design professionals is discussed in Chapter 7.
20. (1986) 38 BLR 36. See, further, Chapter 7.
21. Law Com. No. 156, *Implied Terms in Contracts for the Supply of Services* (1986).
22. [1968] 2 All ER 1169.
23. [1968] 2 All ER 1181.
24. *Ibid*, n.23, p.1124.
25. See, in particular, the speech of Lord Reid, *supra*, n.22, p.1172.
26. [1932] AC 562.
27. For a critique of the doctrine of privity of contract see Law Commission Consultation Paper No. 121 (1991), in particular pp.76–78, and Law Com. No. 242, *Privity of Contract: Contracts for the Benefit of Third Parties* (1996), in particular pp.43–48.
28. See now Sale of Goods Act 1979, sections 12–15.
29. See Law Com. No. 95, *Implied Terms in Contracts for the Supply of Goods* (1979).
30. See section 1(1) of the Sale of Goods Act 1979, where a contract of sale is defined as a contract under which the seller transfers or agrees to transfer the property in goods to the buyer for a money consideration called the price.
31. See section 15(3) of the Supply of Goods (Implied Terms) Act 1973.
32. Law Com. No. 160, *Sale and Supply of Goods* Cm. 137 (1987).
33. This is a truncated version of the definition of satisfactory quality contained in sections 14(2A) and (2B) of the Sale of Goods Act 1979. Section 4(2A) of the 1982 Act is identical to section 14(2A) of the 1979 Act. Section 14(2B) of the 1979 Act is omitted from the definition contained in the 1982 Act.
34. See, in particular, Guest. A.G. (Ed.), *Benjamin's Sale of Goods*, 5th edn, Sweet & Maxwell, 1996; and Atiyah, P.S., Adams J. and MacQueen H., *Sale of Goods*, 10th edn, Longman, 2000.
35. [1987] QB 933.
36. *Ibid*, n.35 p.944.
37. *Ibid*, n.35, p.944.
38. [1977] RTR. 308.
39. [1982] AC 225, p.276.
40. [1989] EGCS 160.
41. Durability is part of the definition of satisfactory quality contained in the Sale of Goods Act: see section 14 (2B)(e).
42. This, of course, is the same as the position under the common law in respect of building contracts: see *Young and Marten* v. *McManus Childs Limited*, *supra*, n.22.
43. (1996) 78 BLR 1.
44. Section 5A was inserted into the 1982 Act by the Sale and Supply of Goods Act 1994, Section 7 and Schedule 2.
45. See *Hong Kong Fir Shipping Co. Ltd* v. *Kawasaki Kisen Kaisha Ltd* [1962] 1 All ER 474.
46. See *Cehave NV* v. *Bremer Handelgesellshaft MbH, The Hansa Nord* [1976] QB44.
47. See *Frost* v. *Aylesbury Dairy Co.* [1905] 1 KB 608, concerning a contract of sale.
48. See, generally, Wilson and Rutherford (1994) 10 Const. LJ 90, and Scriven (1996) 12 Const. LJ 226
49. (1820) 3 Stark 6.
50. [1956] 1 WLR 303.
51. *Ibid*, n.40, p.308.
52. (1974) 21 BLR 27.
53. (1984) 2 Con. LR 1.

54. (1984) 2 Con. LR 43.
55. (1988) 42 BLR 66.
56. (1992) 9-CLD-05–21; (1993) 62 BLR 147. See the author's article (1992) 8 PN 110 for a detailed comment on this case.
57. *Building*, 30 October 1998, p.70.
58. [2000] BLR 137.
59. See, generally, Furmston, M.P., *Cheshire, Fifoot and Furmston's Law of Contract*, 13th edn, Butterworths, 1996, Ch. 6, pp.160–203.
60. See *Smith* v. *Eric S. Bush; Harris* v. *Wyre Forest District Council* [1989] 2 All ER 514.
61. *See Phillips Products Ltd* v. *Hyland* [1987] 2 All ER 620.
62. [1981] SLT 103.
63. (1992) 56 BLR 115.
64. *Supra*, n.62, p.105.
65. *Supra*, n.63, p.133.
66. 7th edn, 2001, p.88.
67. Section 111, paragraph 575.
68. 93/13/EEC, OJ 1993 L.95/29, Article 3(2). This provision is contained in Regulation 5(2) of The Unfair Terms in Consumer Contracts Regulations 1999 (SI 1999 No. 2083).
69. [1988] 1 WLR 321.
70. [1980] AC 827.
71. *Ibid*, n. 70, p. 843.
72. [1983] 2 AC 803.
73. (1992) *Building Law Monthly*, April; (1993) 33 Con. LR 1.
74. [1998] 1 Lloyd's Rep. 403.
75. *Ibid,* n.74, p.414.
76. [1998] 1 Lloyd's Rep. 498.
77. *Ibid*, n.76, pp.507–508.
78. [1996] 4 All ER 481.
79. *Robinson* v. *Harman* (1848) 1 Ex. 850, p.855.
80. (1854) 9 Ex. 341.
81. [1949] 1 All ER 997.
82. [1967] 3 All ER 686.
83. [1978] 1 All ER 525, CA.
84. *East Ham Corporation* v. *Bernard Sunley & Sons Ltd* [1966]AC 406.
85. *Dodd Properties (Kent) Ltd* v. *Canterbury City Council* [1980] 1 All ER 928, CA.
86. (1986) 279 EG 759.
87. *Applegate* v. *Moss* [1971] 2 All ER 747.
88. (1992) Const. LJ 215. The judgement of the Court of Appeal was given on 15 February 1980.
89. [1995] 3 All ER 268. This part of the chapter is based on the author's article in (1996) 12 PN 21.
90. The decision was delivered in the Central London County Court on 13 July 1993. The quote is taken from the speech of Lord Lloyd, *ibid*, n.89, p.280.
91. [1994] 3All ER 801.
92. *Ibid*, n. 91, p.810.
93. *Supra*, n.89, p.277.
94. *Contract Remedies and the Consumer Surplus* (1979) 95 LQR 581.
95. See, in particular, Alfred Marshall, *Principles of Economics*, 8th edn, 1930, pp.124–131.
96. *Supra*, n.94, p.600.

97. *Supra*, n.89, p.277.
98. See, generally, Kim Franklin (1992) 8 Const. LJ 318.
99. [1991] 4 All ER 937.
100. [1909] AC 488.
101. [1987] 1 CR 700.
102. *Ibid*, n.101, p.718.
103. [1982] 3 All ER 705.
104. *Ibid*, n.103, p.712.
105. [1990] 2 All ER 815.
106. *Ibid*, n.105, p.824.
107. (1991) CILL 653.
108. [1990] 48 EG 118.
109. *Supra*, n.99, pp.959–960.
110. [1915] AC 79, at p.86.
111. *Temloc Ltd* v. *Errill Properties Ltd* (1987) 39 BLR 30.
112. [1956] AC 696, at p.729.
113. For an explanation of the principles underlying sections 1(2) and (3) see the judgement of Goff J in *BP Exploration Co. (Libya) Ltd* v. *Hunt (No. 2)* [1982] 1 All ER 925.
114. Beatson, J., *Anson's Law of Contract*, 27th edn, Oxford University Press, 1998, p.610.
115. See *Planché* v. *Colburn* (1831) 8 Bing 14.
116. *Cutter* v. *Powell* (1795) 6 Term Rep. 320.
117. *Parkinson* v. *Commissioners of Works* [1949] 2 KB 632.
118. *BP Exploration Co. (Libya) Ltd* v. *Hunt*, op. cit., n.113.
119. *Dakin (H) & Co Ltd* v. *Lee* [1916] 1 KB 566.

2

Unfair Terms in Construction Contracts

INTRODUCTION

The general principle governing the concluding of contracts, including construction contracts, is that the parties are free to include in their contracts any terms they consider to be to their advantage, and the common law refuses to recognise a general doctrine that a contractual term may be declared void or unenforceable on the ground that its inclusion in a contract is unfair or unconscionable. This doctrine of freedom of contract is closely associated with the doctrine of sanctity of contract. Under this doctrine, a contract is viewed as a bargain or an exchange which the parties have freely negotiated and entered into and, short of misrepresentation, duress or undue influence, the common law holds the parties to that bargain, however one-sided or unjust it may seem ethically. The doctrine of sanctity of contract was stated in the following terms by Sir George Jessel MR in his famous *dictum* in *Printing & Numerical Registering Co. v. Sampson*:

> if there is one thing more than another which public policy requires, it is that men of full age and competent understanding shall have the utmost liberty in contracting, and that their contracts when entered into freely and voluntarily, shall be held sacred and shall be enforced by Courts of Justice.[1]

These twin doctrines of freedom of contract and sanctity of contract are based on the political economy of individualism set out by Adam Smith in *The Wealth of Nations*. According to this philosophy, the economic welfare of the community is maximised if men are permitted to run their affairs with the minimum of outside interference and regulation. In terms of economic policy, this meant a *laissez-faire* approach to the regulation of trade and industry. In terms of the law of obligations, it meant an emphasis on freedom of contract and the idea that men should be at the utmost liberty to settle the content of the bargains into which they entered. Adam Smith, in his seminal book, was at pains to stress that it was by entering bargains that men satisfied their needs. Men enter into bargains, said Smith, not through benevolence but because they consider them to be in their self-interest. It was by allowing men the maximum amount of freedom to pursue their self-interests that their needs would be satisfied. In Smith's lapidary words:

> It is not from the benevolence of the butcher, the brewer or baker that we expect our dinner, but from their regard of their own interest.[2]

The underlying ethic of the classical model of English contract law is, then, one of self-interest; a contract is seen as a vehicle for self-interested exchange and neither party is under any obligation to consider the interests of the other party. Under this model the function of the law is seen as enforcing agreements entered into voluntarily in accordance with their terms. Only if the *process* of contracting was defective should the law intervene, for in such circumstances the agreement is not truly a voluntary one.

In the 20th century, the doctrines of freedom of contract and sanctity of contract and the economic philosophy of individualism and *laissez-faire* have suffered something of a decline and for much of this period a more interventionist and welfarist economic philosophy has been ascendant.[3] This welfarist approach to economic policy views the application of the doctrine of freedom of contract as producing an optimum allocation of resources only if there is equality of bargaining power between the parties to a contract, so that one party cannot impose his terms upon the other party. It is argued that frequently this is not the case; one party to a contract often is in a position to dictate the terms of the contract to his own advantage, with the result that the conclusion of the contract produces a less than optimum distribution of resources.

The concept of inequality of bargaining power has proved a popular official justification for limiting the freedom to contract in the area of consumer law.[4] However, it cannot be said to be a well-defined concept. As a reason for setting limits to the doctrine of freedom of contract, the concept of inequality of bargaining power has been closely, if not inextricably, bound up with the perceived implications of the spread of standard form contracts. Where a contract is concluded on one party's pre-formulated terms the other party is given little, if any, scope to negotiate the content of the contract; he must accept the standard terms offered to him or go elsewhere. Generally, the non-negotiated standard form contract is found in the area of consumer contracts where the consumer frequently is compelled to contract on the supplier's terms. It is argued that freedom to contract must imply some choice or leave room for negotiating the terms of a contract and failure in this respect means that suppliers are able to force consumers into concluding contracts on terms which are less advantageous (to the consumers) than they would otherwise be.[5]

The argument just outlined has been called the exploitation theory of contract and has been put forward, in particular, as a justification for regulating clauses excluding or restricting the liability of one party, generally the supplier, under the contract. It gained judicial recognition in *Instone* v. *Schroeder Music Publishing Co. Ltd*, where Lord Diplock stated:

> This [standard form of contract] is of comparatively modern origin. It is the result of the concentration of particular kinds of business in relatively few hands ...The terms ... have not been the subject of negotiation between the parties to it, or approved by any organisation representing the interests of the weaker party. They have been dictated by that party whose bargaining power ... enables him to say: 'If you want those goods or services at all, these are the only terms on which they are obtainable. Take it or leave it.'[6]

Despite this judicial approval of the concept of inequality bargaining power as a rationale for regulating contract terms, it must be said that it is a very crude concept. Inequality of bargaining power as a rationale for regulating contracts has been subject to intense scrutiny by the law and economics movement.[7] A detailed economic analysis of this concept is beyond the scope of this work, but two points must be highlighted in this context. In the first place, standard form contracts do not necessarily operate to the disadvantage of consumers. They have a particular role to play, namely, they facilitate the conduct of trade and, in so doing, they reduce transaction costs. Secondly, their effect on contractual content cannot be divorced from market power. Arguably, only if a supplier has market power beyond what would obtain in a competitive market structure can he be said to 'exploit' his consumers. The use of standard form contracts is not a measure of market power; the measure of market power is the availability of alternative sources of supply.

The use of standard form contracts has for long been a dominant feature of the construction industry. The JCT and the ICE forms are the two most common contracts in use in the industry. They are the result of extensive negotiation between bodies representing employers and contractors and by no stretch of the imagination can they be said to fit into the exploitation theory of contract. It is in the area of domestic building work that the use of standard form contracts *may* operate to the disadvantage of the employer, who is usually the owner or tenant of a domestic dwelling, equivalent in economic status to a consumer in a contract of sale. This sector of the construction industry consists mainly of small and medium sized firms and it is by no means certain that any particular firm would have sufficient market power to be able truly to impose terms on the building owner or tenant. In analysing the unfairness, or otherwise, of a term in a domestic construction contract this is a crucial point to bear in mind.

The lack of a clearly defined rationale for curbing the operation of the doctrine of freedom of contract has not proved a brake to the introduction of a range of legislative measures controlling the effect of various categories of contractual terms. For present purposes, the most important of these measures is the Unfair Terms in Consumer Contracts Regulations 1999,[8] which are designed to protect consumers against unfair terms in standard form contracts made with businesses. These Regulations are consumer protection legislation implementing an EC directive and they do not affect construction contracts made between a contractor or design professional and a business organisation or public body. That does not mean that they can be ignored for the purposes of Construction Law. If a contractor or design professional enters into a contract on his standard form terms with a building owner or tenant who acts as a consumer the Regulations will apply. It is therefore very much in the interests of the construction industry and its associated design professionals to examine carefully the provisions of these Regulations and to review the content of contracts made with consumer clients to ensure that they comply with these provisions.

The remainder of this chapter has two objectives:

(1) to examine the general principles of the 1999 Regulations and their relationship with the common law of contract; and
(2) to examine the indicative list of unfair terms in Schedule 3 to the Regulations with particular reference to construction contracts.

THE UNFAIR TERMS IN CONSUMER CONTRACTS REGULATIONS 1999

The Unfair Terms in Consumer Contracts Regulations 1999 came into effect on 1 October 1999. They revoke and replace the Unfair Terms in Consumer Contracts Regulations 1994,[9] which introduced into English law a duty of fairness and good faith in relation to terms contained in pre-formulated consumer contracts. They were made under the provisions of s.2(2) of the European Communities Act 1972 and implement in the UK the provisions of the EC Directive on unfair terms in consumer contracts.[10] They came into force on 1 July 1995 and apply to contracts made on or after that date. Their implementation was accompanied by three Department of Trade and Industry (DTI) publications, two consultation papers and a set of guidance notes.[11] Further, the Office of Fair Trading (OFT) has issued an explanatory booklet on the Regulations[12] and, periodically, issues bulletins on their implementation.

It may seem surprising that a new set of Regulations on this subject should be enacted so soon after the first set of Regulations was introduced. There are three essential differences between the 1994 and the 1999 Regulations. First, the wording and layout of the 1999 Regulations modify the 1994 Regulations in order to reflect more closely the wording of the Directive. It is important to bear in mind, however, that the 1999 Regulations do not amend the essential principles of the 1994 Regulations and Regulations 3 to 9 of the 1999 Regulations re-enact Regulations 2 to 7 of the 1994 Regulations. Secondly, the 1999 Regulations confer powers of enforcement on a wider range of bodies than the 1994 Regulations and grant to these bodies powers to obtain documents and information from traders, powers which were not contained in the 1994 Regulations. Thirdly, the 1999 Regulations omit the definition of one of its key concepts, that of good faith, which was contained in the 1994 Regulations and which was based on the definition of that concept in the Directive.

In broad terms, the Regulations state that a consumer is not bound by a standard term in a contract with a seller or supplier which is unfair. They also give the Director General of Fair Trading powers to stop the use of unfair standard terms by businesses and to prevent anyone recommending such terms, if necessary by obtaining a court injunction.

The purpose of the Directive to which the Regulations give effect, as set out in Article 1, is to approximate the laws, regulations and administrative provisions of the Member States relating to unfair terms in contracts concluded between a seller or supplier and a consumer. It is one of the New Approach Directives made under the provisions of the Single European Act 1986, whose principal aim is to create a single market throughout the EC. The Recitals to the Directive make it clear that in order to safeguard consumers in the single market it is essential that they have the confidence to enter into contracts for the purchases of goods in other Member States. To this end, it is essential to remove unfair terms from those contracts.

The scope of the Regulations

Under the provisions of Regulation 3(1), the Regulations apply to any term that has not been individually negotiated in a contract concluded between a consumer and a seller or supplier. The Regulations apply, therefore, only to pre-formulated standard terms. Regulation 4(1) states that the Regulations apply in relation to unfair terms in contracts concluded between a seller or a supplier and a consumer.

Three matters must now be examined:

(i)   Who is a 'consumer' for the purposes of the Regulations?
(ii)   Who is a 'seller or supplier' for the purposes of the Regulations?
(iii) Contracts and terms excluded from the scope of the Regulations.

(i)   Who is a 'consumer'?

Regulation 3(1) provides that for the purpose of the Regulations 'consumer' means a natural person who is acting for purposes which are outside his business or profession. A company cannot be a consumer for the purpose of the Regulations, because although it has separate legal personality it is not a natural person. A partnership in English law does not have separate legal personality; however, a partnership may exist only for business purposes and the issue of whether a partnership may be a consumer is unlikely to arise in practice. It should be noted that the definition of a consumer is narrower than that used in the Unfair Contract Terms Act 1977, section 12(1) of which refers to 'dealing as a consumer' when one party neither makes the contract in the course of a business nor holds himself out as doing so and the goods are of a type ordinarily supplied for private use or consumption.

(ii) Who is a 'seller' or 'supplier'?

Under the provisions of Regulation 3(1), 'seller' or 'supplier' means any natural or legal person who, in contracts covered by these Regulations, is acting for purposes relating to his trade, business or profession, whether publicly owned or privately owned. This definition is wide in scope and it is clear that the activities of government departments and local authorities, as well as business organisations in the private sector are caught by it. This definition of 'seller' and 'supplier' is broader than that contained in the 1977 Act, which requires a seller or supplier to be acting 'in the course of a business'. The courts have interpreted this concept in the context of the 1977 Act as meaning acting with regularity, so that a sale or supply must be an integral part of the seller's or supplier's business before it can be construed as being in the course of his business.[13] The phrase 'acting for purposes relating to his trade, business or profession' arguably catches any sale or supply made in the course of a business, whether regular, irregular or one-off.

The combined effect of these definitions of 'consumer' or 'seller or supplier' is that the Regulations cover only contracts between private persons and businesses trading on standard terms. They do not cover contracts between one business and another (including contracts between a sole trader and a large company), nor do they cover contracts between one private person and another.

(iii) Contracts and terms excluded from the scope of the Regulations

Under the provision of Regulation 4(2) the Regulations do not apply to contractual terms which reflect:

(a) mandatory statutory or regulatory provisions;
(b) the provisions or principles of international conventions to which the Member States or the Community are party.

The provisions of Regulation 5 make it clear that the Regulations apply only to terms which have not been individually negotiated. In other words, the Regulations apply only to pre-formulated standard terms. Regulation 5(2) states that a term shall always be regarded as not individually negotiated where it has been drafted in advance and the consumer has not been able to influence the substance of the term. Regulation 5(3) goes on to state that if a contract term, or certain aspects of it, has been individually negotiated, the Regulations shall apply to the rest of the contract if an overall assessment of it indicates that it is a preformulated standard contract, Regulation 5(4) places the burden of proof in this matter firmly on the seller or supplier; it states that it shall be for any seller or supplier who claims that a term was individually negotiated to show it was. This latter provision is similar in effect to section 12(3) of the Unfair Contract Terms Act 1977, which provides that it is for those claiming that a party does not deal as a consumer to show that he does not.

The 1994 Regulations excluded certain categories of contracts from their scope, the most important of which was contracts of employment. This provision (Schedule 1 to the 1994 Regulations) is not contained in the 1999 Regulations and it would appear, therefore, that the 1999 Regulations apply to a broader range of contracts than did the 1994 Regulations.

We have seen in Chapter 1 that a construction contract is a species of contract known as a contract for the supply of goods and services or a contract for work and materials. There is no doubt that such contracts fall within the scope of the Regulations. However, it is not entirely clear whether contracts relating to the creation, transfer or termination of an interest in land fall within the scope of the Regulations. This matter is of particular importance to a house builder who disposes of building plots on his pre-formulated terms. As we have seen, Regulation 2(1), the interpretation section of the Regulations, refers to the seller of goods and to the supplier of goods or services. Land is neither a good nor a service. It could be argued, therefore, that as the Regulations (and the Directive) make no express reference to land, contracts concerning land are outside their scope. This, however, may be too sweeping a conclusion to draw; in the view of the DTI, until this matter is decided by the European Court of Justice, it would be prudent to assume that the Directive, and hence the Regulations, could extend to transactions in land.[14] Further, McKendrick points out that the French text of the Directive uses the word 'biens'; this word includes both movable and immovable property. Thus, the French text includes land and McKendrick goes on to point out that the European Court of Justice would be unlikely to tolerate English law diverging from French law on this point.[15] The safest conclusion to be drawn, therefore, is that the Regulations do apply to contracts for the sale of land.

Unfairness and good faith

The key concepts in the Regulations are those of unfairness and good faith.

(i)   What is an unfair term?

The approach which the Directive and the Regulations take to the concept of an unfair term is to lay down a general test followed by an indicative and illustrative list of terms which may be regarded as unfair. The general test is contained in Regulation 5(1), which provides that an unfair term is one that, contrary to the requirement of good faith, causes a significance imbalance in the parties' rights and obligations under the contract to the detriment of the consumer. This test can be interpreted in a variety of ways but the general view seems to be that it is a cumulative one, so that before a term can be found to be unfair it must satisfy the following three requirements:

(a) it must be contrary to the requirement of good faith;
(b) it must create a significant imbalance in the parties' rights and obligations under the contract; and
(c) that imbalance must be to the detriment of the consumer.

Under the provisions of Regulation 6(1), in assessing unfairness a court must give consideration to the following factors:

- the nature of the goods or services for which the contract was concluded;
- all circumstances attending the conclusion of the contract; and
- all other terms of the contract or of another contract on which it is dependent.

Under the provision of Regulation 6(2), the core terms of the contract, provided that they are in plain, intelligible language, are not subject to the requirement of fairness. These core terms are terms that:

- define the subject matter of the contract; or
- concern the adequacy of the price of the goods sold or the remuneration of the services supplied.

Thus, in respect of price and defining the scope of a contract the Regulations preserve the principle of freedom of contract. The Regulations, therefore, leave the principle that consideration must be sufficient but need not be adequate intact and they make no attempt to admit the concept of a just or fair price. However, the price paid by the consumer may be relevant in considering whether a non-core term is unfair; a seller or supplier may be successful in arguing that a price lower than that charged by competitors justifies the inclusion in the contract of what would otherwise amount to an unfair term on the ground that considering the contract as a whole there is no significant imbalance in the parties' rights and obligations under the contract to the disadvantage of the consumer. It must be noted, though, that this exclusion applies only if the core terms are in plain and intelligible language. Thus, the price charged must be transparent to the consumer. If the core terms in a contract are unduly difficult for the consumer to understand they can be deemed to be unfair.

(ii) What is 'good faith'?

The 1999 Regulations do not contain a definition of 'good faith', unlike the 1994 Regulations. Schedule 2 to the former Regulations provided that in making an assessment of good faith, regard should be had in particular to:

(a) the strength of the bargaining position of the parties;
(b) whether the consumer had an inducement to agree to the term;

(c) whether the goods or services were sold or supplied to the special order of the consumer; and
(d) the extent to which the seller or supplier had dealt fairly and equitably with the consumer.

This definition was based on the provisions of Recital 16 to the Directive which also states that the requirement of good faith is satisfied where the seller or supplier 'deals fairly and equitably with the other party *of whose legitimate interests he also takes account.'* This part of Recital 16 was not reproduced in the 1994 Regulations, but its implication is that where the other party's legitimate interests under the contract are not taken into account then the requirement of good faith is not satisfied. As the definition of good faith in the 1994 Regulations is not replaced in the 1999 Regulations by a new definition, but simply omitted, arguably it is open to the courts to have regard to and possibly adopt the 1994 definition when applying the 1999 Regulations. In any case, paragraphs (a) – (d) above were *particular* factors, leaving it open to the courts to develop a wider definition should they so desire.

In relation to contract law, the concept of good faith is a difficult one to define with any precision, but it may be said to consist of a procedural element and a substantive element. Thus Professor Beale states:

> I suspect that good faith has a double operation. First, it has a procedural aspect. It will require the supplier to consider the consumer's interests. However, a clause which might be unfair if it came as a surprise may be upheld if the business took steps to bring it to the consumer's attention and to explain it. Secondly, it has a substantive content; some clauses may cause such an imbalance that they should always be treated as ... unfair.[16]

A clause excluding liability for death or personal injury caused by negligence might be an example.

Procedural good faith is concerned with the behaviour of the parties during the pre-contract negotiations, rather than with the terms of the contract. In this respect, good faith means particularly disclosure of information about the terms of the contract so that the process of entering into the contract is as open as possible. The aim of procedural good faith is to protect consumer choice by correcting any market failure brought about by inadequate information. Procedural good faith is easily reconciled to the classical model of contract law and Adam Smith's philosophy of self-interested exchange. Substantive good faith is not so easy to square with this individualism. Substantive good faith means that the terms of the contract must not be contrary to good faith in the sense that they operate to give the seller or supplier an unfair advantage under the contract. In this sense, good faith extends to control over the drafting of contractual terms; it would enable a term to be unenforceable because unconscionable, something which the classic undividualistic model of contract law does not admit.

Clearly, the concept of substantive good faith is a problematical one for the common law of contract. At this point, several important points may be made about the implications of substantive good faith for English law. In the first place, the English Sale of Goods Act lays down that something is done in good faith where it is done honestly.[17] Thus, certain remedies are available only to a *bona fide,* contracts of the utmost good faith.[18] Secondly, certain categories of contract – most notably, contracts of insurance – are contracts *uberrimae fidei*, contracts of the utmost good faith. In such contracts, one party possesses knowledge not easily accessible to the other party and disclosure of that knowledge is deemed by law to be good faith. The concept of good faith in some circumstances may require more than honesty and disclosure. This is particularly so where the parties are in a fiduciary relationship, where one party reposes trust and confidence in the other. In such a relationship a high standard of conduct is required of the fiduciary; not only must he act honestly but he must place the beneficiary's interests above his own interests.

Carter and Furmston[19] argue that in a substantive sense a duty of good faith is wider than a duty of honesty but falls short of amounting to a fiduciary duty. The essence of such a duty, they say, is a requirement to have regard to the legitimate interests of the other party to the contract. The important point to recognise about this interpretation of good faith is that it does not deny the right to act self-interestedly as in a fiduciary relationship; it merely curtails or sets limits on that right.

Good faith and the common law

The common law has set its face very firmly against a general doctrine of good faith and fairness. That does not mean that it has eschewed the concept entirely. In relation to clauses which exclude or restrict the liability of one party to the contract, it requires that the other party be given adequate notice of such clause before they can be held to be incorporated into the contract.[20] The purpose of this doctrine of notice, as it is known, is that one party must not be taken by surprise by the terms of the contract. In this way, the common law may be said, in effect, to have admitted into its midst some of the principles which govern procedural fairness and good faith. The concept of procedural fairness may be seen also in the approach which the courts have taken towards the application of the reasonableness test in the Unfair Contract Terms Act; a clause restricting or excluding liability is more likely to satisfy this requirement if the other party has been given adequate notice of it and, further, can be seen to be presented with the choice of contracting with or without the clause.

The most important recognition by the common law of a procedural duty of fairness and good faith occurred in the decision of the Court of Appeal in *Interfoto Picture Library Ltd* v. *Stilotto Visual Programmes Ltd*.[21] That case concerned the degree of notice required for the effective incorporation of an onerous condition into an oral contract. The defendants ordered photographic transparencies from the plaintiffs. There had been no previous course of dealing between the parties. The plaintiffs sent 47 transparencies together with a delivery note which contained a condition stating that a holding fee of £5 a day for each transparency was payable for every day that the transparencies were kept in excess of fourteen days. The defendants forgot about the transparencies and did not return them until after one month. The plaintiffs sent them an invoice for £3,783.50. The Court of Appeal held that the above condition was not incorporated into the contract because insufficient notice of its terms had been given to the defendants. They said that a party who seeks to incorporate into a contract a term which is particularly onerous or unusual must prove that the term has been fairly and reasonably drawn to the attention of the other party.

In particular terms, the decision in *Interfoto* is significant for its extension of the rule laid down by the Court of Appeal in *Spurling* v. *Bradshaw*[22] that the more unusual or unreasonable a clause in a contract the greater the degree of notice required by law. More generally, *Interfoto* is of importance for the judgement of Bingham LJ, in which he interpreted the cases on sufficiency of notice in terms of a procedural duty of good faith. In a key philosophical passage he explained the concept of good faith in this context as follows:

> In many civil law systems, and perhaps in most legal systems outside the common law world, the law of obligations recognises and enforces an overriding principle that in making and carrying out contracts parties should act in good faith. This does not simply mean that they should not deceive each other, a principle which any legal system must recognise; its effect is perhaps most aptly conveyed by such metaphorical colloquialisms as 'playing fair', 'coming clean' or 'putting one's cards face upwards on the table'. It is in essence a principle of fair and open dealing.
>
> The well known cases on sufficiency of notice are in my view properly to be read in this context. At one level they are concerned with a question of pure contractual analysis, whether one party has done enough to give the other notice of the incorporation of a term in the contract. At another level they are concerned with a somewhat different question, whether it would in all the circumstances be fair (or reasonable) to hold a party bound by any conditions or by a particular condition of an unusual and stringent nature.[23]

Later in his judgement, Bingham LJ seemed to expressly admit the existence of a *procedural* duty of good faith in the common law:

> The tendency of the English authorities has, I think, been to look at the nature of the transaction in question and the character of the parties to it; to consider what notice the party alleged to be bound was given of the particular condition said to bind him; and to resolve whether in all the

circumstances it is fair to hold him bound by the condition in question. This may yield a result not very different from the civil law principle of good faith, *at any rate so far as the formation of the contract is concerned.*[24]

In the area of procedural good faith, the approach of the common law may therefore be characterised as a pragmatic one. This pragmatism contrasts very sharply to the intransigence shown by the common law to the recognition of a general duty of substantive good faith. Here, the common law clings to an individualistic notion of contract, where the parties are expected to look after their own interests.

This view of contract was stated with robustness by the House of Lords in handing down their decision in *Walford* v. *Miles.*[25] In that case, the parties were involved in negotiations for the sale of a business. The sellers informed the buyers that if they provided a comfort letter from their bank confirming that the bank had offered them loan facilities to make the purchase they would terminate negotiations concerning the business with any third party. The buyers duly provided the comfort letter, but several days later the sellers withdrew from the negotiations and decided to sell to a third party. The buyers brought an action for breach of a collateral 'lock-out' agreement under which they claimed to have been given an exclusive opportunity to reach agreement with the sellers. They alleged that it was an implied term of this agreement that the sellers would continue to negotiate with them in good faith, so long as they desired to purchase the business. The House of Lords held that a lock-out agreement, whereby one party agreed for good consideration not to negotiate with anyone except the other party for a specified period could constitute an enforceable agreement. However, an agreement to negotiate in good faith for an unspecified period was not enforceable.

The rationale of the rule concerning good faith is set out in the speech of Lord Ackner in the following terms:

> [T]he concept of a duty to carry on negotiations in good faith is inherently repugnant to the adversarial position of the parties when involved in negotiations. Each party to the negotiations is entitled to pursue his (or her) own interests, so long as he avoids making misrepresentations ... A duty to negotiate in good faith is as unworkable in practice as it is inherently inconsistent with the position of a negotiating party.[26]

However, although the common law steadfastly refuses to recognise the existence of a general doctrine of good faith that does not mean that the concept is entirely absent from its domain. In addition to the cases where a procedural duty of good faith has been recognised a number of cases may be cited as evidence of a notion of good faith influencing the outcome. Thus, in *D & C Builders* v. *Rees,*[27] Lord Denning laid down the following qualification to the application of the principle of equitable estoppel:

The creditor is only barred from his legal rights when it would be *inequitable* for him to insist on them. Where there has been a *true accord,* under which the creditor voluntarily agrees to accept a lesser sum in satisfaction, and the debtor *acts* on that accord by paying the lesser sum and the creditor accepts it, then it would be inequitable for the creditor afterwards to insist on the balance. But he is not bound unless there has been a true accord between them.[28]

The plaintiffs, *D & C Builders Ltd*, did some work on premises owned by the defendant, Mr Rees. The defendant paid £250 on account and £482 was owing on completion of the contract. The plaintiffs were in financial difficulties and, knowing of this, Mrs Rees offered them £300 by way of final settlement which the plaintiffs accepted. The plaintiffs then sued for the balance. The defendant was barred from raising an estoppel; there had been no true accord between the parties as Mrs Rees had compelled the builders to accept the sum of £300. In essence, Mrs Rees had acted unfairly and contrary to good faith in procuring a settlement by intimidation.

In *Williams* v. *Roffey Bros*,[29] the defendants were main contractors employed to refurbish a block of flats. They subcontracted the carpentry work to the plaintiffs at a price of £20,000. The main contract contained a penalty clause under which the main contractor would incur a liability to the employer in the event of late completion. The plaintiffs' subcontractor ran into financial difficulties after completing part of the work (he had underpriced the job) and the main contractor offered him an additional £10,300 to complete the carpentry work on time. The work was completed on time but the main contractor refused to pay this additional sum. The Court of Appeal held that the promise of additional payment by the defendants was enforceable because they had obtained a practical benefit in the form of avoiding a late finish penalty. The main contractor in effect recognised that the subcontractor had originally underpriced the work and in fact it was the main contractor who had opened negotiations for the variation of the subcontract. The decision of the Court of Appeal is a recognition that it would have been inequitable, or contrary to good faith, to allow the defendants to go back on their promise of an additional payment of £10,300.

In *Balfour Beatty Civil Engineering Ltd* v. *Docklands Light Railway Ltd*,[30] a contractor was employed to carry out civil engineering repairs to the Docklands Light Railway. The contract between the parties was based on the ICE standard form but with two important amendments which were greatly to the employer's advantage. First, the employer's representative took the place of the engineer in the standard conditions. Secondly, the clause providing for the settlement of disputes by arbitration was omitted. A dispute did arise which concerned claims by the contractor for a longer period to complete the contract than granted by the employer and for additional costs for which he alleged the employer was responsible. The Court of Appeal held that the parties' rights and obligations were governed by the contract. Under the contract the contractor's entitlements depended upon the employer's judgement. The court did not have the power to review the exercise of that judgement. Sir Thomas Bingham MR, in giving the judgement of the court said:

> It is not for the court to decide whether the Contractor made a good bargain or a bad one, it can only give effect to what the parties agreed.[31]

Nonetheless, Sir Thomas Bingham went on to say that the employer was subject to a duty of good faith in the sense that he was bound to act honestly, fairly and reasonably in arriving at his judgement even where there was no such obligation in the contract. If the contractor could prove a breach of this duty he would be entitled to a remedy.

In *First Energy (UK) Ltd* v. *Hungarian International Bank Ltd*,[32] Steyn LJ recognised the influence of good faith in shaping the common law in the following terms:

> a theme that runs through our law of contract is that the reasonable expectations of honest men must be protected. It is not a rule or a principle of law. It is the objective which has been and still is the principal moulding force of our law of contract. It affords no licence to a judge to depart from binding precedent. On the other hand, if the *prima facie* solution to a problem runs counter to the reasonable expectations of honest men, this criterion sometimes requires a rigorous re-examination of the problem to ascertain whether the law does indeed compel demonstrable unfairness.

Good faith and the Regulations

The concept of good faith set out in the Regulations is novel to the English common law of obligations. It is derived from civil law and in particular the German Standard Contract Terms Act 1976, which provides for the avoidance of a term which is unreasonably disadvantageous to a party 'contrary to the requirements of good faith'. This civil law principle is difficult to reconcile with the classic individualistic view of contract so uncompromisingly set out by the House of Lords in *Walford*. Nonetheless, the evidence is that neither the bodies charged with enforcing the Regulations nor the courts are shrinking from this task. The approach taken to the requirement of good faith by the OFT, one of the bodies charged with enforcing the Regulations, is a rigorous one and they clearly regard this requirement as more than a procedural duty. The Legal Director of the OFT has stated that the requirement of good faith involves more than the absence of 'bad faith' in the narrow English sense of dishonest or deceptive conduct. It necessitates consideration of two factors:

- the extent of any inequality of bargaining power between supplier and customer; and

- whether, in the circumstances, use of the term by the trader amounts to dealing fairly and equitably with consumers, and taking into account their legitimate interets.[33]

Significantly, she goes on to say that where suppliers are dominant in their markets and where it is difficult for consumers to avoid continuing to deal with them after an initial transaction, the OFT will be unlikely to have accepted their unsupported professions of good faith. In other words, the onus on suppliers with monopoly powers to establish good faith in continuing to use a particular contract term is likely to prove a heavy one.

The OFT are of the opinion that a term is more likely to comply with the duty of good faith if it meets the requirement of plain English contained in the Regulations. Under the provisions of Regulation 6, a seller or supplier must ensure that any written term of a contract is expressed in plain, intelligible language. If there is doubt about the meaning of a written term, the interpretation most favourable to the consumer shall prevail. There is no definition, either in the Directive or in the Regulations, of 'plain, intelligible language', but in the view of the OFT it means avoiding misleading or confusing consumers and using language which an ordinary person can understand without taking legal advice.[34]

The concepts of fairness and good faith under the Regulations came before the Court of Appeal in *Director General of Fair Trading* v. *First National Bank plc*.[35] The First National Bank lent money under its standard form agreement. Condition 8 of the Agreement provided that where the Bank obtained judgement against a borrower in default, interest was payable by the borrower at the contractual rate on the outstanding principal plus accrued interest unpaid at the date of judgement, until the judgement was discharged by payment. The Director General received a number of complaints from members of the public about this standard term. The substance of these complaints was that borrowers were not always aware of the effect of this term and to their surprise they found themselves liable to the Bank for amounts far beyond those provided for in the judgements against them. The Director General sought an injunction against the Bank on the ground that Condition 8 was unfair within the meaning of the 1994 Regulations.

There are two issues in this case: first, whether the term in question was a core term as defined by regulation 3(2) of the 1994 Regulations and secondly, whether the term was unfair. In relation to the first issue, the trial judge, Evans-Lombe J, and the Court of Appeal held that the term was not a core term. Gibson LJ, for the Court of Appeal, said that the test of whether a term is a core term is whether it falls within one or both of paragraphs (a) and (b) of regulation 3(2). He said that it did not fall within the scope of either of these paragraphs. It did not define the subject matter of the contract nor did it concern the adequacy of the price or remuneration. Condition 8 was a default provision dealing with the consequencies of a breach of contract by the borrower, not a provision stipulating the rate at which interest was payable.

In relation to the second issue, whether the term was unfair, Evans-Lombe J held that the term was not unfair because a potential borrower would not have thought that it was unfair if its effects had been drawn to his attention. The trial judge then went on to consider the requirement of good faith. He distinguished substantive unfairness and procedural unfairness. He said that the only substantive advantage of which the term deprived the borrower was his exemption from interest on a judgement debt under the County Court (Interest on Judgement Debts) Order.[36] In the view of the judge that was not a significant advantage because the Order did not prohibit such exemption. On procedural unfairness, the judge concluded that, although steps should have been taken by the Bank to draw Condition 8 to the attention of borrowers, their failure to do so did not amount to procedural unfairness.

The Court of Appeal reversed the judge's decision on the unfairness of the term, holding that it was unfair. Gibson LJ said that the judge was not correct in his approach. The test of unfairness was not to be judged by personal concepts of inherent fairness apart from the requirements of the Directive and the Regulations. The test of unfairness in the Regulations, he said, consists of three elements:

(1)   an absence of good faith;
(2)   a significant imbalance in the parties' rights and obligations under the contract; and
(3)   detriment to the consumer.

In considering these elements, Gibson LJ said that the conceptual roots of good faith lay in civil law. He then went on to refer to Bingham LJ's dictum in *Interfoto*[37] and to cite Beale's distinction between procedural good faith and substantive good faith. In a test which appears to merge these two aspects of good faith, Gibson LJ summed up the concept in the following terms:

> As is aptly said in Anson's Law of Contract, 27th edn (1998), p.293, the 'good faith' element seeks to promote fair and open dealing, and to prevent unfair surprise and the absence of real choice. A term to which the consumer's attention is not specifically drawn but which may operate in a way which the consumer might reasonably not expect and to his disadvantage may offend the requirement of good faith. Terms must be reasonably transparent and should not operate to defeat the reasonable expectations of the consumer. The consumer in choosing whether to enter into a contract should be put in a position where he can make an informed choice.[38]

Gibson LJ, went on to say that the element of significant imbalance would appear to overlap substantially with that of the absence of good faith. A term which gives a significant advantage to the seller or supplier without a countervailing benefit to the consumer (such as a price reduction) might fail to satisfy this aspect of unfairness.

Finally, for a term to be found unfair there must be an element of detriment to the consumer.

Applying these principles to the facts of the case, the Court of Appeal held that the Bank, with its strong bargaining position relative to the consumer, had not adequately considered the consumer's interests. The term created unfair surprise and it caused a significant imbalance in the rights and obligations of the parties by allowing the Bank to obtain interest after judgement in circumstances where statutory interest could not be obtained.

The decision of the Court of Appeal, as well as being of philosophical interest in terms of its analysis of the concepts of unfairness and good faith, is also of practical relevance in terms of the remedy awarded. The Court did not grant the Director General an injunction against the use of the term but, instead, asked the parties to reach agreement on the amendment of the term.

To sum, the duty of good contained in the Regulations consists of two broad elements:

- In a *procedural* sense, there must be fair and open dealing in the formation of a contract, so that, in particular, the consumer is not taken by surprise by its contents.
- In a *substantive* sense, the seller or supplier must take account of the legitimate expectations of the consumer under the contract.

In philosophical terms, the duty of good faith lies somewhere between a duty of honesty and a fiduciary duty and involves suppliers in taking account of the legitimate contractual expectations of their customers. The decision of the Court of Appeal in *DGFT* v. *First National Bank plc* shows that the court was prepared to take into account both the procedural and the substantive elements of good faith and, to that extent, the decision is a significant advance on the approach of Bingham LJ in *Interfoto*. It would be far too sweeping to say that this decision spells the end of the doctrine of freedom of contract in English law, but if the courts continue to take as broad an approach to the application of good faith as taken in the judgement of Gibson LJ then, at the very least, the extreme expression of that doctrine by the House of Lords in *Walford* will require modification.

Remedies and enforcement

The Regulations contain two enforcement mechanisms, an individual enforcement mechanism and a collective enforcement mechanism. The individual enforcement mechanism is contained in Regulation 8. Under the provisions of Regulation 8(1), an unfair term in a contract conducted with a consumer by a seller or supplier is not binding on the consumer. Regulation 8(2) provides that the contract shall continue to bind the parties if it is capable of continuing in existence without the unfair term. Regulation 8 means that a business cannot enforce an unfair term against a consumer. No criminal penalty is involved.

The collective enforcement mechanism is contained in Regulations 10–15. In practical terms these provisions are the most significant part of the Regulations. Their principal features are as follows:

(a) The Director General of Fair Trading has a duty to consider any complaint made that any contract term drawn up for general use is unfair, unless the complaint appears to him to be frivolous or vexatious. If, following a complaint, the Director considers that a contract term is unfair he may, if he considers it appropriate to do so, seek an injunction to prevent the continued use of the term. Before seeking an injunction, the Director may, if he considers it appropriate, try to obtain an undertaking from the business concerned that it will stop using the term. The Director is under an obligation to give reasons for his decisions as to whether or not to apply for an injunction (Regulations 10 and 12).

(b) A qualifying body named in Schedule 1 (statutory regulators, trading standards departments and the Consumers' Association) may also apply for an injunction to prevent the continued use of an unfair contract term. It must first notify the Director of its intention at least 14 days before the application is made (unless the Director consents to a shorter period). A qualifying body has a duty to consider a complaint if it has told the Director General that it will do so (Regulations 11 and 12). It must notify the Director of any undertakings given to it or of any orders made by the court (Regulation 14).

(c) The Director and the qualifying bodies have powers to require traders to produce copies of their standard contracts in order to facilitate investigation of complaints and to ensure compliance with undertakings or injunctions (Regulation 13).

(d) The Director has wide powers to distribute information and to give advice about the operation of the Regulations (Regulation 15).

Two points must be made clear about the duties of the Director and of the qualifying bodies under the 1999 Regulations. In the first place, they cannot act on their own initiative; they can act only when they receive a complaint. Secondly, in relation to the 1994 Regulations, the DTI considered that it was not intended that the Director would exercise his powers to obtain a direct civil law remedy in the case of a particular aggrieved consumer, but that he would act only in the general interest of consumers to ensure that unfair terms, once identified, did not continue in use. There is no reason to believe that this principle does not apply to the powers given to the Director and to the qualifying bodies under the 1999 Regulations.

Following the issue of the 1994 Regulations the Director set up a specialist group within the Office of Fair Trading (OFT), the Unfair Contract Terms Unit, to implement his duties under the Regulations. This Unit produces regular bulletins setting out the approach of the OFT to the Regulations and the outcomes of their investigations into complaints about unfair contract terms.

The relationship between the Regulations and earlier law governing unfair terms

The Regulations add to, and do not replace, the common law and earlier legislation governing unfair terms. Of particular importance is the relationship between the Regulations and the Unfair Contract Terms Act 1977 and in this context two points are worthy of note. First, the Regulations govern a narrower range of contracts than the Act. Thus, only consumer contracts are within the scope of the Regulations, whereas the Act applies to consumer and non-consumer contracts. However, insurance contracts are excluded from the scope of the Act but not from the scope of the Regulations. Secondly, the Act deals only with clauses which attempt to exclude or restrict liability, whereas the Regulations deal with unfair contract terms in general. The Act extends to notices disclaiming liability, but notices appear to fall outside the scope of the Regulations.

There is, of course, considerable overlay between the two legislative measures and it is to be regretted that in implementing the EC directive on unfair terms in consumer contracts Parliament did not see fit to produce one unified piece of legislation. In some cases, the Act and other earlier legislation offer stronger protection against certain types of exemption clauses than the Regulations. Thus, clauses exempting liability for death or personal injury and clauses exempting the liability of a seller or a supplier for breach of the statutory implied terms relating to description, quality and fitness in a contract with a consumer are void under the Act but subject to a fairness test under the Regulations. Further, under the provisions of the Consumer Transactions (Restrictions on Statements) Order 1976[39] the display of a notice by a seller exempting his liability for breach of those statutory implied terms is an offence. The provisions of the Act that declare certain terms void do not fit in with a procedural approach to unfairness; rather they are examples of a substantive approach. The pattern of control in the Act is therefore a mixture of the procedural and substantive approaches to fairness.

THE INDICATIVE AND ILLUSTRATIVE LIST OF UNFAIR TERMS

Schedule 3 to the Regulations (which reproduces the Annex to the Directive) contains a list of (17) terms which *may* be regarded as unfair. At the outset, three points should be noted about this list. In the first place, it is 'indicative and illustrative'. In other words, it is non-exhaustive; the fact that a term does not appear in the list does not create a presumption that it is fair. Any term that, contrary to the requirement of good faith creates an imbalance in the parties' rights and obligations under the contract to the detriment of the consumer is potentially unfair. Secondly, it is *not* a blacklist. It is a greylist of terms which *may* be regarded as unfair and the appearance of a term in the list does not necesssarily mean that it is unfair. Thirdly, it is wide in scope. It is concerned not just with clauses which exclude or limit the liability of a seller or supplier, but sets out a range of clauses which possess as their main unifying theme onerous obligations that are imposed on a consumer, or rights under the contract that are taken away from the consumer, by reasons of the fact that the seller or supplier is the more powerful of the contracting parties.

Arguably, in assessing the fairness or otherwise of a particular term the courts will be required to examine its substance and effect to see if it resembles one (or more) of the indicative and illustrative terms. They will then need to assess the fairness or otherwise of the term in the context of the contract as a whole. It must be emphasised that if a term does not resemble any of the indicative and illustrative terms that is not conclusive of its fairness.

The list reproduced from paragraph 1 of Schedule 3, is as follows:

(a) *excluding or limiting the legal liability of a seller or supplier in the event of the death of a consumer or personal injury to the latter resulting from an act or omission of that seller or supplier;*

(b) *inappropriately excluding or limiting the legal rights of the consumer vis-à-vis the seller or supplier or another party in the event of total or partial non-performance or inadequate performance by the seller or supplier of any of the contractual obligations, including the option of offsetting a debt owed to the seller or supplier against any claim which the consumer may have against him;*

(c) *making an agreement binding on the consumer whereas provision of services by the seller or supplier is subject to a condition whose realisation depends on his own will alone;*

(d) *permitting the seller or supplier to retain sums paid by the consumer where the latter decides not to conclude or perform the contract, without providing for the consumer to receive compensation of an equivalent amount from the seller or supplier where the latter is the party cancelling the contract;*

(e) *requiring any consumer who fails to fulfil his obligation to pay a disproportionately high sum in compensation;*

(f) *authorising the seller or supplier to dissolve the contract on a discretionary basis where the same facility is not granted to the consumer, or permitting the seller or supplier to retain the sums paid for services not yet supplied by him where it is the seller or supplier himself who dissolves the contract;*

(g) *enabling the seller or supplier to terminate a contract of indeterminate duration without reasonable notice except where there are serious grounds for doing so;*

(h)   *automatically extending a contract of fixed duration where the consumer does not indicate otherwise, when the deadline fixed for the consumer to express this desire not to extend the contract is unreasonably early;*

(i)   *irrevocably binding the consumer to terms with which he had no real opportunity of becoming acquainted before the conclusion of the contract;*

(j)   *enabling the seller or supplier to alter the terms of the contract unilaterally without a valid reason which is specified in the contract;*

(k)   *enabling the seller or supplier to alter unilaterally without a valid reason any characteristics of the product or service to be provided;*

(l)   *providing for the price of goods to be determined at the time of delivery or allowing a seller of goods or supplier of services to increase their price without in both cases giving the consumer the corresponding right to cancel the contract if the final price is too high in relation to the price agreed when the contract was concluded;*

(m)   *giving the seller or supplier the right to determine whether the goods or services supplied are in conformity with the contract, or giving him the exclusive right to interpret any term of the contract;*

(n)   *limiting the seller's or supplier's obligation to respect commitments undertaken by his agents or making his commitments subject to compliance with a particular formality;*

(o)   *obliging the consumer to fulfil all his obligations where the seller or supplier does not perform his;*

(p)   *giving the seller or supplier the possibility of transferring his rights and obligations under the contract, where this may serve to reduce the guarantees for the consumer, without the latter's agreement;*

(q)   *excluding or hindering the consumer's right to take legal action or exercise any other legal remedy, particularly by requiring the consumer to take disputes exclusively to arbitration not covered by legal provisions, unduly restricting the evidence available to him or imposing on him a burden of proof which, according to the applicable law, should lie with another party to the contract.*

It is now proposed to examine a selection of these indicative and illustrative terms which appear to be of particular relevance for construction contracts.[40]

Illustrative term 1(a). Excluding or limiting liability for death or personal injury

Under the provisions of section 2(1) of the Unfair Contract Terms Act 1977, this type of clause is void, regardless of fairness. Section 2(1) does not just apply to consumers; it extends to exclusion or limitation of liability for death or personal injury caused to anyone. So, in this respect the 1977 Act provides far stronger protection to consumers than the Regulations.

However, section 2(1) of the 1977 Act governs only exclusion or limitation of liability for death or personal injury *caused by negligence*. The illustrative term in paragraph 1(a) makes no reference to negligence and arguably it extends to exclusion or limitation of liability by a business for breach of a strict liability duty. Thus, under the provisions of Part I of the Consumer Protection Act 1987 a contractor is under a strict liability duty to supply only safe products in carrying out the building works and any attempt by him to exclude or limit this duty would come within the scope of the illustrative term in paragraph 1(a).

Illustrative term 1(b). Excluding or limiting liability for breach of contract

A contractor may incorporate into a construction contract a term which excludes or limits his liability in the event of poor quality workmanship, or total or partial non-performance of the contract or supplying materials which do not comply with the statutory implied terms as to description, quality and fitness. The illustrative term in paragraph 1(b) means that such exclusion or limitation is potentially unfair under the Regulations.

However, as in the case of the illustrative term in paragraph 1(a), the 1977 Act provides the consumer with stronger protection against this kind of term than the Regulations provide. Under the provisions of section 7(2) of the 1977 Act any exclusion or limitation of liability by a contractor in a contract with a consumer for breach of his implied statutory duties as regards the materials used is void, regardless of fairness. Any attempt by a contractor to exclude or limit his liability for death or personal injury resulting from breach of his implied duty to perform the contract with reasonable care and skill is void, by virtue of the provisions of section 2(1) of the 1977 Act. Exclusion or limitation of liability for other loss or damage resulting from performing the contract negligently is subject to the reasonableness test contained in the 1977 Act, by virtue of the provisions of section 2(2).

Any attempt by a contractor to prohibit a consumer's right of offsetting a debt owed to him in the event of his (the contractor) being in breach of contract is not caught by the 1977 Act, but under the Regulations is potentially unfair.

Illustrative terms 1(j) and 1(k). Variation of the contract

The illustrative terms in paragraph 1(j) and 1(k) would apply to a construction contract which gives the contractor the right to change unilaterally terms agreed with the consumer and to change unilaterally any characteristics of the materials or services provided. Such variations may be fair if the consumer is given notice of the terms which may be varied and there is a valid reason for the variation, e.g. the contractor is unable to obtain the materials specified in the contract because the only available source of supply fails.

Illustrative term 1(l). Right of the supplier to increase the price

A contractor may include in a building contract a term giving him the right to increase the agreed price. This is not a core term and is therefore subject to the test of fairness. Arguably, such a term is unfair unless the consumer is given the right to cancel the contract if the price ultimately charged increases too much. This illustrative term does not apply to indexation clauses where the contractual price is linked to a recognised index.

Illustrative term 1(q). Restrictions on legal remedies

This illustrative term covers terms which exclude or restrict the consumer's right to take legal action, e.g. setting a very short deadline by which complaints have to be made. Such terms are caught by the 1977 Act, by virtue of section 13(1). It also covers terms which oblige a consumer to refer a dispute to arbitration; these terms are subject to the provisions of the Consumer Arbitration Agreements Act 1988, which makes them either unenforceable or subject to the discretion of the court which will not allow a compulsory reference to arbitration if that would be against the consumer's interest.

CONCLUDING COMMENT

It is difficult to offer a conclusion on a piece of legislation whose implementation is still in its infancy, but a few brief comments are in order. The Regulations introduce into English law a general duty of fairness and good faith in relation to pre-formulated and non-negotiated terms included in contracts made between businesses and consumers. That, in itself, is a significant reform since, of course, the common law does not develop deductively from general principles but on a case by case basis, extending (if at all) its rules by analogous reasoning. The Regulations are nothing if not radical in a juridical sense. More than that, though, they challenge the orthodox individualistic notion of contract to which the common law has clung so tenaciously. They temper that individualism with a duty of solicitude.

It is far too soon to predict how deeply these generalised concepts will take root in English law; suffice it to say that they arm the judges with powerful intellectual tools with which to reshape the law of contract should they so choose. Arguably, though, the most far reaching feature of the Regulations is the powers of enforcement it gives to the OFT. The OFT appear to be using these powers rigorously and have persuaded many suppliers to discontinue or amend what they consider to be unfair terms.[41] The principal beneficiary of the Regulations may well prove to be contractual practice rather than the law of contract.[42]

SUMMARY

1. The English law of contract is based on an individualistic view of contract under which the parties are free to include in their contracts any terms they consider to be to their advantage.

2. There is no general doctrine at common law by which a term of a contract may be declared unfair.

3. The Unfair Terms in Consumer Contracts Regulations 1999 are an important exception to the common law in this respect.

4. The Regulations implement into English law the EC Directive on unfair terms in consumer contracts.

5. They apply to non-negotiated pre-formulated terms in a contract concluded between a consumer and a seller or supplier.

6. A consumer is a natural person who, in making a contract to which the Regulations apply, is acting for purposes outside his business.

7. A seller or supplier is any person who sells goods or supplies goods or services and who, in making a contract to which the Regulations apply, is acting for purposes relating to his business.

8. Core terms (i.e. terms which define the subject matter of the contract concerned or concern the price of the goods or services supplied) are not subject to the Regulations, provided that they are in plain, intelligible language.

9. Construction contracts, where a contractor supplies work and materials to a building owner or tenant who acts for purposes outside his business, are within the scope of the Regulations. A design contract whereby a design professional supplies his services to such a person are similarly caught by the Regulations.

10. Contracts for the sale of land, as where a developer sells a domestic dwelling to a person who acts for purposes outside his business, are not contracts of sale or contracts for the supply of goods and services but the general view is that they come within the scope of the Regulations.

11. The core of the Regulations are the concepts of unfairness and good faith.

12. A term is unfair if:
    (i) it is contrary to the requirements of good faith; and
    (ii) it causes a significant imbalance in the parties' rights and obligations under the contract to the detriment of the consumer; and
    (iii) there is an element of detriment to the consumer.

13. Good faith, broadly speaking, requires the seller or supplier to deal fairly and equitably with the consumer and to take account of his legitimate interests under the contract. The consumer, in choosing whether to enter into a contract, must be put in a position where he can make an informed choice.

14. The Regulations provide some guidance as to the scope of these concepts by including in Schedule 3 an indicative and illustrative list of unfair terms.

15. Inclusion on the list means that a term *may* be unfair; exclusion from the list does not necessarily mean that a term *is* fair.

16. Where a term is held to be unfair it is not binding on the consumer.

17. The Directive General of Fair Trading is given powers to intervene to prevent the continued use of unfair terms in consumer contracts.

18. The Regulations supplement, but do not replace, earlier law governing unfair terms. It is important to bear in mind in this respect that in some circumstances the consumer is provided with greater protection against exclusion and limitation clauses by the Unfair Contract Terms Act 1977 than by the Regulations.

NOTES

1. (1875) LR 19 Eq 462, p.465.
2. Adam Smith, *The Wealth of Nations*, Everyman's Library edn. 1991, p.13.
3. For a detailed analysis of these philosophical trends and their effect on the law of contract see Atiyah, P.S., *The Rise and Fall of Freedom of Contract*, Oxford University Press, 1979.
4. See, for example, Final Report of the Committee on Consumer Protection, 1962, Cmnd 1781, pp.15–17; Report of the Committee on Consumer Credit 1971, Cmnd 4596, para. 6.1.12; and Law Com. Second Report on Exemption Clauses, No. 69, 1975, paras 11, 146.
5. For an analysis of these influences on the general law of contract see Beatson J, *Anson's Law of Contract*, 27th edn, Oxford University Press, 1998, Ch. 1.
6. [1974] IWLR 1308, p.1316. Lord Diplock's doctrine of superior bargaining power was applied by Lord Denning in *Levison* v. *Patent Carpet Cleaning Co.* [1977] 3 WLR 90, where the issue was whether an exemption clause on the back of an order form provided an effective defence to an action for fundamental breach of contract.
7. The law and economics movement has spawned a considerable amount of literature. For an economic analysis of standard form contracts and a general doctrine of unconscionability, the reader is directed to Trebilcock, 'Economic Criteria of Unconscionability' in *Studies in Contract Law* (eds. Reiter and Swann), pp.390–396, 404–408 and Kessler, 'Contracts of Adhesion – Some thoughts about Freedom of Contract' (1943) 43 Col. LR 629, pp.631–632. The relevant parts of these publications are reprinted in Beale, H.G., Bishop, W.D. and Furmston, M.P., *Contract Cases and Materials*, 3rd edn, Butterworths, 1995, pp.831–835 and 827–828.
8. SI 1999 No. 2083.
9. S.I 1994 No. 3159.
10. 93/13/EEC, OJ No. L95, 21.4.93, p.29.
11. Implementation of the EC Directive on Unfair Terms in Consumer Contracts (93/13/EEC): A Consultation Document (October 1993); Implementation of the EC Directive on Unfair Terms in Consumer Contracts (93/13/EEC): A Further Consultation Document (September 1994); and The Unfair Terms in Consumer Contracts Regulations 1994 (SI 1994, No. 3159) Guidance Notes, July 1995.

12. OFT Briefing, *Unfair Standard Terms*, November, 1997.
13. See *R & B Customs Brokers Co. Ltd* v. *United Dominions Trust Ltd* [1988] 1 All ER 847. This case was distinguished by the Court of Appeal in *Stevenson* v. *Rogers* [1999] 1 All ER 613, where, in relation to section 14(2) of the Sale of Goods Act 1979, it was held that there was no requirement of regularity of dealing for a sale to be made in the course of a business.
14. DTI Guidance Notes, *op. cit.*, n.10, paras 3.19 and 3.20.
15. McKendrick, E., *Contract Law*, 4th edn, Macmillan Press Ltd (now Palgrave), 2000, p.365.
16. Beale, 'Legislative Control of Fairness. The Directive on Unfair Terms in Consumer Contracts' in Beatson J and Friedman, *Good Faith and Fault in Contract Law*, Oxford University Press, 1995, p.245.
17. Section 61(3).
18. See section 23 of the Sale of Goods Act 1979 (as amended).
19. [1994] 8 JCL 1–15.
20. See, for example, *Olley* v. *Marlborough Court Ltd* [1949] KB 532 and *Thornton* v. *Shoe Lane Parking* [1971] 2 QB 163.
21. [1989] QB 433.
22. [1956] 1 WLR 461.
23. *Supra*, n.21, p.439.
24. *Supra*, n.21, p.445.
25. [1992] 1 All ER 453.
26. *Ibid*, n.25, pp.460–461.
27. [1966] 2 QB 617.
28. *Ibid*, n.27, p.625.
29. [1991] 1 QB 1.
30. [1996] 78 BLR 42.
31. *Ibid*, n.30, p.57.
32. [1993] 2 Lloyd's Rep. 194, at p.196.
33. Pat Edwards, 'The Challenge of the Regulations' in OFT, *Unfair Contract Terms Bulletin 4*, December 1997, p.23.
34. OFT, *Unfair Contract Terms Bulletin 4*, December 1997, pp.12–17.
35. [2000] 2 All ER 759.
36. SI 1991, No. 1184.
37. *Op. cit.* n.21.
38. *Supra*, n.35, p.769.
39. SI 1976 No. 1813.
40. For guidance on the complete list of indicative and illustrative terms see the notes in the appendix to the OFT Briefing, *Unfair Standard Terms*, *op. cit.*, n.11, to which the author is indebted in the preparation of this part of the chapter. A detailed analysis of the list is contained in Lockett, N. and Egan, M., *Unfair Terms in Consumer Agreements*, Wiley, 1995. See Howells, G., *Consumer Contract Law*, Blackstone Press Ltd, 1995, pp.46–48 for a categorisation of the illustrative terms.
41. See OFT, *Unfair Contract Terms Bulletin No. 5*, October 1998, p.17.
42. For a general critique of the 1994 Regulations see Brownsword and Howells (1995) JBL 243. For a philosophical analysis of good faith and the Regulations see Adams, J. and Brownsword, R., *Key Issues in Contract*, Butterworths, 1995, Ch. 7 and Ch. 8 (pp.281–291). For an analysis of the enforcement activities of the DGFT's Unfair Contract Terms Unit see Bright, S. (2000) 20 LS 331. Further change in this area of law is likely. The European Commission is consulting on amendments to the Directive and the DTI issued a consultation paper on this matter in July 2000, *European Commission Review of Directive 93/13/EEC on Unfair Terms in Consumer Contracts*.

3

Builders' Liability in Negligence

INTRODUCTION

This chapter is concerned first with the liability of the builder to a subsequent owner of a building. In such a case there is no contractual relationship between the parties and the basis of the builder's liability under the common law is the tort of negligence. The liability of the builder in negligence may, in certain cases, also be of relevance to the first purchaser. Thus, where a defective house has been purchased from a developer, rather than the builder, and the developer then goes into liquidation, the purchaser's only worthwhile cause of action will be against the builder. Under the common law this will have to be based on tortious negligence, since in such circumstances there will be no privity of contract between the purchaser and the builder. In the event of a purchase of a defective house from a vendor/builder who goes into liquidation, the purchaser's only means of recovery will be against any subcontractor if he has been responsible for the defect. Again, under the common law such recovery will have to be based on the tort of negligence. It must also be remembered that, as we have seen in Chapter 1, the purchaser of a defective building will in any case rarely have an action against his vendor because of the doctrine of caveat emptor, and so he is forced to seek elsewhere for a remedy.

This area of Construction Law gives rise to a number of problematical issues. These issues are where the boundaries of the law of tort should be drawn where the loss suffered is purely economic, the relationship between contract and tort, and whether the law should impose different obligations on a builder from those imposed on a manufacturer of chattels. It is an area of the law which has seen great change during the last twenty years. The pendulum has swung from a position where the law did not permit recovery in tort for a defective building to a position where recovery for such loss could be recovered in the tort of negligence in certain circumstances and then back to its original position.[1] It is the purpose of this chapter to trace these movements of the pendulum and to examine the arguments which the courts have advanced to justify these swings and counter-swings.

THE ORTHODOX VIEW

The orthodox view of liability in negligence for defective buildings, which may be said to have existed up to the period of the 1970s, was clear, if rigid in its application. It was that there was no liability in negligence on the part of the builder for any defective building work which he may have carried out, even if such works led to the death or personal injury of the occupier. Two cases can be cited as authority for that proposition. In *Cavalier* v. *Pope*,[2] the owner of a dilapidated house contracted with his tenant to repair the floor in the kitchen, but failed to do so. The tenant's wife, who lived in the house and was well aware of the danger from the floor, was injured when she fell through it. The House of Lords, although sympathetic to the wife, held that she had no claim for damages against the owner as she was not a party to the contract between the owner and the tenant. In *Bottomley* v. *Bannister*,[3] a firm of builders sold a new house to Mr Bottomley. It was agreed that they would make the house fit for habitation. By agreement Mr and Mrs Bottomley moved in before the house was completed. The boiler in the house was defectively installed in that no flue had been fixed to carry the fumes from it to the air outside, and, shortly after moving in, Mr and Mrs Bottomley were found dead in the bathroom from carbon monoxide poisoning. The administrators of Mr and Mrs Bottomley brought an action in contract and in tort against the builders. The Court of Appeal, rather surprisingly, held that there had been no breach of contract because the boiler was part of the realty and if properly regulated was not dangerous. In relation to the claim in tort, Scrutton LJ said:

> Now it is at present well established English law that, in the absence of an express contract, a landlord of an unfurnished house is not liable to his tenant, or a vendor of real estate to his purchaser, for defects in the house or land rendering it dangerous or unfit for occupation, even if he has constructed the defects himself or is aware of their existence.[4]

Greer LJ denied the claim in tort in somewhat wider terms, stating:

> English law does not recognise a duty in the air, so to speak; that is, a duty to undertake that no one shall suffer from one's carelessness ... . It seems to me that this principle ... applies to the case of a builder or other owner of property, when the question is whether he owes any duty towards people who may with his consent either as purchasers, tenants, or licensees or purchasers or tenants, come on to his property and be damaged by its defective condition.[5]

Some seven months after the judgements in *Bottomley* v. *Bannister* were delivered the House of Lords handed down their decision in *Donoghue* v. *Stevenson*,[6] during the course of which Lord Atkin set out his famous neighbour principle for determining when relations give rise to a duty of care in tort.[7] The exact status of that principle is still a matter for debate,[8] and it certainly did not bring about a revolution overnight in the scope of tortious relations. However, for present purposes, it is the importance of the case for the law on liability for defective products that must be considered. The facts of the case are of course extremely well known, but for the sake of demonstrating the seminal importance of the case they are worth repeating. The appellant drank a bottle of ginger-beer manufactured by the respondent, which a friend had bought from a retailer and given to her. She alleged that the bottle contained the decomposed remains of a snail, as a result of which she suffered from shock and severe gastro-enteritis. The bottle was opaque and the remains were not, and could not be, detected until the greater part of the contents of the bottle had been consumed. She did not have a contract with the retailer and she accordingly instituted proceedings against the manufacturer. The House of Lords held, by a bare majority of three to two, that these facts disclosed a cause of action and that the manufacturer of an article owed a duty to the ultimate consumer of it to take reasonable care to see that it is free from defect likely to cause injury to health. This has become known as the narrow rule of the case and it was expressed by Lord Atkin in the following terms:

> A manufacturer of products, which he sells in such a form as to show that he intends them to reach the ultimate consumer in the form in which they left him with no reasonable possibility of intermediate examination, and with the knowledge that the absence of reasonable care in the preparation or putting up of the products will result in an injury to the consumer's life or property, owes a duty to the consumer to take that reasonable care.[9]

There are a number of significant aspects of this narrow rule that need to be noted. Firstly, it created a new duty in the English law of tort (and also the Scottish law of delict) in that it demonstrated that there could be liability in negligence for a defective product independent of a contractual relationship. In this respect it disposed of what became known as the 'privity of contract fallacy', whereby it was said that the manufacturer of a defective product could not owe a duty of care to the ultimate consumer of that product because it would enable that consumer to take the benefit of a contract to which he was not a party. Secondly, the duty created was concerned with safety; that is, it is a duty owed by the manufacturer of a dangerous product, not simply a defective product. There is nothing in the speeches of the majority to suggest that the manufacturer would have been liable if the ginger-beer had been simply flat. Thirdly, the duty has not been confined to food and drink but has been extended to a wide range of products.[10] It has also been extended to include repairers.[11]

Buildings, however, were at first thought to be outside the scope of the rule. Thus, in *Otto* v. *Bolton*,[12] Atkinson J stated very firmly that the law as stated by Scrutton LJ and Greer LJ in *Bottomley* v. *Bannister* was not altered by the decision of the House of Lords in *Donoghue* v. *Stevenson*. He said:

> That was a case dealing with chattels and there is not a word in the case from beginning to end which indicates that the law relating to the building and sale of houses is the same as that relating to the manufacture and sale of chattels.[13]

If the orthodox principle governing this area of Construction Law can be stated clearly, the same cannot be said of the rationale underlying that principle. On examination, a number of factors can be seen to have influenced the courts in this area of the law. First and foremost, the doctrine of privity of contract, that only a person who is a party to a contract can sue on it, has had, and continues to have, immense influence on the development of the law of tortious liability for defective buildings. The question, of course, is why so many of the judiciary have felt bound by that doctrine. The answer lies partly in the fear of creating unlimited liability – a fear which has dominated and continues to dominate the whole law of negligence. The fear was expressed in the following terms by Alderson B in *Winterbottom* v. *Wright*:

> If we were to hold that the plaintiff could sue in such a case, there is no point at which such actions would stop. The only safe rule is to confine the right to recover to those who enter into a contract: if we go one step beyond that, there is no reason why we should not go fifty.[14]

As we have seen, that did not deter the majority of the House of Lords in *Donoghue* v. *Stevenson*, but their decision did not pave the way for the creation of a duty of care in negligence on the part of the builder. The reason for that seems to be that in the case of products the manufacturer does not intend his article to be examined either by the consumer or by any intermediate party. In this way, he is said to bring himself into a direct, or proximate, relationship with the consumer. In the case of buildings, however, it was felt that examination by a purchaser was much more likely, particularly in view of the fact that there is no implied obligation as to quality on the sale of a house.[15]

One final point needs to be made at this juncture on the rationale governing negligence and defective buildings. That is, in the cases so far discussed, the issue has always been liability for death or personal injury. No question has so far arisen of liability for a building – or a product, for that matter – which is defective but not dangerous.

THE ABANDONMENT OF ORTHODOXY

The orthodox view of the duty of care owed by a builder was abandoned in the 1970s and early 1980s when, in a series of decisions, the courts significantly enlarged the builder's liability in negligence. The two most significant of these cases are *Dutton* v. *Bognor Regis UDC* [16] and *Anns* v. *Merton LBC*.[17] Both these cases involved claims against local authorities, so that the question of the builder's liability was not before the court. However, in each of these cases the court felt it necessary to consider this issue.

The decisions in *Dutton* and *Anns* were foreshadowed by the High Court ruling in *Sharpe* v. *E.T. Sweeting & Son Ltd*.[18] The facts of that case are that the defendant company built a number of houses for Middlesbrough Corporation and the plaintiff's husband went into possession, as first tenant, of one of them when it was completed. The plaintiff lived there with him. Over the front door of the house was a reinforced concrete canopy which the defendants had constructed. One evening the plaintiff went outside the door and the concrete canopy fell on her, causing her injury. The cause of its fall was the faulty and negligent reinforcement by the defendant builders of the concrete. The legal issue in the case was whether or not the principle laid down in *Donoghue* v. *Stevenson* applied to these circumstances. Nield J held that it did. After considering the decisions in *Bottomley* v. *Bannister* and *Otto* v. *Bolton* which he thought were based on the fact that the defendants in those cases were owners, he summarised the law in the following terms:

> ... the fact that the owner is also the builder does not remove the owner's immunity, but when the builder is not the owner he enjoys no such immunity.[19]

It was in *Dutton* and *Anns*, however, that the most significant development in the builder's liability in negligence occurred. These two decisions are almost certainly the most radical in the recent history of tort law and are an integral part of the expansionist and plaintiff-oriented phase of that branch of the law. In *Dutton*, a builder developing a housing estate on land owned by him applied to the local council for permission to build a house and for approval under the building by-laws made under the Public Health Act 1936. Permission was granted and one of the council's building inspectors approved the foundations, which were then covered up. The house was completed and sold to C, who nearly one year later sold it to the plaintiff, Mrs Dutton. As the house was almost new, she did not have it surveyed, but it was passed by the surveyor to the building society from whom she had obtained a mortgage. Soon after the plaintiff moved in serious defects developed in the internal structure of the house. Expert investigation revealed that the foundations were unsound because the house was built on the site of an old rubbish tip, and that if the council's inspector had been careful, he would have detected that fact.

The plaintiff began an action against the builder and the council, though her action against the builder was settled for £625 on advice that as the law stood a claim in negligence against him could not succeed. At first instance, the judge held that the neighbour principle in *Donoghue* v. *Stevenson* applied to land as well as chattels and that accordingly the council were in breach of the duty of care owed to the plaintiff. The council appealed, but their appeal was dismissed by a majority of the Court of Appeal. In considering the position of the builder Lord Denning MR said:

> the distinction between chattels and real property is quite unsustainable. If the manufacturer of an article is liable to a person injured by his negligence, so should the builder of a house be liable.[20]

After referring to the distinction between cases in which the builder was only a contractor and cases in which he was the owner of the house itself, he went on to say:

> There is no sense in maintaining this distinction. It would mean that a contractor who builds a house on another's land is liable for negligence in constructing it, but that a speculative builder, who buys land and himself builds houses on it for sale, and is just as negligent as the contractor, is not liable. That cannot be right. Each must be under the same duty of care and to the same persons.[21]

Lord Denning MR held that *Bottomley* v. *Bannister* and *Otto* v. *Bolton* were no longer authority and overruled them. He said that *Cavalier* v. *Pope* was reversed by the Occupiers Liability Act 1957, section 4(1). The other member of the majority, Stamp LJ, was more cautious in his approach. He simply disapproved of *Bottomley* v. *Bannister* and *Otto* v. *Bolton* and said that *Cavalier* v. *Pope* did not affect the liability of a local authority.

The decision in *Dutton* was approved by the House of Lords in *Anns*. Lord Wilberforce, with whom the other Law Lords agreed, did, however, qualify the reasoning of the majority of the Court of Appeal by saying that a cause of action only arose when the state of the building is such that there is a present or imminent danger to the health of the persons occupying it. With reference to the position of the builder Lord Wilberforce said:

> I agree with the majority of the Court of Appeal in thinking that it would be unreasonable to impose liability in respect of defective foundations upon the council, if the builder, whose primary fault it was, should be immune from liability.[22]

Lord Wilberforce went on to say that the doctrine of *Donoghue* v. *Stevenson* did apply to realty, and he expressed approval with Lord Denning's judgement in *Dutton* on that point.

Strictly, the *dicta* in *Dutton* and *Anns* as to the legal position of the builder were *obiter* and for that reason those decisions did not completely dispel the doubt as to whether a builder of defective premises did come within the scope of the principle laid down in *Donoghue* v. *Stevenson*. However, the legal position of the builder arose directly in *Batty* v.

Metropolitan Property Realisations Ltd.[23] In that case, developers built a house on sloping ground which was subject to subsidence. Part of the garden slipped away, though the house itself was undamaged. However, expert evidence showed that at some point in the following ten years the house was likely to suffer damage. The Court of Appeal held that the developers were liable to the building owner. They said that the damage to the garden could be considered physical loss, and the threatened damage to the house could be considered to come within the scope of Lord Wilberforce's doctrine of present or imminent danger to the occupant.

The implications of *Dutton*, *Anns* and *Batty* were far-reaching for the whole common law of obligations.

In the first place, the duty established in those cases was owed not just to the first owner or occupier of the defective premises, but to any subsequent owner or occupier who suffered injury or whose health and safety was endangered. Privity of contract was no longer a prerequisite for a successful suit against a negligent builder. The significance of this for the builder was that in an action by a third party he could not rely on any exemption clause in his contract for sale. In other words, establishment of a tortious duty of care circumvented both the doctrine of privity of contract and any contractual exemption clause.

Secondly, the establishment of such a duty provided the first owner or occupier of defective premises with a tortious action as well as a contractual action.[24] This was a significant advantage to him from the standpoint of limitation. In contract a plaintiff has six years from the date of the breach of contract in which to commence an action; in an action for personal injury resulting from negligence the plaintiff has three years from the date when he suffers injury in which to commence an action.[25] In building cases, damage invariably takes a great deal longer than six years in which to manifest itself, and a plaintiff in such a case will often be out of time in contract but still in time in tort. Thus, if a builder had built a house with unsafe foundations in 1980 and sold it to the plaintiff in that year and the plaintiff was injured by collapse of the ceiling in 1992, he would of course be out of time in contract but he would have until 1995 in which to bring an action for damages in tort.

The most significant aspect of those decisions, however, lies in the nature of the loss suffered by the plaintiff. In each of these cases a remedy was granted in respect of the cost of remedying *threatened* structural failure. Thus, Mrs Dutton complained not that she had suffered personal injury nor that the defective house had damaged other property, but that a defect in the house had damaged the house itself. Counsel for Bognor Regis UDC argued that the council should not be liable for this loss and that liability would only arise where the defects had caused personal injury or damage to the occupier's chattels. Lord Denning MR, replying to counsel's submission, stated:

If Mr Tapp's submission were right, it would mean that if the inspector negligently passes the house as properly built and it collapses and injures a person, the council are liable: but if the owner discovers the defect in time to repair it – and he does repair it – the council are not liable. That is an impossible distinction. They are liable in either case.[26]

Lord Denning MR classified Mrs Dutton's loss as physical damage to the house and, in *Anns*, Lord Wilberforce said that the relevant damage was physical, though subject to the qualification that what is recoverable is the amount of expenditure necessary to restore the dwelling to a condition in which it is no longer a danger to the health or safety of the occupants. Arguably, however, the loss in those cases, and in *Batty*, was economic in the sense that the plaintiffs succeeded in tort for a defect in the quality of their premises. This was of great significance in the law of negligence because until those decisions it had been thought that such loss, if resulting from a negligent act, could not be recovered.[27] In the field of product liability, the decision in *Donoghue* v. *Stevenson* was concerned solely with physical injury. Lord Wilberforce's notion of endangering health and safety seems to bring the building cases within the scope of the narrow rule in *Donoghue* in the sense that the loss suffered in those cases can be regarded as a mitigation of the potential damage, to both persons and other property, that might occur if the premises were left in a dangerous state. Even this test, however, involves a form of economic loss.[28] Thus, Weir states, 'by making a bad thing you do not damage it; you damage a thing by making it worse than it was'.[29]

The extension of tortious liability for defective buildings following *Anns* reached its high water mark in the decision of the House of Lords in *Junior Books Ltd* v. *Veitchi Co. Ltd.*[30] *Junior Books* (the pursuers) employed contractors to construct a factory, the flooring work being carried out by the defenders as nominated subcontractors. Some two years after it had been laid, the floor developed cracks and it had to be replaced. There was no danger to personal safety but Junior Books sued for the cost of replacing the floor and the consequential economic loss suffered during the period of replacement. The House of Lords held, by a majority of four to one, that where the relationship between the parties was sufficiently close the scope of the duty of care in tort extended to this form of loss. On the assumption that the defective floor resulted from the negligence of the subcontractors, the Law Lords held that there was a sufficient degree of proximity between the parties to give rise to a duty of care and that there were no policy factors negativing that duty. This was a remarkable decision and it seemed to pave the way for a general principle allowing recovery for economic loss in the tort of negligence. There are, in fact, differences of emphasis in the speeches. The most radical in its approach was Lord Roskill's speech, who thought that the question of the scope of the tort of negligence should be determined by considerations of principle rather than policy. He said:

> the proper control lies not in asking whether the proper remedy should lie in contract or instead in delict or tort ... but in the first instance in establishing the relevant principles and then in deciding whether the particular case falls within or without those principles.[31]

It must be emphasised that such a wide approach to the common law of obligations was not echoed in the other speeches. As we shall see, although the decision has not been overruled, it has been confined to its own facts in subsequent cases and today it is most significant for the dissenting speech of Lord Brandon. He argued that to impose a duty on the subcontractors for the losses suffered by the pursuers would be to depart from long-established authority and that there was no sound policy reason for imposing a duty on the subcontractors in these circumstances because it would create contractual obligations between two parties who were not in any contractual relationship with each other. In view of the subsequent approval of Lord Brandon's speech by the House of Lords, his remarks on the matter are worth quoting *in extenso*:

> There are two important considerations which ought to limit the scope of the duty of care which it is common ground was owed by the defendants to the pursuers on the assumed facts of the present case.
>
> The first consideration is that, in *Donoghue* v. *Stevenson* itself and in all the numerous cases in which the principle of that decision has been applied to different but anologous fact situations, it has always been either stated expressly, or taken for granted, that an essential ingredient in the cause of action relied on was the existence of danger, or the threat of danger, of physical damage to persons or their property, excluding for this purpose the very piece of property from the defective condition of which such danger, or threat of danger, arises. To dispense with that essential ingredient in a cause of action of the kind concerned in the present case would, in any view, involve a radical departure from long-established authority.
>
> The second consideration is that there is no sound policy reason for substituting the wider scope of the duty of care put forward for the pursuers for the more restricted scope of such duty put forward by the defenders. The effect of accepting the pursuers' contention with regard to the scope of the duty of care involved would be, in substance, to create, as between two persons who are not in any contractual relationship with each other, obligations of one of these two persons to the other which are only really appropriate as between persons who do have such a relationship between them.
>
> In the case of a manufacturer or distributor of goods, the position would be that he warranted to the ultimate user or consumer of such

goods that they were as well designed, as merchantable and as fit for their contemplated purpose as the exercise of reasonable care could make them.

In the case of subcontractors such as those concerned in the present case, the position would be that they warranted to the building owner that the flooring, when laid, would be as well designed, as free from defects of any kind and as fit for its contemplated purpose as the exercise of reasonable care could make it.

In my view, the imposition of warranties of this kind on one person in favour of another, when there is no contractual relationship between them, is contrary to any sound policy requirement.

It is, I think, just worth while to consider the difficulties which would arise if the wider scope of the duty of care put forward by the pursuers were accepted. In any case where complaint was made by an ultimate consumer that a product made by some person with whom he himself had no contract was defective, by what standard or standards of quality would the question of defectiveness fall to be decided? In the case of goods bought from a retailer, it could hardly be the standard prescribed by the contract between the retailer and the wholesaler, or between the wholesaler and the distributor, or between the distributor and the manufacturer, for the terms of such contracts would not even be known to the ultimate buyer. In the case of subcontractors such as the appellants in the present case, it could hardly be the standard prescribed by the contract between the subcontractors and the main contractors, for, although the building owner would probably be aware of those terms he could not, since he was not a party to such contract, rely on any standard or standards prescribed in it. It follows that the question by what standard or standards alleged defects in a product complained of by its ultimate user or consumer are to be judged remains entirely at large and cannot be given any just or satisfactory answer.[32]

THE RETURN TO ORTHODOXY

Following the decision in *Junior Books*, the courts have adopted a much more cautious and pragmatic approach to the question of tortious liability for defective buildings. Both the Court of Appeal and the House of Lords have been at pains to emphasise that, despite the decisions in *Anns* and *Junior Books*, the law of negligence ordinarily does not permit recovery for purely economic loss consequent upon negligent acts.

The return to orthodoxy began in 1984 with the case of *Governors of the Peabody Donation Fund* v. *Sir Lindsay Parkinson & Co. Ltd.*[33] There the House of Lords held that a local authority's statutory powers to approve plans and inspect drainage systems were not intended to protect developers from sustaining economic loss. Their purpose was to safeguard the occupiers of houses built in the area, and members of the public generally, against dangers to their health arising from defective drainage. This new approach was supported by the Australian appeal court in the case of *Sutherland Shire Council* v. *Heyman*.[34] The facts of that case were similar to those of *Anns* but the court reinterpreted Lord Wilberforce's proximity test as requiring 'a close relationship' and not simply one where there was 'reasonable contemplation of damage'. So defined, there was insufficient proximity because there was no evidence that the occupier had ever relied on the council's approval of the house foundations as assuring that the house would be free of subsidence defects.

The implications of *Junior Books* were considered in *Muirhead* v. *Industrial Tank Specialties Ltd*.[35] A negligent manufacturer of water pumps was sued by the operator of a lobster farm whose lobsters had died because defects had prevented the pumps circulating adequate supplies of fresh water. In the event, the manufacturer was held liable, as the defect had led to damage to the plaintiff's property (the lobsters). But Goff LJ made it clear that the manufacturer would not have been liable for the defect alone. He argued that the key to *Junior Books* seemed to be that the House of Lords through the conceptions of proximity and reliance, was treating the nominated subcontractors as having voluntarily assumed responsibility with respect to the work which arose. However, such an analysis seemed not to fit the facts, as the parties' contractual relationship was so structured as to avoid any direct contractual liability of the subcontractors to the clients. The implication of *Muirhead* was clear, however: *Junior Books* was now to be looked on as establishing an exception to non-liability for defects rather than as a general basis for liability.

Another blow to *Junior Books* was delivered by the Court of Appeal in *Simaan General Contracting Co.* v. *Pilkington Glass Ltd (No. 2)*.[36] A manufacturer supplied a subcontractor with glass panels for the exterior cladding of a building in Abu Dhabi. The glass should have been green but it was alleged that, owing to negligent manufacture, the glass turned red under the Middle Eastern sun. The main contractor, who had to bear the cost of replacing the defective glass, sued the manufacturer in tort. The relationship between the manufacturer and the main contractor appeared very similar to that between the subcontractor and the owner in *Junior Books*, but the Court of Appeal had no hesitation in distinguishing that decision as limited to its particular facts.

This trend culminated in a trilogy of cases: *D & F Estates* v. *Church Commissioners of England*,[37] *Murphy* v. *Brentwood DC*[38] and *Department of the Environment* v. *Bates*.[39] The importance of these cases is that the House of Lords discussed the nature of the damages involved (in *Peabody*, etc., that issue had not been directly addressed). In *D & F Estates*, the plastering work in a block of flats had been subcontracted by the builders. The plaintiffs were lessees and occupiers of one of the flats. Fifteen years after construction it was discovered that the plastering had not been carried out in accordance with the manufacturer's instructions, causing peeling from ceilings. The plaintiff sued the builders in negligence for the cost of the remedial work. The House of Lords held that the cost of repairing a defect in a building before the defect had actually caused personal injury or physical damage to other property was not recoverable in negligence from the builder responsible for causing the defect, because the cost of repair was pure economic loss, and pure economic loss was not generally recoverable in the law of tort. The two main speeches were delivered by Lords Bridge and Oliver. Lord Bridge put forward the following view regarding the liability of a builder of a building which is dangerously defective:

> ... liability can only arise if the defect remains hidden until the defective structure causes personal injury or damage to property other than the structure itself. If the defect is discovered before any damage is done, the loss sustained by the owner of the structure, who has to repair or demolish it to avoid a potential source of danger to third parties, would seem to be purely economic.[40]

Both of their Lordships, with whom the other Law Lords concurred, said that defective buildings were to be treated in the same way as defective products. In the case of a defective product where the defect was discovered before it caused injury to persons or other property, the loss was recoverable in contract by a buyer or hirer of the chattel, but was not recoverable in tort by such persons. There was no non-contractual or transmissible warranty of quality attaching to the goods.

The House of Lords were not able to overrule *Anns* under the *Practice Statement* of 1966,[41] because the facts of *D & F Estates* did not raise the issue of local authority liability. That issue did arise in *Murphy* and on that occasion the House of Lords, consisting of seven Law Lords, did overrule *Anns*. The facts of *Murphy* are that in 1970 the plaintiff purchased from a construction company one of a pair of semi-detached houses. The houses were newly constructed on an in-filled site on a concrete raft foundation to prevent damage from settlement. The plan and calculations for the raft foundations were submitted to the local council for building regulation approval and the council approved the design after first referring them to consulting engineers. In 1981 the plaintiff noticed serious cracks in his house and discovered that the raft foundation was defective. In 1986 he sold the house subject to its defects for £35,000 less than its market value in sound condition. He sued the local authority for negligence in approving the plans. The House of Lords held that when carrying out its statutory function of building control, a local authority was not liable in negligence to a building owner or occupier for the cost of remedying a dangerous defect in the building which resulted from the negligent failure of the authority to ensure that the building was designed and erected in accordance with the Building Regulations.[42] Their Lordships advanced two reasons for this ruling. Firstly, the damage suffered by the building owner in *Murphy* was not physical but the purely economic loss of the expenditure occurred in remedying the defect. Secondly, a dangerous defect once known became merely a defect in quality and to permit the building owner or occupier to recover his loss would lead to an unacceptably wide category of claims in respect of defective buildings and products; in effect, it would introduce transmissible warranties of quality into the law of tort by means of judicial legislation. For these reasons their Lordships felt that the decision in *Anns* had not been based on any recognisable principle and consequently they overruled it.

One final point needs to be made on the speeches in *Murphy*. The decision in *Junior Books* was not overruled; rather it was almost given approval in that it was explained in terms of the doctrine of reliance contained in *Hedley Byrne & Co. Ltd* v. *Heller & Partners*.[43] The relationship between the building owner and the subcontractor in *Junior Books* was so close that the building owner could be said to have relied on the expertise of the subcontractor.

The decision in *Murphy* was applied by the House of Lords to builders in *Department of the Environment* v. *Bates*. In that case the plaintiffs were the underlessees of the upper nine storeys of an eleven storey office in a building complex constructed by the defendants in 1970–71. It was discovered in 1981 that, because low-strength concrete had been used in the pillars, the building, although capable of supporting its existing load safely, was not capable of supporting its design load. The plaintiffs sued for the cost of carrying out remedial works to strengthen the pillars. The House of Lords held that the loss suffered by the plaintiffs was purely economic and therefore not recoverable at the time when the work was carried out. The building was not unsafe but merely suffered from a defect in quality.

The judicial reasoning underlying Murphy, etc.

The general significance of *D & F Estates*, *Murphy* and *Bates* is that they have re-established the orthodox view of the law regarding recovery for economic loss resulting from negligence. From that point of view, these decisions are good news for builders and local authorities, but they will leave many owners of defective buildings without a remedy. It is because of this last point that they have attracted much comment and criticism.[44]

The reasons given for denying recovery for economic loss are often obscure and it is essential that they be subject to scrutiny. The usual reason given is the floodgates argument, i.e. to permit recovery would open the floodgates to a potentially unlimited number of claims, thereby exposing any particular defendant to the prospect of indeterminate liability. This argument is by no means as straightforward as it seems at first sight.[45] It was not, however, the reason for denying the claims in *D & F Estates* and *Murphy*, etc., because in each of those cases there was only one potential defendant. The arguments put forward by the Law Lords for denying recovery were:

(i) that it would create a large new area of tortious liability and this would amount to judicial legislation which is not a proper exercise of judicial power;[46]

(ii) that consumer protection is best left to the legislature and that this area has received full treatment by Parliament in the form of the Defective Premises Act 1972;[47]

(iii) that to allow recovery in negligence for defective buildings would be to impose a non-contractual and transmissible warranty of quality on builders and local authorities which would be contrary to principle;[48] and

(iv) that to allow recovery for economic loss in English law would be contrary to recent decisions of certain of the Commonwealth courts and the US Supreme Court.[49]

Each of these arguments needs to be examined closely.

In relation to the argument that *Dutton* and *Anns* were judicial legislation, it needs to be remembered that they both gave rise to a new point in law and that the resolution of any such point must be judicial legislation. Even if *Dutton* and *Anns* had been decided to the contrary, that would still have been judicial legislation. To that extent the decisions in *D & F Estates*, *Murphy* and *Bates* all amount to judicial legislation just as much as the decisions in *Dutton* and *Anns*. It would be more accurate to say that the decisions in *Dutton* and *Anns* belonged to an expansionist, plaintiff-oriented and welfarist phase in the law of tort, whereas the *Murphy* line of cases belongs to a phase which is more defendant-oriented and cautious in the creation of new duties.

In relation to consumer protection, the passing of the Defective Premises Act 1972 was a recognition by Parliament that in the case of dwellings the law should have a consumer protectionist role. The existence of that Act was thought by the Law Lords in *Murphy* to preclude the upholding of the decisions in *Dutton* and *Anns*. Further, it may be thought that the duties specified in the 1972 Act, together with the NHBC scheme,[50] make the imposition of a general tortious duty on housebuilders and local authorities unnecessary.[51] Two points can be made in answer to these views. Firstly, section 6(2) of the Act expressly provides that any duty imposed by or enforceable by virtue of any provision of the Act is in addition to any duty a person may owe apart from that provision. In other words, it seems that the intention of the Act is not to put a brake on the development of wider common law duties as circumstances require. Secondly, there are a number of limitations on the legislative duty which have prevented the Act from being as valuable a piece of consumer protection legislation as it might otherwise have been.[52]

The overriding consideration in *D & F Estates*, *Murphy* and *Bates* was a desire on the part of the Law Lords to re-emphasise the distinction between contractual and tortious obligations and to assert that liability for defective buildings and defective products belong to the domain of contract law. It was in this context that the (dissenting) speech of Lord Brandon in *Junior Books* was expressly approved. This is the argument that the manufacturer of a defective product, or builder of a defective building, cannot be liable to the ultimate consumer or occupier of such product or building because such loss is a form of expectation loss. When a consumer purchases an article, he has certain expectations of the quality of that article based on its price, any description attached to it by the seller, and so forth, and if the quality of the article does not match those expectations, only the immediate seller can be responsible. However, this argument does not explain why such obligations should lie solely in the province of the law of contract. There seems no reason in logic why strict contractual obligations of quality should preclude the existence of a tortious obligation of quality based on reasonable care. To the argument that it would be impossible to define the standard required of the manufacturer or builder in these circumstances it may be said that the law has not found it impossible to define standards of safety in the absence of express contractual obligations. And more to the point, these safety standards are based on a consumer expectations test.[53] Further, this judicial argument seems to ignore the commercial reality that in a modern economy consumers frequently do rely on manufacturers for the quality of their products.

In relation to Commonwealth and US developments concerning negligence and economic loss, the references to these developments by the Law Lords have been heavily criticised as misleading and one-sided. The most important point to make in this connection, however, is that since *Murphy* was decided the appellate courts in New Zealand, Australia and Canada, in a trilogy of important decisions laid down in 1994 and 1995, all departed from the exclusionary rule governing economic loss laid down in that case. Instead, they followed, in varying degrees, the principles which the House of Lords laid down in *Anns* and which the decision in *Murphy* so infamously overruled.[54]

The New Zealand case in question is *Invercargill City Council* v. *Hamlin*.[55] The facts of this case bear an all too familiar ring. Mr Hamlin's house was constructed in 1972, since when it suffered from a number of minor defects, such as jamming doors and cracks in the walls. In 1989, when the back door stuck badly, Mr Hamlin commissioned an engineer's report. That report stated that the foundations should be replaced as they had not been built to an acceptable standard. In 1996 Mr Hamlin commenced proceedings against the council for negligent inspection of the foundations by their building control inspector. In addressing the issue of the common law duty of a council to the owner and subsequent owners of a building in the exercise of its building function, the New Zealand Court of Appeal unanimously departed from the decision in *Murphy*. They held that local authorities were liable to house owners and subsequent owners for defects in a building caused by the negligence of their building inspectors.

The two principal judgements in *Invercargill* were those of Cooke P and Richardson J. Cooke P said that homeowners in New Zealand traditionally relied on local authorities 'to exercise reasonable care not to allow unstable houses to be built in breach of the byelaws'. He went on, 'the linked concepts of reliance and control have underlain New Zealand case law in this field from *Bowen*[56] onwards'. He also noted a number of New Zealand cases where other types of public authority had been held liable in negligence for economic loss. Richardson J's judgement lays great emphasis on the policy considerations which affect house building in New Zealand, in particular that it is not common practice for purchasers of dwellings to commission their own surveys. The judgement contains a detailed historical and socio-logical account of the New Zealand housing market and of the New Zealand building control legislation. He concluded:

> ... there is nothing in the legislation to preclude private damages claims in accordance with the existing New Zealand law for losses arising out of the negligent exercise of building control functions.[57]

The decision of the New Zealand Court of Appeal was upheld by the Privy Council.[58] The judgement of the Privy Council was delivered by Lord Lloyd who said that the New Zealand Court of Appeal was entitled to develop the common law of New Zealand according to local policy considerations in areas of the common law that were developing and not settled. Liability in negligence for defective buildings, said Lord Lloyd, was especially unsuited for a single monolithic solution. More importantly, Lord Lloyd went on to stress that the Privy Council should not ignore the policy considerations set out in the judgement of Richardson J.

The decision in *Invercargill*, of course, concerns the tortious duties owed by *local authorities* to owners and subsequent owners of dwellings; it does not concern the liability of the builder to subsequent owners of the building. That matter was considered by the New Zealand Court of Appeal in *Bowen v. Paramount Builders (Hamilton) Ltd.*[59] There, the majority held that a builder who negligently constructed a house was liable for the loss suffered by a subsequent owner of the house. However, the loss was not classified as economic, because it was directly connected with the structural damage to the building. Cooke J referred to cases in other areas in which liability for purely economic loss had been recognised and suggested it could be recognised in this field also. It would, of course, be open to a future New Zealand Court of Appeal to overrule the decision in *Bowen* in light of the decision of the House of Lords in *Murphy*. However, given the strength of the reasoning of the court in *Invercargill*, in particular the judgement of Richardson J, it is unlikely to do so. Instead, it is much more likely to affirm the decision in *Bowen*, perhaps taking such opportuntiy to be less equivocal about the nature of the loss concerned.

The decision of the Supreme Court of Canada in *Winnipeg Condominium Corporation No. 36* v. *Bird Construction Co. Ltd*[60] did concern the liability of a builder for losses suffered by a subsequent owner of the building. An apartment building was constructed in 1972, and the plaintiff became the owner of it in 1978. In 1989, a section of exterior stone cladding collapsed, necessitating repairs. The plaintiff brought an action against the contractors, the cladding subcontractors and the architects employed by the owner in 1972.

The judgement of the court was given by La Forest J. He proceeded on the assumption that the plaintiff's losses were purely economic and held that they were recoverable. He refused to follow the decision of the House of Lords in *D & F Estates*, for two reasons. In the first place, La Forest J said, that case rests upon the assumption that liability in tort for the cost of repair of defective houses is an unjustifiable intrusion of the law of tort into the contractual sphere. However, it is well-established in Canada that a duty in tort may exist co-extensively with a duty in contract. The second of La Forest J's reasons for not following *D & F Estates* was that it was part of a line of cases leading ultimately to the rejection of *Anns*. However, the Supreme Court of Canada had continued to apply the *Anns* principle.

The key point in La Forest J's judgement is that the duty in tort arises *only if there is a danger to the health and safety of the occupants which is foreseeable*. He went on to say:

> I do not find it necessary to consider whether contractors should also in principle be held to owe a duty to subsequent purchasers for the cost of repairing non-dangerous defects in buildings.[61]

In relation to the relationship between duties in tort and duties in contract in this context, La Forest J said that the tortious duty to construct a building without dangerous defects arises independently of the contractual duty to build according to standards of quality. He said that as the tortious duty arises independently of any contract, there is no logical reason for allowing the contractor to rely upon a contract made with the original owner to shield him from liability to subsequent purchasers ensuing from dangerously constructed building. Finally, La Forest J said that there were no adequate policy considerations which existed to negate the contractor's duty in tort.

The Australian case of *Bryan* v. *Maloney*[62] also concerned the liability of a builder for losses suffered by a subsequent owner of the building concerned.

A professional builder built a house for a Mrs Manion in 1979. Mrs Manion sold the house to a second person who sold it to Mrs Maloney in 1986. Some six months after Mrs Maloney's purchase the fabric sustained substantial damage when the soil on which it stood underwent seasonal changes. The damage was caused by inadequate foundations. As a result, Mrs Maloney suffered financial loss caused by a diminution in the value of the house. She sued the builder for recovery of these losses.

The High Court of Australia held, by a majority of four to one, that the builder was liable in these circumstances. The case gave rise to two issues: (1) the proximity of the relationship between the builder and Mrs Maloney, and (2) whether the relationship of proximity extended to the recovery of pure economic loss.

In relation to the issue of proximity the majority judgements of Mason CJ, Deane J, Gaudron J and Tooley J held that the existence of a duty of reasonable care owed by the builder to Mrs Maloney depended upon there being a relationship of sufficient proximity between the parties. They pointed to a number of factors which established such a relationship in these circumstances:

(1) The house was a permanent structure intended to be used indefinitely and represented a significant investment by the ultimate purchaser. This, said Mason CJ etc., was 'a substantial connecting link' between the parties.
(2) It was obviously foreseeable by the builder that negligent construction of the house, in the form of inadequate foundations, would cause economic loss to a subsequent purchaser when the defects manifested themselves.
(3) A subsequent owner of a house would have less opportunity to inspect the foundations than the first owner.[63]

The more difficult question which faced the court in this case was whether the relationship of proximity and consequent duty of care extended to pure economic loss. The majority held that it did. Both majority judgements firmly set their face against the approach of the House of Lords in *D & F Estates* and *Murphy* to pure economic loss and rejected the main arguments there put forward against allowing recovery for economic loss resulting from the negligent construction of a building.

The judgement of Mason CJ, etc. lists the following factors as favouring the recovery of pure economic loss in the circumstances of this case:

(1) The distinction between the kind of economic loss suffered by Mrs Maloney (i.e. diminution in the value of her house upon discovery of the inadequate footings) and ordinary physical damage to property is essentially a technical one. The economic loss suffered by the owner of a house when the inadequacy of the footings manifests itself is,

arguably, less remote and more readily foreseeable than ordinary physical damage to other property of the owner.

(2) The policy considerations of liability in an indeterminate amount to an indeterminate class underlying the reluctance of the courts to recognise a duty of care in cases of more economic loss are largely inapplicable in the relationship between builder and subsequent owner.

(3) The similarities between the relationship between builder and first owner and the relationship between builder and subsequent owner as regards the particular kind of economic loss are of much greater significance than the differences namely, the absence of direct contract or dealing and the possibly extended time in which liability may arise. Both relationships are characterised, to a comparable extent, by assumption of responsibility on the part of the builder and likely reliance on the part of the owner. No distinction can be drawn between the two relationships as far as foreseeability is concerned. If the foundations of a building are inadequate it is obviously foreseeable that loss will be sustained by either the first or a subsequent owner, whichever happens to be the owner at the time when the defect manifests itself.

(4) The relationship between builder and subsequent owner had to be distinguished from that between the manufacturer and the purchaser of a chattel with a latent defect. Holding a builder liable in negligence to a subsequent owner in respect of a diminution in value of the building did not necessarily mean that a manufacturer owed a similar duty to a purchaser or subsequent owner of a chattel.

Mason CJ etc. conclude their analysis in the following robustly pro-*Anns* terms:

> It is difficult to see why, as a matter of principle, policy or common sense, a negligent builder should be liable for ordinary physical injury caused to any person or to other property by reason of the collapse of a building by reason of the inadequacy of the foundations but be not liable to the owner of the building for the cost of remedial work necessary to remedy that inadequacy and to avert such damage. Indeed, there is obvious force in the view expressed by Lord Denning MR in *Dutton* v. *Bognor Regis Urban District Council* that, as a rational basis for differentiating between circumstances of liability and circumstances of no liability such a distinction is an 'impossible' one.[64]

To sum up this review of the reasons put forward by the House of Lords for their decisions in *D & F Estates* and *Murphy*, whereas the appellate courts of New Zealand, Canada and Australia have taken a consumer-protectionist, plaintiff oriented approach to this area of law and have emphasised the policy arguments in favour of the *Anns* principle, the approach of the House of Lords is based on legal doctrine. Should purchasers of defective buildings – in particular, homeowners – be protected by the law of negligence? In answer to this question, a number of things need to be pointed out. Firstly, many defects in buildings, in particular, dwellings, are not covered by first party insurance.[65] Secondly, it seems wrong to put defective buildings on a par with defective products. The purchase of a domestic dwelling is the most important financial transaction most persons enter into, and, if such a dwelling proves defective, the occupier concerned will almost certainly be unable to absorb the loss. This is in contrast to products, many of which are of trivial monetary value. Moreover, whereas a tortious duty of care extending to quality in the case of products may involve the manufacturer concerned in an indeterminate volume of claims, the same cannot be said of buildings. The courts have accepted that in the event of a negligent survey of a low or moderately priced house, the surveyor should be liable in tort to the buyer of the house.[66] There seems to be no sound reason in policy to distinguish between builders and local authorities and surveyors in this context.

Exceptions to the exclusionary rule in Murphy

Despite the robust re-assertion of the orthodox approach of the House of Lords to the recovery in the tort of negligence of the cost of repairing a defective, but not dangerous, building in *D & F Estates, Murphy* and *Bates,* they nevertheless left open the door to recovery in three exceptional circumstances. These exceptions are as follows:

(i) where the building may be regarded as a complex structure and a defect in one part of the building causes damage to another part;
(ii) where expenditure is necessary to repair a defective building in order to avoid liability to third parties; and
(iii) where the loss suffered as a result of the defect can be brought within the scope of the reliance principle in *Hedley Byrne & Co. Ltd* v. *Heller & Partners.*

(i) The complex structure theory

As we have seen, the House of Lords in *D & F Estates* was at pains to stress that a defective building should be viewed in the same way as a defective product. In the law of product liability no transmissible warranty of quality attaches to goods, so that, for example, a buyer who purchases goods from a retailer cannot sue the manufacturer in the law of negligence for non-dangerous defects in the goods. In such a case the buyer is a third party and consequently has no contractual relationship with the manufacturer. Further, the *Donoghue* v. *Stevenson* duty of care owed by manufacturers to final buyers had not been extended to include the cost of repairing a defective product. The problem for the House of Lords was that the decision in

Anns seemed to imply that there was such a warranty attached to buildings. In order to reconcile this inconsistency their Lordships distinguished between complex and simple structures. In the case of complex structures one element of the structure should be regarded as distinct from another element so that damage to one part of the structure caused by a hidden defect in another part may qualify as damage to 'other property'. In this way, Lords Bridge and Oliver attempted to reconcile *Anns* with *Donoghue* v. *Stevenson*.

This decision produced a great deal of confusion in this area of law.[67] The complex structure theory seemed tailor made for litigation. The notion of when different parts of a building may be regarded as 'other property' is by no means clear. The concept of 'other property' has not been without its problems in the field of product liability.[68] Further the concept of the complex structure did not entirely reconcile *Anns* with *Donoghue* v. *Stevenson*, because under the *Anns* principle the cause of action accrues when the building 'becomes a present or imminent danger' which means that the plaintiff does not have to wait until damage to the building itself occurs.

In the course of their speeches in *Murphy* the Law Lords reviewed the complex structure theory and no doubt mindful of the criticism to which it had been subjected, rejected the version of it contained in *D & F Estates*. They said that any defect in the structure is a defect in the quality of the whole and that it is quite artificial to treat a defect in an integral structure which weakens the structure as damage to 'other property'. Thus cracking in walls and ceilings caused by defective foundations cannot be treated as damage to 'other property'. Lord Bridge distinguished between a part of a complex structure which is a danger because it does not perform its proper function of sustaining the other parts and a distinct item incorporated in the structure which malfunctions thereby causing damage to the structure in which it is incorporated. To illustrate this form of the theory he gave the following example:

> Thus, if a defective central heating boiler explodes and damages a house or if a defective electrical installation malfunctions and sets the house on fire, I see no reason to doubt that the owner of the house, if he can prove that the damage was due to the negligence of the boiler manufacturer in the one case or the electrical contractor in the other, can recover damages in tort on *Donoghue* v. *Stevenson* principles. But the position of the law is entirely different where by reason of the inadequacy of the foundations of the building to support the weight of the superstructure, differential settlement and consequential cracking appears.[69]

The complex structure theory was applied in *Jacobs* v. *Moreton & Partners*.[70] In that case, the plaintiffs were the freehold owners of a semi-detached house in Northolt, Middlesex. In 1986 the plaintiffs' predecessors in title retained the defendants, consulting civil and structural engineers, to advise them in connection with remedial work to repair cracking in the property caused by ground movement and to design and supervise such remedial work. The defendants approved a design for the construction of a piled raft foundation supported on small diameter bored piles, which had been prepared by consultants to specialist sub-contractors. The defendants supervised the execution of these works which were completed in October 1987.

The plaintiffs purchased the property in June 1988. By November 1988 further cracking had occurred. This was found to be caused by heave and by the failure of the 1987 remedial works sufficiently to accommodate this. The only practical method of rectifying the fault was by the demolition and rebuilding of the property. The plaintiffs sued the defendants in negligence seeking the cost of demolition and rebuilding. One of the preliminary issues in the case was whether the defendants owed the plaintiffs a duty of care at common law.

The Official Referee, Mr Recorder Jackson, QC, held that the damage suffered by the plaintiffs was properly to be characterised as damage to property and not economic loss because the case fell within the complex structure exception to the exclusionary rule in *Murphy*. He said that the scope of the complex structure exception is a question of fact and degree to be determined by reference to the circumstances. He identified four considerations as relevant to the question:

(1) whether the item in question was constructed by someone other than the main contractor responsible for the main building works;
(2) whether the item in question has retained its separate identity – for example a central heating boiler – or whether it has merged with the remainder of the building – for example, a wall;
(3) whether the item positively inflicts damage on the building – for example, faulty electrical wiring which causes a fire – or whether it simply fails to perform its function and thus permits damage to occur; and
(4) whether the item in question was constructed at a different time from the rest of the building.[71]

Applying these considerations to the instant case, the Official Referee said that the defective raft foundation was designed and constructed by persons who had no responsibility for any other element in the building; it had to some degree, but not entirely, merged with the rest of the building; it had inflicted harm on the rest of the house; and it had been inserted into the property some eight years after the house had been built. The Official Referee concluded, therefore, that the case fell within the complex structure exception.[72]

In *Bellefield Computer Services Ltd* v. *E. Turner & Sons Ltd*,[73] the Court of Appeal considered the question of whether the rooms on one side of the compartment wall of a dairy should be treated as a different building from the rooms on the other side. The dairy was extensively damaged by a fire which broke out in 1995. The fire would have been restrained had a compartment wall built between the storage area and the rest of the building been constructed properly and the owner of the dairy, Unigate (UK) Ltd, brought an action in negligence against the building contractor for repairs and cleaning to the building, damage to the equipment and contents and loss of profits. The plaintiff's claim was unsuccessful, the court applying the exclusionary rule laid down in *Murphy*. However, the court went on to consider whether the complex structure theory applied to the circumstances of the case. They held that it did not, saying that to regard the rooms on one side of the compartment wall as a different building from the rooms on the other side would be 'a thoroughly undesirable approach'. They emphasised that the whole of the dairy was built at the same time by the builders and marketed and built as a unit. The fact of 'compartmentalisation' did not mean that the structure ceased to be a single building.

(ii)   Expenditure necessary to avoid liability to third parties

In *Murphy*, Lord Bridge said that there may be an exception to the exclusionary rule where expenditure was needed to prevent a defective building from causing injury to persons or property on neighbouring land or on the public highway. He expressed the point in the following terms:

> if a building stands so close to the boundary of the building owner's land that after discovery of the dangerous defect it remains a potential source of injury to persons or property on the neighbouring land or on the highway, the building owner ought, in principle, to be entitled to recover in tort from the negligent builder the cost of obviating the danger, whether by repair or demolition, so far as that cost is necessarily incurred in order to protect himself from potential liability to third parties.[74]

(iii)   The *Hedley Byrne* reliance principle

Lord Oliver in *D & F Estates*[75] and Lords Bridge and Keith in *Murphy*[76] suggested that economic loss may be recoverable in the case of a defective building by means of the application of the reliance principle in *Hedley Byrne & Co. Ltd.* v. *Heller & Partners*. The essential principle laid down by the House of Lords in this case is that a duty of care is owed in the making of statements if there is a 'special relationship' between the parties concerned. Their Lordships did not provide a unanimous formulation of the nature and extent of this relationship. However, the speeches highlight that two requirements had to be satisfied before such a relationship could arise: there had to be reliance on the statement by the recipient and there had to be an assumption of responsibility on the part of the maker of the statement.

Thus, it was thought that a subsequent owner of a defective building may be able to successfully sue the builder for his loss if he could show that he had relied on the builder in the *Hedley Byrne* sense of reliance and that the builder had assumed a responsibility to him in respect of the quality of the building. The *dicta* of Lords Oliver, Bridge and Keith are based upon a particular interpretation of the rule in *Junior* Books: namely that the relationship between the employer and the subcontractor in that case was so close, or proximate, that it could be interpreted as a special relationship in the sense that the employer could be said to have relied on the skill and expertise of the subcontractor.

This extension of the *Hedley Byrne* principle into Construction Law is difficult to reconcile with the reformulation of that principle by the House of Lords in *Caparo* v. *Dickman*.[77] In that case, Lord Oliver laid down the following requirements for the existence of a special relationship:

(i)   the advice is required for a purpose known, either actually or inferentially, to the adviser at the time when the advice is given;

(ii) the adviser knows, either actually or inferentially, that his advice will be communicated to the advisee,

(iii) it is known, either actually or inferentially, that the advice is likely to be acted upon by the advisee; and

(iv) it is so acted upon by the advisee to his detriment.[78]

This formulation of the special relationship effectively put paid to any hope that the *dicta* of Lords Oliver, Bridge and Keith in *D & F Estates* and *Murphy* might prove a means of circumventing the exclusionary rule. It can be seen at a glance that the relationship between builder and subsequent owner is very unlikely to meet the above requirements.

Although the decisions in *Murphy* etc., put a brake on construction negligence in the form of duties owed to third parties, the years following these decisions have seen a re-emergence of negligence in the form of concurrent liability in contract and tort. This revival of concurrent liability received the *imprimatur* of the House of Lords in *Henderson and Others* v. *Merrett Syndicates Ltd.*[79] That case was not a building case but concerned the question of whether or not Lloyd's Names were owed concurrent duties of care in contract and tort by their agents. The House of Lords answered this question in the affirmative. The decision of their Lordships was delivered by Lord Goff and he examined the issue in terms of the decision of the House of Lords in *Hedley Byrne*. The key passage in his speech referring to this point states:

> if a person assumes responsibility to another in respect of certain services, there is no reason why he should not be liable in damages for that other in respect of economic loss which flows from the negligent performance of these services. It follows that once the case is identified

as falling within the *Hedley Byrne* principle, there should be no need to embark upon any further enquiry whether it is 'fair, just and reasonable' to impose liability for economic loss.[80]

The key phrase in this *dictum* for the question of construction negligence is, 'respect of certain services'; the significance of this phrase is that it extends the *Hedley Byrne* principle beyond statements to the provision of services and, as such, it seemed, *prima facie*, to re-open the possibility of that principle providing an exception to the exclusionary rule. However, it is essential to realise that in this *dictum* Lord Goff was referring to the basis of tortious liability owed by professional persons to their clients, *to whom they are contractually bound.* There is nothing in Lord Goff's speech which even hints at extending this form of liability to third parties. Moreover, Lord Goff placed a very important limitation on his principle in relation to the liability of contractors and subcontractors. He said that in an ordinary construction project there is a well defined chain of contractual liability under which the building owner contracts with the main contractor for the construction of the building works and the main contractor then contracts with various subcontractors and suppliers. If the subcontracted work or materials do not come up to the required standard it is not open to the building owner to sue the subcontractors or the supplier under the *Hedley Byrne* principle. There is no assumption of responsibility by the subcontractors or suppliers towards the building owner; the parties structure their relationships so that assumption of responsibility cannot arise.[81]

The conclusion from *Henderson* in relation to the third party liability of building contractors is inescapable: the principle laid down by Lord Goff in *Henderson* has in no way breached the exclusionary rule relating to negligence and defective buildings laid down in *Murphy*. The rule in *Murphy* is still the cornerstone of this area of law.

CONCLUDING COMMENT

The return to orthodoxy in this area of law has had, and will continue to have, important practical consequences for the construction industry. Most prominently, the shift of judicial emphasis back to contractual obligations has meant increased pressure on architects, engineers and contractors from occupiers for collateral warranties, i.e. guarantees of fitness for use in the absence of any tortious duty.[82] From the standpoint of the occupier of a defective dwelling the decisions in *Murphy* etc. have led to a renewal of interest in the provisions of the Defective Premises Act 1972 as a means of redress.[83] The principle of reliance, first set out in *Hedley Byrne* v. *Heller*, is now the only basis of liability in negligence for economic loss and this has meant that in many cases of defective buildings the only chance of a successful suit will lie against the surveyor of the building. One commentator has summed up the common law of defective buildings in the following terms:

> ... the victim often finds himself caught in a pair of pincers, one jaw of which is the doctrine of privity of contract, and the other the tortious principle that there is no liability in negligence for 'purely economic loss.[84]

The doctrine of privity of contract is now considerably modified by the Contracts (Rights of Third Parties) Act 1999, which gives third parties such as subsequent purchasers, tenants and financial institutions who fund construction projects the right to enforce a contract term if the contract expressly provides that they may or if it appears that the contracting parties intended a term to be enforceable by such third parties.[85] Third party rights are likely to be included in the standard form construction contracts, but it remains to be seen whether a subsequent purchaser of a domestic dwelling will benefit from this important reform of the English law of contract. For persons who find themselves in a *Murphy* situation the jaws of the proverbial pincers may well maintain their tight grip.

SUMMARY

Dramatic changes have occurred in this area of law in this century, but the essential principles may be summarised as follows:

1. Where the defect in a building causes death or personal injury or damage to property other than the defective building itself, the builder will be liable under the *Donoghue* v. *Stevenson* principle.
2. If the defect is simply one of quality and does not render the building a danger to the health or safety of its occupants, then such loss is pure economic loss and not recoverable.
3. If the defect does render the building an imminent danger to the health and safety of its occupants, the cost of averting that danger is again economic loss and irrecoverable.
4. If an item, such as a boiler, incorporated in the structure malfunctions and damages the structure, then the supplier of that item will be liable for the damage to the structure.
5. If expenditure is necessary to repair a building which is potentially dangerous to persons or property on neighbouring land, such expenditure is recoverable in tort from the negligent builder.

NOTES

1. This has been described in terms of the military analogy of advance and retreat in Farrar, J.H. and Dugdale, A.M., *Introduction to Legal Method*, 3rd edn, Sweet & Maxwell, 1990, Ch. 8.
2. [1906] AC 428.
3. [1932] 1 KB 458.
4. *Ibid*,n.3, p.468.
5. *Ibid*,n.3, p.476.
6. [1932] AC 562.
7. *Ibid*,n.6, p.580.
8. See, in particular, the speeches of their Lordships in *Caparo* v. *Dickman* [1990] 1 All ER 568.
9. *Supra*, n.6, p.599.
10. For example, underpants (*Grant* v. *Australian Knitting Mills* [1936] AC 85); and chemicals (*Vacwell Engineering Co. Ltd* v. *B.D.H. Chemicals Ltd* [1971] 1 QB 88).
11. See *Haseldine* v. *Daw & Son Ltd* [1941] 2 KB 343.
12. [1936] 2 KB 46.
13. *Ibid*, n.12, p.54.
14. (1842) 10 M & W 109, p.115, and quoted by Lord Denning in *Dutton* v. *Bognor Regis UDC* [1972] 1 QB 373, p.393.
15. See Atkinson J's judgement in *Otto* v. *Bolton, supra*, n.12, p.58.
16. *Supra*, n.14.
17. [1978] AC 728.
18. [1963] 1 WLR 665.
19. *Ibid*, n.18, p.675.
20. *Supra*, n.14, p.393.
21. *Supra*, n.14, pp.393–94.
22. *Supra*, n.17, p.758.
23. [1978] QB 554.
24. This is known as concurrent liability: see *Midland Bank Trust Co. Ltd* v. *Hett, Stubbs & Kemp* [1978] 3 All ER 571.
25. This matter is explored further in Chapter 8.
26. *Supra*, n.14, p.396.
27. See, in particular, *Cattle* v. *Stockton Waterworks* (1871) LR 10 QB 453; *Weller* v. *Foot and Mouth Disease Research Institute* [1966] 1 QB 569.
28. See the remarks of Lord Oliver in *Murphy* v. *Brentwood DC* [1990] 2 All ER 908, p.932.
29. *Casebook on Tort*, 4th edn, p.29.
30. [1983] 1 AC 520.
31. *Ibid*, n.30, p.545.
32. *Ibid*, n.30, pp.551–52. The speech of Lord Fraser also discusses the difficulty of ascertaining the standard of duty owed by the subcontractor to the employer.
33. [1984] 3 All ER 529.
34. (1985) 60 ALR 1 (H.C.).
35. [1985] 3 All ER 705.
36. [1988] 1 All ER 791.
37. [1988] 2 All ER 992.
38. *Supra*, n.28.
39. [1990] 2 All ER 943.
40. *Supra*, n.37, p.1006.

41. [1966] 3 All ER 77.
42. See, further, Chapter 5.
43. [1964] AC 465. Discussed further in Chapter 8.
44. See Cane (1989) 52 MLR 200; Brown (1990) 6 PN 150; Olowofoyeku (1990) 6 PN 158; Sir Robin Cooke (1991) 107 LQR 46; Wallace (1991) 107 LQR 228; Stapleton (1991) 107 LQR 249; National Consumer Council, *Murphy's Law*, 1991.
45. See Stapleton, *supra*, n.44, pp.253–256.
46. *Per* Lord Keith, *supra*, n.28, pp.922–923; Lord Bridge, *supra*, n.28 at p.924; and Lord Oliver, *supra*, n.28, p.937.
47. *Per* Lord Bridge, *supra*, n.37, p.1007; Lord Mackay LC, *supra*, n.28, p.912; Lord Keith, *supra*, n.28, p.923; Lord Bridge, *supra*, n.28, p.93; Lord Oliver, *supra*, n.28, p.938; Lord Jauncey, *supra*, n.28, pp.942–943.
48. *Per* Lord Keith, *supra*, n.28, pp.917–920; Lord Bridge, *supra*, n.28, pp.925–926; Lord Oliver, *supra*, n.28, pp.934–936; and Lord Jauncey, *supra*, n.28, pp.940–941.
49. *Per* Lord Keith, *supra*, n.28, pp.920–922; Lord Bridge, *supra*, n.28, pp.924–928; and Lord Jauncey, *supra*, n.28, pp.940–941.
50. The detailed provisions of this scheme are set out in Chapter 4.
51. This has been suggested by Professor J. A. Smilie in [1990] NZLJ 310, p.314 and quoted by Sir Robin Cooke, *supra*, n.46, p.69.
52. See Chapter 4.
53. See Section 3 of the Consumer Protection Act 1987.
54. See James (1995) 11 PN 132 and (1996) 12 PN 94. For a detailed comparison of the Canadian and Australian approaches to liability for defective buildings see Stychin (1996) 16 LS 387.
55. [1994] 3 NZLR 513.
56. That is, *Bowen* v. *Paramount Builders (Hamilton) Ltd* [1975] 2 NZLR 546.
57. *Supra*, n.55, p.526.
58. [1996] 1 All ER 756.
59. *Supra*, n.56.
60. (1995) 121 DLR (4th) 193.
61. *Ibid*, n.60, p.215.
62. (1995) 128 ALR 163.
63. *Ibid*, n.62, p.171.
64. *Ibid*, n.62, p.173.
65. But see Chapter 9 for a discussion of BUILD.
66. See *Eric S. Smith* v. *Bush* [1989] 2 All ER 514, discussed further in Chapter 8.
67. See Ross (1989) 5 PN ll.
68. See *Aswan Engineering Establishment Co. V. Lupdine Ltd* [1987] 1 All ER 135.
69. *Supra*, n.28, p.928.
70. (1994) 72 BLR 92.
71. *Ibid*, n.70, p.103.
72. See the commentary on *Jacobs* by the editor of the Building Law Reports (*ibid*, n.70, pp. 94–96) for a critique of the complex structure theory.
73. [2000] BLR 97.
74. *Supra*, n.28, p.926.
75. *Supra*, n.37, p.1014.
76. *Supra*, n.28, p.919.
77. [1990] 2AC 605.
78. *Ibid*, n.77, p.638.
79. [1994] 3 All ER 506.
80. *Ibid*, n.79, p.521.
81. *Ibid*, n.79, p.534.

82.   See further Chapter 9.
83.   See Duncan Wallace [1991] 107 LQR 228, p.243.
84.   J.R. Spencer [1974] CLJ 307, p.309.
85.   The Act is discussed fully in Chapter 9.

4

The Defective Premises Act and the NHBC Scheme[1]

INTRODUCTION

This chapter examines the liability of the builder under the provisions of sections 1 and 2 of the Defective Premises Act 1972 and the National House-Building Council (NHBC) scheme.

The 1972 Act is based on a report of the Law Commission, *Civil Liability of Vendors and Lessors of Defective Premises*.[2] It is a consumer protection measure which provides a remedy to any person who acquires an interest in a residential dwelling and who suffers financial loss as a result of its defective construction. This remedy is wide ranging, is based on strict liability and is additional to any common law remedies that may be available in this situation.

At the time of passing of the Act the common law in this area was considered generally to be deficient. In the first place, the sale of houses is governed by the doctrine of *caveat emptor*; the purchaser of a defective house generally has to bear the consequences unless the vendor has undertaken a contractual responsibility for the defects, which is rare. Secondly, this doctrine not only applies to the sale of an existing house by a private seller but extends also to the builder who builds a house on his own land and later sells or lets the house (the case of the vendor/builder). The only exception to this rule would be if the builder is registered with the NHBC, in which case the buyer would be provided with express contractual warranties. Thirdly, if a builder builds a house on another person's land, then he owes certain duties to that person in relation to the standard of workmanship and the quality of the materials provided. These duties provide some measure of protection for the person on whose land the house was built. But that protection does not extend to a lessee or subsequent purchaser of the house; such persons have no privity of contract with the builder, and unless the house is dangerous and causes them personal injuries or damages other property belonging to them, they cannot successfully sue in negligence.

The attempt made by the Act to remedy these deficiencies in the common law has so far proved largely unsuccessful and the provisions of the Act in

103

relation to defective dwellings have been little used by plaintiffs. One of the principal reasons for this was the radical developments which occurred in the common law shortly after the passing of the Act. These developments, in the shape of the decisions of the Court of Appeal in *Dutton* v. *Bognor Regis UDC*[3] and the House of Lords in *Anns* v. *Merton LBC*,[4] extended the builder's liability in tort by allowing recovery of the cost of repairing defective building, such loss to the purchaser being regarded as the mitigation of personal injury or damage to other property which could eventually ensue. However, the overruling of these decisions in *Murphy* v. *Brentwood DC*,[5] and the ruling in that case that such repair costs are a form of economic loss and as such irrecoverable in the tort of negligence, save where the relationship between the plaintiffs and the builder can be brought within the reliance doctrine, has given the 1972 Act a new importance for plaintiffs who seek redress for defective buildings and who fall outside the scope of the implied contractual obligations imposed on the builder and outside the scope of the NHBC scheme.

THE DEFECTIVE PREMISES ACT 1972

The nature of the duty

The duty in respect of building created by the Act is contained in section 1(1). This states:

> A person taking on work for or in connection with the provision of a dwelling (whether the dwelling is provided by the erection or by the conversion or enlargement of a building) owes a duty –
>
> (a) if the dwelling is provided to the order of any person to that person; and
>
> (b) without prejudice to paragraph (a) above, to every person who acquires an interest (whether legal or equitable) in the dwelling;
>
> to see that the work which he takes on is done in a workmanlike or, as the case may be, professional manner, with proper materials and so that as regards that work the dwelling will be fit for habitation when completed.

These requirements are virtually identical with the obligations implied by the common law to a contract for work and material and to the express warranties contained in the NHBC scheme. However, the duty in section 1(1) is additional to the common law duties (section 6(2)). Further, it cannot be excluded by agreement to the contrary (section 6(3)).

The duty is qualified by the provisions of sections 1(2) and (3) of the Act. Section 1(2) states:

> A person who takes on any such work for another on terms that he is to do it in accordance with instructions given by or on behalf of that other

shall to the extent to which he does it properly in accordance with those instructions, be treated for the purposes of this section as discharging the duty imposed on him by subsection (1) above except where he owes a duty to that other to warn him of any defects in the instructions and fails to discharge that duty.

This means that a builder will discharge his duty under section 1(1) if he is instructed to build according to a particular specification and follows such instructions. However, if the instructions are defective then he may incur liability under the Act if he fails to warn of those defects. It is not clear when this duty to warn arises.

Section 1(3) states:

A person shall not be treated for the purposes of subsection (2) above as having given instructions for the doing of work merely because he has agreed to work being done in a specified manner, with specified materials or to a specified design.

The purpose of this subsection is to circumvent the rule in *Lynch* v. *Thorne*,[6] that where a builder builds according to specifications then, in the absence of some other express provision, that is the extent of his obligation under the contract. In other words, under the provisions of section 1(3) of the Act, if a builder is provided with defective specifications, then he is under a duty to warn the employer of those defects.[7]

One of the problematical aspects of the duty contained in section 1(1) is whether it is contractual or tortious in nature. This is not merely an academic issue, since it involves the practical questions of the kind of defects which are covered by the duty, the losses which are recoverable under it and, in particular, the meaning of 'fit for habitation'. In one sense, the duty may be looked on as in essence a contractual warranty which is transmissible to 'every person who acquires an interest ... in the dwelling'. Support for this view can be found in the fact that in the event of the NHBC scheme being in operation rather than the provisions of section 1(1), then the rights under such a scheme are extended to subsequent purchasers. If this is the correct interpretation of section 1(1), then the duty would seem to extend to defects of quality. On the other hand, the Law Commission, in their report which forms the basis of the Act, appear to take the view that the duty is more tortious than contractual in nature.[8] The report draws a firm distinction between defects of quality and dangerous defects. It goes on to state the view that in the law of tort it is only dangerous defects for which a builder should be liable; defects of quality are seen as the sole province of the law of contract. The long title of the Act seems to reflect that view:

An Act to impose duties in connection with the provision of dwellings and otherwise to amend the law of England and Wales as to liability for injury or damage caused to persons through defects in the state of premises.

The meaning of 'fitness for habitation' has been considered in *Alexander* v. *Mercouris*[9] and, more recently, in *Thompson* v. *Alexander*.[10] In *Alexander* v. *Mercouris*, the Court of Appeal said, *obiter*, that 'fitness for habitation' was a measure of the standard to be achieved through the use of proper work and materials, not a separate, third obligation. Thus, Buckley LJ said:

> The reference to the dwelling being fit for habitation indicates the intended consequences of the proper performance of the duty and provides a measure of the standard of the requisite work and materials. It is not, I think, part of the duty itself.[11]

In other words, the duty in section 1(1) is to carry out work on a dwelling in a workmanlike manner and with proper materials so that when complete the dwelling is fit for habitation.

This *obiter dictum* was relied upon by Judge Esyr Lewis in *Thompson* v. *Alexander*. In that case, three house owners brought proceedings under section 1(1) against the architects and engineers whom they alleged designed and supervised the construction of their houses. The architects and engineers contended that it was an essential ingredient of a cause of action under section 1(1) that, in addition to proving that the defect arose out of a failure to carry out the work in a professional manner or with proper materials, the defect should also render the dwelling unfit for habitation. In respect of many of the defects complained of, the house owners did not contend that they made the dwellings concerned unfit for habitation. However, they argued that section 1(1) imposed three separate obligations. The judge accepted the contention of the architects and engineers. He said that the duty imposed by section 1(1) is intended to ensure that the persons concerned in the design or construction of a dwelling will carry out their work in a manner which will result in the building's being fit for habitation when completed. In other words, before a duty can arise under the Act the dwelling must be rendered unfit for habitation by the defect complained of. The judge then went on to say that it would not be reasonable to construe section 1(1) in a way which would make builders and designers of a dwelling liable to a subsequent purchaser for trivial defects in design and construction. He thought that the existence of such defects would be reflected in the price paid for the dwellings by such a purchaser.

The result of these decisions seems to be that the duty extends only to defects of a major (structural) kind; more minor defects are outside its scope.

When does the duty apply?

The rules concerning the application of the duty in section 1(1) are as follows:

(a) The duty arises when a party to a contract agrees to carry out work and, in any event, not later than the start of the work. This rule was laid down by the Court of Appeal in *Alexander* v. *Mercouris*. On 20 November 1972 the defendants entered into an agreement with the plaintiff for the sale of a dwelling-house. It was part of that agreement that the defendants would modernise the house and convert it into two flats and they employed a firm of builders to carry out this work. The work was completed in February 1974. It was not satisfactory and the plaintiff brought an action under section 1(1) of the Act. The question for determination was whether or not the Act applied in this case. Under the provisions of section 7(2) the statutory duty applies only if the work was taken on after 1 January 1974. The Court of Appeal held that the duty arose when the work was taken on, i.e. in November 1972. This was before the Act came into force and therefore the defendants owed no duty under its provisions to the plaintiff.

(b) It applies only to the construction, conversion or enlargement of a *dwelling*. It does not extend to industrial or commercial premises. This limitation is based on the Law Commission's view that in such cases the parties are generally able to protect their own interests.

(c) It imposes liability for *nonfeasance* as well as *misfeasance*. In *Andrews* v. *Schooling*,[12] the defendant company acquired, in 1986, two adjacent Edwardian semi-detached houses and employed subcontractors to convert them into flats. One of these flats was on the ground floor and included a cellar. The subcontractors did not put a damp-proof course into this cellar, but merely pointed the walls. In 1987 the defendants leased the ground floor flat to the plaintiff. Shortly after moving in she complained that the flat suffered from penetrating damp coming from the cellar and she sued the defendants for breach of the duty imposed by section 1(1) of the Act. The defendants argued that this provision only applied to liability for misfeasance and they could not be liable, therefore, for *omitting* to put in a damp-proof course. The Court of Appeal rejected this argument. They held that the provisions of section 1(1) applied as much to a failure to carry out the necessary work as to the carrying out of such work badly.

(d) It does not apply to building works covered by an approved scheme. This is the effect of section 2, which provides that the duty contained in section 1(1) is not applicable if at the time of the first sale or letting an 'approved scheme' conferring rights in respect of defects in the dwelling was in operation. The only scheme to have obtained such approval is that operated by the NHBC and since almost all new dwellings are covered by this scheme this meant that section 1(1) was rendered virtually redundant. Thus Spencer in his article on the Act comments:

> Section 1 gets all dressed up, and Section 2, by excluding any case where the NHBC scheme applied, leaves it with virtually nowhere to go.[13]

That view is no longer correct. After 31 March 1979 the NHBC scheme was no longer officially approved and it seems that section 1(1) does apply to *all* new dwellings erected since that date.[14] In other words, dwellings covered by the 1985 and 1992 editions of the NHBC scheme do come within the scope of the section 1(1) duty.

(e) In *Jacobs* v. *Moreton & Partners*,[15] the Official Referee, Mr Recorder Jackson QC, held that the phrase 'the provision of a dwelling' in section 1 meant that the section applies only to the creation of a new dwelling and does not extend to works of rectification to an existing building.

Who owes the duty?

The duty in section 1(1) is imposed upon those who take on work in relation to the provision of a dwelling. It is beyond doubt that this includes builders, subcontractors, architects and engineers. The subsection, however, is wider than simply imposing a duty on the actual person who carried out the work; section 1(4) provides that the duty extends to a person who in the course of a business or in the exercise of a statutory power arranges for another to take on work for or in connection with the provision of a dwelling. In other words, the statutory duty covers developers and local authorities.

To whom is the duty owed?

Under the provisions of section 1(1) the duty is owed to:

(a) the person who orders the building; and
(b) every person who acquires a legal or equitable interest in the dwelling.

In other words, the statutory duty extends to both the first purchaser of the dwelling and every subsequent owner.

Limitation

Section 1(5) provides that the limitation period for the statutory duty is normally six years *from the time when the dwelling was completed*. This is a much more unfavourable limitation period to the plaintiff than in a common law action for negligence, where the basic rule is that the limitation period is six years *from the date when the damage occurred*.[16]

The effect of section 1(5) is to exclude many householders from the protection of the Act, a point illustrated by *Rimmer* v. *Liverpool City Council*.[17] In that case, the local authority designed and built a large block of flats in 1959. The flats contained inside walls consisting of glass panels which were only three millimetres thick. In 1975, the plaintiff, one of the tenants of the flats, fell and injured himself when his left hand broke one of these glass panels. The Court of Appeal held that the local authority were liable for breach of their common law duty of reasonable care towards the plaintiff. However, the plaintiff's claim under section 1 of the 1972 Act was barred by section 1(5) because his cause of action was deemed to have accrued in 1959.

THE NHBC SCHEME

The NHBC was founded in 1936. It is a private company limited by guarantee and registered under the Companies Acts in England and Wales. The council consists of nominees of all the main bodies concerned with new housing, including the professions (RIBA, RICS, ICE, Law Society, etc.), the Building Societies Association, the Consumers Association and local authority bodies. The chairman is nominated by the Secretary of State for the Environment. In effect it is the consumer protection body of the house-building industry.

The NHBC serves two particular functions. Firstly, it keeps a National Register of approved house-builders, who are entitled to build houses either for sale direct to the public or for developers, and developers, who are not entitled to build houses themselves but must employ a registered house-builder as a main contractor. Most builders are registered with the NHBC; they have a strong, if not overwhelming, commercial incentive to register, since building societies and banks are reluctant to lend on the security of new houses not guaranteed by the NHBC. Secondly, the NHBC inspects new houses under construction in order to ensure that the NHBC's standards are being met and in order to see that the Building Regulations are being observed.

The NHBC scheme, known as 'Buildmark', is in essence a method of self-regulation on the part of the building industry of setting minimum standards for the construction of new dwellings. The scheme began in 1936 and by 1969–70 98 per cent of new private sector housing was covered by it.[18]

Under the Buildmark scheme builders who are members of the NHBC have a threefold duty to the NHBC when building new dwellings:

(i)   a duty to comply with the NHBC's requirements;
(ii) a duty to offer the purchaser of the dwelling the House Purchaser's Agreement (Form HB5); and
(iii) a duty to complete the work to a standard sufficient to obtain the Council's Notice of Insurance Cover (Form HB7).

If a builder fails to apply for the inspection of a dwelling and/or to offer the Buildmark, NHBC may take disciplinary action under its Rules. The ultimate sanction is deletion from the Register.

The House Purchaser's Agreement

This is nominally a separate contract made between the vendor and the purchaser, for the benefit of which the purchaser provides a consideration of 5p. It is the rights conferred by this agreement that form the primary remedy for the purchaser of a defective new dwelling-house.

Under the agreement the builder warrants to the purchaser that the dwelling has been or will be built:

(a) in accordance with the NHBC's requirements; and
(b) in an efficient and workmanlike manner and of proper materials and so as to be fit for habitation.

(b) above is, of course, virtually identical with the obligations imposed on a builder by the common law. The rights conferred by the House Purchaser's Agreement are, however, additional to the common law rights.[19]

Under the Agreement there are two guarantee periods:

(i)   the initial guarantee period; and
(ii) the structural guarantee period.

The initial guarantee period

During this period the builder warrants that he will put right *any* defects which are:

(i)   due to non-compliance with the NHBC's Technical Requirements; and
(ii) which occur within two years of the date of the Notice of Insurance Cover.[20]

During this period the Council acts as underwriter of this obligation, i.e. if the vendor does not satisfy an award or judgement made against him for breach of this undertaking, the Council will do so. The liability of the Council in this respect is limited to the purchase price of the dwelling, subject to a maximum of three times the national average purchase price. These limits are increased in line with inflation, up to a maximum of 12 per cent per annum compound from the date of purchase.

The structural guarantee period

This runs from the third to the tenth years after the Notice of Insurance Cover has been issued. During this further eight-year period the NHBC will pay the cost of putting right any 'major damage' which first appears and is reported to the NHBC before the end of the period. 'Major damage' is defined as damage which is:

(a) caused by a defect in the structure; or
(b) caused by subsidence, settlement or heave affecting the structure.

The liability of the NHBC during the structural guarantee period is subject to the same financial limits as during the initial guarantee period.[21]

Subsequent purchasers[22]

The rights under the House Purchaser's Agreement extend to subsequent purchasers of the dwelling. That is, second and subsequent purchasers are safeguarded against new defects which appear after they bought the dwelling. However, this aspect of the NHBC scheme suffers from the doctrine of privity of contract, that no one who is not a party to a contract can take the benefit of it. The House Purchaser's Agreement is a contract made between the vendor and the first purchaser and confers rights on no one save the first purchaser. The fact that Form HB5 is expressed to be for the benefit of subsequent purchasers is no help in this matter, firstly, because it is not under seal, and secondly, because a subsequent purchaser will not have provided consideration for it. In order to ensure that a subsequent purchaser does take the benefit of the Agreement, it must be assigned to him under the provisions of section 136 of the Law of Property Act 1925. In this way the problem of privity of contract can be overcome.

The NHBC has a rule forbidding its members from taking the privity point in litigation. However, if the HB5 form was not validly assigned and the builder chose to ignore that rule, then a subsequent purchaser could well find that he did not have the benefit of the Buildmark scheme.

CONCLUDING COMMENT

By way of summary the following points can be highlighted.

In the case of the first purchaser of a defective new dwelling the principal course of action will be under the NHBC scheme. But that scheme does not cover extensions or improvements to existing dwellings. In those cases a plaintiff will have to seek a remedy either under the Defective Premises Act or for breach of the common law implied obligations.

It is the case of the subsequent purchaser of a defective dwelling, however, to which attention needs to be drawn. He is still at a disadvantage in respect of the rules governing privity of contract and economic loss. The privity rule may operate to the effect that the benefits of the NHBC scheme are not available to him. Further, following the decision in *Murphy* he will have no remedy in tort against the builder. This means that section 1 of the Defective Premises Act may well be a last straw for him to clutch. But that section does not appear suited to play this role; the duty contained in it is subject to too short a limitation period, and, moreover, it is not clear as to whether this duty covers economic loss. The courts are not at present in the mood to take a liberal view of this last factor!

SUMMARY

1. Section 1(1) of the Defective Premises Act 1972 places a duty on a person taking on work for or in connection with the provision of a dwelling to see that the work is done in a workmanlike manner with proper materials so that the dwelling will be fit for habitation when completed.

2. This duty is imposed upon anyone who takes on work in relation to the provision of a dwelling. Thus, it extends to builders, subcontractors, architects and engineers, developers and local authorities.

3. The duty is owed to the first purchaser or lessee of the dwelling and every subsequent owner or lessee.

4. The duty in section 1(1) does not impose a three-fold obligation on those taking on work in connection with the provision of a dwelling. Fitness for habitation is a measure of the standard imposed by the duty, not a separate obligation.

5. As a consequence, the duty appears to extend only to defects of a major (structural) kind.

6. A builder will not be liable under section 1(1) if he carries out work according to specifications or an architect's instructions. However, if the specifications or instructions are defective he may be under a common law duty to warn the employer of that fact.

7. The duty does not extend to industrial or commercial premises.

8. The limitation period for the duty is six years from the time when the dwelling was completed.

9. More than 95 per cent of new private sector dwellings built in the UK are covered by the NHBC guarantee.

10. The NHBC maintains a register of approved house-builders.

11. Builders who are members of the NHBC undertake that every home built and sold complies with the NHBC's requirements.

12. The NHBC issue a Buildmark form of guarantee to the purchaser, under which the builder warrants that the home has been or will be built (a) in accordance with the NHBC's requirements and (b) in an efficient and workmanlike manner and of proper materials and so as to be fit for habitation.

13. The Buildmark guarantee requires the builder to put right at his expense any defects resulting from non-compliance with the NHBC's requirements during the initial guarantee period (two years from the date of the Notice of Insurance Cover)

14. From the end of the initial guarantee period to the end of the tenth year after the date of the Notice of Insurance Cover the NHBC will pay the cost of putting right major damage caused by structural defects or by subsidence, settlement or heave affecting the structure.

NOTES

1. See, generally, J.R. Spencer (1974) CLJ 307; and Holyoak, J.H. and Allen, D.A., *Civil Liability for Defective Premises*, Butterworths, 1982, pp.93–106 and 116–118.
2. Law Com. No. 40 (1970).
3. [1972] 1 QB 373.
4. [1978] AC 728.
5. [1990] 2 All ER 908.
6. [1956] 1 WLR 303.
7. See *Lindenberg* v. *Canning* (1992) *Construction Law Digest* (May) p.21; and (1993) 62 BLR 147.
8. *Supra*, n.2. The courts, of course, must ignore Law Commission reports when construing the provisions of an Act of Parliament.
9. [1979] 1 WLR 1270.
10. (1992) 59 BLR 77.
11. *Ibid*, n.9, p.1274
12. [1991] 3 All ER 723.
13. *Supra*, n.1, p.320.
14. See *Keating on Building Contracts*, 7th edn, Sweet & Maxwell, 2001, pp.450–451, and I.N. Duncan Wallace (1991) 107 LQR 228, pp.242–243.
15. (1994) 72 BLR 92, p.105.
16. See *Anns, supra*, n.4; and *Pirelli* v. *Oscar Faber* [1983] AC 1. Limitation is a problematic issue in Construction Law and it is an important enough topic to merit its own chapter, Chapter 10.
17. [1985] QB 1.
18. The latest edition of the NHBC scheme was published in 1992. Copies can be obtained from NHBC, 58 Portland Place, London, W1N 4BU.
19. This point is recognised in the NHBC's Explanatory Notes to Form HB5.
20. Defects due to normal shrinkage or drying out are excluded, and purchasers must notify defects in writing to the vendor as soon as practicable after they appear.
21. It should be noted that the Buildmark booklet provides a list of items for which the builder will *not* be liable under the scheme during the initial guarantee period and a list of items for which the NHBC will *not* be liable under the scheme during the structural guarantee period.
22. This section of the chapter is based on J.R. Spencer's analysis, *supra*, n.1

5

The Building Regulations[1]

ORIGINS AND PURPOSE OF THE BUILDING REGULATIONS

The Building Regulations are a comprehensive set of rules which provide a detailed system of quality control for all stages of building work. They cover a wide range of matters including drains, sewage and sanitary conveniences, foundations and building materials. They were originally model by-laws which were made under the Public Health Act 1875 and which many local authorities adopted with modification. The Public Health Act 1961 replaced these by-laws by the Building Regulations, which came into effect in 1966.

Historically, the Regulations have been seen as a cornerstone of the maintenance of general standards of public health. The need for such detailed controls was created by the very poor housing conditions which were all too common a feature of the industrial towns which grew so rapidly in the nineteenth century. This public health role was emphasised by the House of Lords in *Anns* v. *Merton LBC*.[2] Lord Wilberforce pointed out that the purpose of the Regulations is to provide for the health and safety of owners and occupiers of buildings, including dwelling-houses, by setting standards to be complied with in construction and by enabling local authorities to supervise and control the operations of builders.[3] Lord Salmon expressed this point as follows:

> The Public Health Act 1936 and the building byelaws made under it confer ample powers on the council for the purpose, among other things, of enabling it to protect the health and safety of the public in its locality against what is popularly known as jerry-building.[4]

To say that the Building Regulations are an aspect of public health is to say that a poorly constructed building may well have harmful effects, not just for the occupiers of the building, but on the environment of the locality in which it stands. In other words, poor-quality buildings may well subject their locality to what economists refer to as external diseconomies, i.e. they may impose costs, not just on their occupiers, but on the community at large. The principal purpose of the Regulations, therefore, is to eliminate or at any rate reduce these externalities.

The more controversial question is whether the Regulations have a wider consumer protection role. Clearly they provide protection for the person who employs a builder to build on land which he, the employer, owns; at the very least the building must come up to the standards prescribed by the Regulations. But what of the subsequent purchaser of such a building or the person who buys or leases a building from a developer? The key issue in those circumstances is whether the building control authority in whose area the building was erected can be said to owe a duty in tort to these persons to adequately enforce the Regulations. In *Anns* the House of Lords said that there was such a common law duty, but in the more recent case of *Murphy* v. *Brentwood DC*[5] *Anns* has been overruled and the House of Lords has said that such a duty cannot be founded on principle. The Law Lords in *Murphy* strenuously denied that the courts had any such consumer protection role. Lord Jauncey put this point bluntly:

> Parliament imposed a liability on builders by the Defective Premises Act, a liability which falls far short of that which would be imposed on them by *Anns*. There can therefore be no policy reason for imposing a higher common law duty on builders, from which it follows that there is equally no policy reason for imposing such a high duty on local authorities. Parliament is far better equipped than the courts to take policy decisions in the field of consumer protection.[6]

Given the much more conservative approach of the present Judicial Committee of the House of Lords to the creation of new tortious duties, it is clear that any broader consumer protection role for the Building Regulations must await another day. None the less, it cannot be denied that the Building Regulations were, and still are, an important part of that governmental paternalism to the protection of the industrial environment which grew up in the nineteenth century. This philosophy has been summed up as follows:

> The Building Regulations may be seen as a classic example of the increase in governmental control over day-to-day living where a small initial degree of intervention has burgeoned into a comprehensive panoply of what may, depending on one's political viewpoint, be regarded as useful controls or excessive interference. They also illustrate the ever increasing tendency to place the responsibility for state intervention in the hands of central, rather than local government. The history of the Regulations is in essence a gradual realisation during the nineteenth century that Britain's housing conditions were often intolerable – inadequately constructed houses surrounded by squalor in unhygienic surroundings were the norm for many in newly industrialised towns and cities.[7]

Modern governments have tended to see the Regulations more in the nature of 'excessive interference' than 'useful controls', and much of the detail of the Regulations is now contained in approved documents, with the Regulations themselves providing a broad framework of control. However, it is hard to imagine building work ever being entirely free of detailed quality control in some form or other.

SCOPE OF THE BUILDING REGULATIONS

The present system of building control is based on the Building Act 1984. Section 1 of that Act empowers the Secretary of State to make regulations with respect to the design and construction of buildings and the provision of services, fittings and equipment in or in connection with buildings for the following purposes:

(a) securing the health, safety, welfare and convenience of persons in or about buildings and of others who may be affected by buildings or matters connected with buildings;
(b) furthering the conservation of fuel and power; and
(c) preventing waste, undue consumption, misuse or contamination of water.

The Building Regulations 1985 were made under these powers and they operated from 11 November 1985 until 31 May 1992. They revoked and replaced the Building Regulations 1976. The 1985 Regulations differed in form from those they replaced in that they were expressed in broad functional terms and the technical details contained in the 1976 Regulations were replaced by approved documents. The Regulations now in force are the Building Regulations 1991.[8] They revoked and replaced the 1985 Regulations with effect from 1 June 1992 and they brought into effect a major review of technical and procedural requirements. In their turn they also have been amended.

The Building Regulations apply throughout England and Wales. At first the Inner London boroughs remained outside their scope and were subject instead to the London Building Acts. However, they have now, for the most part, been brought within the national system.[9]

Under Regulation 4 of the 1991 Regulations, building work must be carried out so that it complies with the requirements set out in Schedule 1. These requirements are in 13 parts, and are as follows:

> Part A (Structure)
> Part B (Fire Safety)[10]
> Part C (Site Preparation and Resistance to Moisture)
> Part D (Toxic Substances)
> Part E (Resistance to the Passage of Sound)
> Part F (Ventilation)

Part G (Hygiene)
Part H (Drainage and Waste Disposal)
Part J (Heat Producing Appliances)
Part K (Stairways, Ramps and Guards)
Part L (Conservation of Fuel and Power)
Part M (Disabled People)
Part N (Glazing – Materials and Protection)[11]

Regulation 7 (as amended)[12] contains general obligations with regard to the standard of building work. It states:

Building work shall be carried out –
(a) with adequate and proper materials which
    (i) are appropriate for the circumstances in which they are used,
    (ii) are adequately mixed or prepared, and
    (iii) are applied, used or fixed so as adequately to perform the functions for which they are designed; and
(b) in a workmanlike manner.

At first sight, these obligations seem very similar to the familiar obligations concerning work and materials which the common law and the provisions of Part I of the Supply of Goods and Services Act 1982 impose upon a building contractor. However, in addition to these traditional duties, Regulation 7 imposes two specific duties on a building contractor: materials used in building work must be adequately mixed or prepared and they must be used so as adequately to perform the functions for which they are designed. Arguably, this latter requirement imposes more than a duty of reasonable care and skill upon a contractor; it imposes a limited duty of result upon him.

Lest the specific requirements contained in Regulation 7 be thought to impose onerous obligations, it should be remembered that by Regulation 8 the obligations are merely to do that which is 'necessary to secure reasonable standards of health and safety for persons in or about the building and others who may be affected by any failure to comply with that requirement.' Regulation 8 reflects the historical concern of the Building Regulations with the maintenance of general standards of public health.

'Building work' is defined in Regulation 3 of the 1991 Regulations as:

(a) the erection or extension of a building;
(b) the provision or extension of a controlled service or fitting in or in connection with a building;
(c) the material alteration of a building, or a controlled service or fitting;
(d) work relating to material change of use;
(e) the insertion of insulating material into the cavity wall of a building; and
(f) work involving the underpinning of a building.

Certain buildings are exempted from the Building Regulations by section 4 of the Building Act 1984. They are educational buildings and buildings belonging to statutory undertakers, the United Kingdom Atomic Energy Authority, the British Airports Authority, and the Civil Aviation Authority. Under the provisions of section 5 of the 1984 Act certain public bodies – in particular, local authorities – are exempt from the procedural, as opposed to the substantive, requirements of the Regulations. Further, Schedule 2 to the Regulations contains a list of exempt buildings and work.

Finally in this section, some comment must be made upon the nature of the 'approved documents'. They were first introduced in 1985 and are a key feature of the modern system of building control. Prior to 1985 the Building Regulations contained much technical detail; now they provide the broad framework of control and the approved documents provide the technical detail and the guidance as to how to comply with the Regulations. The argument for these documents is that they are a better way of accommodating technical information than the Regulations themselves which are published by way of statutory instrument; in particular, they can be updated much more easily than statutory instruments.

Under the provisions of section 7 of the Building Act 1984 legal status of these approved documents is evidentiary rather than substantive and compliance with their provisions is not mandatory. Section 7 provides as follows:

> A failure on the part of a person to comply with an approved document does not of itself render him liable in any civil or criminal proceedings; but if, in any proceedings whether civil or criminal, it is alleged that a person has at any time contravened a provision of the Building Regulations
>
> (a) a failure to comply with a document that at any time was approved for the purposes of that provision may be relied upon as tending to establish liability, and
>
> (b) proof of compliance with such a document may be relied on as tending to negative liability.

This means that if, say, a builder does not comply with the requirements of an approved document, then he will not be liable under the 1984 Act if he can show that he has complied with the requirements of the Regulations themselves by another, and equally satisfactory, method.

SUPERVISION OF THE BUILDING REGULATIONS

There are now two methods by which a builder or architect can have the building work supervised: (1) by a local authority, or (2) by an approved inspector.

Local authority control

Under local authority control, two options are available. The first option is the deposit of full plans, together with the prescribed fee. Local authorities have no discretion when considering such plans; under the provisions of section 16 of the Building Act 1984 they must approve the plans unless they are defective or in contravention of the Regulations. They have five weeks in which to pass or reject the plans, although this period can be extended, by agreement, to two months. The second option, which is available essentially for small scale domestic work, involves the applicant serving a 'building notice' on the local authority together with the prescribed fee. The notice must contain a short description of the work, the site, size and use of the building, proposals for drainage and a block plan of the new building or extension. The local authority does not issue any approval of the work, but it has powers to seek additional information and to check work in progress.

Approved inspector control

This form of supervision was introduced by Part II of the 1984 Act, though the detailed procedures are set out in regulations.[13] In broad terms Part II provides that responsibility for ensuring compliance with the Building Regulations may, if the person intending to carry out the work so chooses, be given to an approved inspector rather than a local authority. The provisions of Part II also enable approved public bodies to approve their own work.

Under this method of supervision the developer and the approved inspector jointly serve an 'initial notice' describing the proposed work on the local authority. This notice can only be rejected by the local authority on very limited grounds. On acceptance the local authority's powers to enforce the Regulations are suspended and the approved inspector becomes responsible for inspecting the plans and the work and for issuing the final certificate on completion.

At present the only approved inspector is the National House-Building Council (NHBC). No other bodies seem likely to be approved in the near future because of the difficulties of obtaining professional indemnity insurance for this work.

ENFORCEMENT

Under the provisions of section 35 of the Building Act 1984 contravention of the Building Regulations is a criminal offence. Under the provisions of section 36 a local authority may serve a notice (known as a section 36 notice) on an owner requiring the building work to be pulled down or altered if it does not comply with the Regulations. If the owner fails to comply with such a notice, the local authority may pull down the work itself and recover the cost from the owner.

CIVIL LIABILITY

Builders

Section 38 of the Building Act 1984 provides that breach of a duty imposed by the Building Regulations shall, if it causes damage, be actionable except in so far as the Regulations provide otherwise. However, this section has not yet been brought into force. If it is eventually brought into effect, then it would have a number of advantages for a plaintiff. Firstly, *vis-à-vis* an action in negligence, there would be no need for a duty of care to be established by the plaintiff, since the statute spells this out. Secondly, and more importantly, the obligations imposed by the Building Regulations are clear, concise and comprehensive; in this respect section 38 has the potential to render redundant the provisions of section 1 of the Defective Premises Act 1972.

There appears to be no common law liability for breach of statutory duty independent of the provisions of section 38. In *Anns*, Lord Wilberforce, in considering this matter, said:

> ... since it is the duty of the builder to comply with the byelaws, I would be of the opinion that an action could be brought against him, in effect, for breach of statutory duty by any person for whose benefit or protection the byelaw was made.[14]

These remarks were *obiter* and they have not been applied in subsequent cases. In *Murphy,* Lord Oliver said:

> There is nothing in the terms or purpose of the statutory provisions which support the creation of a private law right of action for breach of statutory duty.[15]

Apart from an action for breach of statutory duty, a builder who builds in contravention of the Building Regulations may be in breach of an *express* term of his contract with the employer. Thus, under the provisions of clause 6 of the JCT '80 the contractor must comply with all statutory requirements and is therefore in breach of contract if he builds the works in contravention of the Building Regulations. There appears to be no *implied* obligation imposed upon the builder that he will construct the works according to the Building Regulations. However, a contravention of the Building Regulations may well be strong evidence that the builder was in breach of his implied obligation to construct the works in a workmanlike manner, using reasonable care and skill.

If the design is in breach of the Building Regulations and the builder builds according to that design, then, if he knew of the contravention, he may well be liable for failing to use reasonable care and skill.[16] It seems that in the circumstances his duty is to warn the architect or the employer of the contravention.[17]

Local authorities

Section 91 of the 1984 Act imposes on local authorities the general duty of implementing the Act and enforcing the Building Regulations in their area. In 1972 the Court of Appeal in *Dutton* v. *Bognor Regis DC*,[18] and in 1978 the House of Lords in *Anns*, held that, in addition to this statutory duty, local authorities had a common law duty to take reasonable care to see that the Building Regulations were complied with.

In *Dutton*, the foundations of a house were inspected and approved by one of Bognor Regis DC's building inspectors. In fact they did not comply with the by-laws because the house was being built on an old rubbish tip, a fact which a competent inspection would have revealed. The plaintiff, Mrs Dutton, bought the house as a second owner. It subsided and serious cracking in the walls occurred. Cusack J at first instance held that the council owed Mrs Dutton a duty of care and that they were liable for breach of that duty. His decision was upheld by the Court of Appeal. Lord Denning, MR said that the Public Health Act 1936 and the by-laws made under it conferred on the local authority a control so extensive over building work and the manner in which it was performed that it carried with it a common law duty to exercise that control with reasonable care. That duty was owed to everyone who the inspector knows or ought to know is relying on his plaintiff.

The decision in *Dutton* was approved, subject to certain modifications, by the House of Lords in *Anns*. In 1962 the local council approved building plans for a block of flats, the construction of which was completed that year. In 1970 structural movements led to walls cracking and other damage. In 1972 the lessees commenced proceedings against the council, alleging that they had either negligently inspected the foundations or not inspected them at all. The House of Lords held that where an inspection was made there was a common law duty to take reasonable care to secure compliance with the building by-laws. The main speech was given by Lord Wilberforce and in its implications it was one of the most radical in the modern history of tort law. He said that the damages recoverable included damages for personal injury, damage to property and damage to the dwelling-house itself. He added:

> If classification is required, the relevant damage is in my opinion material, physical damage, and what is recoverable is the amount of expenditure necessary to restore the dwelling to a condition in which it is

> *no longer a danger to the health or safety of persons occupying* ...
> [author's italics][19]

Lord Wilberforce also considered the legal position if a local authority decided not to inspect. He said that it can still be challenged in the courts; although councils are under no duty to inspect, they are under a duty to give proper consideration to the question whether or not they should inspect. Essentially this means that before a local authority can be liable in negligence for an omission to inspect, that omission must be *ultra vires*. Lord Wilberforce emphasised that a local authority has to strike a balance between the claims of efficiency and thrift and that they are entitled not to inspect in certain circumstances. In other words, as long as a decision not to inspect is a properly taken policy decision, then a local authority cannot, it seems, be liable in negligence.

The decisions in *Dutton* and *Anns* were a radical development for the tort of negligence in general and for the duties of building control authorities in particular. They were controversial decisions, representing as they did the potential for further radical developments in the scope of this tort.[20] Not surprisingly, it was not long before the appellate courts began to place limitations on the extent of these decisions.[21] In these (subsequent) cases the issue for consideration was whether or not a local authority in exercising their building control duties owed a common law duty to the original building owner or developer. This issue came before the House of Lords in *Governors of the Peabody Donation Fund* v. *Sir Lindsay Parkinson & Co. Ltd.*[22] The plaintiffs in that case were developers. Their architects submitted plans for the construction of a flexible system of drainage to the local authority concerned. These plans were approved. However, the plaintiffs' contractors, on instructions from the architect, installed a rigid system of drainage. This fact came to the attention of the local authority but they took no action. The drains proved defective and had to be reconstructed, causing delay and substantial loss to the plaintiffs. They sued the local authority for negligence in carrying out their building control duties. The House of Lords held that the plaintiffs as owners of the building site were responsible for seeing that the drainage scheme conformed to the design approved by the local authority. The fact that they suffered loss because they were in breach of that duty did not make it reasonable or just to impose on the local authority a liability to indemnify the plaintiffs.

The principle in *Peabody* was applied by the Court of Appeal in *Investors in Industry Commercial Properties Ltd* v. *South Bedfordshire DC.*[23] The Court said that the purpose of the supervisory powers of the building control authorities is to protect the occupiers of buildings and members of the public generally against dangers to health or personal safety. It is not to safeguard the building developer himself against economic loss.

In *Richardson* v. *West Lindsey DC*,[24] the Court of Appeal reiterated that view. They said that it is the duty of a building owner who intends to develop his building to observe the provisions of the Building Regulations. They also said that the local authority owed no common law duty to the building owner himself to ensure that he complied with the Regulations, *whether the loss he suffered was physical or economic.*

Clearly these decisions put significant limitations on the *Anns* principle. But it was not until *Murphy* that the House of Lords confronted the crux of that principle, the nature and classification of the loss suffered by the occupier of a building which is *potentially* dangerous. The facts of *Murphy* are as follows. In 1970 the plaintiff purchased from a construction company one of a pair of semi-detached houses newly constructed on an in-filled site. They were supported by a concrete raft foundation to prevent damage from settlement. The plans and calculations for the foundations were submitted to the local council for approval. The council approved them after referring them to consulting engineers for checking. In 1981 the plaintiff noticed serious cracks in his house and investigation showed that the foundation was defective. In 1986 he sold the house subject to its defects for £35,000 less than its market value in sound condition. The plaintiff sued the council for negligence and the judge at first instance held that the council were liable for the consulting engineers' negligence. The judge's decision was upheld by the Court of Appeal. The council then appealed to the House of Lords, who upheld their appeal.

The House of Lords held that when carrying out its building control functions, a local authority was not liable in negligence to a building owner or occupier for the cost of remedying a defect in the building which resulted from the negligent failure of the local authority to ensure that the building was constructed in accordance with the Building Regulations. The Law Lords were at pains to emphasise that such loss was not physical damage but economic loss. They said that once a dangerous defect became known it was a defect in quality. If a duty to avoid such loss was to be imposed on the local authority, then a similar duty would have to be imposed on the builder. There would be no grounds in principle for not extending such liability to the manufacturer of a chattel and that in turn would lead to an exceedingly wide field of claims involving the introduction of a transmissible warranty of quality into the English law of tort. *Dutton* and *Anns* were overruled.

There is no doubt that the decision in *Murphy* has ended a period of great uncertainty in this area of law as to the true extent of the *Anns* doctrine. The underlying reasoning of these two seminal decisions has been extensively examined in Chapter 2. Suffice it to say here by way of summing up that essentially the decision in *Anns* was a consumer protection decision, allowing the occupier of a defective building to recover his losses from the deepest pocket, which in the event of the insolvency of the builder means the local authority. It meant in effect that local authorities became insurers of buildings constructed in their area in the sense that they guaranteed that they were constructed in accordance with the Building Regulations. That doctrine was criticised by some commentators as being contrary to principle.[25] In *Murphy*, the House of Lords clearly accepted that criticism and, as already stated, emphatically eschewed any consumer protection role for this area of law.

That leaves to be decided the question of what is the nature of the local authority's supervisory role in relation to building control. Is it simply to protect subsequent occupiers of a building from personal injury and damage to property other than the building itself? In appearing to overrule *Anns* in its entirety in *Murphy*, the House of Lords has implied that even that much may now be in doubt. The concluding words of the Lord Chancellor sound rather ominous in this respect:

> I should make it clear that I express no opinion on the question whether if personal injury were suffered by an oocupier of defective premises as a result of a latent defect in these premises, liability in respect of that personal injury would attach to a local authority which had been charged with the public law duty of supervising compliance with the relevant building by-laws or regulations in respect of a failure properly to carry out such duty.[26]

SUMMARY

1. The Building Regulations are a form of quality control over building work.

2. Their primary purpose, as set out in section 1 of the Building Act 1984, is to protect the health and safety of 'persons in or about buildings and of others who may be affected by buildings'.

3. The Building Regulations currently in force were made in 1991, though they have been amended.

4. With regard to the standard of building work the general obligation imposed by the Regulations is that it must be carried out with adequate and proper materials and in a workmanlike manner.

5. More detailed requirements are contained in Schedule 1 to the Regulations, though much technical detail is to be found in what are called 'approved documents'.

6. The task of ensuring that building work complies with the Building Regulations is carried out by local authorities or, in some cases, by an approved inspector.

7. Section 38 of the Building Act 1984 provides that a person who suffers damage as a result of a breach of the Building Regulations may bring

an action for breach of statutory duty against the builder concerned. However, this section is not yet in force.

8. There appears to be no right of action under the common law against the builder for breach of the Building Regulations.

9. In *Murphy*, the House of Lords held that a local authority is not liable under the common law of negligence to a building owner or occupier for the cost of remedying defects in the building which result from its failing to carry out with reasonable care its building control function.

10. Whether a building owner who suffered personal injury as a result of a local authority failing to carry out properly its building control function may recover damages under the common law of negligence was left undecided in *Murphy*.

NOTES

1. See, generally, *Knight's Building Regulations*.
2. [1978] AC 728.
3. *Ibid*, n.2, p.753.
4. *Ibid*, n.2, p.761.
5. [1990] 2 All ER 908.
6. *Ibid*, n.5, pp.942–943.
7. Holyoak, J.H. and Allen, D.K., *Civil Liability for Defective Premises*, Butterworths, 1982, p.119.
8. SI 1991 No.2768.
9. See the Building Regulations (Inner London) Regulations 1985 and 1987 (SI 1985 No.1936 and SI 1987 No.798).
10. In addition to requirements imposed under the Building Act 1984, the provision of adequate means of escape from certain buildings is controlled by the Fire Precautions Act 1971. This requires designated buildings to have a fire certificate which, among other matters, certifies that the means of escape is adequate considering the use and occupancy of the building. See, further, Allen, D., Holyoak, J. and Everton, A., *Fire Safety and Law*, 2nd edn, Paramount Publishing, 1990, Chapter 2.
    The Building Regulations (Amendment) (No.2) Regulations 1999 (SI 1999 No.3410) have substituted a new Part B. The new Part B adds to the pre-existing Part B a requirement for appropriate provision for early warning of a fire. This addition makes it clear that the resistance to fire must be adequate and that the facilities and access for the fire service must be reasonable.
11. This part was added by the 1991 Regulations.
12. See Regulation 4 of the Building Regulations (Amendment) Regulations 1999 (SI 1999 No. 77). Regulation 4 replaces the original Regulation 7 in the 1991 Regulations. The original Regulation 7 was in two parts; the second part contained requirements to be met by proper materials. These requirements have been replaced by practical guidance contained in a document approved by the Secretary of State: *Approved Document to Support Regulation 7: Materials and Workmanship*, 1999, published by TSO Publications Centre, P.O. Box 276, London, SW8 5DT.
13. The Building (Approved Inspectors) Regulations 1985, SI 1985 No. 1066. An approved inspector is a person approved by the Secretary of State under the provisions of section 49 of the Building Act 1984.

14. *Supra*, n.2, p.759.
15. *Supra*, n.5, p.943.
16. *Equitable Debenture Assets Corporation* v. *William Moss* (1984) 2 Con. LR 1.
17. *Lindenberg* v. *Canning* (1992) *Construction Law Digest* (May), p.21. See also sub-clauses 6.1.2 and 6.1.5 of the JCT '80.
18. [1972] 1 QB 373.
19. *Supra*, n.2, p.759.
20. See, in particular, the decision of the House of Lords in *Junior Books Ltd* v. *Veitchi Co. Ltd* [1983] 1 AC 520 (allowing a building owner's claim against a subcontractor for replacement of defective flooring and thereby opening the door to general recovery for economic loss in the tort of negligence).
21. Fleming has described Lord Wilberforce's speech in *Anns* as 'an affirmation of judicial sovereignty, a provocation to the partisans of judicial restraint': (1990) 106 LQR 525, p.525.
22. [1984] 3 WLR 953.
23. [1986] 1 All ER 787.
24. [1990] 1 All ER 296.
25. See especially Duncan Wallace (1991) 107 LQR 228.
26. *Supra*, n.5, p.912.

6
Liability of Subcontractors

INTRODUCTION

Under the traditional form of contracting in the construction industry, initially one contractor, known as the main contractor, is engaged to construct the whole of the works. However, it is usual for the majority of the work on a substantial construction contract to be carried out by a large number of (specialist) subcontractors. The subject of this chapter is the duties and liabilities of these subcontractors and the liability of the main contractor for their work.

These duties and liabilities will be examined from three points of view:

(1) the relationships between the employer and each subcontractor;
(2) the relationships between the principal contractor and each subcontractor; and
(3) the liability of the main contractor for the work of the subcontractors.[1]

EMPLOYER AND SUBCONTRACTOR

Liability in contract

Under the traditional JCT form of contract, a subcontractor is not a party to the contract between the contractor and the employer. In technical language, there is no privity of contract between employer and subcontractor. The employer, therefore, cannot sue a subcontractor in contract for deficiencies or delays in the performance of his contractual work.

The doctrine of privity of contract can be bypassed by the employer obtaining a direct warranty from a subcontractor, known as a collateral warranty. The JCT has produced a standard form of employer/nominated subcontractor agreement.[2] Under clause 2.1 of this form a contractor warrants that he has used reasonable care and skill in:

(1) the design of the subcontract works in so far as the subcontract works have been or will be designed by the subcontractor;
(2) the selection of materials and goods for the subcontract works in so far as such materials and goods have been or will be selected by the subcontractor; and

127

(3) the satisfaction of any performance specification or requirement in so far as such performance specification or requirement is included or referred to in the description of the subcontract works included in or annexed to the tender.

The essential point to note about such a warranty is that it adds nothing to the implied duties owed by the supplier in a contract for work and materials: it simply allows a third party (the employer) to take the benefit of those duties.

Liability in tort

In the absence of any direct warranty the only means by which the employer can sue a subcontractor is in the tort of negligence. In practice, any losses sustained by the employer as a result of the negligence of a subcontractor are likely to be economic and as we have seen in Chapter 2, this is a problematical area of law. Construction cases, including those involving the liability of subcontractors, have played a prominent part in the recent history of negligence and economic loss and it is, therefore, worth recounting that history.

Until the 1960s the law concerning negligence and economic loss seemed to be clear: where a negligent act or negligent words *forseeably* led to another person suffering economic (i.e. financial) loss, then the defendant was not liable for that loss. In the 1960s and 1970s there occurred a number of developments which, in effect, created exceptions to this rule.

(1) The House of Lords in *Hedley Byrne* v. *Heller*[3] said, *obiter*, that a person who suffers financial loss through relying on a false statement made negligently has, in certain circumstances, a claim in negligence against the maker of the statement.[4]
(2) In the so-called 'building cases' a builder's liability in tort for defective premises was extended to include what, in effect, was economic loss.[5]
(3) In *Spartan Steel & Alloys Ltd* v. *Martin & Co. (Contractors) Ltd*[6] the Court of Appeal held that economic loss resulting from a negligent act was recoverable where it was consequent upon damage to property.

These developments culminated in the decision of the House of Lords in *Junior Books Ltd* v. *Veitchi Co. Ltd*,[7] a Scottish case involving the liability of a subcontractor for negligence. A firm of builders was engaged to construct a factory for the building owner. The defendants were engaged as subcontractors to lay a composition floor. Because of their negligence the floor was defective and cracked up. There was no danger to health or safety or any other property of the building owner but the floor needed to be replaced. The building owner sought to recover the cost of replacement, including the loss of profits incurred while the floor was being relaid, from the subcontractors. There was no contract between the parties and the building owner therefore sued in the tort of negligence. The House of Lords treated the building owner's loss as economic and they held, by a majority, that his allegations disclosed a cause of action. The majority said that where the relationship between the parties was sufficiently close the scope of the duty of care extended to a duty to avoid causing economic loss consequent upon defects in the work and to avoid defects in the work itself.

The leading speech for the majority was given by Lord Roskill. He based his analysis on Lord Wilberforce's famous two-stage test for establishing a duty of care in *Anns*. Lord Wilberforce said that in order to establish that a duty of care arises in a particular situation, it is not necessary to bring the facts of that situation within those previous situations in which a duty of care has been held to exist. Rather the question has to be approached in two stages:

(1) Is there a sufficient relationship of proximity between the plaintiff and defendant for a duty to arise?
(2) If the first question is answered affirmatively, are there any considerations which ought to negative or limit the scope of the duty? [8]

In applying the first stage of Lord Wilberforce's test, Lord Roskill in his speech referred to two specific factors which gave rise to an adequate degree of proximity for the subcontractors to owe a duty of care to the pursuers. Firstly, the subcontractors had expert knowledge of the flooring trade and of the requirements of the factory owners and they relied on that expertise. Secondly, the relationship between the parties was all but contractual in character and it must have been clear to the subcontractors that bad workmanship on their part would result in increased expenditure by the factory owners. As to the second stage of Lord Wilberforce's test, Lord Roskill said that there were no policy factors which negatived or restricted the duty: in particular, there was no question of the subcontractors being liable to an indeterminate class.

In general terms, the decision in *Junior Books* seemed to open up the possibility of a general rule of recovery for economic loss in an action in negligence. In relation to defective buildings it was thought that the law might develop so that any owner of a building in disrepair because of negligence on the part of those constructing it would be able to recover the expense of repair, subject to satisfying the two parts of the *Anns* test and subject to the rules relating to the limitation of actions. Those hopes were soon dashed. Subsequent cases in this area have regarded *Junior Books* as a special case confined to its own facts, and the decision of the House of Lords there has been distinguished on all these occasions. Moreover, as we have seen in Chapter 2, the *Anns* line of cases was overruled in *Murphy* v. *Brentwood DC*.[9]

It is not even clear now as to whether *Junior Books* could be relied upon by an employer suing a subcontractor. In four cases involving claims in tortious negligence by employers against subcontractors the courts have distinguished *Junior Books*. In *Southern Water Authority* v. *Carey*,[10] the predecessors of Southern Water Authority entered into a contract for the construction of a sewage works. The actual works were carried out by subcontractors. Under the *main* contract the main contractors were to be responsible for making good defects in the works arising within twelve months of completion as a result of defective materials, workmanship or design. The main contract also stated that the acceptance of this liability by the main contractor was to be *instead of* any condition or warranty implied by law as to quality and fitness for any particular purpose of the work. The work proved to be defective, with the result that the whole sewage scheme was a failure. The plaintiff sued the subcontractor for negligence in the design and supply of defective equipment and the installation of this equipment. The High Court held that the subcontractors could not be liable in tort because the main contract negatived the duty of care which would otherwise have been owed by the subcontractors. In other words, the wording of the main contract defined the area of risk which the plaintiff had chosen to accept and in doing this it had limited the scope of the subcontractor's liability.

In *Norwich City Council* v. *Paul Clarke Harvey & Briggs Amasco Ltd*,[11] the plaintiff entered into a contract with Bush Builders Ltd to build an extension to a swimming pool complex. Bush entered into a subcontract for felt-roofing with Briggs Amasco Ltd. In the course of the felt roofing work an employee of Briggs Amasco set fire with a blowtorch to both the existing buildings and the new extension, causing extensive damage. The terms of the subcontract contained a provision which bound Briggs Amasco to the terms and conditions of the main contract. The main contract provided that as between the plaintiff and Bush the existing structures and works would be at the sole risk of the plaintiff as regards loss or damage by fire. The plaintiff therefore tried to recover their losses from the subcontractors in tort. The High Court held that the duty of care owed by the defendants to the plaintiff was qualified by the terms of the main contract. Accordingly, the subcontractors were not liable to the plaintiff.

In *Greater Nottingham Co-operative Society Ltd* v. *Cementation Piling and Foundations Ltd*,[12] the plaintiff building owner entered into a contract with a contractor for the extension and alteration of his office premises. Subcontractors were engaged to provide piles for the extension. The subcontractors entered into a collateral contract with the building owner which required them to exercise reasonable care and skill in the design of the piling works and in the selection of materials. That collateral contact was silent as to the manner in which the piling works were to be executed. In the event, the piling equipment was operated negligently by one of the subcontractors' employees and damage was caused to an adjoining building. Work was suspended while a revised piling scheme was worked out and the plaintiff sued the subcontractors in tort for his economic loss resulting from delayed completion of the building. The Court of Appeal held that the collateral contract entered into by the subcontractors defined the extent of their responsibility to the plaintiff building owner. As that collateral contract made no mention of liability for the execution of the piling work, the subcontractors were not responsible in tort for the building owner's economic loss.

In *Simaan General Contracting Co.* v. *Pilkington Glass Ltd (No. 2)*,[13] the plaintiffs were the main contractors for the construction of a building in Abu Dhabi. The supply and erection of curtain walling was subcontracted to an Italian company. The terms of the subcontract required the subcontractors to obtain specified double-glazed units of green glass from Pilkingtons, the defendants. When erected, the glass was found to be not of a uniform colour and the building owner withheld part of the contract price from the main contractors. The main contractors sought to recover this loss from Pilkingtons by suing them in negligence. The Court of Appeal distinguished this case from *Junior Books* and held that the defendants were not liable for the plaintiffs' losses. There was not a sufficiently close relationship between the plaintiffs and Pilkingtons to give rise to a duty of care; there had been no technical discussions about the product between the plaintiffs and Pilkingtons, and the plaintiffs could not be said to have relied on Pilkingtons in this matter.

A number of factors can be identified in this retreat from *Junior Books*. Firstly, it is part of the general retreat of the law of negligence. The courts now see the function of the law of negligence as being to protect the plaintiff's interest in his person and his property but not his purely financial interests. Secondly, the giving of a warranty by the subcontractor will restrict the subcontractor's liability in tort towards the building owner. The warranty is seen as defining the extent of the subcontractor's liability to the building owner and the courts do not regard it as proper for the law of tort to add to that liability. Thirdly, the courts have laid great stress on the risk of a tort action disturbing the allocation of responsibilities down the chain of contracts. In particular, emphasis has been laid on the possibility that if the employer is allowed to sue a subcontractor directly in tort then this could outflank an exemption clause either in the main contract or in the contract between the main contractor and the subcontractor.[14] All of these factors can be reduced to the general point that the dominant trend in this area of law since *Junior Books* has been to emphasise the law of contract as the means for recovering economic loss.

The conclusion from this survey is therefore clear: as a general rule, an employer will not be able to successfully sue a subcontractor directly in tort for economic loss suffered as a consequence of the subcontractor's negligence. However, there may be two exceptions to this general rule. Firstly, the employer may be able to successfully sue a subcontractor in negligence if he can show that his relationship with the subcontractor can be brought within the scope of the reliance doctrine first laid down in *Hedley Byrne*. Secondly, an action in negligence against a subcontractor may succeed if the loss suffered can be brought within the scope of the complex structure theory.

The first of these exceptions is based on the interpretation of *Junior Books* by Lord Keith in *Murphy*.[15] He said there that *Junior Books* is an application of the *Hedley Byrne* principle: the subcontractors owed a duty to the building owner because the building owner relied on their expertise.

In *Henderson and Others* v. *Merrrett Syndicates Ltd*,[16] Lord Goff extended the *Hedley Byrne* principle beyond the making of statements to the provision of services. He stated:

> if a person assumes responsibility to another in respect of certain services, there is no reason why he should not be liable in damages for that other in respect of economic loss which flows from the negligent performance of those services. It follows that once the case is identified as falling within the *Hedley Byrne* principle, there should be no need to embark upon any further enquiry whether it is 'fair, just and reasonable' to impose liability for economic loss.[17]

At first sight, this *dictum* seems to widen Lord Keith's exception to the general exclusionary rule governing economic loss. But it is important to realise the context in which it was made, namely the concurrent liability in contract and tort of managing agents to Lloyd's Names. There is nothing in Lord Goff's speech which suggests that his principle of assumption of responsibility may form a basis for independent liability in tort to third parties. True, he said that in the context of *Henderson* itself he saw no reason why indirect names should not be free to sue the managing agents in tort and thus bypass the contractual chain of indirect names, members' agents and managing agents. But he stressed that that context was an unusual one.

More important, for the purposes of Construction Law, is the very important limitation which Lord Goff placed on his principle in relation to the liability of contractors and subcontractors. Lord Goff referred to the contractual chain of liability which exists in an ordinary construction project under which the main contractor contracts with the building owner for the construction of the relevant building and the main contractor then subcontracts with various subcontractors and suppliers. Lord Goff said that if the subcontracted work or materials did not come up to the required standard it was not open to the building owner to sue the subcontractor or supplier under the *Hedley Bryne* principle. There was no assumption of responsibility by the subcontractor or supplier towards the building owner; the parties had structured their relationships so that such assumption of responsibility could not arise.[18]

It would be an unwise, if not reckless, observer, therefore, who suggested that the reliance principle, or its subsequent application, had in any way breached the exclusionary rule relating to negligence and economic loss laid down in *Murphy*. In relation to third party liability, the rule in *Murphy* is still the cornerstone of the law of negligence in general and of the law of construction negligence in particular.

The second exception derives from the attempts of the Law Lords in *D & F Estates* v. *Church Commissioners for England*[19] to reconcile their decision in that case with *Anns*. They introduced a distinction between simple and complex structures and said that damage to one part of a structure caused by a defect in another part could be treated as damage to other property.[20] Not surprisingly, such a theory is fraught with problems and in *Murphy* it was considerably modified. Lord Bridge said there that it applied only to a distinct item incorporated in the structure (e.g. a central heating boiler which malfunctions so as to damage the structure) and not to the structure itself. Thus, where the foundations of a building were inadequate to support its superstructure, that was a defect of quality.[21] Lord Jauncey said that the only context in which the complex structure theory could arise in the case of a building would be where one integral component of the building was built by a separate contractor and where a defect in that component caused damage to other parts of the structure. He gave an example of a steel frame erected by a specialist contractor which failed to support adequately the floors and walls. Lord Jauncey went on to say that defects in such ancillary equipment as central heating boilers or electrical equipment which caused damage to other parts of the building were subject to *Donoghue* v. *Stevenson* principles.[22]

It seems that before a subcontractor can be sued by the employer under the complex structure theory it must be established that the subcontractor supplied a distinct component within the building but did not also supply the part damaged by a defect in this component. It is obviously difficult to determine what constitutes 'other property' for the purposes of this theory. Why is damage caused by defective foundations regarded differently from damage caused by a defective steel structure? The law in this area can hardly be said to be crystal clear.

Concurrent liability in contract and tort

Where a subcontractor provides the employer with a direct warranty the terms of such a warranty may affect the scope of any tortious liability owed concurrently by that subcontractor to the employer. Such concurrent liability in tort to the employer must be distinguished from liability in tort to the employer as a third party. The general position governing concurrent liability in the employer/subcontractor relationship is summed up in the following terms by *Emden*:

> It is now clear that where a subcontractor makes a direct collateral contract with the employer, that contract will normally be treated as con-

taining the whole of the subcontractor's liabilities towards the employer in respect of economic loss caused by negligence. If, therefore, the contract does not place responsibility for such loss on the subcontractor, the employer cannot recover by suing alternatively in tort, the contract will be regarded as the exhaustive definition of the subcontractor's responsibility for economic loss.[23]

Two authorities support this general statement of principle: *Henderson* v. *Merrett Syndicates* and *Barclays Bank* v. *Fairclough*.[24] In *Henderson*, Lord Goff expressed the relationship between a contractual duty of care and a tortious duty of care in the following terms:

> My own belief is that, in the present context, the common law is not antipathetic to concurrent liability, and that there is no sound basis for a rule which automatically restricts the claimant to either a tortious or a contractual remedy. The result may be untidy; but given that this tortious duty is imposed by the general law, and the contractual duty is attributable to the will of the parties, I do not find it objectionable that the claimant may be entitled to take advantage of the remedy which is most advantageous to him, subject only to ascertaining whether the tortious duty is so inconsistent with the applicable contract that, in accordance with ordinary principle, the parties must be taken to have agreed that the tortious remedy is to be limited or excluded.[25]

In *Barclays Bank* v. *Fairclough*, Lord Goff's principle of concurrent liability was extended to subcontractors. In that case a specialist subcontractor was employed by a contractor, Fairclough, to clean the asbestos roof of two buildings owned by Barclays. He did the job so negligently that he created asbestos slurry which, when it dried, created a serious health hazard. Fairclough was held liable to Barclays for the cost of the necessary remedial works, which was nearly £4 million. Fairclough then sued their subcontractor in tort for recovery of these damages. This was pure economic loss. Beldam LJ, in delivering the decision of the Court of Appeal, applied the principle laid down by Lord Goff in *Henderson* and held that the subcontractor owed a concurrent duty of care in tort to the contractor to avoid causing economic loss by failing to exercise the care and skill of a reasonably competent contractor. He said:

> A skilled contractor undertaking maintenance work to a building assumes a responsibility which invites reliance no less than the financial or other professional adviser does in undertaking his work. The nature of that responsibility is the same though it will differ in extent.[26]

The liability to which the duty in *Barclays* gave rise was no greater than liability for breach of the equivalent contractual term. In *Holt* v. *Payne*

Skillington,[27] the Court of Appeal considered the question of whether a con-current duty in tort meant a duty that was co-extensive with the duty in con-tract or whether the duty in tort could be wider than the duty in contract. The plaintiffs in *Holt* employed a firm of valuers to value a property which they wished to acquire for the purpose of short-term holiday lets. This agree-ment made no reference to the valuers investigating whether the property had the necessary planning permission. In fact, the valuers did make such enquiries and they (wrongly) informed the plaintiffs that the property in question had established use as serviced self-contained accommodation let on a short-term basis.

The trial judge, Judge Hague QC, rejected a claim for breach of contract on the grounds that there was no express or implied term obliging the valuers to investigate the planning permission or making it a condition that the property should have the necessary authorised use. However, he upheld a claim in tort. On appeal, it was found as a fact that the valuers had not been negligent in giving the planning advice because the plaintiffs had not relied to their detriment on it. Nonetheless, the decision of the Court of Appeal is significant because they held that a concurrent duty in tort can arise between two contracting parties which goes beyond the scope of the con-tractual duties. Hirst LJ, in giving the judgement of the Court of Appeal, said that there was no reason in principle why a *Hedley Byrne* type of duty could not arise in an overall set of circumstances where, by reference to certain limited aspects of those circumstances, the same parties entered into a con-tractual relationship involving more limited obligations than those imposed by the duty of care in tort. In such circumstances, the duty of care in tort and the duties imposed by the contract would be concurrent but not co-extensive. A consideration of the individual facts and circumstances of each case would determine whether any duty of care in tort which the general law might impose was of wider scope than any contract between the parties.

Hirst LJ went on to say that the difference in scope between the two duties would reflect 'the absence of any term in the contract which precluded or restricted the wider duty of care in tort'. In other words, even though a con-current duty in tort may be wider than a duty under the contract it is still open to the parties to exclude or limit that tortious duty.

The decision in *Holt* is one of great importance, both to professional advisers and others. It means that if a professional adviser goes beyond the contract with his client and provides advice which the client is intended to, and does, rely on the professional adviser will be liable in tort to the client should that advice turn out to have been negligently given. The most obvious implication of *Holt* for the construction industry would be where a contractor or subcontractor employed under the usual JCT form of contract, went beyond that contract and provided, say, advice on design. If that advice was negligently given he might now be held liable in tort for the client's losses resulting from it. The decision is a controversial one and it has been criticised as being unsound in principle by the editor of the Building Law Reports.[28]

PRINCIPAL CONTRACTOR AND SUBCONTRACTOR

The duties owed by the subcontractor to the main contractor in relation to the quality of the subworks are based on contract. These duties are of two kinds: express and implied.

Express duties

There will generally be a written agreement between the main contractor and each subcontractor and this agreement will contain the express obligations of the subcontractor. A standard form of agreement between main contractor and subcontractor is published by the JCT – Sub-Contract NSC/C.[29] This is the form most frequently used in the industry.

The subcontractor's obligations for the quality of the subcontract works under this form are contained in clause 1.9. They are as follows:

(1)   The subcontractor must carry out and complete the subcontract works in compliance with the subcontract documents and in conformity with the directions and requirements of the main contractor.

(2)   All materials and goods supplied by the subcontractor must be of the kinds and standards described in the subcontract documents. Where the architect has responsibility for approval of the quality of the materials and goods supplied they must be to his satisfaction.

(3)   All workmanship must be of the standards described in the subcontract documents. If no such standards are specified, then the workmanship must be of a standard appropriate to the subcontract works. Where approval of workmanship is subject to the opinion of the architect, then such workmanship must be to his satisfaction.

(4)   All work must be carried out in a proper and workmanlike manner.

More specifically, clause 2.1 states that the subcontractor must carry out and complete the subcontract works in accordance with the agreed programme details in the tender and in accordance with the progress of the main contract works. If the subcontractor is in default of this obligation, then under clause 7.1 the main contactor must inform the architect. If the architect so instructs, the main contractor must then issue a notice to the subcontractor specifying the default. If the subcontractor continues with such default for 14 days after the receipt of such notice the main contractor may terminate the employment of the subcontractor.

In substance these express obligations add little or nothing to the subcontractor's obligations under the general law.

Implied duties

A subcontract is, like the main contract, a contract for work and materials. As such, a subcontractor will be subject to the same implied obligations in relation to the work and materials as is the main contractor under the main contract. They are as follows:

(1) that the subcontractor carry out the works with reasonable care and skill; and
(2) that any materials supplied by the subcontractor be of good quality and fit for any particular purpose specified by the main contractor.

These duties are now contained in the Supply of Goods and Services Act 1982.[30] A detailed commentary on these implied duties is provided in Chapter 1, but two points are worth repeating here. Firstly, liability attaching to a breach of the duties relating to the materials supplied is strict, in contrast to liability attaching to defective workmanship which is negligence based. Secondly, if the main contractor does not rely on the expertise of the subcontractor in the selection of the materials, the implied duty of fitness for purpose is excluded; however, the subcontractor will still be responsible for the quality of the materials supplied.[31]

LIABILITY OF THE MAIN CONTRACTOR FOR THE WORK OF SUBCON- TRACTORS

The main contractor is entitled under the provisions of the JCT '98 to subcontract the work. Even if the main contract is not subject to the provisions of this standard form, the main contractor will almost certainly have implied powers to subcontract, since subcontracting is such an established custom in the construction industry.

When the main contractor subcontracts part of the work, he is not liable in tort to either the owner or the occupier of the building for the negligence of the subcontractor. The main contractor's only duty is to employ a competent subcontractor. This rule was explained by Lord Bridge in *D & F Estates* in the following terms:

> It is trite law that the employer of an independent contractor is, in general, not liable for the negligence or other torts committed by the contractor in the course of the execution of the work.[32]

Lord Bridge subsequently went on to say that if the fact of employing a contractor does not involve the assumption of any duty of care by the employer, then the contractor assumes no such liability when he employs an apparently competent subcontractor to carry out part of the work for him. This means that in the event of a subcontractor's negligence in the execution of the subcontract works the employer's only remedy lies against the sub-contractor in the tort of negligence, and, as we have seen in the first part of this chapter, where the employer's loss is purely economic it will be very difficult for him to establish that the subcontractor owed him a duty of care.

Lord Bridge pointed to one exception to the above rule. If the main contractor exercises a degree of supervision over the subcontractor and in the course of that supervision discovers defects in the subcontractor's work, which he approves, then he will be potentially liable for the consequences jointly with the subcontractor. The result of this proviso is that the main contractor is under a duty to warn the employer of any defects in the work of a subcontractor which comes to his attention.

Where the employer relies on the skill and judgement of the main contractor for the selection of the materials to be used, then the main contractor will remain liable to the employer in the event of a subcontractor supplying materials which are not of good (or merchantable) quality. The main authority for this rule is the decision of the House of Lords in *Young & Marten Ltd v. McManus Childs*.[33] In that case, contractors were building dwelling-houses on their own land. They subcontracted the roofing and they specified that a particular type of tile, Somerset 13, was to be used for the roof. These tiles were made by only one manufacturer and in specifying these tiles the contractor's representative relied on his own skill and judgement. The supplying and laying of tiles was further subcontracted. The tiles had a latent defect, not apparent on inspection, which was the result of a fault in their manufacture. This defect became apparent after the tiles were fixed and exposed to the weather. The House of Lords held that in a contract for work and materials two warranties may be implied in respect of the materials supplied, a warranty of their reasonable fitness for the purpose and a warranty of their good quality – in particular, against latent defects. Where the materials are chosen by the party for whom the work is to be done, a warranty of their fitness is not implied but, unless excluded by the circumstances or by the contact, a warranty of quality will be implied. As the contractors' representative relied on his own skill and judgement in the selection of the tiles in question, the subcontractors were held not liable for breach of the warranty of fitness for purpose, but they were held liable in damages for breach of the implied warranty of quality. Strictly speaking, of course, this case concerns the liability of a subcontractor who then further subcontracted the work in question. The first subcontractor was held liable for the defective tiles which the sub-subcontractor obtained from the manufacturer and used. However, it seems virtually certain in these circumstances that had it been an employer suing the main contractor for the work of a subcontractor, the result would have been the same.

The rationale underlying this rule was discussed most fully in the speech of Lord Reid. He set out two reasons for implying a warranty of quality. The first of these reasons he expressed as follows:

If the contractor's employer suffers loss by reason of the emergence of the latent defect, he will generally have no redress if he cannot recover damages from the contractor. If, however, he can recover damages the contractor will generally not have to bear the loss: he will have bought the defective materials from a seller who will be liable under section 14(2) of the Sale of Goods Act 1893, because the material was not of merchantable quality; and if that seller had in turn bought from someone else there will again be liability, so that there will be a chain of liability from the employer who suffers the damage back to the author of the defect.[34]

This chain may of course be broken because the contractor or an earlier buyer contracted subject to a clause excluding his supplier's liability under the Sale of Goods Act. Lord Reid said that should not deprive the employer of a remedy; in the event of such an exclusion clause the risk should lie with the party concerned if the goods proved defective.

What would be the position if the manufacturer was a monopolist and willing to sell only on terms which excluded or limited his liability? Lord Reid suggested that if this fact was known to the employer it would be unreasonable to impose liability for latent defects on the contractor. That, of course, was some time before the days of the Unfair Contract Terms Act 1977. Under the provisions of that Act the court may strike down a clause in a contract between a monopolistic supplier and a buyer without such market power excluding the supplier's liability under the Sale of Goods Act as unreasonable.[35] Imposing liability for latent defects on the contractor in these circumstances now, therefore, should not prevent such liability being passed on to the manufacturer.

Lord Reid's second reason for implying a warranty of quality in contracts of work and materials was to bring them into line in that respect with contracts for the sale of goods. Thus, if an employer bought a machine and installed it himself, that would be a contract of sale and the employer would have a warranty under section 14(2) of the Sale of Goods Act. If the seller agreed to install the machine that would be a contract for work and materials. Lord Reid said that it would be strange if installation by the seller made any difference.[36] Any doubt about this matter has of course been laid to rest by the Supply of Goods and Services Act 1982.[37]

The decision in *Young & Marten* must be considered alongside the decision of the House of Lords in *Gloucestershire County Council* v. *Richardson*.[38] In that case a contractor contracted with employers to build an extension to a technical college. The employers laid down that certain concrete columns were to be supplied by nominated suppliers at a quoted price. The contract between those suppliers and the contractors contained a clause limiting the supplier's liability for defective goods and excluding their liability for consequential loss or damage. The columns contained latent defects which became apparent when used in the building work. The House of Lords held that in view of these circumstances any warranty by the contractor of the quality or fitness of the columns supplied by the suppliers was excluded.

It must be emphasised that the decision in *Gloucestershire County Council* v. *Richardson* is generally considered to be an exception to the rule laid down in *Young & Marten*. Confirmation for this conclusion is provided by the following *dictum* of Lord Fraser in *IBA* v. *EMI Ltd and BICC Ltd*:

> ... in a building contract for work and materials a term is normally implied that the main contractor will accept responsibility to his employer for materials provided by a nominated subcontractor.[39]

A more interesting and unusual exception to the reasoning of *Young & Marten* occurred in *University of Warwick* v. *Sir Robert McAlpine and Others*.[40] Between about 1963 and 1968 the University erected a number of buildings. They had a uniform white ceramic tile cladding. In about 1969 the tiling began to fail. The contractors, McAlpine, carried out remedial works, but in 1973 it became apparent that they would be far more extensive than anticipated. An epoxy resin injection was considered as an alternative. The sole British licensee of this process was Cementation Chemicals Ltd (CCL). The University instructed McAlpine to employ CCL as subcontractors. McAlpine was not involved in the decision to use the CCL system. In fact, they had substantial reservations about the system and obtained an indemnity from CCL. The system failed and the University sued, *inter alios*, McAlpine for breach of an implied term to supply epoxy resin that was fit for its purpose. (The University accepted that the resin injection was of merchantable quality.) Garland J held that a term that the resin be fit for its purpose could only be implied in the main contract if the University had relied on McAlpine. They had not done so and no such term could therefore be implied.

In the course of his judgement Garland J distinguished between *Young & Marten* and *Gloucestershire County Council*. He said that in *Young & Marten* fitness was never *prima facie* implied (the main contractor's representative selected the tiles) and in *Gloucestershire County Council* only quality was at issue because the columns had been chosen by the architect. Garland J further pointed to the fact that the University could have obtained an express warranty of fitness from McAlpine, which they did not, as evidence of absence of reliance by the University on McAlpine.

Garland J's decision meant that the chain of contractual liability on which so much emphasis was placed in *Young & Marten* was broken at the first stage. In the view of the editor of the *Building Law Reports* the judge's analysis is faced with the difficulty that McAlpine obtained an indemnity from CCL. In his view this indicates that the parties wished to maintain the contractual chain of liability and that the judge was unduly restrictive in his interpretation of the concept of reliance.[41] In the author's view this argument is tenuous and Garland J's conclusion on this aspect of the case is to be preferred. McAlpine's reservations about the epoxy resin system were clear and they made those reservations known to the University. The University, far from relying on that advice, specifically ignored it. To the author, it seems that obtaining an indemnity from CCL indicates not a wish to preserve the usual contractual chain of liability, but caution on McAlpine's part in the event of their being successfully sued by the University; a form of litigation insurance, if you like.

SUMMARY

1. In the traditional tripartite construction project, subcontractors are employed by the main (or principal) contractor to carry out specialist functions.
2. In such a project, carried out under the JCT form of contract, a subcontractor is employed by the main contractor. There is no contract between employer and subcontractor.
3. A subcontractor, however, may provide the employer with a direct warranty that he will use reasonable care and skill in the design and construction of the subcontract works.
4. As a general rule, a subcontractor owes no duty of care in tort to the employer for economic loss suffered by the employer as a consequence of the subcontractor's negligence.
5. There may be an exception to this general rule where a subcontractor provided a component of the building which caused damage to other parts of the building.
6. Where a subcontractor provides the employer with a direct duty of care warranty any concurrent duty of care in tort is generally limited in scope by the obligations contained in that warranty. However, if the subcontractor performs a function which is not contained in the warranty then a tortious duty of care is owed to the employer in respect of that function, unless such duty is excluded or restricted by the terms of the warranty.
7. The relationship between a subcontractor and the principal contractor is contractual.
8. The obligations of the subcontractor for the quality of the subcontracted works will be set out in the express terms of the subcontract.
9. A subcontract, like the main contract, is a contract for work and materials and a subcontractor is subject to the same implied obligation in relation to work and materials as is the main contractor under the main contract, namely:

(i) the subcontract works must be constructed with reasonable care
and skill; and

(ii) any materials supplied by the subcontractor must be of satisfactory quality and reasonably fit for any purpose specified by the main contractor.

10. The main contractor is under a duty to the employer to employ competent subcontractors, but he is not liable if any subcontractor negligently constructs the subworks.

11. If the employer relies on the skill and judgement of the main contractor for the selection of materials to be used by a subcontractor then the main contractor will be liable to the employer in the event of those materials proving to be of unsatisfactory quality.

12. There is no implied obligation on the part of a subcontractor for the quality and fitness of the materials he uses where those materials are selected by the employer or by the employer's architect.

NOTES

1. This structure is based on *Emden's Construction Law*, 8th edn, Butterworths, 1990, Binder 1, Chapter 6.
2. NSC/2. This form is published in *Emden's Construction Law*, Binder 4, Division M.
3. [1964] AC 465.
4. Their Lordships differed in their formulation of these circumstances, but they have subsequently been reformulated by the House of Lords in *Caparo* v. *Dickman* [1990] 1 All ER 568 and further refined by the Court of Appeal in *James McNaughten Paper Group Ltd* v. *Hicks Anderson & Co.* [1991] 1 All ER 134 (per Neill LJ, pp.144–45).
5. *Dutton* v. *Bognor Regis UDC* [1972] 1QB373; *Anns* v. *Merton LBC* [1978] AC 728; and *Batty* v. *Metropolitan Realisations* [1978] QB 554.
6. [1973] QB 27.
7. [1983] 1 AC 520.
8. *Supra*, n.5, *Anns* v. *Merton LBC*, pp.751–752.
9. [1990] 2 All ER 908.
10. [1985] 2 All ER 1077.
11. (1988) 4 Const. LJ 217.
12. [1988] 2 All ER 971.
13. [1988] 1 All ER 791.
14. See, for example, the judgement of Bingham LJ in *Simaan* v. *Pilkington*, *ibid.*, n.13, p.804.
15. *Supra*, n.9, p.919.
16. [1994] 3 All ER 506.
17. *Ibid*, n.16, p.521.
18. *Ibid*, n.16, p.534.
19. [1988] 2 All ER 992.
20. See, for example, the speech of Lord Bridge, *ibid.*, n.19, pp.1006–1007.
21. *Supra*, n.9, p.928.
22. *Supra*, n.9, p.942.
23. *Emden's Construction Law,* 8th edn., 1990, Issue 56, Binder 1, Division I, para. 973.

24. (1996) 76 BLR 1.
25. *Supra*, n.16, pp.532–533. Pages 523–533 of Lord Goff's speech are seminal reading for the student of concurrent liability. See Chapter 7 for a more detailed discussion of this subject.
26. *Supra*, n.24, p.24.
27. *The Times*, December 22, 1995; (1996) 77 BLR 51.
28. *Ibid*, n.27.
29. NSC/C is the JCT standard form conditions of subcontract entered into between a contractor and a nominated subcontractor. They were introduced in 1991 and succeed NSC/4, from which they are derived. They are published in *Emden's Construction Law*, Binder 4, Division M and in *Keating on Building Contracts*, 7th edn, 2001, Ch. 19.
30. See sections 2–5 and section 13.
31. See *Young & Marten* v. *McManus Childs Ltd* [1968] 2 All ER 1169; and section 4 of the Supply of Goods and Services Act 1982.
32. *Supra*, n.19, p.1008.
33. *Supra*, n.31.
34. *Supra*, n.31, p.1172.
35. See Schedule 2 to the Act and in particular guidelines (a) and (b).
36. *Supra*, n.31, p.1172.
37. See section 4.
38. [1968] 2 All ER 1181.
39. (1980) 14 BLR 1, pp.44–45.
40. (1988) 42 BLR 1.
41. See the commentary on the case, *ibid*, n.40, p.4.

7

Liability of Architects, Engineers and Quantity Surveyors

INTRODUCTION

This chapter is concerned with the liability in professional negligence of those professions who provide design and financial services in connection with building and engineering projects, especially large scale ones. The most important of those professions are architecture, engineering and quantity surveying. Essentially the services which they provide in relation to a construction project can be divided into three broad categories:

(i) the preparation of skilful and economic designs for the works:
(ii) the provision of measurements and quantities and the calculation of estimates; and
(iii) the supervision and administration of the works in the best interest of the employer.

1. Architects

An architect has been defined in the following terms by the Divisional Court in *R* v. *Architects' Registration Tribunal, ex parte Jaggar*:

> one who possesses with due regard to aesthetic as well as practical considerations, adequate skill and knowledge to enable him (i) to originate, (ii) to design and plan, (iii) to arrange for and supervise the erection of such buildings or other works calling for skill in design and planning as he might, in the course of his business, reasonably be asked to carry out in respect of which he offers his services as a specialist.[1]

The express duties of the architect employed in a building project cover a range of tasks: surveying the site, producing drawings, advising on building regulations, selecting materials, supervising the works, issuing certificates, etc.[2]

Under section 20(1) of the Architects Act 1997 it is an offence for anyone to practise or carry on business under any name, style or title containing the word 'architect' unless his name appears on the Register of Architects.[3] Under the provisions of section 20(3) a body corporate, firm or partnership is not prevented from carrying on a business under a name containing the word 'architect' if the business is under the control and management of a registered person, or is under the supervision of a registered person.

Section 1(1) of the 1997 Act provides for the continued existence of the Architects Registration Board.[4] The Board maintains the register of architects, it publishes a code of professional conduct and practice and it has the power to discipline architects for unacceptable professional conduct or serious professional incompetence.

Architects also are subject to the rules of any professional body of which they are members. The leading professional body for architects is the Royal Institute of British Architects (RIBA). The RIBA has its own code of professional conduct and if a client is dissatisfied with the professional conduct of any of its members he may apply to the RIBA for conciliation of the complaint.

2 Engineers

There is no precise definition of 'engineer'. The term is used in Construction Law to mean a person who in a contract for engineering works performs functions analogous to those of an architect under a traditional building contract.

There are no statutory controls governing engineers. Anyone may call himself an engineer but use of the term 'chartered engineer' denotes membership of one of the professional bodies. The best known of these bodies is the Institution of Civil Engineers (ICE), which publishes a standard form of civil engineering contract (the *ICE Conditions*, 6th edn, 1991) and which has a code of conduct governing its members, breach of which may result in the ICE taking disciplinary action.

3. Quantity surveyors

The function of a quantity surveyor was defined in *Taylor* v. *Hall* as follows:

> taking out in detail the measurements and quantities from plans prepared by an architect for the purpose of enabling builders to calculate the estimates for which they would execute the plans.[5]

The functions of quantity surveyors have expanded considerably since this case was decided and their present day functions may be put into three categories:

(i) during the development and procurement stage of a building project, the preparation of estimates, bills of quantity and schedules for pricing to enable the contractor to calculate the amounts required to execute the architect's plans;

(ii) during the construction of the project, the valuation of work done for the purpose of interim and final certificates issued by the architect; and

(iii) after the completion of the project, the valuation of the contractor's final account and the estimation of any loss and expense to which the contractor may be due.[6]

Anyone may practise as a quantity surveyor, but to use the term 'chartered quantity surveyor' a person must be an Associate or a Fellow of the Royal Institute of Chartered Surveyors (RICS).

The architect, engineer or quantity surveyor is not a party to the main contract between the contractor and the employer. Nor is he a party to any subcontract, except in the case of a design and build contract.[7] In the traditional form of building contract there will be a contract between the employer and the contractor and another contract between the employer and the architect, engineer or quantity surveyor. Under this traditional form of building contract the architect or engineer has a design function and will play a leading role in the administration of the building contract itself, i.e. the contract between the employer and the contractor. The quantity surveyor's role is to deal with the financial aspect of these different stages in a building project in the form of the provision of measurements and the valuation of work carried out.

The position in law of the architect, engineer or quantity surveyor will vary according to which of their functions they are performing. At the initial (design) stage of the project he will almost certainly be an independent contractor, but in the supervision of the building contract he will have a dual role: first, he will be the employer's agent acting on his behalf and secondly, he will issue certificates (or in the case of the quantity surveyor, measure and make work for such purpose) in which capacity he must act impartially as between the employer and the contractor. We can accordingly divide this chapter into four broad areas:

(1) liability to the employer;
(2) supervision of the building contract;
(3) liability to third parties; and
(4) damages.

Most of the reported case law in this area of Construction Law involves either architects or engineers. There are few reported cases on the liabilities of quantity surveyors.[8] For this reason, the discussion on liabilities in this chapter is confined to architects and engineers. However, the general principles set out in the case law may be extrapolated to the functions carried out by quantity surveyors.[9]

LIABILITY TO THE EMPLOYER

1.   *Liability under the contract*

Architects, engineers and quantity surveyors may be employed directly by the employer under the traditional form of building contract or under a design and build contract, where the employer employs a contractor to design and construct the building works and the design professionals will be employed by the contractor. The discussion which follows concerns the duties of design professionals under the traditional form of building contract.

Under this form of building contract, the primary basis of the duties of the architect engineer or quantity surveyor is the contract under which he is engaged by the employer. Those are his *express* duties. Generally, those duties are set out in one of the standard form contracts used for the engagement of architects, engineers or quantity surveyors.

Architects are usually engaged subject to the RIBA's Standard Form of Agreement for the Appointment of an Architect (SFA/99).[10] This standard form consists of the following parts:

(a) Articles of Agreement.
(b) Four Schedules, namely:
    – Schedule 1: Project Description;
    – Schedule 2: Services, which describes the services to be provided by the architect;
    – Schedule 3: Fees and Expenses; and
    – Schedule 4: Other Appoinments.
c) Conditions of Engagement, which contain *inter alia* provisions relating to:
    – the obligations and authority of the architect;
    – the obligations and authority of the client;
    – payment;
    – copyright; and
    – liabilities and insurance.

The specific terms contained in SFA/99 relate to a wide range of matters, including, in particular, limitation of liability for loss or damage and provision for such sum as is 'just and equitable' for the architect to pay where he is jointly liable with another party or other parties. The architect's responsibilities under this form are subject to an overriding general obligation:

> The Architect shall in providing the services exercise reasonable care and skill in conformity with the normal standards of the Architect's profession.[11]

This is identical to the architect's duty under the general law, which is discussed below.

The most common standard form in use for engineers is the Association of Consultant Engineers (ACE) Conditions of Engagement 1995.[12] This standard form is very similar in structure and content to SFA/99. It contains a limitation of liability clause, a 'fair contribution' clause and a skill and care obligation.

The RICS provides a standard form for the appointment of quantity surveyors, Quantity Surveyor's Appointment and Fees.[13] This form contains the usual obligation that the quantity surveyor will perform his services with reasonable care, skill and diligence, but subject to the proviso that the liability of the quantity surveyor will be limited to the sum covered by his professional indemnity insurance.[14]

It is important to bear in mind that none of the standard forms discussed above comply with the requirements of Part III of the Housing Grants, Construction and Regeneration Act 1996, which came into force on 1 May 1998. Part III puts into effect the recommendations of the Latham Report 1994.[15] The aim of this legislation is to promote fairer construction contracts and to this end a number of clauses are prohibited or restricted. The clauses in question concern adjudication of disputes and late payment. The term 'construction contract' is defined widely by the Act to include agreements:

(a)   to do architectural, design or surveying work; or
(b)   to provide advice on building, engineering, interior or exterior decoration or on the laying out of landscape in relation to construction operations.[16]

Where a construction contract does not comply with the requirements of Part III then the Scheme for Construction Contracts[17] takes effect: The Scheme is in two parts. Part I provides for the selection and appointment of an adjudicator and gives him powers to gather and consider information and to make decisions. Part II makes provision for payments under a construction contract where either the contract fails to make provision or the parties fail to agree. The provisions cover the following matters:

(a)   the method for calculating the amount of any instalment, stage or periodic payment;
(b)   the due date and the final date for payments to be made; and
(c)   prescribes the period within which a notice of intention to withold payment must be given.

2.   The implied duty of reasonable care and skill

The *implied* duty of the architect, engineer or quantity surveyor is to carry out his express duties with reasonable care and skill.[18] As a general rule there appears to be no stricter duty of guaranteeing that a particular result will be produced; an architect, engineer or quantity surveyor is contractually liable only if he has failed to exercise reasonable care and skill.[19] This is in direct contrast to the legal position of the builder. As we have seen in Chapter 1, a builder's contractual duties to his employer are strict duties in a number of respects: he guarantees the quality of the materials used and, if he is building a house, that it will be fit for habitation when completed.

The concept of reasonable care and skill in the context of professional duties means the standard required of the ordinary skilled and competent practitioner in the profession concerned. This is known as 'the *Bolam* standard', after McNair J's famous dictum in *Bolam* v. *Friern Barnet Hospital Management Committee*:

> The test is the standard of the ordinary skilled man exercising and professing to have that special skill ... A man need not possess the highest expert skill; it is well established law that it is sufficient if he exercises the ordinary skill of an ordinary competent man exercising that particular art.[20]

Thus an architect, engineer or quantity surveyor must carry out his duties as would a reasonably competent member of his profession. Essentially the standard of a reasonably competent architect, engineer or quantity surveyor would be decided on the basis of evidence (if any) of accepted standards of conduct in the profession concerned.[21]

The meaning of reasonable care and skill in the context of the particular duties carried out by design professionals must now be examined. Most of the case law involves architects, but the principles laid down apply also to engineers and quantity surveyors.

Design duties

What constitutes reasonable skill and care in the design of a building depends upon the circumstances of each case. The duty will normally be discharged by following established practice. Where there is no established practice, such as where a new construction technique is used, the duty of reasonable care and skill may be discharged by taking the best advice available and by warning the employer of any risks involved. In the mid-nineteenth century case of *Turner* v. *Garland and Christopher*[22] the employer instructed his architect to use a new patent concrete roofing which proved to be a failure. It was held that where an untried process was used, failure might still be consistent with reasonable skill. Erle J said:

> If you employ [an architect] about a novel thing, about which he had little experience, if it has not had the test of experience, failure may be consistent with skill. The history of all great improvements show failure of those who embark on them.

The 20th century cases take a much stricter view of the duties of an architect in relation to a novel or innovative design. The modern approach to this question is more safety conscious than the view of Erle J and was expressed in the following terms by Lord Edmund-Davies in *Independent Broadcasting Authority* v. *EMI Electronics Ltd and BICC Construction Ltd*:

> Justice requires that we seek to put ourselves in the position of BICC when first confronted by their daunting task, lacking all empirical knowledge and adequate expert advice in dealing with the many problems awaiting solution. But those very handicaps created a clear duty to identify and to think through such problems ... so that the dimensions of the 'venture into the unknown' could be adequately assessed and the ultimate decision as to its practicability arrived at.[23]

Lord Edmund-Davies went on to say that the risk of injury to those engaged in a project may be so great that the only proper course is to abandon the project altogether.

In *Victoria University of Manchester* v. *Hugh Wilson*,[24] the architects adopted a novel design for a university building which involved cladding a building of reinforced concrete (which was not waterproof) partly in red Accrington bricks and partly in ceramic tiles. In due course many of the tiles fell off. Judge Newey QC held that it was not wrong in itself to use this relatively untried method of cladding but it did call for special caution. He said:

> [A]rchitects who are venturing into the untried or little tried should be wise to warn their clients specifically of what they are doing and to obtain their express approval.[25]

A professional person is not liable for aspects of design that are outside his usual sphere of expertise. In *Holland Hannen & Cubitts (Northern) Ltd* v. *Welsh Health Technical Services Organisation* (WHTSO)[26] the issue arose of the extent to which a consulting engineer retained by nominated subcontractors responsible for the design and construction of part of a hospital were responsible for the 'serviceability' of the work designed by him. WHTSO employed Cubitts to construct a new hospital and CED were nominated as subcontractors to design the floor. They instructed a firm of structural engineers, AMP, to assist them. The floors suffered from defects and 'visually looked wrong'.[27] The employer's architects amended the specification but the floors failed to comply with that amended specification. The majority of the Court of Appeal held, *inter alia*, that AMP were not negligent as it was a matter for the architects, not them as structural engineers, to consider matters of visual appearance or aesthetic effect. Dillon LJ said:

> As I see it, however, matters of visual appearance or aesthetic effect are matters for the architect and are not within the power of the structural engineer. It is for the structural engineer to work out what the deflection of a floor will be; it is for the architect to decide whether a floor with those deflections will be visually or aesthetically satisfactory when the finishes chosen by the architect have been applied.[28]

It is instructive to note that on this point Goff LJ (as he then was) entered a powerful dissent. He said:

> I accept the proposition that finishes are a matter for the architct, and that in this sense the visual appearance of the structure is a matter for the architect and not for the structural engineer. But it does not follow that structural engineers are not concerned at all with visual appearance. A structural engineer is obviously concerned with the strength and stability of the structure; but he is also concerned with the configuration of the structure which the relevant design may produce, with regard not only to its function but also to its appearance.[29]

Goff LJ went on to say that if the engineer considers that, on the data available to him, there is a risk that the profile of the floor may be unacceptable he is under a duty to warn his clients.

An important point in relation to design duties is the extent to which a design professional may satisfy the standard of reasonable care and skill by conforming to a code of practice or to regulations. In *Holland Hannen and Cubitts (Northern) Ltd* v. *Welsh Health Technical Services Organisation*, the Court of Appeal laid down the principle that a professional is not entitled to follow slavishly the provisions of a code of practice without taking into account their relevance to the project in hand. Goff LJ said:

> It is plain from the evidence that the code of practice is no more than a guide for use by professional men, who have to exercise their own expertise; this must moreover be especially true in cases such as the present, where the design was a novel one ... Practice alone can, I consider, provide of itself no reliable guide where, as here, a novel design concept is being used.[30]

A further question which arises in this context is whether if an architect or engineer does not comply with a relevant code or regulation that is evidence of a failure to meet the required standard of reasonable care and skill. This question was considered by Beattie J in the New Zealand case of *Bevan Investments Ltd* v. *Blackhall and Struthers* (No. 2). He said:

> Bearing in mind the function of codes, a design which departs substantially from them is *prima facie* a faulty design, unless it can be demonstrated that it conforms to accepted engineering practice by rational analysis.[31]

In other words, if an architect or engineer departs from the provisions of a relevant code or regulation the onus will be upon him to establish that the design is consistent with the broad purposes of the code or regulation, in particular safety.

The Construction (Design and Management) Regulations 1994[32]

The Construction (Design and Management) Regulations 1994 impose requirements and prohibitions with respect to design and management aspects of 'construction work'. They give effect to the EC Directive on the implementation of minimum safety and health requirements at temporary or mobile construction sites.[33] By Regulation 3(1) the Regulations apply only to construction work. This term is defined widely in Regulation 2(1) and means the carrying out of any building, civil engineering or engineering construction work.

Under the provisions of Regulation 13 a number of requirements are imposed on designers. Regulation 13(1) prohibits a designer from preparing a design unless he has taken reasonable steps to ensure that the client for the project is aware of the duties to which the client is subject by virtue of the Regulations and of the requirements of any practical guidance issued by the Health and Safety Commission.

Regulation 13(2) imposes three obligations on a designer:

(a) an obligation to ensure that any design he prepares and which he is aware will be used for the purposes of construction work will have regard to the health and safety of persons carrying out the construction work;

(b) an obligation to ensure that the design includes adequate information about any aspect of the project or structure or materials which might affect the health and safety of persons carrying out construction work; and

(c) an obligation to co-operate with the planning supervisor and any other designer involved in the same project.

A designer is defined in Regulation 2(1) as any person who carries on a trade, business or other undertaking in connection with which he

(a) prepares a design; or

(b) arranges for any person under his control (including, where he is an employer, any employee of his) to prepare a design, relating to a structure or part of a structure. A 'structure' is defined widely by Regulation 2(1) to include not only buildings but railways, tunnels, bridges, reservoirs, cables, pipes, drainage works and sea defences.

In *R* v. *Paul Wurth SA*,[34] the decision of the Court of Appeal seemed to narrow the scope of the duties of designers under Regulation 13(2)(a). In that case, Paul Wurth was employed to install a conveyor in a steelworks. It employed another company to convert its design into manufacturing and construction drawings. That company in turn subcontracted the manufacture to a third company. That third company prepared a drawing for the latching part of the machinery. This drawing had no locking or securing pin. Paul Wurth was given the drawing to approve but did not comment on the omission, which caused a fatal accident. The Court of Appeal held that Regulation 13(2)(a) applied only to a designer that prepared the design and Paul Wurth had not prepared the design of the latching device. The Court of Appeal also said that Regulation 13(2)(a) does not apply to a designer who comes within the second part of the definition of designer in Regulation 2(1). Thus a designer would not be in breach of Regulation 13(2)(a) if an employee of his prepared the design.

In order to counteract the effect of the Court of Appeal's judgement in *Paul Wurth* the Health and Safety Commission has proposed amending the definition of designer in the 1994 Regulations so that this term will include the employees of the firm carrying out the design and other persons under the firm's control, such as specialist consultants.

The specialist practitioner

Where a design professional is employed because of his specialist skills his duty is to exercise reasonable care and skill in the light of that specialist knowledge. The relevant standard is that of the ordinary and skilled practitioner in that speciality.[35]

Conflict of opinion

A design professional will not necessarily be negligent if there is a conflict of opinion within his profession as to the feasibility of a particular design which he has chosen to employ. The legal position in this situation was set out in the judgement of Stephen Brown LJ in *Nye Saunders and Partners* v. *Alan E. Bristow* in the following terms in relation to the duty of care owed by an architect:

> Where there is a conflict as to whether he has discharged that duty, the courts approach the matter upon the basis of considering whether there was evidence that at the time a responsible body of architects would have taken the view that the way in which the subject of enquiry had carried out his duties was an appropriate way of carrying out the duty, and would not hold him guilty of negligence merely because there was a body of competent professional opinion which held that he was at fault.[36]

An obligation of fitness for purpose

The design liability of the architect or engineer may be stricter than reasonable care and skill in two situations. First, a strict duty may be imposed where the architect or engineer delegates part of the design work; as a general rule he will remain liable for the design unless the employer agrees to the delegation. Secondly, a stricter obligation than reasonable care and skill may be implied into the contract between the architect or engineer and the employer from the surrounding circumstances.[37]

The first exception is illustrated by *Moresk Cleaners* v. *Hicks*.[38] An architect was engaged to prepare plans and specifications for the extension of the plaintiff's laundry. He delegated the design of the structure to the building contractor. Within two years of completion cracks appeared in the structure and the roof purlins sagged. Expert investigation showed that these defects were caused by faults in the design. The plaintiff sued the architect. In his defence the architect argued: (1) that it was an implied term of his contract of engagement that he should be entitled to delegate specified design tasks to qualified specialist subcontractors; and (2) that he had implied authority to employ the contractor to design the structure. These defences were rejected by the trial judge, Sir Walter Carter, QC, who said:

> if [the architect] takes upon himself the design of a building, he cannot in my view escape his liability for that design by delegating his duty to the contractor who is going to do the building.[39]

The approach taken to delegation of design duties in *Moresk* was followed by the Court of Appeal in *Nye Saunders and Partners* v. *Alan E. Bristow*. An architect who, in reliance upon an estimate supplied by a quantity surveyor, advised his client of the cost of a project without making it clear that the estimate was based on current costs and did not take account of inflation, was held to be liable to the client for breach of his duty of care.

The architect will not be liable, however, if he reasonably relies on the manufacturer's expertise. In *London Borough of Merton* v. *Lowe*[40] the plaintiffs engaged the defendants, a firm of architects, to design and supervise the erection of a new indoor swimming pool. The design included the use of a proprietary plaster manufactured by Pyrok Ltd for the ceiling. After completion cracks appeared in the ceiling and the architects asked Pyrok Ltd to remedy them. This they did. The architects did nothing further and issued a final certificate. Later more cracks appeared in the ceiling which expert examination revealed was unsafe. The trial judge, Judge Stabb, QC, held that the architects were not liable to the plaintiffs for accepting and approving Pyrok's specification for the ceiling. They were, however, held liable for failing to check the design and for failing to see that the defective design was replaced by an effective one. The judge further held that they were negligent in issuing the final certificate. In the course of his judgement Judge Stabb adopted the words of Sachs LJ in *Brickfield Properties* v. *Newton*:

> The architect is under a continuing duty to check that his design will work in practice and to correct any errors which may emerge.[41]

The judgement of Judge Stabb was upheld by the Court of Appeal.

It is the second exception which has attracted the most attention. At the outset it needs to be stressed that the nature of the general duty owed by professionals involved in the design of construction projects has not always been entirely free from doubt. Indeed, for a time, it was thought that architects and engineers were subject to a general regime of strict liability. The authority most often quoted for this view is *Greaves & Co (Contractors) Ltd v. Baynham Meikle.*[42] In that case contractors agreed to design and construct a warehouse and office for a company who intended to use the warehouse as a store for oil drums. Those oil drums were to be kept on the first floor and moved into position by fork-lift trucks. The contractors engaged structural engineers to design the structure of the warehouse and the contractors told them the purpose for which it was required. The engineers in their design did not take into account the effect of the vibrations from the fork-lift trucks. The result was that the floor cracked under the weight of the oil drums and of the trucks. It was held that the defendants were in breach of an implied warranty that the floor would be fit for the purpose for which they knew it was required. Lord Denning said:

> the owners made known to the contractors the purpose for which the building was required, so as to show that they relied on the contractor's skill and judgement. It was therefore the duty of the contractors to see that the finished work was reasonably fit for the purpose for which the building was required. It was not merely an obligation to use reasonable care.[43]

However, the Court of Appeal was careful to emphasise that there was no such general implied term in contracts for the supply of services and that the decision depended upon the particular facts of the case. Thus Lord Denning stated:

> The law does not usually imply a warranty that [a professional person] will achieve the desired result, but only a term that he will use reasonable care and skill. The surgeon does not warrant that he will cure the patient. Nor does a solicitor warrant that he will win the case. But, when a dentist agrees to make a set of false teeth for a patient, there is an implied warranty that they will fit his gums: see *Samuels* v. *Davis* [1943] 2 All ER 3.[44]

Geoffrey Lane LJ said:

> No great issue of principle arises in this case ... The suggestion that by reason of this finding every professional man or every consultant engineer by implication of law would be guaranteeing a satisfactory result is unfounded.[45]

Even without these caveats, *Greaves* would not be an entirely satisfactory case on which to base a general principle of professional liability in the construction industry because the case involved a package deal, or design and build contract, instead of the usual JCT form of contract where the architect or engineer is employed directly by the building owner and has no contractual relationship with the contractor. Further the leading judgement in the case, that of Lord Denning, was not entirely unequivocal on the question of professional liability in the construction industry. After his remarks on the standard of duty required of the professional person in general he went on to say of construction industry professionals:

> What then is the position when an architect or an engineer is employed to design a house or a bridge? Is he under an implied warranty that, if the work is carried out to his design, it will be reasonably fit for the purpose? Or is he only under a duty to use reasonable skill and care? This question may require to be answered some day as a matter of law. But, in the present case I do not think we need answer it.[46]

The door to the imposition of a general duty of strict liability on construction professionals was not, it seems, shut tight and in *Independent Broadcasting Authority* v. *EMI Ltd and BICC Ltd*, certain *dicta* of Roskill, LJ in the Court of Appeal and Lords Fraser and Scarman in the House of Lords seemed to push it open a little further. That case concerned a contract to erect a 1250 ft high TV mast for the IBA. EMI were the main contractors and BICC the subcontractors who were responsible for the design of the mast. In bad, though not exceptional, weather conditions the mast collapsed, after just over three years in service. The Court of Appeal held that there was an implied term in the contract for the construction of the mast that it should be fit for its intended purpose and there was nothing in the contractual documents to exclude that implied term. The contractors had promised to erect a mast, and it was implicit in that promise that the mast would achieve the desired object, insofar as it was within the power of the contractors to determine that. Roskill LJ in referring to a builder employed to build a house said:

> We see no good reason ... for not importing an obligation as to reasonable fitness for the purpose into these contracts or for importing a different obligation as to design from the obligation which plainly exists in relation to materials.[47]

The House of Lords upheld the Court of Appeal's decision, though on different grounds. The basis of their decision was that BICC had been negligent in the design of the mast and EMI were under a contractual responsibility to IBA for the design of the mast which included responsibility for a negligent design.

In effect, the House of Lords' decision amounted to an imposition of strict liability on the main contractor, though by a different route from the decision of the Court of Appeal. The main significance of their Lordships' decision for design professionals, however, was certain dicta of Lords Fraser and Scarman which appear to lend support to the Court of Appeal's importation of an implied term as to fitness for purpose in building contract. Lord Fraser said:

The principle that was applied in *Young* v. *Marten Ltd* in respect of materials, ought in my opinion to be applied here in respect of the complete structure, including its design. Although EMI had no specialist knowledge of mast design, and although IBA knew that and did not rely on their skill to any extent for the design, I see nothing unreasonable in holding that EMI are responsible to IBA for the design seeing that they can in turn recover from BICC who did the actual designing.[48]

Lord Scarman said:

In the absence of any term (express or implied) negativing the obligation, one who contracts to design an article for a purpose made known to him undertakes that the design is reasonably fit for the purpose.[49]

Further support for the view that the law was moving towards an obligation of fitness for purpose on the part of design professionals seemed to be provided by the decision of Judge Davies QC in *Viking Grain Storage Ltd* v. *T.H. White Installations Ltd*[50] The defendants entered into a design and build contract to construct a grain storage and drying installation on the plaintiffs' land. The plaintiffs alleged that: (i) some of the materials used by the defendant were defective; (ii) aspects of the construction work were inadequately performed; and (iii) the ground of the site was not adequately prepared. One of the preliminary issues in the case was whether the defendants' duty was one of reasonable care and skill or whether they were under a duty to produce a building which would be suitable for its contemplated purpose. The judge held that the defendants were liable if the installation fell below the standard of reasonable suitability for purpose and the exercise of reasonable care and skill would not amount to a defence.

The question of whether or not an architect or engineer is under an implied warranty that his design will be reasonably fit for the purpose was considered again by the Court of Appeal in *George Hawkins* v. *Chrysler (UK) Ltd and Burne Associates.*[51] The defendants (Chrysler) wished to have new showers installed in their foundry and they employed Burne, a firm of engineers, to prepare the design and specifications and to supervise the installation. After the work was completed the plaintiff, Hawkins, slipped on a puddle of water in the shower room after using the shower and sued Chrysler and Burne for his resulting injuries. He argued that (a) it was a term of the contract that Burne would use reasonable care and skill in selecting the material to be used for the floor and (b) there was an implied warranty that the material used for the floor would be fit for use in a wet shower room. At first instance, the judge found that Burne was not negligent but was in breach of an implied warranty that they would provide as safe a floor as was practicable.

The Court of Appeal upheld the judge's finding on negligence but they were unanimous that there was nothing in the case to give rise to the implication of a warranty other than to take reasonable care and skill in preparing the design. Thus Fox LJ stated unequivocally:

> a professional man, in the exercise of his profession, is normally obliged only to use reasonable care and skill. That is reflected in the standard conditions of employment of architects in the RIBA Conditions, and in the standard conditions of engagement for design of engineering projects which is the ACE document – both of which stipulate for the use of reasonable care and skill.[52]

The decision in *George Hawkins* v. *Chrysler* must remove much of the doubt that the ordinary duty of an architect or engineer is one of reasonable care and skill and that any higher duty will be the exception from this general rule. If confirmation for this conclusion is needed then it is provided by a medical case, that of *Thake* v. *Maurice*.[53] The plaintiffs, who were husband and wife, contracted with the defendant surgeon for a vasectomy to be performed. The surgeon emphasised to the plaintiff the irreversible nature of the operation but he failed to point out the risk of it not proving successful. In the event, the operation was not successful, as was evidenced when Mrs Thake became pregnant for the sixth time. The plaintiffs' action for breach of contract succeeded at first instance, Pain J stating that the surgeon had contracted to produce a particular result, namely rendering Mr Thake permanently sterile. However, his judgement on this point was reversed by a majority of the Court of Appeal who said that the surgeon's statements did not amount to a guarantee.

These two latest decisions of the Court of Appeal on this subject must strengthen the view that there is *no* general duty of fitness for purpose imposed upon a supplier of professional services. Such a duty will, however, exist if the supplier expressly or implicitly agrees that the provision of his services will achieve a particular result – on reflection, a not dissimilar position from that obtaining in contracts for the sale of goods by virtue of section14(3) of the Sale of Goods Act 1979.

A continuing duty?

We have seen that there is a *dictum* of the Court of Appeal to the effect that a design professional has a duty to see that his design works in practice.[54] This was referred to as a continuing duty, though in fact it is simply an aspect of the normal duty to use reasonable care and skill to produce an effective design. If, some years later, defects in the design are revealed this is merely evidence that on completion of the design contract the design was defective.[55]

In *Eckersley* v. *Binnie*,[56] the question of whether a professional person may continue to owe a duty to his client to advise him of professional developments after the terms of his engagement have been completed arose.

Between 1972 and 1979 a link was designed and built between the River Lune and the River Wyre at Abbeystead. The link was designed by the first defendants, Binnie & Partners (Binnie) between 1972 and 1978, constructed by the second defendants (Nuttalls), tunnelling contractors, and after 1979 operated by the third defendants, the *North West Water Authority*. In May 1984 a party of 38 people visited the pumping works at Abbeystead. While they were at the pumping works there was an explosion in the valve house caused by an accumulation of methane in a void in the ground which was pumped into the valve house and probably ignited there by a match or cigarette lighter. All those in the valve house were injured and sixteen died. The trial judge held all three defendants to be negligent and apportioned the losses between them. All three appealed. The Court of Appeal held:

(1) The first defendant's appeal failed because there was a risk of methane being present which should have been taken account of in the design. The presence of the methane would have been detected by adequate testing and the later activities of the third defendants did not break the chain of causation.

(2) Although the tunnelling contractors were in breach of their contractual duty to test for methane, that did not give rise to breach of any duty of care to the plaintiffs because the scope of that duty was restricted to ensuring that the tunnel was safe for those who used it in the construction process.

(3) There was no negligence on the part of the water authority because at the date of the accident they had no reason to suspect that the first defendants had negligently failed to supervise the construction of the link.

At first sight, this decision suggests that the design engineers had a duty to monitor developments in the tunnel after completion of the design stage of the project. Bingham LJ, while not ruling out entirely the existence of such a duty, struck a very cautious note about it, pointing out how novel and burdensome such an obligation would be. He said:

> What is plain is that if any such duty at all is to be imposed, the nature, scope and limits of such a duty require to be very carefully and cautiously defined. The development of the law on this point, if it ever occurs, will be gradual and analogical. But this is not a suitable case in which to launch or embark on the process of development, because no facts have been found to support a conclusion that ordinarily competent engineers in the position of the first defendants would, by May 1984, have been alerted to any risk of which they were reasonably unaware at the time of handover. There was, in my view, no evidence to support such a conclusion. That being so, I prefer to express no opinion on this potentially important legal question.[57]

Examination of site

Architects and engineers owe a duty of care to the employer to see that the site is suitable for the construction works. In *Moneypenny* v. *Hartland*,[58] an engineer was held negligent in failing to examine the nature of the soil in which to place the foundations of a bridge. In *Eames London Estates Ltd.* v. *North Hertfordshire District Council*,[59] an industrial building was constructed on made-up ground. The architect, who was entrusted with the design, including the foundations, was held to be negligent in not ascertaining whether the ground was suitable for the loadings.

This duty is a delegable one. In *Investors in Industry Commercial Properties* v. *South Bedfordshire District Council*,[60] Judge Sir William Stabb QC held that architects engaged to design four warehouses which were to be constructed on an infill site were entitled to rely upon their consulting engineers' judgement as to the suitability of the foundations.

Supervision

The architect or engineer has a duty to see, so far as is reasonably practicable, that the works are carried out in accordance with the contract. This does not require him to be on site continuously but his supervision must be such as to allow him to certify honestly that the work has been done as the contract requires. The precise level of supervision required will depend on the particular job and the contract under which the architect or engineer is employed. It is important to note in this respect that the RIBA's conditions of engagement refer to a duty to *inspect*, rather than a duty to supervise.[61]

There is very little case law directly relating to the duty of supervision, but the following *dictum* of Judge Bowsher QC in *Corfield* v. *Grant* may be considered instructive:

> What is adequate by way of supervision and other work is not in the end to be tested by the number of hours worked on site or elsewhere, but by asking whether it was enough. At some stages of some jobs exclusive attention may be required to the job in question (either in the office or on site): at other stages of the same job, or during most of the duration of other jobs, it will be quite sufficient to give attention to the job only from time to time. The proof of the pudding is in the eating. Was the attention given enough for the job?[62]

But, whatever level of supervision or inspection is appropriate it is essential to remember that '[a]n architect's duty is to exercise reasonable skill and care in seeking to achieve a particular result not to guarantee that a particular result will be achieved'.[63]

Liability for materials

The architect or engineer owes a duty of care to ensure that the materials which are to be used by the contractor are suitable for the purpose. No stricter duty is generally implied, i.e. the architect or engineer does not normally guarantee that the materials to be used are fit for the purpose. The key question for the architect is: what does he have to do in order to fulfil this duty? Such authority as there is on this point suggests that it is not sufficient for the architect to rely solely on the recommendations, if any, of the supplier or the manufacturer of the product. The architect appears to be obliged in law to conduct his own investigations into the suitability of the building materials that he recommends. In *Holland Hannen & Cubitts Ltd* v. *Welsh Health Technical Services Organisation*, the architects were held to be under a duty to ask probing questions of a subcontractor about the design of window assemblies used in the construction of a hospital. In *George Hawkins v. Chrysler (UK) Ltd and Burne Associates*, an engineer selected shower room tiles after careful investigation of RIBA product data sheets and trade brochures and after consulting a specialist flooring firm. The tiles turned out to be slippery and an employee of the building owner sustained injuries in the shower room. The engineer was held on these facts not to have been negligent.

If the materials are selected by the employer without reference to the architect or engineer then the only duty imposed upon the architect or engineer is a duty to warn of any defects in the materials known to him.

There is one exception to the rule of reasonable care and skill in these circumstances: where the architect or engineer supplies materials as well as services as part of his contract with the employer he will be strictly liable for the quality and fitness of those materials.[64]

Recommending a builder

If the architect selects a builder then he must exercise reasonable care in that selection. In *Pratt* v. *George J. Hill Associates*,[65] the plaintiff retained a firm of architects for the construction of a bungalow. They obtained tenders from builders including two whom they described as 'very reliable'. The plaintiff accordingly entered into a contract with one of those builders, Swanmore Builders Ltd. Swanmore proved to be very unreliable and failed to complete the work. They subsequently became insolvent. The plaintiff commenced proceedings against the architects claiming damages for negligence in recommending Swanmore. The Court of Appeal upheld her claim, stating that the architect was in breach of his duty to recommend a suitable reliable builder.

Compliance with the law

Architects and engineers have a duty to ensure that the works comply with the relevant statutory obligations. In particular, the architect is under a duty to ensure that the building complies with the Building Regulations.

3.   *Concurrent liability in tort and contract*[66]

The English law of obligations is sharply segregated into a law of contract and a law of tort. Concurrent liability means that a professional person can be subject to claims by a client under these two branches of the law arising from the same breach of duty. Thus, in the event of the professional person's negligent conduct of the contract the client will have a choice of remedy. The importance of this concept for professional negligence is two-fold: first, different limitation periods exist in contract and tort and secondly, the rules relating to remoteness of damages in tort differ from those in contract.

The essential principles governing limitation periods are as follows. Under the provisions of sections 5 and 8 of the Limitation Act 1980, an action for breach of contract cannot be brought after the expiration of six years from the date of the breach of contract or twelve years in the case of a contract made under seal. In the tort of negligence, where the damage is to the plaintiff's property or is economic loss the common law limitation period is six years from the date when the cause of action accrued; in the case of a professional person providing advice, this will be when the plaintiff relied to his detriment on that advice. The provisions of section 1 of the Latent Damage Act 1986 extend this tortious period to three years from the date when the damage was discovered or should have been discovered, subject to an overriding time limit (or 'long-stop') of fifteen years from the date on which the negligence occurred. The overall effect of a concurrent duty in tort is therefore to extend the period during which a professional person may be liable to his client. The practical importance of this extension was emphasised by Lord Goff in *Henderson* v. *Merrett Syndicates Ltd* in the following terms:

> If concurrent liability in tort is not recognised, a claimant may find his claim barred at a time when he is unaware of its existence. This must moreover be a real possibility in the case of claims against professional men, such as solicitors or architects, since the consequences of their negligence may well not come to light until long after the lapse of six years from the date when the relevant breach of contract occurred. Moreover the benefits of the Latent Damage Act 1986, under which the time of the accrual of the cause of action may be postponed until after the plaintiff has the relevant knowledge, are limited to actions in tortious negligence. This leads to the startling possibility that a client who has had the benefit of gratuitous advice from his solicitor may in this respect be better off than a client who has paid a fee.[67]

In relation to remoteness of damages, the ambit of liability is likely to be much wider in tort than in contact. In contract, the defendant is liable for such loss if the probability of its occurrence should have been within the reasonable contemplation of both parties at the time when the contract was made, having regard to their knowledge at that time.[68] In tort, however, a defendant is liable for any damage which is of such a kind as should have been foreseen by a reasonable man, however unlikely its occurrence might have been.[69]

Concurrent liability in tort has had an uncertain history in the common law and it did not become firmly established until the decision of the House of Lords in *Henderson*. In *Donoghue* v. *Stevenson*, the following *obiter dictum* of Lord Macmillan's supported such a principle:

> The fact that there is a contractual relationship between the parties which may give rise to an action for breach of contract, does not exclude the co-existence of a right of action founded on negligence as between the same parties, independently of the contract, though arising out of the relationship in fact brought about by the contract. Of this the best illustration is the right of the injured railway passenger to sue the railway company either for breach of the contract of safe carriage or for negligence in carrying him.[70]

However, Lord Macmillan's approach was not followed by the English courts in the years following the decision in *Donoghue* v. *Stevenson*; rather they insisted that a claimant should pursue his remedy in contract alone. Thus, in *Groom* v. *Crocker*,[71] a claim against a firm of solicitors for damages for injured feelings and reputation, the Court of Appeal held that the claim had to be in contract, not in tort. Scott LJ said:

> A solicitor, as a professional man, is employed by a client just as much as is a doctor, or an architect, or a stockbroker, and the mutual rights and duties of the two are regulated entirely by the contract of employment.[72]

That view of the duties of a professional practitioner was affected radically by the decision of the House of Lords in *Hedley Byrne & Co. Ltd* v. *Heller & Partners*.[73] Until that decision it was thought to be the law that a professional person could only be liable *in tort* for losses incurred as a result of relying on his advice if that advice was given fraudulently. In *Hedley Byrne*, the House of Lords laid down that, in certain circumstances, there could be liability for losses caused by relying on a negligently prepared statement.

Hedley Byrne was concerned with liability of bankers for a negligently prepared financial reference which was relied on by a third party; it was concerned with concurrent liability. However, the relationship of the *Hedley Byrne* principle with the rule in *Groom* v. *Crocker* was considered by the Court of Appeal in *Esso Petroleum* v. *Mardon*.[74] The defendant entered into pre-contractual negotiations with the plaintiffs with a view to becoming tenant of a garage. During the negotiations the plaintiffs made estimates of annual throughput which were prepared negligently. In reliance on the estimates, the defendant entered into a contract with the plaintiff and suffered loss for which he conterclaimed when sued by them for the price of petrol supplied. The Court of Appeal found the plaintiff liable both in contract and in tort under the principle in *Hedley Byrne*. Lord Denning expressly disapproved *Groom* v. *Crocker* and said:

> ... in the case of a professional man, the duty to use reasonable care arises not only in contract, but is also imposed by the law apart from contract, and is therefore actionable in tort. It is comparable to the duty of reasonable care, which is owed by a master to his servant, or vice versa.[75]

That decision was followed in *Midland Bank Trust Co. Ltd* v. *Hett Stubbs & Kemp*.[76] After a comprehensive review of the authorities (both before and after *Groom* v. *Crocker*), Oliver ɟ held that there was no rule of law which precluded a claim in tort for breach of a duty to use reasonable care and skill if there was a parallel contractual duty of care. He preferred the decision in *Esso* to that in *Groom*.

The effect of these decisions was clearly to establish that a professional person would face concurrent liability i.e. liability in tort and in contract. However, doubt was cast upon the existence of concurrent liability by the following *dictum* of Lord Scarman in *Tai Hing Cotton Mill Ltd* v. *Liu Chong Hing Bank Ltd*:

> Their Lordships do not believe that there is anything to the advantage of the law's development in searching for a liability in tort where the parties are in a contractual relationship. This is particularly so in a commercial relationship ... [T]heir Lordships believe it to be correct in principle and necessary for the avoidance of confusion in the law to adhere to the contractual analysis: on principle because it is a relationship in which the parties have, subject to a few exceptions, the right to determine their obligations to each other, and for the avoidance of confusion because different consequences do follow according to whether liability arises from contract or tort, e.g. in the limitation of action.[77]

This case was not concerned with concurrent liability; it was concerned with the question of whether the customer owed the bank a duty of care as part of the banker/customer relationship. The Privy Council decided that he did not, and Lord Scarman said that it was not necessary to investigage the relationship of banker and customer to see whether it is possible to identify tort as well as contract as a source of the obligations owed by one party to the other. He then went on to say:

> Their Lordships do not, however, accept that the parties' mutual obligations in tort can be any greater than those to be found expressly or by necessary implication in their contract.[78]

This *dictum* cast a great deal of uncertainty over this area of law. Taken at its face value, it rules out any liability in tort where the parties are in a contractual relationship. Indeed, the Court of Appeal in *Lee* v. *Thompson*[79] appeared to take that view.

An alternative view of Lord Scarman's *dictum* is that it does not rule out liability in tort where the parties are in a contractual relationship. Rather it means that in the professional/client relationship any duty in tort owed by the professional cannot be any greater in scope than that owed in contract. That interpretation means, of course, that it is possible for a professional person to exclude a tortious duty in his contract with the contract. This was the approach taken to concurrent liability by the Court of Appeal in *Greater Nottingham Co-operative Society* v. *Cementation*.[80] In this case the plaintiffs were building owners and the defendants were subcontractors for piling. The subcontractors entered into a collateral warranty agreement requiring them to exercise reasonable care and skill in the design of the works and the selection of materials. This contract was silent as to the manner in which the piling works were to be executed. As a result of the negligent operation of the piling equipment by one of subcontractors' employees, damage was caused to an adjoining building and work was suspended while a revised piling scheme was worked out. The plaintiffs claimed, *on the basis of tort,* damages for:

(i)   the additional cost to them paid under the main contract as a result of executing the revised piling scheme (£68,606);
(ii) the additional sums which they paid to the main contractor as a result of the delay in putting in piles (£79,235); and
(iii) their consequential loss resulting from delayed completion of the building (£282,697).

This was a claim for economic loss. The Court of Appeal held that if there was a contract between the parties it was to be assumed that they had defined in that contract on what basis, if any, one party was to be liable to the other for economic loss. On the facts, the parties had defined their relationship in the collateral contract. That contract did not provide for the defendants to be liable for the manner in which they executed the piling work or for them to be directly responsible to the plaintiffs for economic loss.

The case of *Greater Nottingham Co-operative Society* did not resolve the question of the status of concurrent liability in the common law. That was left to the House of Lords in *Henderson* v. *Merrett*.[81] *Henderson* was not a building case but involved claims by Lloyd's names against their agents for economic losses resulting from the negligent writing of insurance business which the names had guaranteed. The names had contracts with their agents but the House of Lords held that, notwithstanding these contracts, the agents owed concurrent duties of care in tort to their names. The decision of the

House of Lords was delivered by Lord Goff. Lord Goff took as the basis for analysing concurrent liability the decision of the House of Lords in *Hedley Byrne*. He said that the principle laid down in that case was based on the concept of one party having assumed or undertaken a responsibility towards the other. The key passage in his speech referring to this point states:

> if a person assumes responsibility to another in respect of certain services, there is no reason why he should not be liable in damages for that other in respect of eonomic loss which flows from the negligent performance of those services. It follows that once the case is identified as falling within the *Hedley Byrne* principle, there should be no need to embark upon any further enquiry whether it is 'fair, just and reasonable' to impose liability for economic loss. [82]

Lord Goff went on to discuss the Privy Council decision in *Tai Hing Cotton Mill* v. *Liu Chong Hing Bank*. He said that Lord Scarman's *dicta* on concurrent liability should not be taken as suggesting that there may be no remedy on tort where the parties had a contract; rather Lord Scarman's remarks were concerned with the issue of whether a tortious duty of care would be more extensive than the duty under the relevant contract. Lord Goff later stated the principle governing concurrent liability in the following terms:

> an assumption of responsibility coupled with the concomitant reliance may give rise to a tortious duty of care irrespective of whether there is a contractual relationship between the parties, and in consequence, unless the contract precludes him from doing so, the plaintiff, who has available to him concurrent remedies in contract and tort, may choose that remedy which appears to him to be the most advantageous.[83]

Lord Goff's speech is of significance in two respects. In the first place, it dispels any doubt that a professional person owes a duty of care both in contract and in tort to his client. Secondly, it extends the *Hedley Byrne* principle to include not only statements but also services. It is in this second respect that Lord Goff's speech has particular implications for construction law. The law on economic loss and negligence has been bedevilled by the dichotomy between acts and statements. In the case of many of the professional activities of architects, engineers and surveyors it was never clear into which of these categories these activities fell. Now that Lord Goff has placed professional services firmly within the scope of the *Hedley Byrne* principle it is clear that the professional activities of architects, engineers and surveyors are caught by that principle, whether they are statements, such as advice, or other activities, such as plans, designs or surveys.

The principle of concurrent liability was recognised in two further decisions of the House of Lords reported in 1995. Both of these decisions involved an extension of the *Hedley Byrne* principle. In *White* v. *Jones*,[84] the

House of Lords held that the assumption of responsibility by a solicitor to his client in the drawing up of the client's will extended to an intended beneficiary under the will, even though the beneficiary could not be said to have relied on the solicitor's advice. Lord Mustill said that the decision in *Henderson* resolved a long standing controversy about the co-existence of liability in contract and in tort. He went on:

> Since the House recognised the possibility of concurrent liabilities even as between immediate parties, it would be impossible now to contend that the mere presence of a contract or contracts linking participants in the transaction is an absolute bar to liability in negligence for pure financial loss.[85]

In *Spring* v. *Guardian Assurance plc*,[86] the House of Lords held that an employer who provided a reference for a former employee owed that employee a duty to take reasonable care in its preparation. In his speech, Lord Goff said that this duty arose either from an implied term of the contract of employment or in tort under the *Hedley Byrne* principle. The tortious duty, said Lord Goff, applied after the employee had left his employment and when there was no contract between the parties and also concurrently with a contractual duty.[87]

Before the decision in *Henderson* was handed down the Official Referee in two cases had reached the conclusion that a design professional could be liable to his client in tort for economic loss resulting from a defective design: *Lancashire and Cheshire Association of Baptist Churches Inc* v. *Howard Seddon Partnership*[88] and *Wessex Regional Health Authority* v. *HLM Design and Others*.[89] The editor of *Keating on Building Contracts* comments that 'these cases, which wrestled with uncertain law before *Henderson* v. *Merrett Syndicates Ltd*, are plainly to be taken as correctly decided.'[90]

In *Lancashire and Cheshire Association of Baptist Churches Inc* v. *Howard Seddon Partnership*, the plaintiffs engaged a firm of architects to design and supervise the building of a new sanctuary for their church. On completion, the plaintiffs alleged that the design was defective in relation to ventilation and the avoidance of condensation. The plaintiffs' claim in contract was statute-barred and one of the issues in this case was whether they could sue in the tort of negligence in order to take advantage of the longer limitation period for actions in tort. Judge Michael Kershaw said that the existence of a duty in tort is not precluded by the existence of a contract. However, he went on to say that the express and implied terms of the contract would limit the scope of that duty.

Judge Kershaw's approach to concurrent liability was adopted by Judge James Fox-Andrews QC in *Wessex Regional Health Authority* v. *HLM Design & Others*. In that case, an architect and an engineer were engaged under standard terms of appointment to design and supervise the building of a hospital between 1984 and 1988 for Wessex Regional Health Authority. There were substantial delays and the architect granted extensions of time in respect of most of them. In 1992 the employer issued writs alleging that the architect had been negligent in his assessments of the extensions of time and had over-certified loss and expense. It was further alleged that the architect and engineer had caused delays to the building work. Some of the delays and certificates dated from 1984/85 and were therefore outside the six year contractual limitation period. If the employer was to be successful in his claim for these losses he had to be able to establish that the architect and engineer owed him a tortious duty to take reasonable care to avoid economic loss.

Judge Fox-Andrews held that where there is a contractual relationship between a person and someone professing special skills, for which professional qualifications are necessary and the contract relates to the exercise of these skills and the case falls within the principles of *Hedley Byrne* v. *Heller and Partners*, there may be a concurrent duty to take reasonable care to avoid or prevent economic loss so long as it is fair and reasonable. The judge said that there is nothing unfair or unreasonable in architects and engineers being liable for economic loss over a longer period than they would under their contracts. Underlying the existence of a duty in respect of negligent advice, statement or information is reliance, and the judge considered that where a person enters into a contract with a professional practitioner he relies on that practitioner not just to exercise care in the performance of his skill, but also to take care to avoid or prevent economic loss.

The most significant aspect of his judgement is the wide view taken of the concept of reliance, much wider than that of Judge Kershaw's in *Lancashire and Cheshire Churches*. Judge Fox-Andrews emphasised that reliance can take many forms. In relation to architects he stated:

> it appeared to me to be artificial to select certain aspects of an architect's work such as written certificates, and regard those aspects alone as matters on which the client placed reliance ... In circumstances of a case such as the present, either the professional man owes a duty in tort to his client to take reasonable care to prevent economic loss in respect of all aspects of his work, or he owes no such duty at all.[91]

Subsequent to *Henderson*, two decisions of the Court of Appeal have extended the principle of concurrent liability. In *Barclays Bank* v. *Fairclough*,[92] Lord Goff's principle was extended to subcontractors. A specialist subcontractor was employed by a contractor, Fairclough, to clean the asbestos roofs of two buildings owned by Barclays. He did the job so negligently that he created asbestos slurry which, when it dried, created a serious health hazard. Fairclough was held liable to Barclays for the cost of the necessary remedial works, which was nearly £4 million. Fairclough then sued their subcontractor in tort for recovery of these damages. This was pure economic loss. Beldam LJ, in delivering the decision of the Court of Appeal, applied the principle laid down by Lord Goff in *Henderson* and held that the subcontractor owed a concurrent duty of care in tort to the contractor to avoid causing economic loss by failing to exercise the care and skill of a reasonably competent contractor. He said:

> A skilled contractor undertaking maintenance work to a building assumes a responsibility which invites reliance no less than the financial or other professional adviser does in undertaking his work. The nature of that responsibility is the same though it will differ in extent.[93]

The liability to which the duty in *Barclays* gave rise was no greater than liability for breach of the equivalent contractual term. In *Holt* v. *Payne Skillington*,[94] the Court of Appeal considered the question of whether a concurrent duty in tort meant a duty that was co-extensive with the duty in contract or whether the duty in tort could be wider than the duty in contract. They held that a concurrent duty in tort can arise between two contracting parties *which goes beyond the scope of the contractual duties.* This ruling is of great importance for design professionals. It means that if a design professional goes beyond the scope of the contract with his client and provides advice which the client is intended to, and does, rely on then he will be liable in tort to the client if that advice is negligently given.[95]

SUPERVISION OF THE BUILDING CONTRACT

In supervising the building contract the architect (or, in the case of an engineering contract, the engineer) takes on three quite separate and distinct roles. In the first place, he becomes the agent of the employer to see that the works are executed in accordance with the design. Secondly, he has the task of issuing certificates authorising payment to the contractor when each stage of the project has been completed satisfactorily, up to and including the issue of the final certificate when the project has been completed. Thirdly, the architect or engineer may have the task of resolving disputes between employer and contractor in the capacity either of arbitrator or of adjudicator. Each of these roles requires independent examination in this section of the chapter.

Duties as agent

Agency is a concept central to commercial law but it is possible in this work to deal with its application to the role of the architect or engineer in supervising the works in outline only.[96]

The most important concept in the law of agency is that of the agent's authority. A distinction is usually made between the express authority, the implied authority and the ostensible authority of an agent. The express authority of an agent is the authority which is conferred on him by agreement with the principal. The implied authority of an agent is the power which he has to do everything which is necessary to the carrying out of his express duties or which an agent of his type would usually be empowered to do. The ostensible authority of an agent is his authority as it appears to others.

The express powers of the architect or engineer are contained in the standard form building contracts.[97] These powers do not normally extend to entering into contracts on behalf of the employer. Essentially they amount to representing the interests of the employer during the course of the works. As a consequence the implied authority of the architect or engineer is very limited. He has an express duty to certify payments to the contractor and this will usually mean that he has implied authority to ensure that the work is carried out according to the terms of the contract. He has no implied authority to vary the terms of the contract or to order variations of the works.

Duties as certifier

A certificate is a written confirmation by the architect or engineer in the form stipulated by the contract that the contractor has complied with the contract specifications. Under the provisions of JCT '98 (clause 30.1.1.1) no payment is due to the contract until a certificate is issued. Certificates may be interim or final. An interim certificate certifies that the contractor is entitled under the contract to an interim payment for the work performed to date. A final certificate certifies that the contractor has satisfactorily completed his obligations under the contract.

In *Sutcliffe* v. *Thackrah*, Lord Salmon expressed the architect's duty as certifier in the following terms:

> The building owner and the contract make their contract on the understanding that in all such matters the architect will act in a fair and unbiased manner and it must therefore be implicit in the owner's contract with the architect that he shall not only exercise due care and skill but also reach such decisions fairly, holding the balance between his client and the contractor.[98]

The architect's duty of impartiality in acting as certifier has raised the question of whether he can be successfully sued if he performs this role negligently. For reasons of public policy,[99] judges and arbitrators have immunity from actions for negligence and it was once thought that this immunity extended to an architect in his role as certifier. The main authority for this point of view is *Chambers* v. *Goldthorpe*,[100] where the Court of Appeal, by a majority, held that in issuing certificates the arbitrator occupied the position of an arbitrator and so could not be sued for negligence in the exercise of those functions.

That view was overruled by the House of Lords in *Sutcliffe* v. *Thackrah*. In that case the plaintiff employed the defendants, a firm of architects, to design a house for him. Subsequently, he entered into a contract with a firm of builders to build the house. The defendants were appointed architects and quantity surveyors. During the carrying out of the works they issued interim certificates to the builders. Before the builders had completed the works the plaintiff turned them off the site, and another firm completed the works at higher cost. The original builders subsequently went into liquidation. The plaintiff brought an action against the defendants for damages for negligence and breach of duty in supervising the building of the house and in certifying for work not done or improperly done by the original builders. The House of Lords held that in issuing interim certificates an architect did not, apart from specific agreement, act as an arbitrator between the parties, and that he was under a duty to act fairly in making his valuation and was liable to an action in negligence at the suit of the building owner. The rationale of this decision was expressed with characteristic robustness by Lord Reid:

> There is nothing judicial about an architect's function in determining whether certain work is defective. There is no dispute. He is not jointly engaged by the parties. They do not submit evidence as contentious to him. He makes his own investigations and comes to a decision. It would be taking a very low view to suppose that without his being put in a special position his employer would wish him to act unfairly or that a professional man would be willing to depart from the ordinary honourable standard of professional conduct.[101]

Under both the JCT and the ICE standard form contracts, power is given to an arbitrator to open up, revise and review certificates. The question of whether the High Court has the same powers was discussed by the Court of Appeal in *Northern Regional Health Authority* v. *Crouch*.[102] The Court of Appeal held that the High Court does not have the same powers as an arbitrator under the JCT form of contract to open up, review and revise certificates, since to do so would be to modify the contractual obligations of the parties. The jurisdiction of the High Court was limited to determining and enforcing the contractual rights of the parties and did not extend to substituting its own discretion simply because it would have reached a different conclusion. The arbitrator, on the other hand, was entitled to modify the parties' contractual rights by substituting his own discretion for that of the architect, because the contract expressly gave him such power.

The decision in *Crouch* has been subject to much criticism and it was overruled by the House of Lords in *Beaufort Developments (N.I.) Ltd* v.

Gilbert Ash N.I. Ltd.[103] The House of Lords held that clause 41.4 of the JCT '80', giving the architect power to open up, review and revise any certificate, could not be construed as curtailing the court's power to rectify the contract. By the same token, the court's power to open up and revise interim certificates is not excluded by the express power to open up and revise certificates conferred on the arbitrator.

The decision in *Beaufort* is a very significant one; its effect is that the court is not bound by an architect's certificate and can consider the dispute on the basis of the evidence. Lord Lloyd, in his speech, said that there is no need for the contract to confer on the court the power to open up and review interim certificates since the power already exists as part of the court's ordinary power to enforce the contract in accordance with its terms. Their Lordships were highly critical of the decision in *Crouch*, in particular the implication that the arbitrator had the right to modify contractual rights. Lord Hoffman, in his speech, emphasised that in submitting a dispute to an arbitrator the parties were simply agreeing to abide by the ruling of a third party, whose role was to act as an independent expert in the interpretation of the contract.

Duties as arbitrator or adjudicator

Arbitration is a private alternative to litigation. It is an agreement whereby the parties to a contract submit any disputes concerning the contract to a formal tribunal (an arbitrator) of their own choosing rather than to the courts. The decision of the arbitrator is binding and final, and there is only limited appeal to the courts.

In contrast to certification, an architect or engineer in discharging the function of an arbitrator will have immunity from legal action. Such immunity is contained in section 29(1) of the Arbitration Act 1996:

> An arbitrator is not liable for anything done or omitted in the discharge or purported discharge of his functions as arbitrator unless the act or omission is shown to be in bad faith.

Further, the Supply of Services (Exclusion of Implied Terms) Order 1985[104] exempts an arbitrator from the provisions of section 13 of the Supply of Goods and Services Act 1982, which imposes a duty on persons who supply a service in the course of a business to carry out that service with reasonable care and skill.

Adjudication is a statutory procedure, contained in section 108 of the Housing Grants, Construction and Regeneration Act 1996, which entitles either party to a construction dispute to refer the matter to an independent third party. There is no established legal framework for adjudication, but it is intended to be a speedy process which avoids the atmosphere of arbitration or litigation. The decision of the adjudicator is temporarily binding until any later court or arbitration proceedings are concluded.

Section 108(4) of the 1996 Act extends the legal immunity enjoyed by arbitrators to adjudicators within the construction industry:

> The contract shall also provide that the adjudicator is not liable for anything done or omitted in the discharge or purported discharge of his functions as adjudicator unless the act or omission is in bad faith, and that any employee or agent of the adjudicator is similarly protected from liability.

The 1996 Act makes it compulsory for all construction contracts (with certain limited exceptions) to contain a provision for disputes arising out of the contract to be referred to an adjudicator. Under the provisions of section 108, eight points concerning adjudication must be included in all construction contracts. If they are not then the Scheme for Construction Contracts (SCC) contained in the Scheme for Construction Contracts Regulations 1998[105] comes into operation. Under the SCC, a construction contract must require the adjudicator to reach a decision within 28 days of referral, although the parties may agree a longer period after the dispute has been referred.

The 1996 Act came into effect on 1 May 1998. It has no effect on contracts entered into before that date.

A question of profound importance is the effect of the Human Rights Act 1998 on arbitration and adjudication. The Act came into force on 2 October 2000. It incorporates the European Convention on Human Rights into English law. The convention guarantees for everyone certain basic rights and it requires public bodies to act in a way that is compatible with those rights. A public body includes anyone fulfilling a public function and would therefore include a judge, an arbitrator and, arguably, an adjudicator. UK courts are bound, where possible, to interpret and to give effect to prior and subsequent Acts of Parliament so as to comply with these basic rights.

The most relevant right for present purposes is that contained in Article 6, which guarantees the right to a fair trial. Every dispute must be determined in a reasonable time by an independent, impartial tribunal and there must be an effective and fair public hearing. Arbitrators and adjudicators are under a duty to ensure that their procedures comply with Article 6. Two questions which arise immediately in this context are whether an arbitration hearing held in private and the 28 day period laid down by the Construction Act 1996 for an adjudicator to reach a decision comply with Article 6. Until these questions are determined, there will be a good deal of uncertainty surrounding arbitration and adjudication.[106]

LIABILITY TO THIRD PARTIES

Personal injury

The liability of the architect or engineer in negligence for personal injuries sustained by third parties has been laid down in a trilogy of cases reported in the *Building Law Reports: Clayton* v. *Woodman & Son (Builders) Ltd;* [107] *Clay* v. *A.J. Crump (Contractors) Ltd and Others;* [108] and *Oldschool* v. *Gleeson (Contractors) Ltd and Others.*[109]

In *Clayton* v. *Woodman*, the plaintiff was a bricklayer employed by Woodman & Son, who were building contractors. They were engaged by the South Western Regional Hospital Board to install a lift in one of their hospitals. The lift was designed by a firm of architects. The design provided for the demolition of part of a roof adjacent to a gable wall. This work weakened the gable wall and the plaintiff tried (unsuccessfully) to persuade the architect to instruct that it should be demolished. When the plaintiff, during the course of construction work, removed part of the wall the wall toppled and fell onto him, injuring him. The trial judge held that the contractors, the regional hospital board and the architects were liable. The architects appealed and the Court of Appeal held that they were not liable in these circumstances. They said that an architect does not undertake to advise a builder as to what safety precautions should be taken or as to how the building operations should be carried out. That is the function of the builder.

In *Clay* v. *Crump*, an architect supervising some demolition work instructed the demolition contractor to leave a wall temporarily standing. He accepted the contractor's word that the wall was safe and did not check it himself. In fact, the wall was tottering unstably over a six foot trench and collapsed injuring one of the contractor's men. The Court of Appeal held that the architect, together with the demolition contractor and the contractor, was liable because the plaintiff's injuries were a foreseeable consequence of his not inspecting the wall.

In *Oldschool* v. *Gleeson*, the plaintiffs owned two houses. They employed the first defendants, the contractors, to redevelop them. The second defendants were the consulting engineers. The works required one of the houses to be demolished. When this was done the party wall between that house and the adjoining property collapsed. Under a party wall agreement the owners of that property were awarded damages of £16,788 against the plaintiffs. The first defendants admitted their liability to indemnify the plaintiffs, but sought to recover that indemnity from the consulting engineers. Judge Stabb dismissed their claim. He said that the duty of the consulting engineers to the contractors did not extend to the execution of the works. It was no more than a duty to warn the contractors to take the necessary precautions. This they had done.

In conclusion, it may be said that the architect or engineer visiting the site in a supervisory capacity does so in order to ascertain if the works are being constructed in accordance with the design, and not in order to control the contractor's execution of the work. The architect or engineer may be liable for personal injuries which result from a defect inherent in the design or from his actual control of the works. However, he will not be liable if the plaintiff's injuries result from the contractor negligently constructing the works.

Liability to the purchaser for defects in the building

As we saw in Chapter 2, the law of negligence in the area of defective, but not dangerous, buildings has been the subject of considerable change over the last two decades. In *Dutton* v. *Bognor Regis UDC* [110] and *Anns* v. *Merton LBC* [111] it was held that purchasers or tenants of properties, who were not party to any contract with the contractors or design professionals, could claim against them in negligence if the building was a danger to the health and safety of the occupants. Those decisions were overruled by the House of Lords in *Murphy* v. *Brentwood DC*.[112] Their Lordships in that case strongly emphasised that a dangerous defect in a building once it became apparent was a defect in quality and the building was therefore worth less than it was supposed to be. The cost of repairing such a building was a form of economic loss and the view of the House of Lords was that to permit the purchaser to recover such loss would lead to an unacceptably wide category of claims. The Law Lords laid great stress on the fact that they saw the existence of such a duty as leading to liability in negligence for defective, though not dangerous, products. It is now virtually impossible, therefore, for the purchaser or lessee of a building which is defective because of a negligent design to successfully sue the architect or engineer who produced that design. The only circumstances in which such purchaser or lessee may be able to succeed against the design professional is if he can show that he relied on the design.[113] In practice, such reliance will be very difficult to establish.

We have seen in the section of this chapter on concurrent liability in tort that the courts have used the *Hedley Byrne* principles of reliance and the assumption of responsibility to establish concurrent liability as a principle of the common law. In *White* v. *Jones*[114] and *Spring* v. *Guardian Assurance plc*[115] these concepts were used to extend the scope of third party liability in tort. It is doubtful, however, if those decisions have opened the door to imposing liability for third party economic losses on design professionals. There are two reasons which can be given for this view. The first reason concerns the concept of assumption of responsibility which is the basis of the principle laid down by Lord Goff in *Henderson*. Clearly, design professionals can be taken to have assumed a responsibility (for advice and services) towards their clients to whom they are contractually bound. But it is doubtful if this *Hedley Byrne* category of liability will be extended to third parties. Thus, an architect or a builder is unlikely to be held liable in negligence to a *subsequent* owner of the building for defective design or defective construction. There is nothing in Lord Goff's speech to even hint at what would be a remarkable change of fortune in the law of negligence and economic loss. True, he said that in the context of *Henderson* itself he saw no reason why indirect names should not be free to sue the managing agents in tort and thus bypass the contractual chain of indirect names, members' agents and managing agents. But he stressed that that context was an unusual one.

The second reason is the very important limitation which Lord Goff placed on his principle in relation to the liability of contractors and subcontractors. Lord Goff referred to the contractual chain of liability which exists in an ordinary construction project under which the main contractor contracts with the building owner for the construction of the relevant building and the main contractor then subcontracts with various subcontractors and suppliers. Lord Goff said that if the subcontracted work or materials did not come up to the required standard it was not open to the building owner to sue the subcontractor or supplier under the *Hedley Bryne* principle. There was no assumption of responsibility by the subcontractor or supplier towards the building owner; the parties had structured their relationships so that such assumption of responsibility could not arise.[116]

Liability to the contractor for economic loss

The principal question which arises in this context is the extent, if any, to which the architect/engineer can be held liable for economic loss to the contractor resulting from his negligence. If the contractor's economic loss can be said to result from a negligent *act* of the architect/engineer then it must be clear, following *Murphy*, that such loss will not be recoverable. If however, the contractor's economic loss can be said to result from a negligent *statement* made by the architect/engineer then the position is not so clear cut.

Following the decisions in *Dutton* and *Anns*, the courts were willing to extend the scope of the liability of design, professionals to third parties. In *Arenson* v. *Cason Beckman Rutley & Co*. Lord Salmon stated:

> The architect owed a duty to his client, the building owner, arising out of the contract between them to use reasonable care in issuing his certificates. He also, however, owed a similar duty of care to the contractor arising out of their proximity.[117]

Since then the courts have been less willing to create new tortious duties and have re-emphasised the network of contractual relationships as the means of recovering losses. In *Murphy*, the House of Lords reasserted the rule that pure economic loss is not recoverable in the tort of negligence unless it can be shown that the relationship between the plaintiff and the defendant falls within the scope of the reliance principle laid down in *Hedley Byrne*. We have seen that this reliance principle has been extended in scope subsequent to the ruling in *Murphy*. It would be unwise, if not reckless, to conclude, however, that its scope had extended to the point where the law regards a contractor as relying on the architect or engineer to produce an accurate design. In the construction industry there is a well established chain of contracts and, as we have seen, in *Henderson* Lord Goff was careful to emphasise that the concept of assumption of responsibility was not intended to short circuit this chain. It must be concluded, therefore, that the exclusionary rule laid down in *Murphy* is still the cornerstone of this area of law.

Before the decision of the House of Lords in *Henderson*, the Official Referee's Court and the Court of Appeal had already begun to restrict severely the extent of the duty of care owed by architects and engineers to contractors. In *Michael Salliss & Co. Ltd* v. *Calil and William F. Newman & Associates*,[118] the architect was alleged by the contractors wrongfully to have granted an extension of 12 weeks instead of the 29 claimed. Judge James Fox-Andrews held that the contractor could have a right of action against an architect who failed to exercise reasonable care and skill in certification. However, the judge went on to say that in many respects the architect owes no duty to the contractor:

> He owes no duty of care to contractors in respect of the preparation of plans and specifications or in deciding matters such as whether or not he should cause a survey to be carried out. He owes no duty of care to a contractor whether or not he should order a variation.[119]

In *Pacific Associates* v. *Baxter*,[120] the plaintiffs were contractors who had tendered 'for dredging and reclamation' work on the basis, *inter alia*, of reports prepared by the defendant engineer. The contractor claimed that the dredging process was rendered more expensive and more difficult due to the presence in the creek to be dredged of a high percentage of hard material which necessitated the use of more powerful machinery. He contended that the information given by the engineer in his reports at the tender stage was inaccurate in that it failed to indicate the extent of the presence of the hard rock. The plaintiffs argued that the relationship between themselves and the engineer was so close that the engineer would be aware that any negligence by him would lead to loss on the part of the contractor and that the engineer must be taken to have assumed responsibility for any such foreseeable losses. This argument was rejected by the Court of Appeal because under the terms of the contract between the engineer and the contractor the engineer was not to be liable for any such losses incurred by the contractor. The main judgement was that of Purchas LJ, and the key passage in his judgement is as follows:

> I have come to the conclusion ... that no liability can be established in tort under which the engineer owed a direct duty to the contractor in the circumstances disclosed in this case. I emphasise, however, in coming to this conclusion it does depend on the particular circumstances of the case, not the least of which were the contractual provisions in the contract which afforded an avenue enabling the contractor to recover from the employer.[121]

The decision in *Pacific Associates* has been followed by the High Court of Hong Kong[122] and by the Supreme Court of Canada.[123] Following Lord Goff's speech in *Henderson*, all of these decisions must be regarded as of considerable authority.

The Defective Premises Act 1972

Section 1 of the Defective Premises Act 1972 creates a general duty on all persons taking on work for or in connection with the provision of dwellings to see that the work is done in a workmanlike or professional manner, with proper materials and so that the dwelling will be fit for habitation. The duty applies to professional persons such as architects or engineers as well as to builders and developers. It may be enforced independently of any contract which may exist, by any person acquiring an interest in the dwelling.

In a number of ways, the duty imposed by this statutory provision is narrow. First, it applies only to dwellings; there is no liability under the provision for defective work on factories, offices and warehouses. Secondly, section 2 excludes actions for breach of the duty created by section 1 in respect of losses covered by an 'approved scheme'. The scheme principally envisaged by this section was the NHBC scheme, but the last NHBC scheme to be approved was their 1979 scheme. The 1985 and 1992 schemes are not approved, and owners of houses covered by these schemes can claim against builders and construction professionals under section 1.

Until recently the 1972 Act was not relied upon by owners of defective homes because the contractual and tortious duties imposed upon builders and construction professionals provided more effective remedies. However, the retreat of the law of negligence may well mean that owners of defective dwellings will seek to use its provisions as a means of obtaining a remedy. As we saw in Chapter 4, the key question for determination is the meaning of 'fitness for habitation' and, thereby, the extent of the loss recoverable under the Act.

DAMAGES

If a design professional is in breach of his duty to his client or to a third party then the usual remedy is damages. There are two areas for consideration here:

(i)   remoteness; and
(ii) the measure of damages.

Remoteness

For damages to be awarded for a breach of duty the plaintiff's loss must have been caused by the breach and have been foreseeable.

Causation is essentially an issue of fact to be determined in the circumstances of each case. One problem that may arise in this area is whether an intervening act of a third party breaks the chain of causation. Such an issue arose in *Clay* v. *A.J. Crump & Sons Ltd*,[124] where the defendant architect and demolition contractors argued that as the building contractors had the last opportunity of examining the site this broke the chain of causation and that, as a consequence, they did not cause the accident. The Court of Appeal rejected that argument. Upjohn LJ, in addressing this point, said:

> The real truth of the matter, as I think, is that causation is almost entirely a question of fact in each particular case. 'It is a fallacy to suppose that the last cause is the sole cause, ' said Lord Denning in *Miller* v. *South of Scotland Electricity Board* 1958 SC (HL) 20, p.39.[125]

Upjohn LJ concluded that the principal cause of the accident was the failure of the architect to perform his duties. The second cause (in order of importance) was that of the demolition contractor and the third cause (least in importance) was the building contractor, who was not entitled to assume that the other two parties had performed their duties.

As well as showing that his loss was caused by the breach of duty of the architect, engineer or quantity surveyor, the plaintiff must also show that the loss was foreseeable. If the claim is in contract this means that at the time that the contract was entered into the damage was reasonably foreseeable as likely to result from the breach.[126] If the claim is in tort then it must have been reasonable at the time that the tort was committed that the kind of damage which occurred would result.[127]

The measure of damages

There are two ways in which the loss suffered by the plaintiff as a consequence of a breach of duty by the architect, engineer or quantity surveyor may be assessed. The first, and principal, way is that of assessing the cost of rectifying the defects in the building works which are the result of the breach of duty. In *Ruxley Electronics* v. *Forsyth*,[128] the House of Lords emphasised that in awarding such costs the court must consider whether such an award is in proportion to the benefit to be obtained by such rectification. In the circumstances of the case, the plaintiff had suffered an amenity loss, in the sense that the building works were worth less to him than to a reasonable buyer on the open market. The House of Lords held that damages should be awarded for this amenity loss, which was far less than an award based on the costs of rectification.

The alternative measure of damages is to award the diminution in value of the building works which results from the breach of duty.[129]

SUMMARY

1. The design of the construction works is the responsibility of the architect. In the case of engineering works, the design function will generally be carried out by an engineer.

2. The role of a quantity surveyor is to provide measurements and quantities and to value the work carried out at the different stages of a construction project.

3. These design professionals are employed directly by the employer and are not parties to the main contract between the contractor and the employer.

4. The express duties of the architect or engineer and the quantity surveyor will generally be set out in the relevant standard form of agreement.

5. The implied duty of the architect, engineer or quantity surveyor is to carry out his express duties with reasonable care and skill and to exercise the care and skill of an ordinary competent member of his profession.

6. There is no general duty imposed on an architect or engineer that the works will be fit for a particular purpose.

7. The implied duty of reasonable care and skill in relation to design professionals has been applied in detail by the courts to the particular functions which they perform.

8. Apart from their common law duty of reasonable care and skill, a design professional has a statutory duty to see that the design is safe for the persons carrying out the construction work.

9. As well as a duty of care in contract, a design professional has also a concurrent duty in tort to his client.

10. This concurrent duty in tort may be excluded by the contract.

11. Where a design professional carries out functions that are not part of the contract with his client (e.g. where an architect is employed to design a building but goes on to advise on marketing the building) then it appears that a tortious duty is owed in respect of the non-contractual functions.

12. The architect or engineer, in addition to his design duties, will usually perform the role of supervising the building or engineering works.

13. In his supervisory capacity, the architect or engineer has several roles. In the first place, he is the agent of the employer in seeing that the works are built in accordance with the design. Secondly, he has the task of certifying that each stage of the project has been completed satisfactorily. Thirdly, he may act as arbitrator or adjudicator in the resolution of disputes concerning the contract. In these second and third roles, the architect or engineer must act impartially between employer and contractor and has legal immunity.

14. The architect or engineer may be liable for personal injury suffered by third parties as a result of a defect in the design, but he is not liable to third parties for defects in the building itself which result from the design. In other words, the architect or engineer owes a duty of reasonable care to third parties to see that the design is safe but he owes no such duty where the design is defective but not dangerous.

15. If a design professional is in breach of his duty to his client or to a third party then the usual remedy is damages.

16. For damages to be awarded for a breach of a design professional's duty the plaintiff's loss must have been caused by the breach.

17. Causation is a question of fact in each particular case.

18. The loss must also be foreseeable.

19. The general measure of damages is the cost of rectifying the defects in the building works which are the result of the breach of duty.

20. If the cost of repair is out of all proportion to the benefit obtained by the plaintiff, the court may instead award damages on the basis of the loss of amenity suffered by the plaintiff.

NOTES

1. [1945] 2 All ER 131, at p.134. This definition is adopted by the Tribunal of Appeal from the Architects' Registration Council (as it then was) and is cited by Jackson and Powell, *Professional Negligence*, 4th edn, Sweet & Maxwell, 1997, p.111, n.3.

2. For a full list of these duties see Duncan Wallace, I.N., *Hudson's Building and Engineering Contracts,*11th edn, Sweet & Maxwell, 1995, Vol. 1, pp.266–267.

3. The Architects Act 1997 consolidates the law relating to the registration of architects. It repeals the Architects Registration Act 1931 and the Architects Registration Act 1938, both Acts being amended by the provisions of Part III of the Housing Grants, Construction and Regeneration Act 1996. Section 20(1) of the 1997 Act re-enacts the offence of practising while not registered, which was introduced by section 1 of the 1938 Act.

4. Under the 1931 Act, the Architects Registration Board was known as the Architects Registration Council of the United Kingdom; it was given its present title by the 1996 Act.

5. (1870) 4 IRCI 467, at p.476. Cited in Neil F. Jones & Co, *Professional Negligence in the Construction Industry*, LLP Reference Publishing, 1998, p.115.

6. For a detailed description of these functions see Neil F. Jones, *Professional Negligence in the Construction Industry, ibid*, pp.115–117.

7. See *Greaves & Co (Contractors) Ltd* v. *Baynham Meikle & Partners* [1975] 3 All ER 99; and *Independent Broadcasting Authority* v. *EMI Electronics and BICC Construction* (1980) 14 BLR 1.

8. The reasons for this phenomenon are set out in Neil F. Jones, *Professional Negligence in the Construction Industry, ibid*, n.5, pp.121–122.

9. See Neil F. Jones, *Professional Negligence in the Construction Industry, ibid*, n.5, pp.123–143.

10. This form supersedes *The Architect's Appointment*, issued in 1992. It is reprinted in *Emden's Construction Law*, 8th edn, Butterworths, 1990, Binder 4,

Division F, and in Appendix C of *Keating on Building Contracts*, 7th edn, Sweet & Maxwell, 2001.

11. Condition 2(1) of the Conditions of Engagement.
12. This form is reprinted in Emden, Binder 4, Division F.
13. This form is reprinted in Emden, Binder 5, Division Y.
14. Clause 9.1.
15. Sir Michael Latham, *Construction the Team*, HMSO, 1994.
16. Section 104(2).
17. The Scheme for Construction Contracts (England and Wales) Regulations 1998 – SI 1998 No. 649.
18. This duty is laid down in *Lamphier* v. *Phipos* (1838) 8 C & P 475 and is now contained in section 13 of the Supply of Goods and Services Act 1982.
19. But see *post* for a discussion on the question of whether an obligation of fitness for purpose can be imposed on an architect or engineer.
20. [1957] 2 All ER 118, p.121.
21. The *Bolam* standard is discussed more extensively in Chapter 8.
22. (1853) cited in *Hudson's Building and Engineering Contracts*, 11th edn, p.293 and in *Jackson & Powell on Professional Negligence*, 4th edn, 1997, pp.180 and 143, n.98.
23. (1980) 14 BLR 1, at p.31.
24. (1980) 2 Con. LR 43.
25. *Ibid*, n.24, p.74.
26. (1981) 35 BLR 1.
27. *Ibid*, n.26, p.16.
28. *Ibid*, n.26, p.31.
29. *Ibid*, n.26, p.23.
30. *Ibid*, n.26, pp.25–26.
31. [1973] 2 NZLR 45, pp.65–66, cited in *Jackson and Powell, op. cit.*, n.1, p.175.
32. SI 1994 No. 3140.
33. 92/57/EEC, OJ No. L.245, 26.8.92, p.6.
34. 26 January 2000. Discussed by Barnes, *Building*, 21 January 2000, on which the following discussion is based.
35. See *Wimpey Construction UK Ltd* v. *Poole* [1984] 2 Lloyd's Rep. 499, at p.506 (*per* Webster J)
36. (1987) 37 BLR 92, at p.103.
37. Section 16(3) of the Supply of Goods and Services Act 1982 expressly permits a duty stricter than that contained in section 13 to be imposed on the supplier of a service.
38. (1966) 14 BLR 50.
39. *Ibid*, n.38, p.55.
40. (1981) 18 BLR 130.
41. [1971] 1 WLR 862, p.873.
42. [1975] 3 All ER 99.
43. *Ibid*, n.42, p.103.
44. *Ibid*, n.42 p.163.
45. *Ibid*, n.42, p.106.
46. *Ibid*, n.42, p.104.
47. (1979) 11 BLR 29, p.52.
48. (1980) 14 BLR 1, p.45.
49. *Ibid*, n.48, p.48.
50. (1985) 33 BLR 103.
51. (1986) 38 BLR 35.
52. *Ibid*, n.51, p.51.

53. [1986] QB 644.
54. *Brickfield Properties* v. *Newton, op. cit.*, n.41.
55. Similarly, in a contract for the sale of supply of goods, where defects in the goods appear sometime after the contract was made, that may be evidence that the seller or supplier was in breach of his statutory duty to supply goods under the contract of satisfactory quality.
56. (1988) 18 Con. LR 1.
57. *Ibid,* n.56, p.147.
58. (1824) 1 Car & P 351.
59. (1980) 259 EG 491.
60. [1986] 1 All ER 781.
61. For a critique of inspection clauses see Melinda Parisotti, *Building,* 11 August 2000, p.51.
62. (1992) 29 Con. LR 58, cited in *Jackson and Powell, op. cit.*, n.1, p.209.
63. *Ibid, Jackson and Powell,* p.209.
64. Section 4 of the Supply of Goods and Services Act 1982; see also *Young and Marten* v. *McManus Childs* [1969] 1 AC 454.
65. (1987) 38 BLR 25.
66. This section of the chapter is based on the author's article in (1995) PN 16. See also Issaka Ndekugri, *Concurrent Liability in Contract and Tort in the Construction Industry* (2000) 16 Const. LJ 13.
67. [1995] 2 AC 145, at p.185. Lord Goff's speech is seminal reading in this subject.
68. *Koufos* v. *Czarnikow, The Heron II* [1969] 1 AC 350.
69. *The Wagon Mound* [1961] 1 All ER 404.
70. [1932] AC 562, at pp.609–10.
71. [1939] 1 KB 194.
72. *Ibid*, n.71, p.222.
73. [1964] AC 465.
74. [1976] 2 All ER 5.
75. *Ibid*, n.74, p.15.
76. [1978] 3 All ER 571.
77. [1985] 2 All ER 947, at p.957.
78. *Ibid*, n.77, p.957.
79. [1989] 40 EG 89.
80. [1988] 2 All ER 971.
81. *Op. cit.*, n.67.
82. *Op. cit.*, n.67, p.181.
83. *Op. cit.*, n.67, p.194.
84. [1995] 2 AC 267.
85. *Ibid*, n.84, p.288.
86. [1995] 2 AC 296.
87. *Ibid,* n.86, p.320.
88. [1993] 3 All ER 467.
89. (1994) 10 Const. LJ 167.
90. 7th edn, Sweet & Maxwell, 2001, p.220, n.46.
91. *Ibid*, n.89, p.187.
92. (1996) 76 BLR 1.
93. *Ibid*, n.92, p.24.
94. (1996) 77 BLR 51.
95. See the commentary in the Building Law Reports for a critique of this decision.
96. For a detailed discussion of this subject see *Keating on Building Contracts*, 7th edn, 2001, pp.379–387.

97.   See, in particular, JCT '98, subclauses 13.2 and 13.3; and SFA/99, conditions 2(2) and (3) of the Conditions of Engagement.
98.   [1974] AC 727, p.737.
99.   See *Randel* v. *Worsley* [1969] 1 AC 191.
100. [1901] 1 KB 624.
101. *Supra*, n.98, pp.737–738.
102. [1984] 2 All ER 175.
103. [1999] 1 AC 266.
104. SI 1985 No. 1.
105. *Op. cit*, n.17.
106. For discussion of the implications of the Human Rights Act for arbitration and adjudication see *Building*, 22 September 2000, pp.58–64.
107. (1977) 4 BLR 65 (judgement given on 9 March 1962).
108. (1977) 4 BLR 80 (judgement given on 30 July 1963); [1964] 1QB 533.
109. (1977) 4 BLR 103.
110. [1972] 1 QB 373.
111. [1978] AC 728.
112. [1990] 2 All ER 908.
113. See the *dicta* of Lord Keith and Lord Oliver in *Murphy, ibid*, n.111, p.919 and p.930, respectively.
114. *Op. cit.*, n.84.
115. *Op. cit.*, n.86.
116. *Op. cit.*, n.67, p.196
117. [1977] AC 405, p.438.
118. (1987) 13 Con. LR 68.
119. *Ibid,* n.118, p.79.
120. [1989] 2 All ER 159.
121. *Ibid*, n.120, pp.179–180.
122. *Lean Engineering and Construction Co. Ltd* v. *KA Duk Investment Co. Ltd* (1989) 47 BLR 139.
123. *Edgeworth Construction Ltd* v. *ND Lea & Associates* (1991) 54 BLR 11.
124. *Op. cit.*, n.108.
125. *Op. cit.*, n.108, pp.568–569.
126. See *Hadley* v. *Baxendale* (1854) 9 Ex. 341; *Victoria Laundry (Windsor) Ltd* v. *Newman Industries Ltd* [1949] 1 All ER 997; and *Czarnikow Ltd* v. *Koufos, The Heron II* [1967] 3 All ER 686. These cases are discussed more extensively in Chapter 1.
127. See *The Wagon Mound* [1961] AC 388.
128. [1995] 3 WLR 118. This case is discussed fully in Chapter 1.
129. See *East Ham Corporation* v. *Bernard Sunley* [1966] AC 406, pp.434–435 (*per* Lord Cohen).

8

Liability of Surveyors for Valuation and Survey

INTRODUCTION

We have seen in Chapters 3 and 7 that in the absence of a contract it is extremely difficult now for the purchaser of a defective building to bring a successful action against either the builder or the designer of the building. The reason for this is that the loss in such circumstances is likely to be economic and such loss is irrecoverable in the tort of negligence except where the relationship between the plaintiff and defendant can be brought within the scope of the principle in *Hedley Byrne & Co.*v. *Heller & Partners.*[1] This has had vital implications for surveyors because, following the decisions of the House of Lords in *Murphy* v. *Brentwood District Council*[2] and *Department of the Environment* v. *Bates*,[3] the only means by which a purchaser of a defective building may be able to recover his losses is to sue his surveyor. The liability of surveyors has, therefore, assumed a unique and, for surveyors an ominous, importance in Construction Law.

In order to grasp fully this particular subject it is necessary to make clear at the outset that a surveyor may be employed to carry out one of three different types of survey:

(i)   a structural survey, which is a report on the structural soundness of the property concerned;

(ii)   the RICS House Buyer's Report and Valuation (HBRV), which is a standard survey and report following a limited inspection of the property and which contains an indication of the value of the property; and

(iii) a mortgage valuation survey carried out under section 13 of the Building Societies Act 1986[4] in order to indicate whether the property is adequate security for a loan.

In the case of the first two types of survey, the surveyor's client is usually the purchaser of the property concerned and any liability on the part of the surveyor will be contractual. In the case of a mortgage valuation survey, however, the client is the mortgagee and any liability owed by the surveyor to the purchaser will be tortious. It is in the case of mortgage valuation

185

surveys that the most controversial developments in surveyors' liability have occurred, controversial in that they raise the vexed question of the true extent of a professional person's liability to third parties.

This chapter is divided into the following components of liability: the duty of care, the standard of care, damages recoverable for breach of the duty of care and exclusion of liability. These are, of course, the components of the tort of negligence. Surveyors' liability has been at the forefront of recent developments in this tort but it must not be forgotten that a surveyor's principal obligation is contractual.

THE DUTY OF CARE

(A)   To the client

In considering the duty which is owed by a surveyor, the most obvious starting point is to consider the duty which he owes to his client, with whom he will have a contract. The contract will normally be set out in writing and the written terms will determine the extent of the surveyor's obligations. Such a contract is known as a contract for services and the common law implies a term into this category of contract which requires the supplier of the service to carry out his duties under the contract with reasonable care and with the skill and competence of an ordinarily competent member of his profession or calling.[5]

A contract for services does not normally contain a term that the supplier will achieve a particular result and there is no term implied by law to that effect. However, the law does not prevent the supplier from taking on an obligation stricter than that of reasonable care and skill,[6] and there may be circumstances where such a term can be implied as a matter of fact.[7] The important point for the surveyor to remember is that in giving oral answers to questions from his client he must take great care to stress the limitations of his survey and avoid making statements which could amount to the giving of a guarantee and the imposition of strict liability.

Following developments in the law of professional negligence in the 1970s, a surveyor also owes a duty in tort (under the principle of *Hedley Byrne* v. *Heller*) to his client.[8] Following the dicta of the Privy Council in *Tai Hing Cotton Mill* v. *Liu Chong Hing Bank Ltd*,[9] that where the parties are in a contractual relationship, there is nothing to the law's advantage or the law's development in searching for a liability in tort, these developments were of uncertain authority.[10] However, the authority of the rule that a surveyor owes a concurrent duty in tort to his client was put beyond doubt by the House of Lords in their decision in *Henderson* v. *Merrett Syndicates Ltd*.[11] In *Holt* v. *Payne Skillington and De Groot Collis*,[12] the Court of Appeal went further than the rule laid down in *Henderson* and said that, in the absence of a contractual term which precluded or restricted the duty of care in tort, it was open to the court to find that the concurrent duty in tort was wider than the duties under the contract. In this case, an employee of a firm of surveyors went beyond the surveyors' contract of retainer and gave advice to the plaintiff about the application of planning laws. The Court of Appeal upheld the finding of the trial judge that the surveyors owed a duty of care in tort in respect of this advice.

(B) To third parties

The most controversial development in the law of professional negligence has concerned the question of whether or not a professional person should owe a duty of care to a third party with whom he has no contract. In relation to surveyors this question has arisen in a case concerning a vendor's survey, *Shankie-Williams* v. *Heavey*,[13] and in three cases involving mortgage valuation surveys: *Yianni* v. *Edwin Evans & Sons*,[14] *Smith* v. *Bush* and *Harris* v. *Wyre Forest District Council*.[15]

Vendors' surveys

In *Shankie-Williams* v. *Heavey*, the owners of a house which had been converted into flats entered into negotiations for the sale of the ground-floor flat. The prospective purchasers and plaintiffs Mr and Mrs Shankie-Williams, suspected that the flat had dry-rot. To reassure them, the owners called in a dry-rot specialist who reported that the flat contained no evidence of dry-rot, though as a precaution he sprayed the timbers and gave a 30 year guarantee against re-infestation. As a result of these assurances the purchase went ahead. Meanwhile, the surveyor's report had been passed on to a prospective purchaser of the first-floor flat who took it as an indication that the whole house was free from dry-rot and so he too went ahead with his purchase. Two years later substantial infestation of dry rot was discovered in both flats. The Court of Appeal held that the surveyor owed the ground-floor purchasers a duty of care because he knew that his report would be passed on to them (that was the whole purpose of the survey). In legal terms, there was sufficient proximity between the parties to give rise to a duty of care. In the case of the purchaser of the first-floor flat, the Court of Appeal held that the surveyor owed no duty to him because there was insufficient nexus or proximity between the parties.

Mortgage valuation surveys

Mortgage valuation surveys are the most controversial of all the situations involving the liability of a surveyor to a third party. In *Yianni*, the plaintiff, who wished to buy a house at a price of £15,000, applied to the Halifax Building Society for a mortgage. The Halifax engaged the defendants, a firm of valuers and surveyors, to value the property. The plaintiff had to pay for their report. They valued the property at £15,000 and assessed it as suitable for maximum lending. The Halifax offered the plaintiff a loan of £12,000 which he accepted and he purchased the house. After he moved in, cracks caused by subsidence were discovered and two years later the cost of repairing the property was estimated to be £18,000. The defendants admitted that they had been negligent in preparing the valuation report but they argued that they did not owe a duty of care to the plaintiff because his loss was the result of his own negligence in failing to commission an independent survey. This argument was dismissed by Park J, who found for the plaintiff. The judge held that a surveyor who carried out a mortgage valuation survey of a property for a building society which is contemplating advancing a loan to a prospective purchaser of that property, owes a duty of care in tort to that purchaser.

The facts of *Smith* v. *Bush* are similar to those of *Yianni*. Mrs Smith bought a home, valued at £16,500, for £18,000 with the aid of a £3500 mortgage from the Abbey National Building Society. The building society, in pursuance of its statutory duty under section 13 of the Building Societies Act 1986, instructed Eric S. Bush, a firm of surveyors and valuers, to report on the value of the house. Mrs Smith paid a fee to the building society in respect of that report and she was sent a copy of it. The report contained a disclaimer of liability for the accuracy of the report covering both the building society and the surveyor. It also stated that it was not a structural survey and advised Mrs Smith to obtain independent professional advice. Nonetheless, she relied on it and purchased the house without an independent survey. The building society's surveyor negligently failed to check the chimney supports which were defective, and later a flue collapsed causing substantial damage to the property. The surveyor conceded that he owed a duty of care to Mrs Smith and relied as a defence on the disclaimer in his report. The House of Lords approved the rule in *Yianni*, held that the disclaimer of liability was caught by the Unfair Contract Terms Act 1977, and ruled that it did not satisfy the reasonableness test in that Act.

The existence of the valuer's duty in tort to the mortgagor was unequivocally recognised by Lord Templeman in the following terms:

> in the absence of a disclaimer of liability the valuer who values a house for the purpose of a mortgage, knowing that the mortgagee will rely and the mortgagor will probably rely on the valuation, knowing that the purchaser mortgagor has in effect paid for the valuation, is under a duty to exercise reasonable care and skill and that duty is owed to both parties to the mortgage for which the valuation is made.[16]

It must be noted, however, that Lords Griffiths and Jauncey said that this duty applied essentially to valuations of dwelling houses of modest value. They hinted strongly that the duty would be much more difficult to establish in the cases of valuations of industrial property and very expensive houses where it would seem reasonable for the purchaser to obtain his own structural survey.[17] However, in *Beaumont* v. *Humberts*,[18] the Court of Appeal rejected the dividing line between modestly priced and more expensive dwellings and held that a duty of care is owed to all house purchasers.

In *Harris* v. *Wyre Forest*, Mr and Mrs Harris purchased a small terraced house for £9000 with the aid of a 95 per cent mortgage from the defendant council. They completed and signed the council's standard mortgage application form and paid the inspection fee. The form stated that the valuation was confidential and intended solely for the benefit of the council and that no responsibility was accepted by the council for the value or condition of the property by reason of such inspection and report. It also advised the mortgagors to instruct their own surveyors, though it was found that neither Mr nor Mrs Harris read those words. The council's valuation surveyor valued the house at £9450 and recommended a mortgage subject to certain repairs. He noticed various signs of settlement but concluded that all the symptoms were referable to movement which had long since ceased. The purchasers were not shown the report but they were subsequently offered, and accepted, a mortgage by the council. Three years later they attempted to sell the house, but a survey revealed that structural repairs amounting to £13,000 were required. The house was regarded as uninhabitable and thus unsaleable.

This case differed from *Smith* v. *Bush* in that the valuation was carried out by an in-house valuer. Essentially this raised the issue of whether or not a mortgagee owes a duty of care to a mortgagor in respect of a valuation report on the property to be negotiated. In *Odder* v. *Westbourne Park Building Society*,[19] Harman J held that a building society owed no duty of care to purchasers in respect of a valuation report for mortgage purposes prepared by the chairman of the society. The Lordships in Harris overruled that decision and concluded that the valuer owed a duty of care to the purchasers and that the local authority, as his employers, were vicariously liable for breach of that duty.[20] In coming to this conclusion, the view of the Court of Appeal of Northern Ireland in *Curran* v. *Northern Ireland Co-ownership Housing Association Ltd*[21] that a mortgagee who accepts a fee to obtain a valuation of a small house owes no duty of care to the mortgagor in the selection of the valuer to whom he entrusts the work, was disapproved.[22]

The theoretical basis of the valuer's duty in tort

Although the existence of the duty owed by a valuer to a mortgagor can now be stated with a reasonable degree of certainty the same cannot be said of its conceptual basis. There has in fact been considerable criticism of this duty, judicial as well as professional, and in *Smith* v. *Bush*, etc. there were differences of emphasis in the speeches on this point. Lords Templeman and Jauncey traced in detail the historical development of the valuer's tortious duty of care and if the difficulties in defining the rationale of that duty are to be fully appreciated then it is necessary to recount this history.

In *Cann* v. *Willson*,[23] a valuer instructed by a mortgagor sent his report to the mortgagee, who made an advance in reliance on the valuation. The valuer was held liable in the tort of negligence to the mortgagee for failing to carry out the valuation with reasonable care and skill on the ground that he knew that the valuation was for the purpose of a mortgage and would be relied on by the mortgagee. In *Le Lievre* v. *Gould*,[24] however, the Court of Appeal declared that decision to be wrong on the ground that it was inconsistent with, and overruled by, *Derry* v. *Peek*,[25] where the House of Lords held that the maker of a statement could only be liable in the tort of deceit when the statement was made with knowledge of its falsity or recklessly. In other words, there could be no liability where the maker of a statement possessed an honest belief in its truth, i.e. where the statement was made negligently or innocently.

This remained the law for another 70 years and various attempts to argue that the law had changed following the decision of the House of Lords in *Donoghue* v. *Stevenson*[26] failed. The one exception was the famous dissenting judgement of Denning LJ in *Candler* v. *Crane, Christmas and Co.*[27] In that case, the accountants of a company were asked by the company to prepare their accounts expressly for the purpose of being shown to a potential investor in the company. Denning LJ said that the accountants owed a duty to the investor to exercise reasonable care and skill in preparing the draft accounts. In considering the question of whom accountants owe a duty to he said:

> They owe a duty, of course, to their employer or client, and also, I think, to any third person to whom they themselves show the accounts, or to whom they know their employer is going to show the accounts so as to induce him to invest money or take some other action on them. I do not think, however, the duty can be extended still further so as to include strangers of whom they have heard nothing and to whom their employer without their knowledge may choose to show their accounts.[28]

The most significant development in the relationship of professional persons to third parties occurred in the seminal case of *Hedley Byrne & Co.* v. *Heller & Partners*. Since that decision, it has been clear that the absence of a contractual relationship is no longer a bar to a successful claim for economic loss resulting from a negligent mis-statement. The plaintiffs were advertising agents who booked advertising space for their clients, Easipower Ltd, on terms which stated that they were to be personally liable if Easipower defaulted. The plaintiffs sought advice on the financial standing of Easipower from Easipower's bankers, the defendants. The defendants, who knew the purpose of the plaintiff's request, carelessly stated that

Easipower was financially sound. As a result, the plaintiffs, in reliance on the banker's reference, placed orders for advertising space to the value of £17,000. Easipower defaulted and the plaintiffs were personally liable for this sum. They sought to recover this sum from the defendant bankers, in an action based on the defendants' negligence. The House of Lords held that the defendants owed a duty of care to the plaintiffs, but since that advice had been given expressly 'without responsibility' there was no liability. The essential principle of this case is that a duty of care is owed in the making of statements if there is 'a special relationship' between the parties. The precise nature and extent of such a relationship has provided much scope for academic discussion and for subsequent judicial development. In *Hedley Byrne* itself, their Lordships did not provide a unanimous formulation of this relationship; their speeches differ as to its precise conceptual basis, though the overall approach taken was one of caution.

Lord Reid said that a special relationship existed:

> Where it is plain that the party seeking information or advice was trust-
> ing the other to exercise such a degree of care as the circumstances
> required, where it was reasonable for him to do that, and where the
> other gave the information or advice when he knew or ought to know
> that the enquirer was relying on him.[29]

Lord Reid went on to say that a reasonable man, knowing that his skill and judgement were being relied on, had three courses open to him. He could stay silent and decline to give the information or advice sought; he could provide an answer with a qualification that no responsibility was accepted; or he could answer without such qualification. Lord Reid said that if he adopted the last course he must be held to have accepted responsibility for his answer being given carefully or to have accepted a relationship with the inquirer which requires him to exercise such care as the circumstances require.

Lord Morris expressed the special relationship in the following words:

> My Lords, I consider that it follows and that it should now be regarded
> as settled that if someone possessed of a special skill undertakes, quite
> irrespective of contract, to apply that skill for the assistance of another
> person who relies upon such skill, a duty of care will arise. The fact that
> the service is to be given by means of or by the instrumentality of words
> can make no difference. Furthermore, if in a sphere in which a person is
> so placed that others could reasonably rely upon his judgement or his
> skill or upon his ability to make careful inquiry, a person takes it upon
> himself to give information or advice, or allows his information of
> advice to be passed on to another person who, as he knows or should
> know, will place reliance upon it, then a duty of care will arise.[30]

Lord Devlin, in his speech, stressed that the special relationship is not a responsibility imposed by law upon certain types of persons or in certain sets of situations. Rather, he went on, it is a responsibility that is voluntarily accepted or undertaken. In the key passage of the speech, Lord Devlin said:

> ... wherever there is a relationship equivalent to contract, there is a duty to care.[31]

The speeches do not make it clear whether it is the assumption of responsibility on the part of the maker of the statement or reliance by the party seeking the information or advice that is the foundation of the relationship. Two points are, however, clear from the speeches. First the special relationship is not limited to cases of fiduciary relationship. Secondly, their Lordships were in general agreement that the concept of reasonable foreseeability as the basis of a duty of care for acts as set out in the speech of Lord Atkin in *Donoghue* v. *Stevenson*[32] had little bearing on the problem of negligent mis-statement.

The implications of the decision in *Hedley Byrne* for the disclosure by a building society to a house-buyer of a mortgage valuation report have been the subject of much debate. The decision of Park J in *Yianni* v. *Evans* was a landmark in that debate. His judgement is interesting on two counts. First, he applied Lord Wilberforce's well known two-stage test to the facts and held that there was a sufficient degree of proximity between the surveyor and the mortgagor for a duty of care to arise. Secondly, he seemed to greatly extend the scope of the concept of reasonable reliance by stating that there was a sufficient degree of proximity between the surveyor and the mortgagor for a duty of care to arise, principally because evidence showed that most mortgagors did not arrange to have their own independent survey carried out and therefore the surveyor knew, or ought to have known, that the mortgagor would rely on his report to the building society.

That reasoning was subsequently criticised on the grounds that Park J's view of reasonable reliance was overgenerous; the mortgagor had not asked the building society for advice and the purpose of the survey was to assess the value of the security offered for the loan. In *Harris* v. *Wyre Forest*, Kerr LJ referred to the 'inherent jurisprudential weakness' of the reasoning in *Yianni* and subjected it to intensive scrutiny.[33] Significantly, however, he went on to say that the particular circumstances of purchasers of houses with the assistance of loans from building societies or local authorities are capable of leading to a different analysis and conclusion. In these circumstances it is now the practice of the lending institutions to show their valuer's report to the intending purchaser. Thus, in *Roberts* v. *Hampson & Co.*,[34] Ian Kennedy J said that the valuer knew, from the fact that a building society survey was being undertaken, that it was very unlikely that the intending purchaser was relying on an independent survey of the property. In *Davies* v. *Parry*,[35] McNeill J concluded that a sufficiently proximate relationship existed between the valuer and the purchaser in that case because the valuer had known that his report would be made available to the purchaser and there was only a one in four chance that he would arrange for a structural survey to be carried out.

In *Smith* v. *Bush*, Lord Templeman said that the relationship between the valuer and the purchaser is 'akin to contract' in the sense that the valuer assumes responsibility to both mortgages and purchaser, because he knows that the valuation fee has been paid for by the purchaser and the purchaser will probably rely on the valuation in deciding whether or not to purchase the house. Lord Griffiths doubted whether the voluntary assumption of responsibility was likely to be a helpful or realistic test in most cases.[36] He went on to say that a duty of care for advice was owed where three conditions were satisfied: (1) it must be foreseeable that if the advice is negligent the recipient is likely to suffer damage; (2) there must be a sufficiently proximate relationship between the parties; and (3) it must be just and reasonable to impose the liability.[37] Lord Griffiths said that in the case of a surveyor valuing a small house for a building society or local authority the application of all three criteria led to the imposition of a duty of care. The requirement of foreseeability was satisfied because, if the valuation was negligent and relied upon, the purchaser would obviously suffer economic loss. The necessary proximity arose from the fact that the surveyor must know that the overwhelming probability is that the purchaser will rely on the valuation. It was just and reasonable for a duty of care to be imposed because the advice was given in a professional, as opposed to a social, context and there was no danger of creating liability in an indeterminate amount to an indefinite class. Lord Jauncey drew attention to the difference between the cases of *Cann* v. *Willson*, *Candler* v. *Crane, Christmas & Co.* and *Hedley Byrne* v. *Heller*, and *Smith* v. *Bush*.[38] In each of the three former cases, there was direct contact between the provider of the advice on the one hand and the plaintiff or his agent on the other hand; in *Smith* v. *Bush*, however, there was no direct contact between Mrs Smith and the valuer. Lord Jauncey thought that the relationship between valuer and purchaser was not 'equivalent to contract' in the sense used by Lord Devlin in *Hedley Byrne* v. *Heller*, but there was sufficient proximity between the parties for the valuer to be deemed to have assumed responsibility towards her; the valuer knew that Mrs Smith would be likely to rely on his valuation without obtaining independent advice and she had paid the valuation fee.

Given the lack of agreement on a test for determining when a duty of care for words arose, it is hardly surprising that *Smith* v. *Bush* has proved of little significance in the development of the tort of negligent mis-statement as a whole. Of more significance in that respect was the decision of the House of Lords in *Caparo Industries plc* v. *Dickman*,[39] where it was held that auditors owe no duty of care either to members of the public or to existing shareholders who buy shares in a company in reliance on its audited accounts. Their Lordships restated the test for the existence of a duty of care for statements in the following terms:

(i)   the person making the statement must be fully aware of the nature of the transaction which the plaintiff had in mind;

(ii) he must know that the statement would be communicated to the plaintiff either directly or indirectly;

(iii) he must know that it is very likely that the plaintiff would rely on that statement; and

(iv) it is so relied on by the plaintiff to his detriment.[40]

In relation to the duty of care of a mortgage valuation surveyor, their Lordships emphasised that the crucial feature of *Smith* v. *Bush*, etc. was that the existence and scope of that duty were limited to the very person and the very transaction which were in the contemplation of the valuer at the time of the valuation, ie. the mortgagor and the purchase of the property. In other words, the facts of the *Smith* v. *Bush* situation met the criteria laid down by the *Caparo* test.

It must be pointed out that the status of the *Caparo* test is still uncertain. In *Beaument* v. *Humberts*,[41] where the defendant valuer was instructed by the mortgagee bank to carry out a valuation for insurance reinstatement purposes as well as a mortgage valuation, the question of whether the valuer owed a duty of care to the mortgagers was decided without reference to the test laid down by the House of Lords in *Caparo*. Instead the duty issue was approached on the basis of the three-stage test first put forward by the Court of Appeal in *Caparo*, i.e.:

(i)   it must be foreseeable that if the advice is negligent the recipient is likely to suffer damage;

(ii) there must be a sufficiently proximate relationship between the parties; and

(iii) it must be just and reasonable to impose the liability.

The overall result of these decisions is that the scope of surveyors' liability is now much wider than that of other professional advisers, in particular accountants. The reasons for this disparity in treatment seem to rest largely on policy factors. These factors were explored by Hoffman J (as he then was) in *Morgan Crucible Co.* v. *Hill Samuel*,[42] He said that the differences between *Smith* v. *Bush* and *Caparo* consist in the different economic relationships between the parties and the nature of the markets in which they were operating. He sets out these factors in the following terms:

> First, Mr. Smith had paid for the survey; although he had no contract with the surveyor, the relationship was, as Lord Templeman said, 'akin to contract'. Economically there was no distinction. Caparo Industries plc, on the other hand, had not paid for the audit.
>
> Second, the typical plaintiff in a *Smith* v. *Bush* type case is a person of modest means and making the most expensive purchase of his or her life. He is very unlikely to be insured against the manifestation of inher-

ent defects. The surveyor can protect himself relatively easily by insurance. The take-over bidder, on the other hand, is an entrepreneur taking high risks for high rewards and while some accountants may be able to take out sufficient insurance, others may not. Furthermore, the take-over bidder is a limited liability company and the accountants are individuals for whom, save so far as they are covered by insurance, liability would mean personal ruin.

Thirdly, the imposition of liability on surveyors would probably not greatly increase their insurance and push up the cost of surveys because the typical buyer who relies on a building society survey is buying a relatively modest house. Take-overs on the Stock Exchange involve huge amounts and the effects on accountants' insurance and fees are unpredictable. [43]

In brief, Hoffman J's policy factors are that the typical mortgagor is more likely to be in need of protection from the law than the take-over bidder and the fact that the damages awarded against a negligent mortgage valuation surveyor are more easily insurable than the damages awarded against a negligent auditor.[44]

In *Smith* v. *Bush* and *Caparo*, there was criticism by some of the Law Lords of the concept of assumption of responsibility by the defendant as the basis of a special relationship. However, in subsequent decisions the House of Lords has recognised the importance of this concept rather than reliance by the plaintiff as the basis of negligent mis-statement. In *Henderson* v. *Merrett Syndicates Ltd*, Lord Goff said:

> In addition, the concept provides its own explanation why there is no problem in cases of this kind about liability for pure economic loss; for if a person assumes responsibility to another in respect of certain services, there is no reason why he should not be liable in damages for that other in respect of economic loss which flows from the negligent performance of those services. It follows that, once the case is identified as falling within the *Hedley Byrne* principle, there should be no need to embark upon any further enquiry whether it is 'fair, just or reasonable' to impose liability for economic loss ...[45]

In *White* v. *Jones*, Lord Browne-Wilkinson also emphasised the importance of the concept of assumption of responsibility. He said:

> ... the crucial element [in *Hedley Byrne*] was that, by choosing to answer the enquiry, the bank had assumed to act, and thereby created the special relationship on which the necessary duty of care was founded.
>
> ... If the responsibility for the task is assumed by the defendant he thereby creates a special relationship between himself and the plaintiff in relation to which the law (not the defendant) attaches a duty to carry out carefully the task so assumed.[46]

THE STANDARD OF CARE

The Bolam *test*

In circumstances where a duty of care is owed the key question is, what must a surveyor do to meet that duty? The essential principle governing this aspect of surveyors' liability is that a surveyor or valuer must carry out his duties with the care and skill of an ordinarily competent member of his profession. This is often referred to as the *Bolam* standard, after the dictum of McNair J. in *Bolam* v. *Friern Barnet Hospital Management Committee*:

> The test is the standard of the ordinary skilled man exercising and professing to have that special skill. A man need not possess the highest expert skill at the risk of being found negligent ... it is sufficient if he exercises the ordinary skill of an ordinary competent man exercising that particular art.[47]

This test of professional negligence was approved by the House of Lords in *Whitehouse* v. *Jordan*,[48] a case involving medical negligence. In *Maynard* v. *West Midlands Regional Health Authority*,[49] another medical negligence case, Lord Scarman endorsed the following passage from Lord President Clyde's judgement in *Hunter* v. *Hanley*:

> In the realm of diagnosis and treatment there is ample scope for genuine difference of opinion and one man clearly is not negligent merely because his conclusion differs from that of other professional men ... The true test for establishing negligence in diagnosis or treatment on the part of a doctor is whether he has been proved to be guilty of such failure as no doctor of ordinary skill would be guilty of if acting with ordinary care ...[50]

In *Sidaway* v. *Bethlem Royal Hospital Governors and Others*,[51] the *Bolam* test was applied to the question of what information a medical practitioner must give to a patient about the risks involved in a course of treatment. That is, on deciding whether to warn his patient of any risks inherent in a course of treatment a doctor was required to act in accordance with a practice accepted at the time as proper by a responsible body of medical opinion.

The principles set out in the above medical negligence cases were applied to the valuation of pictures in *Luxmoore-May and Another* v. *Messenger May Baverstock*.[52] In that case, the defendants, a provincial firm of auctioneers and valuers, were asked their opinion as to the sale value of two paintings. A fine art consultant valued them at £30 to £50 for the pair. They sold for £840. They were subsequently cleaned and auctioned by Sotheby's, who described them as being by George Stubbs. They sold for £88,000. The Court of Appeal held that the defendants had not been negligent.

In his judgement, Slade LJ said that the nature of the legal duty falling on the defendants was set out in the following propositions, which had been submitted to the trial judge and which he had accepted:

1. the required standard of skill and care allows for differing views, and even a wrong view, without the practitioner holding that view (necessarily) being held in breach of his duty;
2. the standard is to be judged by reference only to what may be expected of the general practitioner, not the specialist – here provincial auctioneers, rather than one of the leading auction houses; and
3. compliance with the required standard is to be judged by reference to the actual circumstances confronting the practitioners at the material time, rather than with the benefit of hindsight.[53]

Slade LJ went on to say that the valuation of pictures of which the artist is unknown was pre-eminently a matter of opinion and judgement. He concluded that provided that the valuer has done his job honestly and with due diligence the court should be cautious before finding him negligent in failing to spot a 'sleeper'.

One aspect of the *Bolam* standard that is clear is that a mere error of professional judgement will not *necessarily* amount to negligence. This point was expressed in the following terms by Lord Fraser in *Whitehouse* v. *Jordan*:

> Merely to describe something as an error of judgement tells us nothing about whether it is negligent or not. The true position is that an error of judgement may, or may not, be negligent; it depends on the nature of the error. If it is one that would not have been made by a reasonably competent professional man professing to have the standard and type of skill that the defendant held himself out as having, and acting with ordinary care, then it is negligent. If, on the other hand, it is an error that a man acting with ordinary care, might have made, then it is not negligence.[54]

For a valuation to be negligent it must be outside the range of valuation to which a reasonably competent valuer could properly come. This point was expressed by Staughton LJ in *Nykredit Mortgage Bank plc* v. *Edward Erdman Group Ltd* as follows:

> There was evidence, which the judge accepted, that careful and skilled valuers did not inevitably arrive at precisely the same answer. If a given figure is taken as the true value, the range within which a valuer could arrive at some different amount without negligence was plus or minus 15 per cent.[55]

In *Craneheath Securities* v. *York Montague Ltd*,[56] restaurant premises were valued at £5.25 million on the basis of turnover for the purposes of a loan. The restaurant later closed and the property was sold for £475,000. The plaintiffs claim that the defendants' valuation was negligent was dismissed by the trial judge. The plaintiffs appealed contending that there were errors in certain stages of the defendants' valuation. The Court of Appeal dismissed the plaintiffs' appeal. The plaintiffs' submission that if the court were satisfied that there were a sufficient number of errors in the defendants' valuation the court should infer that the valuer's final result was wrong, was rejected. The Court of Appeal held that it was not enough for the plaintiffs to show that there were errors at some stages of the valuation, unless they could also show that the final valuation was wrong. Balcombe LJ said:

> Valuation is not a science, it is an art, and the instinctive 'feel' for the market of an experienced valuer is not something which can be ignored.[57]

It is quite common for there to be differing views within a profession about the way certain of its functions should be carried out. In *Zubaida* v. *Hargreaves*,[58] a valuer was appointed to determine the rent of a restaurant on a rent review. The Court of Appeal held that he was not negligent in using as comparables the rent of similar shop units, as that was a practice which a competent and respected body of professional opinion accepted as proper. In applying the *Bolam* test, Hoffman LJ stated:

> In an action for negligence against an expert, it is not enough to show that another expert would have given a different answer. Valuation is not an exact science; it involves questions of judgment on which experts may differ without forfeiting their claim on professional competence. The fact that a judge may think one approach better than another is therefore irrelevant ... The issue is not whether the expert's valuation was right, in the sense of being the figure which a judge after hearing the evidence would determine. It is whether he has acted in accordance with practices which are regarded as acceptable by a respectable body of opinion in his profession.[59]

In *Michael Hyde and Associates Ltd* v. *J.D. Williams & Co Ltd*,[60] the Court of Appeal held that if a profession embraced different views then the competence of a professional person was to be gauged by the lowest acceptable standard. Sedley LJ said of the *Bolam* test:

> [it] was typically appropriate where the neglect was said to lie in conscious choice of available courses made by a trained professional.
>
> It was typically inappropriate where it was in an oversight that the neglect was said to lie. That was because it was likely to be much easier to characterise the former than the latter as errors of judgement.

The *Bolam* standard will sometimes require a professional person to warn his client that his advice should be treated with caution. That was the ruling of the Court of Appeal in *Merivale Moore plc and Another* v. *Strutt & Parker*.[61]

The defendant valuers advised the plaintiffs on the purchase of a commercial property in the West End of London. They based their valuation on the rental value of the property, converting that into a capital value by the use of a figure for percentage yield, which was 7.5 per cent. This method of valuation led to an overvaluation of the property. The trial judge, Mr Graeme Hamilton QC, found that the use of the figure of 7.5 per cent was not in itself negligent, but the defendants were negligent in not stating that this figure carried an enhanced risk and in not attaching an appropriate qualification or warning to it. The judge's decision was upheld by the Court of Appeal, where Buxton LJ said:

> there was no doubt that if the plaintiffs had been told anything of the process whereby the yield figure had been arrived at they would have rejected the valuation. A qualification would have had the effect not merely as a warning that the advice should have been treated with caution, but in effect a warning that the whole basis of the valuation could not be vouched for.

The *Bolam* standard seems to imply that the courts are prepared to accept that professional negligence is a question to be determined by evidence from other practitioners. It is generally accepted, however, that the courts have the power to set the standard required of a profession, though in practice a court will rely heavily on expert evidence and any codified standards adopted by a profession.

Until 31 December 1995 chartered surveyors were under a professional duty to comply with all practice statements published by the Royal Institute of Chartered Surveyors (RICS). These practice statements were contained in the RICS's *Statement of Asset Valuation Practice and Guidance Notes* (the 'Red Book') and its *Manual of Valuation Guidance Notes* (the 'White Book'). Neither of these publications applied to valuations of domestic houses or valuations for mortgages or loans secured on commercial property.

With effect from 31 December 1995 these two publications were replaced by one publication, the RICS *Appraisal and Valuation Manual*.[62] This manual is divided into two sections:

– Section One, which contains Practice Statements; and
– Section Two, which contains Guidance Notes on good valuation practice.

Compliance with Section One is made mandatory by the RICS. Compliance with Section Two is not mandatory but the RICS is at pains in the introduction to the manual to stress that surveyors should depart from its provisions only if they have good reason:

> 'when an allegation of professional negligence is made against a surveyor, the court is likely to take account of any relevant practice statement published by the RICS in deciding whether or not the surveyor has acted with reasonable competence. Failure to comply with practice statements is likely to be adjudged negligent.'

In addition to the 1995 RICS *Appraisal and Valuation Manual*, the RICS and the Incorporated Society of Valuers and Auctioneers (ISVA) have published a number of guidance notes on domestic and commercial surveys and valuations. They are as follows:

– *Buying a home*,[63] which describes the nature of a valuation and the purposes for which a Home Buyer's Survey is provided;
– *Comments and Guidance on the Standard Conditions of Engagement and Guidance on Reporting*;[64] and
– *Building Surveys of Residential Property: A Guidance Note.*[65]

Despite the warning of the RICS in the introduction to its *Appraisal and Valuation Manual*, the exact legal status of these practice statements and guidance notes remains uncertain. Whether compliance with these guidelines will be sufficient to satisfy the duty imposed upon valuers has yet to be determined by the courts, but in *PK Finans International (UK) Ltd* v. *Andrew Downs & Co. Ltd* the judge passed the following comment upon them:

> These ... are not to be regarded as a statute. I suspect that they are as much for the protection of surveyors as anything else, in that they set out various recommendations which, if followed, it is hoped will protect the surveyor from the unpleasantness of being sued. *In any event, mere failure to comply with the guidance notes does not necessarily constitute negligence.* [author's italics][66]

Whatever their true legal status, it has been pointed out that one should not be naive about their true purpose: not simply improving standards in the surveying profession, but providing surveyors with a potential defence against claims for negligence in the conduct of surveys and valuation.[67]

In concluding this discussion of the *Bolam* test, three points need to be emphasised about it in the context of surveyors. First, it is the standard which the surveyor must meet whether his duty is owed in contract to his client or in tort to a third party. Secondly, it is a negligence standard and, as such, this aspect of surveyors' liability is an application of the ordinary principles of negligence. Thirdly, in those circumstances where a surveyor owes a duty of care to a third party the scope of that duty is governed by the terms of the contract which he has made with his client.

The surveyor's contract

The first point of reference in determining whether or not a surveyor has been negligent is the contract which he has entered into. The basic obligation which the law imposes upon a surveyor is that he must carry out his instructions with reasonable care and skill. In other words, in determining whether or not a surveyor is guilty of negligence, it is first necessary to know what he was employed to do. If he was employed to carry out a valuation survey then his duty is to conduct that kind of survey with the standard of care and skill which would be expected of an ordinary competent surveyor who performs valuations surveys. This point is illustrated by *Sutcliffe* v. *Sayer*.[68] In that case the plaintiffs, realising that the house which they wished to buy was priced rather lower than other apparently comparable properties, asked the defendant, a local estate agent who was experienced but unqualified, to report on its price and any defects which might affect its value. The defendant identified various defects but none the less recommended a purchase at about the asking price. The plaintiffs went ahead with the purchase at this price, but three years later when they put the property on the market they found that it was unsaleable because it was built on a substratum of peat (a factor which the defendant had not mentioned). The Court of Appeal held that the defendant was not negligent; the evidence established that his valuation of the property was accurate and he had not been asked to do anything more, such as investigating structural factors affecting resaleability.

The essentials of the negligence standard

The problem with the concept of reasonable care and skill is that it is difficult to determine in advance what must be done in a given situation to meet that requirement. Each case will turn on its own facts and in that sense the question of whether a surveyor has been negligent is one of fact rather than law. However, the law does lay down general guidelines to aid the courts in determining whether or not the standard of reasonable care and skill has been met in a particular situation, and in that respect the standard is a legal standard. A detailed treatment of these guidelines can be found in any text on the law of tort and it is necessary here only to outline them. They are:

(i)   unforeseeable harm;
(ii) the magnitude of the risk;
(iii) the social utility of the defendant's conduct; and
(iv) the practicability of precautions.

First, if the danger could not reasonably have been foreseen then the defendant has not acted negligently.[69] Secondly, if the damage is foreseeable then the defendant is only negligent if he fails to exercise a degree of care which is commensurate with the risk attaching to the activity concerned; the greater the risk of harm the greater the precautions that need to be taken.[70] Thirdly, the social utility of the defendant's activity may justify taking greater risks than would otherwise be the case.[71] Fourthly, reasonableness involves striking a balance between the risks involved and the expenditure required to eliminate, or at any rate reduce, that risk.[72]

It now remains to examine how the courts have applied these general principles to the various surveys undertaken by surveyors.

The HBRV

As already stated, this is a modified form of structural survey. The question of the difference between the two kinds of survey was discussed in *Cross* v. *David Martin & Mortimer*.[73] In that case, the plaintiffs, a husband and wife, employed the defendant surveyor to conduct a HBRV on a house that they were considering purchasing. He reported that there was no evidence of structural fault or significant disrepair and they went ahead with the purchase. After moving in, the plaintiffs discovered that the lounge floor was irregular and that the hall had a noticeable 'hump'. Independent advice revealed subsidence, misalignments of doors on the first floor, and problems with the loft conversion. Phillips J found that the defendant was negligent on all three of the above counts, although he added that the survey was not slap-dash and was not a reflection on his general competence. In general terms, the significance of the case is that in coming to this decision the judge noted the view of an RICS Working Party that the same level of expertise was expected from a surveyor carrying out a HBRV as for a structural survey. This seems a surprising piece of evidence, given that a HBRV is less comprehensive than a structural survey and consequently carried out for a lower fee. The decision seems contrary to the general principles outlined above.

Mortgage valuations

It is the standard required of a reasonably competent mortgage valuation which has caused the most concern in recent years. Following the decision in *Yianni* it was feared by surveyors that a mortgage valuation would have to become in effect a structural survey. These fears were increased by Kennedy J's (infamous) description of a competent mortgage valuation in *Roberts* v. *J. Hampson & Co*.[74] After stating the general principle that a mortgage valuation was an appraisal by a professional man and that his basic duty was to take reasonable care in providing a valuation, the judge went on to say:

The second aspect of the problem concerns moving furniture and lifting carpets. Here again, as it seems to me, the position the law adopts is simple. If a surveyor misses a defect because its signs are hidden, that is a risk that his client must accept. But if there is specific ground for suspicion and the trail of suspicion leads behind furniture or under carpets, the surveyor must take reasonable steps *to follow the trail* [author's italics] until he has all the information which is reasonable for him to have before making his valuation.[75]

That *dictum* was quoted with approval by Lord Templeman in *Smith* v. *Bush*. However, Lord Griffiths defined the valuer's duty in more moderate terms:

the inspection carried out is a visual one designed to reveal any obvious defects in the property which must be taken into account when comparing the value of the property with other similar properties in the neighbourhood ... It is only defects which are observable by a careful visual examination that have to be taken into account.[76]

Recent decisions show that it is the more moderate approach which is prevailing in the courts. In *Whalley* v. *Roberts & Roberts*,[77] the plaintiff mortgagors purchased a detached bungalow, built in 1978, with the aid of a mortgage from the Royal Bank of Scotland. The valuation for the mortgage was made by the defendant firm of surveyors. The mortgage valuation report stated that its purpose was to provide a valuation for a mortgage and was not a structural survey. It reported the standard of construction and the condition of the main structure to be satisfactory. On the day that the plaintiffs moved in they noticed that the floor of the bungalow sloped, though they had not noticed this on visits before moving in. The valuer's report made no mention of this defect and he said in evidence that it was not something for which he would have checked unless there was evidence of movement. In fact the fall from right to left, looking at the bungalow was 3 1/2 in. over a total width of 23 ft 6 in. There were no signs of subsidence but there was evidence of steps taken to camouflage the existence of the slope. Auld J after referring to Lord Griffiths's dictum in *Smith* v. *Bush*, held that the valuer had not been negligent. In essence, this judgement illustrated the principle that a mortgage valuer is not negligent if the risk of harm suffered by the plaintiff was not reasonably foreseeable.

In *Lloyd* v. *Butler*,[78] the plaintiff purchased a filthy and dilapidated property for £37,500 with the aid of a mortgage of £20,000 from the Alliance Building Society. The society instructed the defendant surveyor to carry out a mortgage valuation of the property. He reported that although it was a poorly maintained house of very basic quality it provided the basis for a comfortable home and was acceptable as a security in its present condition. In a box on the report form headed 'Essential Repairs' he wrote 'None'. The plaintiff, relying on this, completed the purchase, but when, with the aid of a builder, she started to repair and improve the house she discovered a number of serious defects, in particular that it was heavily infested with woodworm, many of the roof tiles needed replacing, the bay window was in a state of collapse, and the wiring and central heating pipes needed to be replaced. Henry J in his judgement set out his view of the nature and scope of a mortgage valuation. He said:

> It is clearly not a structural survey; it is a valuation. It is taken on the basis of the inspection which on average should not take longer than 20–30 minutes. It is effectively a walking inspection by someone with a knowledgeable eye, experienced in practice, who knows where to look ... to detect either trouble or the potential form of trouble. *He does not necessarily have to follow up every trail* [author's italics] to discover whether there is trouble or the extent of any such trouble. But where such an inspection can reasonably show a potential trouble or the risk of potential trouble, it seems to me that it is necessary ... to alert the purchaser to that risk, because the purchaser will be relying on [the valuation report].[79]

He held that the valuer had been negligent for failing to warn of the defects in the property.

The decisions in *Whalley* and *Lloyd* provide evidence that the courts are applying the basic principles of negligence to the question of the standard of care required of a mortgage valuer. In both cases the judges seemed well aware that a mortgage valuation was only a limited survey carried out for a limited price and did not amount to a structural survey. In practical terms the significance of the decisions can be stated as follows:

(i)   if there are visible defects in the property or defects are discovered, the valuer's duty is to warn the mortgagee and the mortgagor of those defects, rather than investigate fully as in a structural survey; and

(ii) there is no duty on the valuer to discover unusual defects in the property, i.e. to guard against unusual risks.

A surveyor must, however, take steps to acquire the necessary information to make a competent mortgage valuation survey. This is a point well illustrated by *Izzard and Another* v. *Field Palmer (a firm) and Others*.[80] In that case, in 1988 the plaintiffs applied to Allied Dunbar for a mortgage to finance the purchase of a maisonette which had been constructed according to the Jesperson 12M system which combined large concrete panels and timber cladding. In 1988 it was known that such a construction system gave rise to problems and there were articles in the professional literature about those problems. Allied Dunbar instructed the defendant surveyor to provide a simple valuation report. In his report, the surveyor noted that the property was built to the Jesperson system but did not provide any other additional warning. He certified that the property was suitable for mortgage purposes. The plaintiffs purchased the property, but parts of it subsequently failed. The trial judge, Scott-Baker J, accepted the evidence of a building surveyor expert for the plaintiffs that a reasonably competent surveyor, carrying out a mortgage valuation report in 1988, would have armed himself with the requisite knowledge from the literature or taken other appropriate steps to obtain the necessary information to make a skilled professional valuation. The Court of Appeal upheld the judge's decision.

One of the most important points to emerge from this case is Scott-Baker J's view of the surveyor's argument that he was doing only what other surveyors would have done, and were doing, in the circumstances. The judge rejected this defence and Kennedy LJ unequivocally supported him on that point:

> In many cases, what other professionals do is persuasive evidence as to what is acceptable (see, for example, *Bolitho (Dec'd)* v. *City and Hackney Health Authority* [1998] AC 232, at p.241), but such evidence cannot be conclusive, and here the weight of evidence was clearly as the judge found it to be.[81]

Later in his judgement, Kennedy LJ said this:

> The incompetent do not set the standards. Neither do the experts. Nothing in the judgement suggests to me that the judge failed to address himself to the correct standard, which is that of reasonable competence.[82]

The approach of the court at first instance and the Court of Appeal in *Izzard* is a robust one. It shows that the courts no longer regard the *Bolam* standard as a matter solely for the professions. Expert evidence is persuasive as to whether or not that standard has been reached, but it is not conclusive; in the final analysis, whether or not the *Bolam* standard has been met is a matter for the court.

Insurance valuations

In *Beaument* v. *Humberts*,[83] the Court of Appeal had to decide the meaning of valuation for insurance re-instatement purposes of a Grade II listed building. The appeal judges said that three meanings could be given to 're-instatement':

(i) an exact copy;
(ii) a replacement which was as near as practicable to an exact copy; or
(iii) a sensible reconstruction in the same style but redesigned in parts to make it more liveable and more convenient.

The valuer adopted the third of these approaches and the majority of the Court of Appeal held that this was not negligent. In their view, the issue turned on the instructions given to the valuer, which were to provide the value for insurance re-instatement purposes; that did not mean an estimate for an exact copy. Dillon LJ in his minority judgement, favoured the second of the above approaches. In the author's view, the minority view is to be preferred; if a house is burnt down completely then surely the owner is entitled to have it rebuilt as nearly as possible to its original specification and not just a reconstruction in the same shape and style. However, the wider principle of the case – that the duty owed by a valuer cannot be divorced from the instructions given to him by his client – is sound.

DAMAGES

There are three issues which arise in relation to the question of damages awarded against a surveyor for a negligent survey:

(i)   the appropriate measure of damages;
(ii)   the scope for awarding compensation for distress to the purchaser and the basis on which it should be calculated; and
(iii)   the measure of damages for a mortgagee relying on a negligent survey.

The measure of damages

There are two possible methods of assessing the general damages to be awarded for a negligent survey. First, they can be assessed on the basis of the difference between the price paid for the property and what it was really worth at the time of purchase. Secondly, the damages can be assessed on the basis of the cost of repairing the defects in the property.

The question of which of these two measures is the correct one came before the Court of Appeal in *Phillips* v. *Ward*.[84] There, the plaintiff instructed the defendant surveyor to carry out a structural survey of a property which he was considering for purchase. The surveyor noted various minor defects in his report and valued the property at between £25,000 and £27,000. In reliance upon this report the plaintiff purchased the property for £25,000. It was subsequently discovered that the timbers in the property were badly affected by death-watch beetle and the cost of remedying that defect was estimated to be £7800. The official referee awarded damages of £4000, representing the difference between the surveyor's valuation (£25,000) and its value in its actual condition (£21,000). The Court of Appeal unanimously upheld that award.

The principles underlying their decision were stated in the judgement of Denning LJ (as he then was). He said that the correct measure of damages was the amount of money which will put the plaintiff into as good a position as if the survey had been properly conducted. This was the difference between the value of the property in its assumed good condition and the value in the bad condition which should have been reported. As to whether the cost of the repairs was the correct measure, Denning LJ said:

> if the plaintiff were to recover from the surveyor £7000, it would mean that the plaintiff would get for £18,000 (£25,000 paid less £7000 received) a house and land which were worth £21,000. That cannot be right.[85]

The reasoning of *Phillips* v. *Ward* was unanimously followed by the Court of Appeal in *Perry* v. *Sidney Phillips & Son*.[86]

The difference in value formula for measuring damages has not gone unchallenged and it has been argued that it needs to be qualified in certain situations:

(i)   where there is no market for the property in its defective state of repair; and

(ii) where it is not reasonable to expect the purchaser to place the property on the market once he has bought.

An example of the first of these situations was provided by *Steward* v. *Rapley*.[87] There, the Court of Appeal held that where the defects in the property are such that the ordinary purchaser would not buy without further investigation then the repair costs were the basis for calculating the difference in value. The plaintiff had purchased a house for £58,500, slightly below the defendant surveyor's valuation of £60.000. Shortly after purchase, dry rot was discovered and there was evidence that an open market valuation of the house immediately after that discovery would have been £50,000. The final cost of repairing the house, once the true extent of the rot was discovered, turned out to be £26,800. The Court of Appeal said that diminution in value was the rule to be applied but refused to accept that £50,000 could be taken as the market value and £8,500 (the difference between the alleged market value and purchase price) as the damages payable. The market value for the speculative buyer might have been £50,000 but for the ordinary purchaser, the house had no market value until the full cost of repair had been calculated. Hence, the true market value was the original valuation of £60,000 minus the cost of repair, £26,800, producing a valuation of £33,200. The difference in value measure was then £58,500 (purchase price) minus £33,200 (market value calculated in accordance with the cost of repair). The result was an award of £25,300.

In a number of recent first instance decisions the cost of repair method has been held to be the proper basis for calculating damages.[88] Those decisions raised the question of whether the difference in value method was still the general rule. However, in *Watts* v. *Morrow*,[89] the Court of Appeal robustly defended the difference in value method and unanimously reaffirmed the principle laid down in *Phillips* v. *Ward*.

In *Watts* the plaintiffs, a professional couple, purchased an old farmhouse in Dorset as a second home. They instructed the defendant to carry out a full structural survey. He produced a 27 page report and advised that the valuation was fair. Although the report listed a number of defects and recommended repairs, the defendant said that none of these would be very expensive. Subsequently, it was discovered that the defendant had overlooked a number of defects, in particular the state of the roof, and that it would cost some £33,000 to put them right. The difference in value between the property in the condition the surveyor described and its actual condition in need of repair was £15,000. At first instance Judge Bowsher awarded damages on the basis of the cost of repair (i.e. £33,961). His award was unanimously set aside by the Court of Appeal who substituted damages of £15,000. In so doing they reaffirmed the rule in *Phillips*. Ralph Gibson LJ said that the decision in *Phillips* is based on the principle that it is the task of the Court to award that sum of money which would, as far as possible, put the purchasers of the house in as good a position as if the contract for the survey had been properly fulfilled. He went on to say that the cost of repairs to put right defects negligently not reported may be relevant to proving the market value of the house in its true condition. But if the cost of repairs exceeds the diminution in value then the ruling in *Phillips* prohibits recovery of the excess because it would put the purchasers in the position of recovering damages for breach of warranty that the condition of the house was correctly described by the surveyor, and in the ordinary case no such warranty was given. Bingham LJ agreed, and added that if on learning of defects which should have been, but were not, reported a purchaser decides not to sell the house then it was doubtful if his losses could be laid at the door of the contract-breaker.

Finally in this particular section it should be noted that the cases have involved assessing damages for the clients of negligent surveyors. Actions by third parties, such as mortgagors, against surveyors have not raised the question of assessing damages. It has been argued that in circumstances where the mortgage valuer's report is not shown to the buyer the true measure of damages is the difference (if any) between the actual value of the property and the mortgage loan.[90]

Damages for distress and inconvenience

It seems now to be an accepted principle that damages can be awarded under this heading, but the crucial question is, on what basis are they made?

In *Perry* v. *Sydney Phillips*, Lord Denning justified the award of a small sum for distress resulting from the purchase of a defective property on the ground that 'if a man buys a house for his own occupation on the surveyor's advice that it is sound and then finds out that it is in a deplorable condition, it is reasonably foreseeable that he will be most upset.' Kerr LJ justified damages for distress in narrower terms, namely that physical consequences to the purchasers were foreseeable as a result of the negligence.

In *Hayes* v. *Dodd*,[91] Staughton LJ stated that distress awards should be made only where the object of the contract was comfort, pleasure or the relief of discomfort. In *Watts*, Judge Bowsher sought to award damages for distress on the basis of that principle. He stated:

> A prospective buyer of a house goes to a surveyor not just to be advised on the financial advisability of one of the most important transactions of his life but also to receive reassurance that when he buys the house he will have 'peace' of mind and freedom from distress. [92]

The Court of Appeal in *Watts* v. *Morrow* stated the grounds on which damages for distress and inconvenience could be awarded much more narrowly. They said that such damages were only recoverable for distress caused by physical discomfort resulting from a breach of contract. There was no express or implied promise on the part of the surveyor for the provision of peace of mind or freedom from distress. The law was stated by Bingham LJ in the following terms:

> A contract breaker is not in general liable for any distress, frustration, anxiety, displeasure, vexation, tension or aggravation which his breach of contract may cause to the innocent party ...
>
> But the rule is not absolute. Where the very object of a contract is to provide pleasure, relaxation, peace of mind or freedom from molestation, damages will be awarded if the fruit of the contract is not provided or if the contrary result is procured instead. If the law did not cater for this exceptional category of case it would be defective. A contract to survey the condition of a house for a prospective purchaser does not, however, fall within this exceptional category.
>
> In cases not falling within this exceptional category, damages are in my view recoverable for physical inconvenience and discomfort caused by the breach and mental suffering directly related to that inconvenience and discomfort.[93]

The rule in *Watts* v. *Morrow* was applied by the majority of the Court of Appeal in *Farley* v. *Skinner*.[94] That case concerned a contract between a chartered surveyor and a prospective purchaser to inspect and report on the condition of a property. The contract included a requirement to advise whether the property might be affected by aircraft noise. The surveyor failed to ascertain that the property was a short distance from a navigation beacon and that on occasions, especially at weekends, its use and enjoyment was badly affected by aircraft noise. It was held that this contract was not one to provide pleasure, relaxation or peace of mind and it did not therefore come within that exceptional class of contract for which damages for non-physical distress and annoyance could be awarded. Further, it was held that the evidence did not support a finding of physical discomfort and inconvenience.

Damages for a mortgagee's losses

If a mortgagor defaults on the loan then it is the mortgagee who stands to lose if the valuer has negligently overvalued the property. The principles on which this loss should be assessed were discussed by the House of Lords in *Swingcastle* v. *Gibson*[95] and *Banque Bruxelles Lambert SA* v. *Eagle Star Insurance Co. Ltd.*[96]

As the law stood before the House of Lords' ruling in *Swingcastle*, the lender who advanced money on the strength of a negligent overvaluation was treated differently from a purchaser who bought the property. The principle underlying the lender's position was stated by the Court of Appeal in *Baxter* v. *FW Gapp & Co. Ltd* as follows:

> The measure of damages ... is that which the plaintiff has lost by being led into a disastrous investment.[97]

In *Baxter*, the mortgagees were unable to recover part of the money due to them under the mortgage and the valuers were liable to restore this shortfall and in addition the unpaid interest owed by the borrower at the date when the security was realised.

In *Swingcastle*, the plaintiff finance company lent £10,000 secured on a property which the defendant valuer said was worth £18,000. The loan was regarded by the plaintiffs as a high risk loan and the interest charged was 36.5 per cent rising to 45.6 per cent on everything outstanding if the borrowers fell into arrears. They did fall into arrears and the plaintiffs took possession of the house and sold it a year later for £12,000. They sued the valuer for, among other things, the interest accrued under the mortgage contract, i.e. they calculated how much *should* have been repaid by the time that the property was resold. In the House of Lords, Lord Lowry, with whom their other Lordships agreed, said that *Baxter* v. *Gapp* was 'not an attractive precedent' because its approach seemed contrary to principle. Lord Lowry said that the principle on which damages should be assessed in this case was as follows:

> The aggrieved party was entitled to be placed in the same position as if the wrong had not occurred, and not to receive from the wrongdoer compensation fo lost interest at the rate which the borrower had contracted to observe.[98]

In other words, the lender is due for compensation on the basis of the rate of interest which the money could have earned if it had not been lent to the mortgagors and *not* on the basis of the (high-risk) rate of interest under the terms of the mortgage. To assess damages on this latter basis would make the valuer, in effect, the guarantor of the mortgagors' creditworthiness.

The rule laid down by the House of Lords in *Swingcastle* did not put to rest the controversy over the extent of the valuer's liability for an over-valuation in a falling market. Arguably it appeared to mean that valuers, or any rate their insurers, bore the risk if the property valued fell in value after the valuation.This matter came to a head in the early 1990s when there was a severe depression in the property market, which followed a prolonged rise in property values in the 1980s. In a falling market, the price achieved for a property sold by a mortgagee in possession may well be considerably lower than the amount of the sum advanced on reliance on the valuation. If that valuation was negligent, the lender is tempted to recover all his loss from the valuer, not merely the difference between the actual valuation and the 'true' valuation of the property at the time of the valuation but also the loss occasioned by the falling property market.

The extent of the valuer's liability in these circumstances came before the courts in the (complex) case of *Banque Bruxelles Lambert SA* v. *Eagle Star Insurance Co. Ltd*. This case concerned large loans made by the plaintiff bank for the purchase of three commercial properties. The borrowers defaulted and the bank suffered heavy losses, caused in part by the fall in the property market. The valuations of the three properties were either admitted or found to be negligent in the sense that the valuers had over-valued them. The trial judge, Phillips J, held that the valuers should not be required to bear that part of the bank's loss which was attributable to the fall in the property market. He said in this respect:

> It does not seem to me that such loss can fairly and reasonably be considered as resulting naturally from [the valuers'] failure to report as they should have done. Where a party is contemplating a commercial venture that involves a number of heads of risk and obtains professional advice in respect of one head of risk before embarking on the adventure, I do not see why negligent advice in respect of that head of risk should, in effect, make the adviser the underwriter of the entire adventure.

The Court of Appeal reversed Phillips J's decision and awarded the bank damages for their loss attributable to the fall in the property market. They based their decision on Gage J's analysis of *Baxter* v. *Gapp* in *United Bank of Kuwait* v. *Prudential Property Services Ltd*:

> That decision is clear authority for the proposition that in non-transaction cases the proper measure of damages is the difference between the sum advanced and the sum recovered on the sale of the property, plus any consequential losses and expenses.[99]

The House of Lords overruled the decision of the Court of Appeal and restored the decision of Phillips J. Lord Hoffman, in giving the decision of the House of Lords, held that the duty of the valuers in each case was to provide the plaintiffs with a correct valuation of the property, i.e. the figure which a reasonable valuer would have considered it most likely to fetch if sold on the open market. If a person was under a duty of care to provide information on which someone else would rely he was, if negligent, responsible not for all the consequences of the information being wrong but only for the foreseeable consequences of the information being wrong. Lord Hoffman held that the valuers were not liable for the loss of the bank resulting from the fall in the property market and the essence of his reasoning in this respect is that such loss would have occurred even if the valuers had not been negligent. A valuer, his Lordship said, is liable for the difference between the valuation and the correct valuation at the date of the valuation.

EXCLUSION OF LIABILITY

The expansion of surveyors' liability in tort to third parties shifted the emphasis from whether such duties existed to whether liability for such duties could be excluded. As we have seen, it is standard practice for surveyors who conduct mortgage valuation surveys to include a clause in their report disclaiming responsibility for the report in the event of their negligence and advising morgagors to commission their own independent survey. Clauses which attempt to exclude a restrict liability for negligence are controlled by the Unfair Contract Terms Act 1977 (UCTA). But before discussing the effect of that Act it must first be asked whether its provisions do in fact apply to the clause in question.

The nature of disclaimers

There are two approaches to contractual clauses and notices which disclaim liability for negligence. First they can be regarded as defining primary obligations in contract or as preventing a tortious duty from arising. The second approach to such disclaimers involves the courts in determining whether or not there has been a breach of contract or whether a tortious duty arises and then seeing whether liability for such breach or duty has been effectively excluded.

Since the coming into effect of UCTA, generally the courts have adopted the second approach. However in *Harris* v. *Wyre Forest DC* the Court of Appeal adopted the first approach. They said that although the local authority's valuation of the plaintiffs' house was negligent and although the plaintiffs as purchasers had relied on that valuation, the local authority owed no duty of care to the plaintiffs because the disclaimer in the mortgage application form prevented a duty of care from arising. The appeal court judges

relied on the approach taken to such disclaimers by the House of Lords in
Hedley Byrne v. *Heller* where Lord Devlin stated:

> A man cannot be said voluntarily to be undertaking a responsibility if at
> the very moment when he is said to be accepting it he declares that in
> fact he is not.[100]

The Court of Appeal's approach in *Harris* was widely criticised. To begin
with, it took no account of section 13(1) of UCTA, which prevents the exclusion or restriction of any liability by reference to terms and notices which
exclude or restrict the relevant obligation or duty. The House of Lords in
Harris were not slow to point out this and they went on to say that the Court
of Appeal's approach would seriously undermine UCTA.

Prior to *Harris*, the effect of exclusion clauses on misrepresentations in
estate agents' particulars of sale had been considered by the Court of Appeal
in *Gremdean Properties* v. *Nash*.[101] It was held that a clause excluding liability for such misrepresentations could have two effects. First, they could
apply to negative liability after the representation of fact and reliance had
been proved. Secondly, they could operate to prevent any actual representation from arising in the first place. In *St Marylebone Property Co. Ltd* v.
Payne,[102] where there was a misdescription in an auctioneer's particulars of
sale, the county court judge, Mr Assistant Recorder Boggis QC, preferred the
former interpretation.The judge said that a notice in the auction catalogue,
stating that all location plans are to enable prospective purchasers to locate
the property only and are not intended to depict the extent of the property,
did not prevent a photograph from being a representation of fact of the
general extent of the property being sold.

In *McCullagh* v. *Lane Fox & Partners Ltd*,[103] however, Hobhouse LJ took
the view that a disclaimer in an estate agent's particulars of sale prevented
the estate agent from owing a duty of care to the purchaser for a negligent
mis-statement. The defendants, Lane Fox & Partners Ltd, advertised a house
for sale for £875,000. During a vist to the property by the plaintiff, the defendants provided him with a copy of the sale particulars. They stated that the
property was set in 0.92 of an acre and also contained a disclaimer of
responsibility for statements in the particulars. The plaintiff informed the
defendants that he was intending to demolish the house and rebuild, that he
was prepared to exchange contracts and would not be relying on a survey
report. After exchange of contracts the plaintiff was informed by his architect that the true area of the gardens was 0.48 acre. Hobhouse LJ said that the
defendants' assumption of responsibility for this mis-statement was negatived by the disclaimer. Applying the reasoning in *Hedley Byrne & Co. Ltd* v.
Heller & Partners Ltd, he held that no duty of care was owed by the defendants to the plaintiffs.

It is difficult to draw any rule of wide application from this case in view
of its particular circumstances. Hobhouse LJ laid great stress on the fact that

the plaintiff was a sophisticated and experienced member of the public. He could be assumed to have the benefit of legal advice and representation. He went on to say that in contracts for the purchase of land the purchaser was able, before exchange of contracts, to make enquiries of the vendor. The use of disclaimers by estate agents to insulate them from responsibility for their misrepresentations was normal. The plaintiff in this case 'had complete freedom of contract and was in a position to negotiate on an equal footing with the vendor'. Hobhouse LJ concluded:

> There was no basis for saying, in the context of the present case, that it would be unfair to [the plaintiff] to allow the defendants to rely upon the disclaimer nor that it would be unreasonable. Indeed, since [the plaintiff] expected that the particulars would contain a disclaimer, it would, in my judgment, be unreasonable and unfair to the defendants to allow him to claim against the defendants as if there had been no such disclaimer.[104]

Nourse LJ and Sir Christopher Slade held that on the particular facts no breach of duty of care could have been established even in the absence of a disclaimer.

The effect of UCTA

The provisions governing exclusion of liability for negligence are found in section 2 of the Act. Occasionally a surveyor's negligence may result in personal injury or even death. By section 2(1) any attempt to exclude or limit liability for these losses is void. Generally, however, a surveyor's negligence will result in financial loss. By section 2(2) any attempt to exclude or restrict liability for loss or damage other than death or personal injury resulting from negligence is subject to the requirement of reasonableness contained in the Act. The Act is not very helpful in defining reasonableness in this context, despite the fact that this concept is central to its strategy. Such guidance as there is is contained in section 11. This section distinguishes between contractual terms and non-contractual notices. Under the provisions of section 11(2), a term will satisfy the requirements of reasonableness if it was a fair and reasonable one to be included in the contract having regard to the circumstances which were, or ought reasonably to have been, known to or in the contemplation of the parties to the contract at the time the contract was made. In relation to a notice, under the provisions of section 11(3) the requirement of reasonableness under the Act is that it should be fair and reasonable to allow reliance on it having regard to all the circumstances obtaining when the liability arose or (but for the notice) would have arisen.

Beyond these (limited) provisions it has been left to the courts to work out the exact meaning of reasonableness in the context of excluding liability for negligence. In *Smith* v. *Bush*, etc. the House of Lords had the opportunity to take a comprehensive view of the matter and Lord Griffiths in his speech laid down a number of guidelines for assessing the reasonableness or otherwise of disclaimers in mortgage valuation reports.[105] These guidelines are as follows:

(1)   Were the parties of equal bargaining power? The requirement of reasonableness is more easily discharged in one-off situation between parties of equal bargaining power than in a case where the disclaimer is imposed upon the purchaser who has no effective power to object.

(2)   In the case of advice would it have been reasonably practicable to obtain the advice from an alternative source taking into account considerations of cost and time? Lord Griffiths said that to require a purchaser to obtain his own report would require him to pay twice for the same advice. This would impose a financial strain on people buying at the bottom end of the market, many of whom are first time buyers.

(3)   How difficult is the task being undertaken for which liability is being excluded? Lord Griffiths said that where a difficult or dangerous undertaking with a high risk of failure is involved it may be reasonable to exclude liability. A valuation, however, did not fall into this category and it was not unreasonable to require a valuer to accept responsibility for 'careful visual examination' where only defects which are observable have to be taken into account.

(4)   What are the practical consequences of the decision on the question of reasonableness? Lord Griffiths said that this must involve the ability of the parties to bear the loss involved, which, in turn, raises the question of insurance. In the present case, Lord Griffiths stressed, the loss was limited to the value of a modest house against which it can be expected that the surveyor will be insured. To the purchaser, on the other hand, it could mean a financial catastrophe. Lord Griffiths admitted that denying the surveyor the right to exclude his liability may result in a few more claims and, as a result, some increase in surveyors' insurance premiums. But his Lordship said that this point should not be exaggerated. He concluded that denying a surveyor the right to exclude liability will result in distributing the risk of his negligence among all house purchasers through an increase in his fees to cover insurance, rather than allowing the whole of the risk to fall upon the one unfortunate purchaser.

Lord Griffiths made it plain that in the case of mortgage valuations of *low and moderately priced dwellings* these guidelines pointed to a disclaimer being unreasonable.

   The decision of the House of Lords in *Smith* v. *Bush* points to the conclusion that it is very difficult for a surveyor to exclude his liability for negligence if his client or the third party concerned is acting as a private individual or consumer. Thus, the guidelines set out by Lord Griffiths were applied by the Queen's Bench Division in *Beaton* v. *Nationwide Building Society.*[106] Like *Smith* v. *Bush,* that case involved the purchase by the plaintiff of a modestly priced house with the aid of a mortgage. The mortgage was provided by the defendants, the Nationwide Building Society, who employed one of their staff valuers to carry out a mortgage valuation. The valuation was conducted negligently and the building society sought to rely on a disclaimer of responsibility in the valuation report. The judge, Mr Neil Butterfield QC, said that the disclaimer was not a contract term but a notice within the meaning of section 11(3) of UCTA and the issue was whether it was fair and reasonable to allow the building society to rely on it. The defendants recognised the guidelines outlined by Lord Griffiths but argued that the plaintiffs had been advised to have a structural survey carried out. The judge, in rejecting this argument, said that only 10 to 15 per cent of all purchasers of modest dwelling-houses obtain their own survey and it was therefore to be anticipated that the plaintiffs would not have a structural survey carried out. He went on to say that the report stressed that certain matters should be brought to the attention of the plaintiffs and in those circumstances the plaintiffs could not be expected to go to the trouble and expense of paying for another report. He concluded that 'the very terms of the report make it unfair and unreasonable to permit the defendant to rely on disclaimers on this ground'.

In one case where a disclaimer in a mortgage valuation report was found to be reasonable the mortgagor was an (unqualified) estate agent.[107] In a commercial transaction a disclaimer of liability in a valuation report is more likely to satisfy the statutory requirement of reasonableness. This conclusion is borne out by the decision of the Court of Appeal in *Omega Trust Co. Ltd and Banque Finindus* v. *Wright Son & Pepper and Another.*[108] There, the defendant valuers provided a borrower with valuations of three commercial properties in London. The valuations contained the following disclaimer:

> This report shall be for private and confidential use of the clients for whom the report is undertaken and should not be reproduced in whole or in part or relied upon by third parties for any use whatsoever without the express written authority of the surveyors.

The borrower applied to Omega for a loan of £350,000. The valuers provided a copy of their valuation report to Omega. Unknown to the valuers, Omega could not lend all of the money that the borrower requested. Omega applied to its associate company, Banque Finindus, for £200,000 and sent them a copy of the defendants' valuation. After completion of the loan, the borrower went into liquidation. The properties proved to be worthless. The valuers applied for a ruling as to whether they owed a duty of care to Banque Finindus. The Court of Appeal held that as an associate company

Banque Finindus was a separate legal entity from Omega. However, they declined to say whether a duty of care was owed by the valuers to Banque Finindus, *a lender unknown to them.*

However, the Court of Appeal held that the disclaimer satisfied the requirement of reasonableness in the UCTA. They stressed the commercial setting of the transaction, as opposed to the domestic nature of the transaction in *Smith* v. *Bush.* In applying the guidelines set out in the speech of Lord Griffiths, Henry LJ said:

> The point that Lord Griffiths was making was that in a transaction involving a lot of money in a commercial context, both parties are well able to look after themselves, and it is not necessary to have any statutory protection for them. It is this point which, in my judgment, distinguishes this commercial case from those purchases of domestic houses with which other cases have dealt.[109]

One final point needs to be made in this section.If a surveyor should seek simply to *limit* his liability then section 11(4) of UCTA provides that in assessing the reasonableness of such limitation regard must be had in particular to:

(a) the resources which he could expect to be available to him for the purpose of meeting the liability should it arise; and
(b) how far it was open to him to cover himself by insurance.

The purpose of this provision is to protect small firms (including small professional firms) with limited financial resources who are able to obtain only limited insurance cover. Thus a clause limiting a firm's liability to its insurance cover is likely to satisfy the requirements of section 11(4).[110]

SUMMARY

1. A surveyor may be employed to carry out one of three different types of survey: a structural survey, a House Buyer's Report and Valuation or a mortgage valuation survey.
2. A surveyor's principal obligation is to his client. He is required to carry out his duties under the contract with his client with reasonable care and skill.
3. A surveyor owes a duty of care in tort to his client.
4. A surveyor owes a duty of care in tort to a third party if he knows, or should know, that his report will be passed on to the third party and relied upon by such person.
5. Thus, a valuer who values a house for the purpose of a mortgage, knowing that the mortgagee will rely on it and the mortgagor will probably rely on it owes a duty of care to both parties.

6. The theoretical basis of the relationship between mortgage valuer and mortgagor is a voluntary assumption of responsibility by the valuer coupled with reliance on the valuation by the mortgagor.
7. The standard of care and skill which the law expects of a surveyor is that of the ordinary competent member of his profession, the *Bolam* standard.
8. A mere error of professional judgement will not necessarily mean that a surveyor has failed to reach the *Bolam* standard. An error will amount to negligence only if it is one which a reasonably competent member of the profession professing to have the standard and type of skill that the defendant held himself out as having would not have made.
9. For a valuation to be negligent it must be outside the range of valuation to which a reasonably competent valuer could properly come. This is taken to be plus or minus 15 per cent of the 'true' value.
10. A surveyor is not negligent merely because his views differ from the views of other members of his profession.If a profession embraces different views then the competence of its members is to be gauged by the lowest acceptable standard.
11. The RICS publishes an *Appraisal and Valuation Manual*, Section One of which contains Practice Statements and Section Two of which contains Guidance Notes on good valuation practice.
12. Compliance with Section One is made mandatory by the RICS. Compliance with Section Two is not made mandatory by the RICS, but the RICS state that surveyors should depart its provision only if they have good reason.
13. The legal status of the RICS Guidance Notes is uncertain, but the High Court has said that mere failure to comply with them is not necessarily negligence.
14. In determining whether or not a surveyor has been negligent the first point of reference for the court is the surveyor's contract.
15. If a surveyor has been employed to carry out a valuation survey then his duty is to conduct that kind of survey with the standard of care and skill of a reasonably competent valuation surveyor.
16. The exact requirements of a reasonable standard of care and skill is a question of fact to be determined in the circumstances of each case.
17. In the case of a mortgage valuation survey the valuer's duty is to carry out a visual inspection in order to discover any observable defects which should be taken into account when comparing the value of the property with other similar properties in the neighbourhood.
18. A valuation survey is more limited than a structural survey and it does not place the valuer under a duty to discover unusual defects in the property.
19. In deciding whether or not a surveyor has reached the *Bolam* standard the courts are guided by expert evidence, but such evidence is not conclusive.

20. In assessing an award of damages for a negligent survey the correct
     measure of the plaintiff's loss is generally the difference between the
     value of the property as reported and its actual value, even if the cost
     of repair exceeds that diminution in value.

21. Damages may be awarded for the distress and inconvenience caused
     by any physical discomfort which results from a negligent survey.

22. If a valuer in conducting a mortgage valuation overvalues the property
     and the mortgager defaults on the loan then the lender is due for com-
     pensation on the basis of the rate of interest which the money could
     have earned elsewhere, not on the basis of any high risk rate of interest
     which may be a term of the mortgage.

23. A valuer who overvalues a property for mortgage purposes is not liable
     for the mortgagee's loss which results from a fall in the property
     market.

24. Disclaimers in valuation reports do not prevent any duty of care from
     arising; rather the question is whether or not they negative any duty
     which has arisen.

25. Any attempt by a surveyor to exclude or limit his liability for death or
     personal injury resulting from his negligence is rendered void by
     section 2(1) of the UCTA.

26. In the case of other loss or damage, a disclaimer will be subject to the
     requirement of reasonableness contained in section 11 of UCTA.

27. Generally, disclaimers in mortgage valuation reports of domestic prop-
     erties will be considered by the courts to be unreasonable.

28. In a commercial transaction, a disclaimer of liability in a valuation report
     is more likely to satisfy the statutory requirement of reasonableness.

NOTES

1. [1964] AC 465.
2. [1990] 2 All ER 908. See Chapter 3.
3. [1990] 2 All ER 943. See Chapter 3.
4. This section, which was originally section 25 of the Building Societies Act 1962,
    imposes a duty on every director of a building society to satisfy himself that
    arrangements are made for an independent assessment of the adequacy of the
    security to be taken in respect of advances made by the society for the purposes
    of purchasing land.
5. This implied term is now contained in section 13 of the Supply of Goods and
    Services Act 1982.
6. Thus, section 16(3)(a) of the Supply of Goods and Services Act 1982 provides that a
    duty stricter than one of reasonable care and skill may be imposed on the supplier.
7. See *Thake* v. *Maurice* [1986] QB 644.
8. See *Midland Bank Trust Co. Ltd* v. *Hett, Stubbs & Kemp* [1978] 3 All ER 571 and
    Batty v. *Metropolitan Property Realisations Ltd* [1978] 2 All ER 445. For an analy-
    sis of the significance of these developments, see Chapter 7.

9.   [1985] 2 All ER 947, p.957.
10. See also *Greater Nottingham Co-operative Society Ltd* v. *Cementation Piling and Foundations Ltd* [1988] 2 All ER 971.
11. [1995] 2 AC 145. The development of concurrent liability in tort is discussed in Chapter 7.
12. [1996] PNLR 179; (1996) 77 BLR 51; (1996) 49 Con. LR 99.
13. [1986] 2 EGLR 139.
14. [1982] QB 438.
15. [1989] 2 All ER 514. These cases were heard as consolidated appeals by the House of Lords.
16   *Supra*, n.15, p.523.
17. *Supra*, n.15, p.532 and pp.541–542.
18. [1990] 2 EGLR 166.
19. (1955) 165 EG 261.
20. See in particular the speech of Lord Griffiths.
21. (1986) 8 NILR 1.
22. The question of a possible duty owed by the mortgagee to the mortgagor is discussed further, though not conclusively, in *Berrisforde* v. *Chesterfield District Council* [1989] 39 EG 176. See also *Beaton* v. *Nationwide Building Society, The Times*, October 8, 1990, and *Halifax Building Society* v. *Edell* [1992] 3 All ER 389.
23. (1888) Ch.D.39. This decision was approved by the House of Lords in *Hedley Byrne* v. *Heller, supra*, n.1.
24. [1893] 1 QB 491.
25. [1889] 14 App. Cas. 337.
26. [1932] AC 562. See Chapter 3.
27. [1951] 2 KB 164.
28. *Ibid*, n.27, p.179. Denning LJ's judgement was approved by the House of Lords in *Hedley Byrne* v. *Heller, supra*, n.1.
29. *Supra*, n.1, p.486.
30. *Supra*, n.1, pp.502–503.
31. *Supra*, n.1, p.530.
32. [1932] AC 462, p.580.
33. [1988] 1 All ER 691, at p.701.
34. (1988) NLJ 166.
35. [1988] 20 EG 92.
36. *Supra*, n.15, p.534.
37. This is the same test as that used by the Court of Appeal in *Caparo Industries plc* v. *Dickman* [1989] 1 All ER 798.
38. *Supra*, n.15, pp.540–541.
39. [1990] 1 All ER 568.
40. See in particular the speeches of Lords Bridge and Oliver. In laying down this formula for the special relationship, the House of Lords specifically endorsed the conditions for the creation of a duty of care for statements suggested by Denning LJ (as he then was) in *Candler* v. *Crane, Christmas & Co*.
41. *Op.cit.*, n.18.
42. [1990] 3 All ER 330.
43. *Ibid*, n.42, p.335.
44. For a further analysis of why the plaintiffs won in *Smith* and *Harris* but lost in *Caparo*, see Lunney, M. and Oliphant, K., *Tort Law Text and Materials*, Oxford University Press, 2000, pp.354–355.
45. [1995] 2 AC 145, p.181.

46. [1995] 2 AC 267, pp.272–275.
47. [1957] 2 All ER 118, p.121.
48. [1981] 1 All ER 267.
49. [1984] 1 WLR 634, p.638.
50. (1955) SLT 213, p.217.
51. [1985] 1 All ER 643.
52. [1990] 1 WLR 1009.
53. *Ibid*, n.52, p.1020.
54. *Supra*, n.48, p.281.
55. [1996] 1 EGLR 119, p.120. This *dictum* confirms that of Watkin J in *Singer and Friedlander Limited* v. *John D. Wood & Co.* (1977) 243 EG 212 at p.213, in which he said that a valuation which departs from the 'true' value by more than 10 or 15 per cent 'brings into question the competence of the valuer and the sort of care he gave to the task of valuation'.
56. [1996] 1 EGLR 130.
57. *Ibid,* n.56, p.132.
58. [1995] 1 EGLR 127.
59. *Ibid,* n.58, p.128.
60. *The Times*, August 4, 2000.
61. *The Times*, May 5, 1999.
62. RICS Books 1995 – published in A4 looseleaf format.
63. RICS, 1993.
64. RICS and ISVA, August 1993.
65. RICS, July 1996.
66. [1992] 24 EG 138.
67. See Jackson and Powell, *Professional Negligence*, 4th edn, Sweet & Maxwell, 1997, pp.259–262; see in particular note 87 on pp.261–262 thereto.
68. [1987] 1 EGLR 155.
69. See *Roe* v. *Minister of Health* [1954] 2 QB 66.
70. See *Bolton* v. *Stone* [1951] AC 850.
71. See *Watt* v. *Hertfordshire County Council* [1954] 1 WLR 855.
72. See *Latimer* v. *A.E.C Ltd* [1953] AC 643 and *The Wagon Mound* (No. 2) [1967] 1 AC 617.
73. [1989] 1 EGLR 154.
74. [1988] 2 EGLR 181.
75. *Ibid*, n.74, p.185.
76. *Supra*, n.15, p.528.
77. [1990] 06 EG 104.
78. [1990] 47 EG 56.
79. *Ibid*, n.78, p.64.
80. (2000) 1 EGLR 177.
81. *Ibid*, n.80, p.180.
82. *Ibid*, n.80, p.181.
83. *Op. cit.*, n.18.
84. [1956] 1 All ER 874.
85. *Ibid*, n.84, p.876
86. [1982] 3 All ER 705.
87. [1989] 1 EG 159.
88. See in particular *Syrett* v. *Carr and Neave* [1990] 48 EG 118 and *Watts* v. *Morrow* (1991) 7 PN 54, 24 Con. LR 125.
89. [1991] 4 All ER 937.
90. [1988] 07 EG 83.

91. [1990] 2 All ER 815.
92. 24 Con. LR 125, p.145; quoted by Ralph Gibson LJ in his judgement in *Watts* v. *Morrow*, *supra*, n.89, p.956.
93. *Supra*, n.89, pp.959–960.
94. *The Times*, April 14, 2000.
95. [1991] 2 All ER 353. For a critique of this case see Dugdale (1991) 7 PN 84 and Hughes (1992) 8 PN 103.
96. [1994] 2 EGLR 108 Phillips J; [1995] QB 375, CA; [1997] AC 191. See also Jackson and Powell, *Professional Negligence*, 4th edn., Sweet & Maxwell, 1997, pp.365–383.
97. [1934] 2 KB 271, p.274 (*per* Mackinnon LJ).
98. *Supra*, n.95, p.363.
99. [1994] 2 EGLR 110.
100. *Supra*, n 1, p.533.
101. (1977) 244 EG 547.
102. [1994] 2 EGLR 25.
103. [1996] 1 EGLR 35.
104. *Ibid*, n.103, p.46.
105. [1990] 1 AC 831, p.858.
106. [1991] 2 EGLR 145.
107. *Stevenson* v. *Nationwide Building Society* (1984) 272 EG 633.
108. [1997] PNLR 424; [1997] 1 EGLR 120.
109. *Ibid*, n.108, p.429.
110. Since January 1, 1986, the RICS has required its members to take out professional indemnity insurance.

9

Privity of Contract and Construction Law

INTRODUCTION

Under the common law doctrine of privity of contract, a contract cannot confer rights or impose obligations on any person except the parties to it. This doctrine has been one of the pillars of the common law of obligations, though its importance has been modified considerably by the Contracts (Rights of Third Parties) Act 1999. The doctrine falls into two distinct parts:

(1) A third party cannot acquire rights under a contract or, in other words, no person can sue on a contract to which he is not a party.

(2) A third party cannot be subject to liabilities arising under a contract or, in other words, no one can be sued on a contract to which he is not a party.[1]

Whilst the second part of the doctrine of privity – the rule that the burden of a contract cannot be imposed on a third party – is consistent with principle, the first part of the doctrine, concerning the conferring of a benefit on a third party, has attracted considerable criticism from academic writers and judges. The essence of this criticism was expressed forthrightly by Steyn LJ in *Darlington Borough Council* v. *Wiltshier Northern Ltd* in the following terms:

> The case for recognising a contract for the benefit of a third party is simple and straightforward. The autonomy of the will of the parties should be respected. The law of contract should give effect to the reasonable expections of contracting parties. Principle certainly requires that a burden should not be imposed on a third party without his consent. But there is no doctrinal, logical, or policy reason why the law should deny effectiveness to a contract for the benefit of a third party where that is the expressed intention of the parties. Moreover, often the parties, and particularly third parties, organise their affairs on the faith of the contract. They rely on the contract. It is therefore unjust to deny effectiveness to such a contract. I will not struggle with the point further since nobody seriously asserts the contrary.[2]

223

The rule that a third party cannot acquire rights under a contract has caused particular difficulties for construction projects. The Law Commission point out that the rule affects both simple construction projects involving only an employer and a builder and complex construction projects involving a main contractor and many subcontractors and design professionals.[3]

To illustrate the difficulties which the doctrine of privity may cause for a simple construction project the Law Commission gives the example of a client contracting with a builder for work to be done on the home of an elderly relative. If the work is performed defectively, then it is only the client who has the contractual right to sue the builder; the elderly relative could not himself or herself sue the builder because he or she has no privity of contract with him. The client in these circumstances can often recover only nominal damages, since he or she will have suffered no direct financial loss as a result of the builder's defective performance of the contract.

In complex construction projects there will be a web of contracts between the participants. The doctrine of privity of contract means that only the parties within each contractual relationship can sue each other. Thus the contractor's duty to build according to specification or the architect's and engineer's duties of care and skill cannot be extended to tenants, subsequent purchasers of the development or funding instructions. The result is that these three parties have suffered considerable inconvenience through the operation of the doctrine of privity.

The tenant

A commercial lease will normally contain a repairing covenant imposing an obligation on the tenant to repair the premises. The nature and extent of that obligation depends on the precise wording of the repairing covenant. The important question for the tenant is whether such a covenant requires him to remedy latent defects in the premises. The law does not provide a very precise answer to this question. The general principle governing such covenants was laid down by Forbes J. in *Ravenseft Properties Ltd* v. *Davstone (Holdings) Ltd*:

> The true test is, as the cases show, that it is always a question of degree whether that which the tenant is asked to do can properly be described as a repair, or whether on the contrary it would involve giving back to the landlord a wholly different thing from that which he demised.[4]

In any particular case it may not be clear whether a latent defect is within the scope of a repairing covenant. The essential point for a tenant is that it *may* fall within such a covenant and therefore it is important for him to seek a means to protect himself from liability for repairing such defects.

The subsequent purchaser

A contract for the sale of land and buildings contains nothing akin to the implied terms of quality and fitness which are imposed on a seller or supplier of goods. It is subject to the doctrine of *caveat emptor*, which means that the onus to discover any latent defects in building will be on the purchaser. If the purchaser is a subsequent purchaser, or purchases from a developer then he will not have a contract with the builder or designer of the premises and will not therefore receive the benefit of the implied obligations imposed upon the supplier in a contract for work and materials or a contract for services. It is therefore common for a purchaser to survey the property before purchase, but such surveys cannot always be relied upon to reveal a latent defect. Purchasers of dwellings will generally have the benefit of the warranties in the NHBC scheme. That scheme does not extend to commercial buildings and the purchasers of these buildings will therefore frequently require collateral warranties from the builder and the design team.

The funding institution

Many developments are funded by banks, pension funds, etc. If the developer runs into financial difficulties then frequently the funding institution will want to take over the project itself. In other words it will want to stand in the shoes of the developer and enforce his contracts with the contractor and the designer. Such an arrangement is known as a novation.

The difficulties caused by the doctrine of privity were compounded by the diminished role of the tort of negligence as a means of compensation for defective design and building work following the decisions of the House of Lords in *D & F Estates* v. *Church Commissioners for England*,[5] *Murphy* v. *Brentwood District Council*[6] and *Department of the Environment* v. *Thomas Bates & Son Ltd.*[7] As we saw in Chapter 3, in *D & F Estates*, the House of Lords held that a builder was not liable in tort to a subsequent purchaser for the cost of repairing defects to a building. In *Murphy*, the House of Lords overruled *Anns* v. *Merton LBC*[8] and held that a local authority, which negligently failed to ensure that a builder complied with the Building Regulations, owed no duty of care in tort for the resulting defects in the building leading to pure economic loss. In *Bates*, the rule laid down in *Murphy* was extended to builders. The effect of these three decisions is that tortious claims by third parties for economic loss resulting from defective buildings are unlikely to succeed unless they can be brought within the scope of the reliance doctrine first laid down in *Hedley Byrne & Co.* v. *Heller & Partners Ltd*[9] and redefined in *Henderson* v. *Merrett*.[10] There is no reported decision where a third party has so succeeded. As a result, a subsequent purchaser or tenant of a defective building now has little protection in tort.

The problems associated with the doctrine of privity and the diminished role of the tort of negligence have led tenants, subsequent purchasers and funding institutions to seek alternative ways of protecting themselves against the losses caused by defective buildings. These alternatives are as follows:

(1) collateral warranties;
(2) first party buildings insurance; and
(3) assignment of legal rights.

It must be emphasised at this point that these means of circumventing the doctrine of privity and the exclusionary rule in *Murphy* are sought largely, if not wholly, by commercial parties, though the decision in *Murphy* has important implications for consumers.[11] The need for these alternatives has been greatly diminished by the Contracts (Rights of Third Parties) Act 1999. However, as we shall see, the doctrine of privity is likely to remain of cardinal importance in areas, such as complex construction projects, where there are established chains of contracts. Parties to a complex construction project are likely still to pursue one of these alternatives, in particular the collateral warranty, in spite of the provisions of the 1999 Act. Besides which, in the construction industry old habits die hard. It is necessary, therefore, to examine the features of these alternatives before proceeding to the scheme contained in the 1999 Act.

COLLATERAL WARRANTIES

A collateral warranty is a contract which stands alongside the main contract. The existence of such contracts has long been recognised by the common law. The best and most well-known description of this concept is that of Lord Moulton's in *Heilbut Symons & Co* v. *Buckleton*:

> It is evident, both on principle and on authority, that there may be a contract the consideration for which is the making of some other contract. If you will make such and such a contract I will give you £100 is in every sense of the word a complete legal contract. It is collateral to the main contract but each has an independent existence and they do not differ in respect of their possessing to the full the character and status of a contract.[12]

Collateral warranties are of two kinds: (a) implied, and (b) express.

(a)   Implied collateral warranties[13]

The courts have in a number of circumstances implied a contractual warranty. In this sense, a collateral warranty is a device used by the courts to get round what they see as an unnecessarily harsh rule of common law. Thus, the collateral warranty has been used to mitigate the harshness of the parol evidence rule, that if the contract is reduced to writing then only that writing can be used as evidence of the terms of the contract. If a preliminary statement or assurance is not included in the written contract the courts may be prepared to treat such statement or assurance as a contractual warranty collateral to the principal agreement.[14] More commonly, the implied collateral warranty has been employed where the person giving, or the person receiving, the assurance is not a party to the main contract.[15]

One overriding principle governs implied collateral warranties: on the totality of evidence the parties must have intended that there should be contractual liability in respect of the accuracy of the statement.[16]

(b) *Express collateral warranties*

An express collateral warranty is one agreed upon by the parties themselves, rather than implied by the courts. It is this form of collateral warranty which is now so important a feature of legal relationships in the construction industry. It is seen as a means of overcoming the effects of the doctrine of privity of contract and the restrictive view of negligence which the courts now take.

The terms of express collateral warranties

Virtually all express contractual warranties are duty of care warranties. The giver of the warranty rarely, if ever, guarantees to the recipient that he will achieve a particular result. In other words, there is generally no question of a collateral warranty creating strict liability. Thus a client will inevitably state that he wants a building for a particular purpose; the obligation which this requirement imposes on the design professional concerned is to use reasonable care and skill in achieving that purpose.[17] There are three principal reasons for this provision. In the first place, the purpose of a collateral warranty is to create a contractual relationship in circumstances where there are no duties in tort owed by one party to the other. As tortious duties are generally based on the concept of reasonable care and skill it is hardly surprising that this concept should provide the essential basis for a device used to plug gaps left by the law of tort. Secondly, collateral warranties in the construction industry essentially transfer obligations in the main contract to a party who is not privy to that contract. Generally, the main contract imposes an obligation of reasonable care and skill, rather than strict liability. For example, under clause 3.1 of the RIBA standard form, *Architect's Appointment*, the architect's duty in relation to design is expressed as follows:

> The Architect will exercise reasonable care and skill in conformity with the normal standards of the Architect's profession.

This duty is of course owed to the architect's employer, the building owner. If the building is leased and the tenant demands a collateral warranty from the architect in relation to design then in all probability such design warranty will simply repeat the provisions of the above clause. Thirdly, a collateral warranty is only as good as the insurance which backs it up; few, if any, insurance companies are prepared to insure a warranty which provides a guarantee.

Insurance

It is common for collateral warranties provided by an architect or engineer to provide a term that professional indemnity insurance (PII) is in force at the date of the warranty. The reason for the inclusion of such a provision is that most design professionals operate in partnerships, a form of business organisation which does not enjoy limited liability. As a result, they may be held personally liable for any contractual obligations they undertake. If their personal assets do not extend to meeting these obligations then the only way in which they can be met is through PII.

PII, however, contains a number of problems whose effect may be to render the collateral warranty worthless.[18] First, the liability of an architect or engineer under a collateral warranty will arise only when damage to the building concerned actually occurs. It is not uncommon for defects in buildings to manifest themselves many years after they have been completed – by this time any PII taken out by the design team may be either inadequate or have lapsed. Secondly, professional persons frequently change their PII to different insurers. If they fail to inform the new insurer of the existence of a collateral warranty then it will not be covered by the new policy. Thirdly, PII is only for the benefit of the insured. The insured may compromise any claim against his insurers without taking into account the liability owed to the third party. For example, if a professional faced with a claim for, say, £1 million settles with his insurers for £100,000 there is nothing that the third party can do about it. Winward Fearon in *Collateral Warranties*[19] cite a further problem with any PII provision. That problem revolves around the remedy available to the beneficiary of the warranty if the designer fails to honour his obligation to insure. Clearly the designer is in breach of contract under the warranty and would thereby be liable in damages for the amount of the PII premiums to the beneficiary. But it is highly unlikely that the beneficiary would be able to take out PII on behalf of the designer.

Deleterious materials

Many collateral warranties contain a provision for proscribing certain materials for use in the construction of the building. Arguably such a list is unnecessary as use of the most commonly proscribed materials would be a breach of the duty to exercise reasonable care and skill. If a list is to be included then it must be made clear that it is not an exhaustive list and that it is not intended to be a substitute for the duty of reasonable care and skill.

Assignment

A warranty will frequently contain a term allowing the benefit of it to be passed on, i.e. assigned, to subsequent tenants or purchasers.[20] Assignment is a complex subject and these complexities are beyond the scope of this work.[21] All that can be done here is to outline the essential principles governing this topic.

The benefits arising under a contract, including a collateral warranty, is a chose in action, i.e. a personal right of property which can only be claimed or enforced by action, and not by taking physical possession.[22]

It is not necessary for a contract to contain an express term granting a right of assignment in order for the benefit of the contract to be assigned. Assignment is a right which arises either by statute or in equity. The right to make a legal assignment is governed by section 136(1) of the Law of Property Act 1925. This provides that:

> Any absolute assignment by writing under the hand of the assignor (not purporting to be by way of charge only) of any debt or other legal thing in action, of which express notice in writing has been given to the debtor, trustee or other person from whom the assignor would have been entitled to claim such debt or thing in action, is effectual in law (subject to equities having priority over the right of the assignee) to pass and transfer from the date of such notice:
> (a) the legal right to such debt or thing in action;
> (b) all legal and other remedies for the same; and
> (c) the power to give a good discharge for the same without the concurrence of the assignor.

This provision means that certain formalities must be complied with if an assignment is to be an effective legal assignment:

(1) there must be an absolute assignment in writing signed by the assignor;
(2) there must be a debt or other legal thing in action; and
(3) there must be an express notice in writing to the debtor.

If these formalities are not complied with then there may still be an equitable assignment. The essential principle governing an equitable assignment is that it may be in writing or oral, provided that there is a clear and unequivocal intention to assign.[23] If a collateral warranty expressly prohibits assignment then that is likely to be effective at law and any attempt to assign in such a case would be invalid.[24]

Novation

This is a transaction by which, with the consent of all the parties concerned, a new contract is substituted for one that has already been made. A novation provision in a collateral warranty will be for the benefit of the purchaser or funding institution. It gives such parties the right to step into the shoes of the developer or building employer if either of those parties become bankrupt or go into liquidation. In this way the main contract and the design contract can then be completed.

The essential difference between novation and assignment is that assignment does not require the consent of the giver of the warranty, whereas novation does.

The BPF warranty

The British Property Federation (BFP) has drawn up a standard form of collateral warranty for use by funding institutions.[25] This standard form was drawn up in collaboration with the ACE, RIBA and RICS. The essential features of this form are as follows:

(1) Like most, if not all, collateral warranties used in the construction industry it is a duty of care warranty. By clause 1 the firm warrants that it has exercised reasonable care and skill in the performance of its duties to the client. This confirms that the obligation to the third party will be no greater than the obligations owed to the client.

(2) Under the provisions of clause 2 certain materials are proscribed:
   (a) high alumina cement in structural elements;
   (b) wood wool slabs in permanent form work to concrete;
   (c) calcium chloride in admixtures for use in reinforced concrete;
   (d) asbestos products;
   (e) naturally occurring aggregates for use in reinforced concrete which do not comply with British Standard 882.

This is a very limited clause; no attempt is made to include substances which do not comply with the relevant British Standards and Codes of Practice.

(3) By clause 9 the firm must maintain PII provided that such insurance is available at commercially reasonable rates. This clause does not specify the risks against which PII is to be maintained and it does not state where such insurance is to be obtained.

(4) By clause 11 the benefits of the warranty may be assigned to another company providing finance or re-finance in connection with the development project without the consent of the client or the firm being required.

Warranties backed by guarantees

This is a form of strict liability, in that such warranties would impose liability for specific defects and damage on the providers irrespective of negligence. In France, for example, architects and builders are required by the Napoleonic *Code Civil* to repair any defects in building structures or ground movement for a period of ten years. This warranty is backed up by *Dommage Ouvrage* insurance.

The NEDC in their BUILD report[26] identified four potential problems with such guarantees:

(1) If applied to a whole building, strict liability could be a very onerous imposition on the construction industry; contractors could well resist, and even refuse, the imposition of such warranties.
(2) It may be difficult, or even impossible, to obtain the necessary insurance backing at reasonable premiums.
(3) If such a guarantee were to be given by a contractor who, in the event, failed to honour it, the success of any claim by a client would then depend upon the insurance policy taken out by the contractor.
(4) Should a client have a valid claim on a contractor's policy, litigation may be needed to recover damages, and a client may have to join a queue of debtors.

The BUILD report concludes that while building warranties with insurance backed guarantees meet some of the objectives, they fail fully to meet the major requirements of providing clients with a secure route to redress.[27]

FIRST PARTY BUILDINGS INSURANCE

First party buildings insurance is a form of insurance whereby payment is made to the insured when certain specified kinds of damage appear in the building concerned. Such insurance is rare in the case of dwellings because they are usually covered by the provisions of the NHBC scheme during the first ten years of their lives. However, as we have seen in Chapter 3, the NHBC scheme does not extend to commercial buildings and in order to fill this gap a form of first party insurance has been recommended by the NEDC in their BUILD report.

The BUILD report was prepared by the Construction Industry Sector Group of the NEDC. In 1984 it appointed the Insurance Feasibility Steering Committee (IFSC) to investigate the desirability and feasibility of latent defects protection insurance for new commercial, industrial and other non-housing building. The IFSC recommended a form of first party material damage insurance, Building Users and Insurance against Latent Defects (BUILD).

The NEDC in their BUILD report point to a number of reasons why such insurance is important. Fault free buildings cannot be guaranteed, and latent defects – defects which cannot reasonably be discovered at the stage of a building's practical completion or during the period of contractual liability for defects – are a common feature of buildings. The report suggests a number of reasons for the occurrence of these defects. They can be summarised as follows. First, they may arise from what the reports refer to as poor visualisation, i.e. the failure of the client or the builder to envisage how a building will actually perform when in use. Secondly, they may be caused by inadequate design, inappropriate specifications, the use of inadequate materials or lack of care in workmanship. Thirdly, defects may arise through technological change. Presumably, the report has in mind in this respect the use of new building materials and experimental designs.[28]

It should be noted that this report was published in 1988 and to these factors the effects of the decision in *Murphy* must be added.

The essential provisions of a BUILD policy

The most important provisions of a BUILD policy are as follows:

(1) It would be negotiated by the developer or building owner at the preliminary design stage. During its currency, the policy would be transferable to successive owners and whole-building tenants.
(2) It provides non-cancellable material damage insurance against specified latent defects and damage for a period of ten years from the date of practical completion.
(3) The cover is initially limited to structure (including foundations), the weathershield envelope and optionally loss of rent.

There are a number of exceptions from a BUILD policy:

— minor elements (e.g. stairs, partitions and suspended ceilings);
— engineering services; and
— consequential economic loss, i.e. disruption of the occupier's activities resulting from the carrying out of remedial works.[29]

The report states that minor elements are excluded because to include them would be administratively cumbersome. Engineering services are excluded because the risks associated with them are difficult to define and because much depends on their efficient operation and maintenance. The risks of consequential economic loss will differ greatly from one occupier to another and the report states that this form of loss is best insured by the insurer.

The advantages and disadvantages of BUILD[30]

The BUILD report sees BUILD policies as having a number of advantages for clients, producers and insurers. In the first place, all these parties would benefit from the avoidance of the cost, delay and uncertainty of litigation that would normally follow the discovery of defects covered by a BUILD policy. Clients would have the advantage of the cost of repairing the defects speedily and without the need for proof of fault. For designers there should be an easing of the burden of PII because some of the major risks will be removed. Contractors will be protected against currently uninsurable risks. For insurers, BUILD will create a new class of business. Professional indemnity insurers will be relieved of the consequences of many of the more costly defects.

The BUILD report identifies a number of disadvantages of BUILD policies. The cost of BUILD premiums will have to be met, in practice calls on deductibles are unlikely to differ much from PII deductibles and, initially at least, insurers will find the risks difficult to assess. The report also considers the argument that BUILD policies may lead to a decline in the quality of buildings by encouraging poor design and careless workmanship. To counteract any possibility of this occurring the report recommends, *inter alia*, that BUILD policies should contain a provision that the contractor discharges his responsibilities under the contract for correcting defects reported during the defects liability period and that they impose a deductible, i.e. the first amount of the claim (say £5000) would not be covered.

The IFSC concluded that the advantages of BUILD far outweigh its disadvantages and strongly recommended that the construction industry's clients should use BUILD policies as a feature of good management.

ASSIGNMENT OF PROPRIETARY RIGHTS IN BUILDING

This section is concerned with the situation where there is a contract for the construction of a building, under terms which prohibit the employer from assigning the benefit of the contract, and the parties contemplate that the proprietary interest of the employer is going to be assigned to a tenant or purchaser. This is a problematical area of law where the building proves to be defective and is assigned, but the defects do not come to light until after the building has been assigned. In these circumstances, the building contractor has committed a breach of his contract with the original owner but the original owner no longer has a proprietary interest in the building and it is the assignee, a third party, who suffers the loss. The general rule is that damages cannot be recovered by the victim of a breach of contract in respect of a third party's loss. That is, where A commits a breach of his contract with B, then B can recover damages only in respect of his own loss and not the loss suffered by a third party, C.[31] The reason for this rule is that the purpose of an award of damages for breach of contract is considered by the common law to be compensatory.

An exception to this general rule has been created in a recent line of cases involving defective buildings. The essence of these cases is that a defective building has been transferred from the original owner to a subsequent purchaser or a tenant before the defect has become apparent. In these circumstances, the third party transferree has no direct claim in contract against the building contractor, nor (as a result of the decisions in *D & F Estates*, *Murphy* and *Bates*) does he have a claim in tort. The issue which then arises is whether the original owner can recover damages for breach of contract from the building contractor. This matter arose for consideration in the consolidated appeals of *Linden Gardens Trust Ltd* v. *Lenesta Sludge Disposals Ltd* and *St Martin's Corporation Ltd* v. *Sir Robert McAlpine & Sons Ltd,* [32] *Darlington Borough Council* v. *Wiltshier Northern Ltd*[33] and *Alfred McAlpine Construction Ltd* v. *Panatown Ltd.*[34]

Linden Gardens concerned a lease of four floors of a building. The leaseholders, Stock Conversion, employed contractors to carry out substantial refurbishment work, including the removal of all asbestos from the building. The contract was the JCT form, clause 17 of which prohibits assignment of the contract by the employer without the written consent of the contractor. The contract was completed in 1980. In 1985 more asbestos was found in the building and new contractors were employed for its removal. At the same time Stock Conversion commenced proceedings against the first contractors. The second contract was completed in August 1985. In December 1986 Stock Conversion sold their lease to new owners at its full market value and formally assigned their claim for damages against the first contractors. The new owners took over the legal action from Stock Conversion and, when even more asbestos was discovered, joined the second contractors as defendants. The main issue in this case was whether the clause prohibiting assignment barred any claim by the plaintiffs against the first and second contractors.

In the *St Martin's* case, during the course of construction of a building its owners, a property company, transferred its ownership to the group's investment property subsidiary at the full market price, together with an assignment to the investment subsidiary of the benefit of the building contract. As in *Linden Gardens*, clause 17 of the JCT form prohibited assignment without the contractor's consent (which was not obtained). After completion, the podium deck of the main building was found to be leaking, and the new owners carried out the necessary repairs. There are two important differences between this case and *Linden Gardens*. First, it was conceded that at the time of the assignment no relevant breach of the building contract had as yet occurred, in contrast to *Linden Gardens* where breaches already existed at the time of assignment. Secondly, both the assignor and assignee sued as co-plaintiffs.

The House of Lords held that clause 17 of the JCT form prohibited the assignment of any benefit of the contract, including not only the assignment of the right to future performance but also the assignment of accrued rights of action. Accordingly the plaintiffs' claim in *Linden Gardens* and the assignee's claim in the *St Martin's* case failed.[35] The rationale for this was explained by Lord Browne-Wilkinson in his speech. He said that the prohibition on the assignment of accrued rights of action was not void as being contrary to public policy since a party to a building contract may have a genuine commercial interest in seeking to ensure that he was in contractual relations only with the other party to the contract.

The House of Lords further held that the assignor in the *St Martin's* case was entitled to damages from the defendant contractor. These parties were to be regarded as having entered into a contract on the basis that the assignor would be entitled to enforce contractual rights for the benefit of the assignee. In coming to this conclusion the House of Lords relied on a very old exception to the general rule that a party cannot recover damages for breach of contract unless he himself has suffered loss. This exception was laid down in *Dunlop* v. *Lambert*,[36] where it was held that a consigner of goods who had parted with the property in the goods before the date of breach could even so recover substantial damages for the failure to deliver the goods. The rationale of that rule was explained by Lord Diplock in *The Albazero*. He said that:

> in a commercial contract concerning goods where it is in the contempla-
> tion of the parties that the proprietary interest in the goods may be
> transferred from one owner to another after the contract has been
> entered into and before the breach which causes loss or damage to the
> goods, an original party to the contract, if such be the intention of them
> both, is to be treated in law as having entered into the contract for the
> benefit of all persons who have or may acquire an interest in the goods
> before they are lost or damaged, and is entitled to recover by way of
> damages for breach of contract the actual loss sustained by those for
> whose benefit the contract is entered into.[37]

Applying this principle to the *St Martin's* case, the majority of the House of Lords said that both the contractor and the assignor knew that the property was going to be occupied by a third party. It was therefore foreseeable that damage caused by a breach of contract by the contractor would cause loss to a subsequent owner.

However, Lord Griffiths took the view that the employer had himself suf-
fered a loss by reason of the breach of contract in that he did not receive the bargain for which he had contracted. He said:

> I cannot accept that in a contract of this nature, namely for work, labour
> and the supply of materials, the recovery of more than nominal damages
> for breach of contract is dependent upon the plaintiff having a propri-
> etary interest in the subject matter of the contract at the date of breach.
> In everyday life contracts for work and labour are constantly being
> placed by those who have no proprietary interest in the subject matter
> of the contract. To take a common example, the matrimonial home is
> owned by the wife and the couple's remaining assets are owned by the
> husband and he is the sole earner. The house requires a new roof and
> the husband places a contract with a builder to carry out the work. The
> husband is not acting as agent for his wife, he makes the contract as
> principal because only he can pay for it. The builder fails to replace the

roof properly and the husband has to call in and pay another builder to complete the work. Is it to be said that the husband has suffered no damage because he does not own the property? Such a result would in my view be absurd and the answer is that the husband has suffered loss because he did not receive the bargain for which he had contracted with the first builder and the measure of damages is the cost of securing the performance of that bargain by completing the roof repairs properly by the second builder.[38]

Lord Griffiths considered that it was irrelevant in this context that it was the assignee, not the employer, who paid for the cost of the repairs, for '[t]he law regards who actually paid for the work necessary as a result of the defendant's breach of contract as a matter which is raised *inter alios acta* so far as the defendant is concerned'.[39] It must be stressed that although Lord Griffiths decided *Linden Gardens* on a wider basis than the other Law Lords he came to the same conclusion as they did, namely that the employer was entitled to recover substantial damages from the contractor for the benefit of the assignee who suffered from the contractor's defective performance.

In *Darlington* there was no change of ownership. Wiltshier, the contractors, entered into a contract with Morgan Grenfell, a finance company, to build a leisure centre for Darlington Borough Council. Morgan Grenfell assigned its contractual rights against Wiltshier to the council. The leisure centre proved to have been defectively constructed. The Court of Appeal, by extending the principle in *Linden Gardens*, held that the council was entitled to substantial damages. The principle laid down in *Linden Gardens* required extension because the original contracting party, Morgan Grenfell, had never had a proprietary interest in the leisure centre. Further, they said that if Morgan Grenfell had sued in its own name it would have recovered damages as constructive trustee for the council. As we have seen, Steyn LJ, in his judgement, launched a direct attack on the doctrine of privity and this dictum appears to be in conflict with the rule laid down by the House of Lords in *Woodar*.

In *Alfred McAlpine Construction Ltd* v. *Panatown Ltd*, Panatown entered into a building contract with Alfred McAlpine Construction Ltd under which McAlpine undertook to design and build an office building on a site which Panatown did not own. The site was owned by Unex Investment Properties Ltd (UIPL) which was part of the same group of companies as Panatown. Under a duty of care deed McAlpine undertook to UIPL that in all matters within the scope of its duties under the building contract it owed a duty of care to UIPL. It was expressly provided that UIPL could assign this deed to its successors in title or to any other party with the consent of McAlpine, such consent not to be unreasonably withheld. In other words, McAlpine's obligations under the building contract were enforceable not only by Panatown but also by UIPL and its successors in title. The building proved defective and Panatown claimed substantial damages from McAlpine. The Court of Appeal held unanimously that the duty of care deed did not deprive the employers of their right to claim substantial damages for the contractor's breach. That decision was based upon the rationale of *Dunlop* v. *Lambert*, the narrower ground.

The House of Lords, by a majority of three to two, reversed the Court of Appeal's decision.They distinguished this case from the *St Martin's* case and held that Panatown's claim must fail as UIPL had a direct claim under the duty of care deed against McAlpine. When a contract between a builder and an employer was for the construction of a building upon the land of a third party who would own the building, the employer was entitled to claim substantial damages on behalf of the third party from the builder for defects in the building only if the third party who actually suffered the loss had no direct remedy against the builder. Where the third party had a direct remedy by virtue of a duty of care deed the employer was entitled only to nominal damages. Moreover, such a remedy also precluded the existence of any right that the employer might otherwise have to recover substantial damages in his own right for loss of the value to him of the performance of the contract.

In relation to the broader ground on which Lord Griffiths decided the *St Martin's* case, Lord Browne-Wilkinson, for the majority, said that Lord Griffiths had held in effect that the loss suffered by the employer in that case was the loss of the value to him of the performance of the contract. Thus, the employer would be entitled to substantial damages, which in Lord Griffiths' view, was the cost of providing the third party with the benefit of the contract. Lord Browne-Wilkinson said that in the present case, in view of the fact that UIPL and its successors in title had a right to sue McAlpine directly, Panatown had suffered no loss to its performance interest.

Lords Goff and Millett entered powerful dissenting speeches. They upheld the decision of the Court of Appeal, but on the basis of Lord Griffiths' broader approach in the *St Martin's* case rather than the narrower ground of the rule in *Dunlop* v. *Lambert*. Thus, Lord Goff stated:

> It would be an extraordinary defect in our law if, where (for example) A enters into a contract with B that B should carry out work for the benefit of a third party, C, A should have no remedy in damages against B if B should perform his contract in a defective manner.[40]

Lord Goff was strongly of the view that Lord Griffiths' approach was in line with existing authority, such as *Woodar Investments* v. *Wimpey*:

> I do not regard Lord Griffiths' broader ground as a departure from existing authority, but as a reaffirmation of existing legal principle. Indeed, I know of no authority which stands in its way.[41]

Lord Goff described the rule in *Dunlop* v. *Lambert* as 'inapposite', because the present case did not involve privity of contract. UIPL were not seeking to enforce a *jus quaesitum tertio*, i.e. a right arising under a contract between McAlpine and Panatown.

In relation to the existence of the duty of care deed, Lord Goff and Lord Millett said that the fact that McAlpine had entered into such an arrangement with UIPL did not detract from its obligations to Panatown under the building contract. The real purpose of the duty of care deed was to provide a contractual remedy in negligence similar to that formerly available under the *Anns* v. *Merton London Borough Council* principle.

One of the principal difficulties of the broader approach of Lord Griffiths is that it seems to permit the promisee to recover substantial damages for breach of contract even though he may have no intention of using them to repair the property. This is because he has suffered the loss of his performance interest, i.e. not getting the bargain for which he had contracted. However, Lord Goff in his speech said that, having recovered substantial damages, the promisee is under an obligation to use them to remedy the defects. To illustrate this point, Lord Goff provided an example of a wealthy philanthropist who contracts for work to be done on the village hall. The work is defective. The trustees who own the hall suggest that he sue the builder for damages. The philanthropist agrees. It would be absurd to suggest his action will fail because he does not own the hall; he has suffered loss because he did not receive the bargain for which he had contracted. The philanthropist would not be allowed to pocket the damages. It must be an implied term of the licence under which he was permitted to renovate the hall that once the building work began he should take steps to procure its satisfactory completion.Accordingly, Lord Goff concluded, if he recovers damages he must employ another builder to rectify the defects, the damages being available to finance that work.

Another problem with the broader approach is that of double jeopardy for the contractor, i.e. liability to the third party under the duty of care deed and liability to the employer under the main building contractor.

THE CONTRACTS (RIGHTS OF THIRD PARTIES) ACT 1999

As we have seen, the doctrine of privity of contract has caused considerable inconvenience in the commercial world and particularly so for the parties to a construction project. The non-recognition of third party rights by the common law has been much criticised by judiciary, academics and the Law Commission.Indeed, the Law Commission has pointed out that senior judges have criticised the privity rule more than any other rule of English contract law. The judiciary though, in the main, have felt that reform of the rule was the task of the legislature.[42] In carrying out this task the legislature has been aided by the Law Commission, who published a consultation paper on the subject in 1991[43] and a report in 1996.[44] In its report the Law Commission considered that for the sake of clarity and certainty reform should take the form of a detailed legislative scheme which defined in detail third party rights and remedies, the rights of the contracting parties to terminate or modify the contract and the promisor's defences. These recommendations were accepted by Parliament and they form the basis of the Contracts (Rights of Third Parties) Act 1999.

Right of third party to enforce a contractual term

The key provision in the 1999 Act is that which defines the right of a third party to enforce a contractual term. This provision is contained in subsections 1(1), (2), (3) and (5) which state:

(1) Subject to the provisions of this Act, a person who is not a party to a contract (a 'third party') may in his own right enforce a term of the contract if –
   (a) the contract expressly provides that he may; or
   (b) subject to subsection (2), the term purports to confer a benefit on him.
(2) Subsection (1) (b) does not apply if on a proper construction of the contract it appears that the parties did not intend the term to be enforceable by the third party.
(3) The third party must be expressly identified in the contract by name, as a member of a class or as answering a particular description but need not be in existence when the contract is entered into.
(4) For the purpose of exercising his right to enforce a term of the contract, there shall be available to the third party any remedy that would have been available to him in an action for breach of contract if he had been a party to the contract (and the rules relating to damages, injunctions, specific performance and other relief shall apply accordingly).

These subsections are based on the Law Commission's test of enforceability, which itself is closely modelled on the New Zealand Contracts (Privity) Act 1982. Their effect is to give a third party the right to enforce a contractual provision in either of two circumstances:

(1) In the first place, a third party has the right to enforce a contractual provision where that right is given to him by an express term of the contract. The third party may be identified by name, class or description, but he need not be in existence when the contract is entered into. This provision is based on what the Law Commission in their report refer to as the 'first limb' of their test of enforceability.
(2) Secondly, a third party has the right to enforce a contractual provision where that provision purports to confer a benefit on the third party, who is expressly identified as a beneficiary of the provision, by name, class

or description.However, there is no right of enforceability where on the proper construction of the contract it appears that the contracting parties did not intend the third party to have that right. This provision is based on the 'second limb' of the Law Commission's test of enforceability.

Before examining these two limbs in more detail, one general point about the test of enforceability in section 1 must be emphasised: it restricts the range of potential third party beneficiaries to those on whom the contracting parties intend to confer *an enforceable legal obligation.* Section 1 does not state that a right of action arises where the contracting parties intend to confer a benefit on a third party. The Law Commission in their report point out that for a right of action to arise simply on conferment of a benefit would be to state the test of enforceability too widely. To illustrate this point, they provide an example of a contract made between contractors and a highway authority for the construction of a new road. The road is intended for the benefit of all road-users but it would not be acceptable for them to have a right of action in the event of completion of the road being delayed.[45]

The first limb of the test of enforceability

The Law Commission in their report point out that this aspect of the test of enforceability is largely self-explanatory. It is satisfied, they state, where the contract contains words such as 'and C shall have the right to enforce the contract'.[46] Thus, subsequent purchasers, tenants and funding institutions can be granted a right to enforce the contractual obligations of the building contractor or of the design professional without the need for a large number of collateral warranties.

The second limb of the test of enforceability

This limb is more problematical than the first limb. The Law Commission in their report state that it is concerned with those situations where the parties do not expressly contract to confer a legal right on the third party. They go on to explain this limb in the following words:

> *In general terms it establishes a rebuttable presumption in favour of there being a third party right where a contractual provision purports to confer a benefit on an expressly designated third party. But that presumption is rebutted where on a proper construction of the contract the parties did not intend to confer a right of enforceability on the third party.* [The Law Commission's italics][47]

The Law Commission consider that this second limb contains three important features. The first of these features is that express designation by name, class or description is a necessary but not a sufficient condition for raising the rebuttable presumption.A third party could be designated in a contract even though no benefit is to be conferred on that third party. The second feature is that the contracting parties must intend the third party to be benefited by the contractual provision in question.Thus, a design and build contract may expressly confer the benefit of the 'build obligations' on subsequent owners but this will not mean that the subsequent owners are intended to be beneficiaries of the 'design obligations'.

It is the third feature of the second limb which is, arguably, the most important from the stand point of Construction Law. The Law Commission state that the presumption of enforceability is rebutted where the proper objective construction of the contract is that the parties did not intend the third party to have the right of enforceability. In the view of the Law Commission, an unidentified third party will not be able to enforce a contract in circumstances where there is an established chain of contracts, as in a complex construction project. The Law Commission were at pains to point out that the second limb does not cut across the chains of subcontracts that are a feature of such a project. Their words, in this respect, are worth quoting *in extenso:*

> [T]o allay the fears of the construction industry we should clarify that … we do not see our second limb as cutting across the chain of sub-contracts that have traditionally been a feature of that industry. For example, we do not think that in normal circumstances an owner would be able to sue a sub-contractor for breach of the latter's contract with the head-contractor. This is because, even if the sub-contractor has promised to confer a benefit on the expressly designated owner, the parties have deliberately set up a chain of contracts which are well understood in the construction industry as ensuring that a party's remedies lie against the other contracting party only. In other words, for breach of the promisor's obligation, the owners' remedies lie against the head-contractor who in turn has the right to sue the sub-contractor. On the assumption that that deliberately created chain of liability continues to thrive subsequent to our reform, our reform would not cut across it because on a proper construction of the contract – construed in the light of the surrounding circumstances (that is, the existence of the connected head-contract and the background practice and understanding of the construction industry) – the contracting parties (for example, the sub-contractor and the head-contractor) did not intend the third party to have the right of enforceability. Rather the third party's rights of enforcement in relation to the promised benefit were intended to lie against the head-contractor only and not against the promisor.[48]

In support of this view, the Law Commission cite the following statement of Lord Wilberforce in *Reardon Smith Line Ltd* v. *Yngrar Hansen-Tangen:*

No contracts are made in a vacuum; there is always a setting in which they have to be placed. The nature of what it is legitimate to have regard to is usually described as 'the surrounding circumstances' but this phrase is imprecise: it can be illustrated but hardly defined. In a commercial contract it is certainly right that the court should know the commercial purposes of the contract and this in turn presupposes knowledge of the genesis of the transaction, the background, the context, the market in which the parties are operating.[49]

Variation and rescission of third party's right

Section 2 of the 1999 Act provides that where a contract term confers a benefit on a third party, the parties lose the right to rescind or vary it in the following circumstances :

(a) the third party has communicated his assent to the term to the promisor;
(b) the promisor is aware that the third party has relied on the term; or
(c) the promisor can reasonably be expected to have foreseen that the third party would rely on the term and the third party has done so.

This provision is based on the Law Commission's test of reliance for the variation or cancellation of a right conferred on a third party.[50] Its purpose is to strike a balance between allowing the parties an unlimited power to vary the contract, which would mean that the third party would not have a right that he could confidently rely on, and prohibiting any variation or cancellation of a third party right, which the Law Commission consider would be too restrictive.

One particular point about the test contained in section 2 is worthy of note: it is based on reliance, not *detrimental* reliance. In other words, it is sufficient that a third party has relied on the term; he does not have to have relied on it to his detriment. The Law Commission justify a reliance test for variation and cancellation on the ground that the essential injustice caused to a third party by the privity rule is that his reasonable expectations of the promised performance are disappointed. The reliance test, in other words, protects the third party's expectation interest. A test of detrimental reliance, on the other hand, would protect only the third party's reliance interest and would make it difficult to explain why he is entitled to performance of the promise. The Law Commission go on to point out, by way of analogy, that there appears to be a consensus that for the doctrine of equitable estoppel to be invoked it is sufficient for the promissee merely to have relied on the promise.[51]

Defences

Section 3 of the 1999 Act provides that the promisor can raise against the third party any defences that he could have raised in an action by the promisee. Thus, if the promisor has been induced into making the contract by a misrepresentation on the part of the promisee, then he can use that as a defence to any action brought by the third party. Section 3 also permits the main contracting parties to agree that a set-off arising between them in an unrelated contract may be used by the promisor against the third party. For example, A and B contract that A will pay T £10,000 if B transfers his car to A. B owes £5000 to A under a wholly unrelated contract. A and B agree in the contract that A can raise against a claim by T any matter that would have given A a set-off against a claim by B. Thus, if T claims £10,000 against A, A will be able to set-off £5000 against this amount. That is, A will be able to pay T £5000 in satisfaction of his claim.[52]

Protection of promisor from double liability

The provisions of section 5 protect the promisor against double liability. Under these provisions, if the promisee has recovered from the promisor a sum in respect of the third party's losses then this would have the effect of reducing any award made to the third party.

Exclusion clauses and third parties

The main contract between the employer and the contractor may contain a clause restricting the liability of the contractor for defective performance. Under the privity rule it is not possible for a subcontractor to take the benefit of such a clause. An exception to the rule was developed by the Privy Council in *New Zealand Shipping Ltd* v. *AM Satterthwaite & Co. Ltd, The Eurymedon,*[53] a case concerning the carriage of goods by sea, but the courts have been reluctant to extend that exception to the construction context. However, they have said that an exemption clause may negative a duty of care that may otherwise have arisen on the part of a subcontractor towards the employer.[54] The provisions of section 1(6) of the 1999 Act enable a contractor and an employer to extend the benefit of an exemption clause in their contract to subcontractors and other parties. Section 1(6) states:

> Where a term of a contract excludes or limits liability in relation to any matter references in this Act to the third party enforcing the term shall be construed as references to his availing himself of the exclusion or limitation.

The Act and the common law

It should not be thought that the role of the common law in the area of privity of contract has been brought to an end by the Act. A number of cases remain outside its scope, in particular whether a promisee can recover damages for a third party's losses. Lord Goff was at great pains to stress this point in *McAlpine* v. *Panatown*:

> That such developments in the law may be better left to the judges, rather than the subject of legislation, is now recognised by the Law Commission itself, because legislation within a developing part of the common law can lead to ossification and a rigid segregation of legal principle which disfigures the law and impedes future development of legal principle on a coherent basis. It comes as no surprise therefore that, in its report (Law Com. No. 242, para. 5.15), the Law Commission declined to make specific recommendations in relation to the *promisee's* remedies in a contract for the benefit of a third party … and stated that the commission 'certainly … would not wish to forestall further judicial development of this area of the law of damages'.[55]

CONCLUSION

By way of conclusion to this chapter, it must be stressed how important a feature of the construction industry that collateral warranties have become following the abolition of the *Anns* duty of care in *Murphy*. However, collateral warranties and the other substitutes for a tortious duty of care discussed in this chapter cannot be said to be adequate replacements for the *Anns* duty. We have seen the drawbacks to collateral warranties – inadequate, or non-existent PII, the fact that there may be a bar to their assignment or, if there is no such bar, they may not in the event be assigned, etc. Added to this, it must be remembered that even if a third party does receive, and is able to enforce, a collateral warranty that still does not put him in the position that he would have been under *Anns*. Contractual warranties give rise to contractual rights and as such they suffer from the same drawbacks *vis-à-vis* tortious rights as any other contractual right: in particular a shorter limitation period and a different, and to the plaintiff a possibly less advantageous, approach to the calculation of damages.[56] First party buildings insurance may not cover the kind of damage suffered in *Murphy* and there may be deductibles which in effect exclude cover for more minor, though still serious, defects.

The scheme contained in the 1999 Act enables the parties to a construction project to avoid the inconvenience of drafting and entering into separate collateral warranties by setting out third party rights in the main contract. Thus purchasers, tenants and funding institutions may take the benefit of the contractor's or architect's duty of care by being named as beneficiaries of these duties by class. It would not be necessary to assign these third party rights to subsequent purchasers, tenants and financiers, as is the case with collateral warranties.

SUMMARY

1. Under the common law doctrine of privity of contract a third party cannot acquire rights under a contract.

2. For a construction project, the privity rule means that the duties of the contractor and the architect or engineer cannot be extended to tenants, subsequent purchaser or funding institutions.

3. The inconvenience caused by the privity rule to these parties is compounded by the exclusionary rule laid down by the House of Lords in *Murphy* that no duty of care lies in tort for a defective building which causes pure economic loss; such loss includes the cost of repairing the building.

4. As a result of the privity rule and the exclusionary rule, tenants, subsequent purchasers and funding institutions seek to protect themselves by acquiring collateral warranties from contractors and design professionals. Such warranties transfer the duties in the main contract or the design contract to these parties.

5. Collateral warranties possess a number of limitations. In particular, they are generally duty of care warranties, they are only as good as the insurance which backs them up and, if they are to benefit further parties down the line, they must be properly assigned to those parties.

6. Tenants, subsequent purchasers and funding institutions may protect themselves by first party building insurance, whereby payment is made to the insured when certain specified kinds of damage occur to the building concerned. One such form of insurance is a Building Users and Insurance against Latent Defects (BUILD) policy, which protects the insured mainly against damage to the structure and the weathershield envelope.

7. A recent line of construction cases appears to have created an exception to the general rule that damages for breach of contract cannot be recovered for loss suffered by a third party. Thus, where a contractor enters into a contract with an employer for the construction of a building, under terms which prohibit assigning the benefit of the contract, and the building subsequently proves defective, but ownership has passed to a third party, then the employer may claim substantial damages from the contractor.

8. This exceptional principle does not apply where the third party has a direct remedy against the builder by virtue of a duty of care deed.
9. A major exception to the doctrine of privity has been created by the Contracts (Rights of Third Parties) Act 1999.
10. Under the 1999 Act, a third party may enforce a contractual term:
    (a) if the contract expressly provides so; or
    (b) if, on a proper construction of the contract, it appears that the contracting parties intended the term to be enforceable by the third party.
11. Under the first limb of the above test of enforceability, tenants, subsequent purchasers and funding institutions may be given the right to enforce the contractual obligations of the building contractor and the design professional without the need for entering into collateral warranties with these parties.
12. It is the view of the Law Commission that the second limb of the test of enforceability will not make it possible for a third party to bypass the established chain of contracts which exist in a construction project.

NOTES

1. For an account of the development of the doctrine of privity of contract and the exceptions and circumventions to it see Law Commission, *Privity of Contract: Contracts for the Benefit of Third Parties* (Law Com. No. 242, 1996), paras 2.1–2.69, or any of the standard texts on Contract Law.
2. [1995] 1 WLR 68, at p.76. The arguments for reform of the rule in the first part of the doctrine are discussed fully in Law Com. No. 242, paras 3.1–3.33.
3. *Ibid*, paras 3.10–3.23.
4. [1980] QB 12, at p.21.
5. [1989] AC 177.
6. [1991] 1 AC 398.
7. [1990] 2 All ER 943.
8. [1978] AC 728.
9. [1964] AC 465.
10. [1994] 3 All ER 506.
11. See National Consumer Council, *Murphy's Law*, 1991.
12. [1913] AC 30, p.47.
13. What follows is an outline of this subject. For a full discussion of the principles and case law governing implied collateral warranties see any of the established texts on Contract Law.
14. See, for example, *De Lassalle* v. *Guildford* [1901] 2 KB 215.
15. See, for example, *Shanklin Pier Ltd* v. *Detal Products Ltd* [1951] 2 KB 854; and *Andrews* v. *Hopkinson* [1957] 1 QB 299.
16. *Heilbut Symons & Co.* v. *Buckleton*, supra, n.12.
17. For a discussion of the concepts of duty of care and fitness for purpose in relation to warranties, see Ann Minogue, *Building*, 15 November 1996, p.38.
18. See Bates [1990] EG 57.
19. Blackwell Scientific, 1990.

20. Compare chapter 3 of the NHBC scheme.
21. See Furmston, M.P., *Cheshire, Fifoot &. Furmston's Law of Contract*, 13th edn, Butterworths, 1996, chapter 16.
22. *Torkington* v. *Magee* [1902] 2 KB 427, p.430 (*per* Channell J.).
23. *William Brandt's Sons & Co.* v. *Dunlop Rubber Co.* [1905] AC 454.
24. *Helston Securities Ltd* v. *Hertfordshire County Council* [1978] 3 All ER 262.
25. Form of Agreement for Collateral Warranty for funding institutions, Co WA/F.
26. *Building Users Insurance Against Latent Defects*, NEDO, 1988, para. 6.12.
27. *Ibid*, n.26, para. 6.13.
28. For a full list of the suggested causes of defects in buildings, see section 9 of the BUILD report.
29. See section 10 of the BUILD report.
30. See section 11 of the BUILD report.
31. *Woodar Investment Development Ltd* v. *Wimpey Construction UK Ltd* [1980] 1 WLR 227.
32. [1993] 3 All ER 417.
33. *Op. cit.*, n.2.
34. [2000] 4 All ER 97.
35. *Supra*, n.32, p.430.
36. (1839) 6 Cl&F 600, 7 ER 824.
37. [1976] 3 All ER 129, p.137.
38. *Supra*, n.32, pp.421–422.
39. *Supra*, n.32, p.423.
40. *Supra*, n.34, p.115.
41. *Supra*, n.34, p.128.
42. See, for example, *Beswick* v. *Beswick* [1968] AC 58.
43. *Privity of Contract: Contracts for the Benefit of Third Parties* (Consultation Paper No. 121).
44. Law Com. No. 242, *op. cit.*, n.1.
45. Law Commission Consultation Paper No. 121.
46. Law Com. No. 242, para. 7.10.
47. Law Com. No. 242, para. 7.17.
48. Law Com. No. 242, para 7.18(iii).
49. [1976] 1 WLR 989, pp.995–996, cited in n.12 of para. 7.18(iii) of Law Com. No. 242.
50. See in particular Law Com. No. 242, paras 9.18–9.26.
51. *Ibid*, para. 9.19.
52. This example is based on an example contained in the Explanatory Note to the Act when at Bill stage.
53. [1975] AC 154.
54. See *Southern Water Authority* v. *Carey* [1985] 2 All ER 1077 and *Norwich City Council* v. *Harvey* [1989] 1 WLR 828.
55. *Supra*, n.34, p.128.
56. See the discussion on concurrent liability in Chapter 7.

10

Limitation of Actions

INTRODUCTION

The subject of limitation of actions deals with the time period within which a plaintiff must commence his action. A plaintiff who fails to initiate proceedings within the applicable period will be barred from obtaining any remedy. The basis of the current law on limitation is to be found in the Limitation Act 1980 as amended by the Latent Damage Act 1986.

The fundamental principle underlying a statute of limitation is that it is a statute of peace. This principle was expressed in the following terms by Lord Simon in *The Amphthill Peerage*:

> There is a fundamental principle of English law (going back to Coke's Commentary on Littleton [Co Litt (1809) p.303] generally expressed by a Latin Maxim [*interest reipublicae ut sit finis litium*] which can be translated: 'It is in the interest of society that there should be an end to litigation.'[1]

The basis of this principle is that the law must strike a balance between allowing a plaintiff sufficient time in which to bring an action and yet not disadvantaging a defendant by allowing claims to be brought against him in respect of misconduct which occurred many years previously.

The issue of limitation periods is of particular importance in the area of Construction Law. Many defects in buildings are latent, i.e. they are not immediately apparent or discoverable and may not manifest themselves until many years after they have been completed. The classic example is a building with foundations that are too shallow and therefore defective. The foundations are covered up at an early stage in the construction process and thereafter there is no means by which the defect can be discovered. Only when the obvious signs, such as cracking in the walls, appear does such a defect become patent. This may be many years after the building is completed. In such a case too short a limitation period would seriously disadvantage the plaintiff, but if the limitation period were to extend for too long a period then it would cause hardship to the defendant builder, designer or local authority who may not be able to obtain PII cover in respect of the building beyond a certain time-span.

Striking a balance between plaintiff and defendant in this area of law is clearly problematical. It is a balance which has shifted between plaintiff and defendant over the last twenty years or so and equilibrium has still not been achieved, despite recent legislative reform in the form of the Latent Damage Act 1986, which restored the balance in favour of the plaintiff. There has recently been a proposal for further reform in this area of law to shift the balance in favour of the defendant.[2] The effect of the decision of the House of Lords in *Murphy* v. *Brentwood District Council*[3] on the law of limitation is clearly to favour the defendant.

This chapter examines this subject from four standpoints:

(1) limitation in contract;
(2) limitation in negligence in respect of personal injury or death;
(3) limitation in negligence in respect of latent damage to buildings; and
(4) fraud, concealment and mistake.

LIMITATION IN CONTRACT

Under the provision of section 5 of the Limitation Act 1980, an action for breach of a simple contract cannot be brought after the expiration of six years from the date on which the cause of action accrued. Section 8(1) provides that, in the case of a contract made under seal, an action cannot be brought after the expiration of twelve years from the date on which the cause of action occurred. In each case, time begins to run from the moment when the breach of contract occurs not when actual damage is suffered.

It makes no difference to the limitation period in contract whether the plaintiff knows, or ought to know of the breach. Thus, the owner of a building, who has a contractual action against the builder for using materials of unsatisfactory quality, is time-barred where defects become apparent more than six years after the building is completed. The six-year limitation period operates in this case even though the building owner could not reasonably have known of the builder's breach of contract until the defects appeared.

LIMITATION IN NEGLIGENCE – DEATH OR PERSONAL INJURY

Under section 2 of the 1980 Act, actions in tort must be brought within six years from the date on which the cause of action accrued. In the case of personal injuries, however, section 11 of the 1980 Act provides that the limitation period is three years from the date on which the cause of action accrued, or the date (if later) of the plaintiff's knowledge of his injuries. Under the provisions of section 11(5), if the injured person dies before the expiry of three years, the limitation period begins on the date of death or on the date of the personal representative's knowledge of the death, if later. If the claim is under the Fatal Accidents Act 1976 in respect of death caused by the defendant's tort, then under the provisions of section 12 of the 1980 Act the dependant must bring the action within three years of the date of death or the date of the dependant's knowledge, whichever is the later.

Knowledge

Under the provisions of section 14(1) of the 1980 Act, a person has knowledge for the purposes of sections 11(4) and (5) and 12 if he knows:

(a) that the injury in question was significant; and
(b) that the injury was attributable in whole or in part to the defendant's act or omission; and
(c) the identity of the defendant; and
(d) if it is alleged that the act or omission was that of a person other than the defendant, the identity of that person and the additional facts supporting the bringing of an action against the defendant.

Section 14(3) provides that the plaintiff's knowledge includes knowledge which he might reasonably have been expected to acquire –

(a) from facts observable or ascertainable by him; or
(b) from facts ascertainable by him with the help of medical or other appropriate expert advice which it is reasonable for him to seek.

The subsection goes on to state that a person shall not be fixed under it with knowledge of a fact ascertainable only with the help of expert advice so long as he has taken all reasonable steps to obtain (and, where appropriate, to act on) that advice.[4]

The statutory discretion

Under the provisions of section 33(1) of the 1980 Act, the court has discretion to disapply the statutory time limit of three years in actions in respect of personal injuries or death. In other words, under this section the court has a discretion to allow an action for personal injuries or death to be brought, notwithstanding that the limitation period has expired. The subsection provides that in exercising this discretion it must appear to the court to be equitable to do so, having regard to the degree to which:

(a) the provisions of sections 11 or 12 of the 1980 Act prejudice the plaintiff or any person whom he represents; and
(b) whether or not any exercise of this discretion would prejudice the defendant or any person whom he represents.

Section 33(3) provides that in exercising its discretion under section 33(1) the court must have regard to all the circumstances of the case and in particular to:

(a) the length of, and the reasons for, the delay on the part of the plaintiff.
(b) the effect of the delay upon the evidence in the case;
(c) the conduct of the defendant after the cause of action arose, including his response to the plaintiff's reasonable request for information.
(d) the duration of any disability of the plaintiff arising from the accrual of the cause of action;
(e) the extent to which the plaintiff acted promptly and reasonably once he knew he might have an action for damage; and
(f) the steps, if any, taken by the plaintiff to obtain medical, legal or other expert advice and the nature of any such advice as he may have received.

LATENT DAMAGE RESULTING FROM NEGLIGENCE

Latent damage may be defined as damage which does not manifest itself until some time after the act or omission which 'causes' it. This kind of damage clearly poses considerable problems to plaintiffs and defendants. A plaintiff may be held time-barred because of the considerable length of time before the damage manifests itself. A defendant may find himself being sued long after a contract is completed and possibly when his PII cover in respect of such a contract has expired. To a plaintiff, therefore, the law of limitation offers the prospect of being a hapless victim without a remedy; to a defendant, especially an architect or an engineer who operates in a professional partnership, on the other hand, it offers the prospect of personal liability and possible bankruptcy long after a project has been completed. Reconciling these opposing interests has been a perennial problem for this area of law. The following review of the relevant case law and statutory intervention in this area shows that a satisfactory reconciliation has yet to be achieved.

The common law background

Developments in the law of limitation played a critical role in the expansionist phase of the tort of negligence. The origin of the modern law on limitation and latent damage is laid down in the decision of the House of Lords in *Cartledge* v. *E. Jopling & Sons Ltd.*[5] In that case the plaintiff had been exposed to dust, which damaged his lungs and he contracted pneumoconiosis. This condition did not manifest itself until some years later. The House of Lords held that a cause of action in negligence accrues when the injury is suffered and not when it is discovered, *even when that injury is unknown to and cannot be discovered by the sufferer.* Thus, in this case the plaintiff's right of action was barred before he knew he had the disease.

The principle laid down in *Cartledge* is of course a very harsh one for plaintiffs. The Law Lords recognised the injustice of the rule that they laid down but they felt bound by the provisions of section 26 of the Limitation Act 1939. The Limitation Act 1963 was passed to remedy the unjust result produced by this decision. That Act extended the time-limit for commencing claims for damages where material facts of a decisive character were outside the knowledge of the plaintiff until after the action would normally have been time-barred. That provision applied only to actions for damages relating to personal injuries. It said nothing about latent damage to buildings. That was left to the courts to determine. They have developed the law in this area first to the advantage of the plaintiff but subsequently to the advantage of the defendant.

In *Dutton* v. *Bognor Regis UDC,* Lord Denning said that in the case of a defective dwelling caused by inadequate foundations the damage was done when the foundations were badly constructed and the period of limitation of six years began at that time.[6]

In *Sparham-Souter* v. *Town & Country Developments (Essex) Ltd,*[7] Lord Denning withdrew that *dictum* and held that the cause of action in such a case accrues, not at the time of the negligent laying or passing of the foundations, nor at the time when the latest owner bought the house, but at the time when the house begins to sink and the cracks appear. Where a local authority negligently approves defective foundations and other work in progress which is then covered up, the limitation period begins to run only when the damage manifests itself and the person who then has an interest in the property discovers the defects, or should, with reasonable diligence, have discovered them. He justified this change of opinion in the following terms:

> That was the first time that any damage was sustained. None of the previous owners had sustained any damage. Each had bought and sold the house at a full price in the belief that the foundations were sound. The only person to sustain the damage was the man who owned the house at the time when the house sank and the cracks appeared. It is only at that time that he can reasonably be expected to know that he may have a cause of action.It would be most unfair that time should run against him before he knows – or has any possibility of knowing – that he has a cause of action.[8]

That view was supported by the other two members of the Court of Appeal, Roskill and Geoffrey Lane LJJ.

In *Anns* v. *Merton LBC,*[9] Lord Wilberforce, with whom the other Law Lords agreed said that the Court of Appeal was right when in *Sparham-*

Souter it abjured the view that the cause of action arose immediately upon conveyance of the defective house. He went on to say that it can only arise when the state of the building is such that there is present or imminent danger to the health or safety of persons occupying[10] The defects to the maisonettes in question first appeared in 1970 and since the writs were first issued in 1972 the actions were not time-barred.

The decision of the House of Lords in *Anns* clearly favoured plaintiffs. But it left a number of points on the law of limitation in relation to negligence unclear. First Lord Wilberforce did not give any indication of the meaning of 'present or imminent danger to health or safety'. Secondly, it was not clear whether the reasonable discoverability test laid down by the Court of Appeal in *Sparham-Souter* had been approved. Thirdly, it was not clear whether the test laid down by the House of Lords applied only to local authorities or whether it applied also to builders, developers and design professionals.

The meaning of 'present or imminent danger to health or safety' was considered by the Court of Appeal in *Percival* v. *Walsall Metropolitan Borough Council*.[11] In that case the plaintiff was the owner of a house built on inadequate foundations. He sued the local authority for negligence in carrying out its duties under the Building Regulations. The problems that arose included cracking of brickwork, ceilings and internal walls; tilting of the house; differential settlement of the exterior; cracking of the garage floor, sticking of doors; draughts; leaking; a risk to services especially to drains; and a certainty of future deterioration because underpinning was not possible. The Court of Appeal held, *inter alia*, that these problems did not constitute a present or imminent danger to the health or safety of the occupiers.

The second and third of the above questions was considered by Judge Fay QC in *Eames London Estates Ltd* v. *North Hertfordshire District*.[12] This case concerned liability in negligence of a developer, a builder, an architect and a local authority, for defective premises. The judge held that the limitation period began to run upon the occurrence of either the date the plaintiff first acquired an interest in the property or the date upon which he first learned of the damage, whichever was the later.

Another factor which moved the law of limitation in favour of plaintiffs was the development of concurrent liability. This meant that in a contract involving a duty of care owed by one party to the other there could be liability in the tort of negligence to the other contracting party alongside liability in contract for breach of that duty. The particular significance of this development for limitation periods lies in the fact that a cause of action in contract accrues on the date of the breach whereas the starting point for the limitation period in tort may be many years later. Thus a plaintiff who is time-barred in contract may still be in time in tort. In *Esso Petroleum Co. Ltd* v. *Mardon*,[13] the plaintiff entered into the tenancy of a petrol-filling station owned by the defendants, Esso Petroleum Co. Ltd, on the strength of estimates throughout supplied by a representative of Esso. The estimates proved grossly inaccurate. The Court of Appeal held that the defendants were liable for breach of contractual warranty and for negligent mis-statement under the principle laid down in *Hedley Byrne & Co. Ltd* v. *Heller & Partners Ltd*.[14] In *Batty* v. *Metropolitan Realisations Ltd*,[15] the Court of Appeal held that a developer and a builder who built a house on a hill subject to landslips were liable both in contract and in tort to the plaintiff building owners. In *Midland Bank Trust Co. Ltd* v. *Hett, Stubbs & Kemp*,[16] a solicitor negligently failed to register an option to purchase a farm as a land charge with the result that it did not bind a third party who bought the land. Oliver J held that the solicitor was liable to his client in tort independently of any liability in contract. The option was granted in 1961, the sale to the third party took place in 1967 and the writ against the solicitor was issued in 1972. The cause of action in contract accrued in 1961 when the breach of contract occurred and the plaintiffs were therefore time-barred in contract. However the cause of action in tort accrued in 1967 when the damage occurred and the plaintiffs were not therefore time-barred in tort.

The decision in Pirelli

In *Pirelli General Cable Works Ltd* v. *Oscar Faber & Partners*,[17] the House of Lords restored the balance of the law of limitation firmly in favour of defendants. In March 1969 the plaintiffs engaged the defendants, a firm of consulting engineers, to design an addition to their factory premises including the provision of a chimney. The chimney was built in June and July 1969. The material used in its construction was unsuitable and cracks developed not later than April 1970. The plaintiffs discovered the damage in November 1977. It was found that they could not with reasonable diligence have discovered it before October 1972. In October 1978 the plaintiffs issued a writ claiming damages for negligence by the defendants.

The House of Lords held that the date of accrual of a cause of action in tort for damage caused by the negligent design or construction of a building was the date when the damage came into existence and not the date when the damage was discovered or should with reasonable diligence have been discovered. The plaintiffs' cause of action accrued not later than April 1970. Since that date was more than six years before the issue of the writ, the claim was statute-barred.

The leading speech was delivered by Lord Fraser. He reviewed the law of limitation and latent damage and rejected the distinction made in this area of law between personal injuries and damage to property. The key passage in his speech is as follows:

> Unless the defect is very gross it may never lead to any damage at all to the building. It would be analogous to a predisposition or natural weak-

ness in the human body which may never develop into disease or injury
.... The plaintiff's cause of action will not accrue until *damage* occurs,
which will commonly consist of cracks coming into existence as a result
of the defect even though the cracks or the defect may be undiscovered
or undiscoverable. There may perhaps be cases where the defect is so
gross that the building is doomed from the start, and where the owner's
cause of action will accrue as soon as it is built, but it seems unlikely
that such a defect would not be discovered within the limitation period.
Such cases, if they exist, would be exceptional.[18]

This passage, and, in particular, the concept of 'doomed from the start',
proved to be problematical and the decision in *Pirelli* certainly did not
produce equilibrium in this area of law. The concept of a building being
doomed from the start was considered in *Kettman* v. *Hansel Properties
Ltd.*[19] In that case the plaintiffs bought houses from the first defendants, the
builders. The foundations were laid between 1973 and 1975 in accordance
with the design of the architects and they were approved by the local
authority. They were faulty and in 1976 cracks appeared in the walls. In
1980 the plaintiffs issued a writ against the builders claiming damages for
negligence and in 1982 they joined in the architect and the local authority.
The Court of Appeal held that the plaintiffs' claims against the architects
and the local authority were not statute-barred on the ground that the
houses were doomed from the start; the plaintiffs' cause of action accrued
when the physical damage to their houses occurred, i.e. when the cracks
appeared in the walls in 1976. The Court of Appeal said that it was only in
exceptional cases that a building could be 'doomed from the start'.

Like the decision in *Anns* in relation to limitation, the scope of the decision in *Pirelli* is not clear, and in subsequent cases it was not applied to the
liability of local authorities or the liability of professional persons. In *Jones*
v. *Stroud District Council*,[20] the plaintiff in 1975 purchased a house built in
1964. In 1976, following a drought, cracks appeared as a result of subsidence
caused by defective foundations. In 1981 the plaintiff issued a writ claiming
damages against the local authority for negligence in failing to inspect the
foundations. The Court of Appeal held that until the condition of the house
gave rise to danger the authority was not in breach of a duty; the cause of
action did not arise, therefore, until some time after the drought of 1976 and
was not statute-barred.

In *Forster* v. *Outred & Co.*,[21] the plaintiff, at her solicitor's office in
February 1973, executed a mortgage deed charging her freehold property to
a company as security for her son's liabilities to the company. The son went
bankrupt owing money to the company. The company threatened to fore-
close on the mortgage unless the plaintiff paid the amount of her son's liabilities. In March 1980 the plaintiff issued a writ against her solicitor
alleging negligence in that he did not explain the full import of the mortgage

deed. (She had thought that the mortgage was security for a bridging loan.) The Court of Appeal held that where a plaintiff alleged that he had suffered economic loss as a result of a solicitor's negligent advice, actual damage occurred and the plaintiff's cause of action arose when, in reliance on the solicitor's negligent advice, he acted to his detriment. Accordingly, the plaintiff suffered actual damage and her cause of action was complete when she executed the mortgage deed in February 1973. The writ which she issued in March 1980 was therefore issued too late to come within the statutory limitation period.

In *Secretary of State for the Environment* v. *Essex Goodman & Suggitt,*[22] the defendants were surveyors who in February 1975 surveyed a recently erected building on behalf of the plaintiffs who were prospective lessees of the building. In July 1975, in reliance on the surveyors' report, the plaintiffs entered into a 25 year lease of the premises. In February 1976 defects appeared in the building and in January 1982 the plaintiffs issued a writ against the surveyors claiming damages for negligence. The Official Referee, Judge Lewis Hawser, QC, held that the duty of care owed by the surveyors to the plaintiffs was different from the duty owed by the designers or builders of the building. The surveyors had been employed to find out whether there were any defects in existence at the date of the survey and their duty was to report to the plaintiffs any such defects. The judge went on to say that if the damage occurred subsequently, or if it could not have been discovered by the exercise of reasonable care and skill, the surveyors would not have been liable since they would have complied with their duty. Accordingly, the plaintiffs' cause of action arose when they acted on the report, i.e. July 1975, and it was time-barred.

The Latent Damage Act 1986

Prior to this Act the law on limitation and latent damage could be summed up as follows:

(1) In an action alleging negligence in the design or construction of a building, the cause of action accrued when damage occurred to the building.
(2) If the defendant was a local authority, the cause of action accrued when there was a present or imminent threat to the health or safety of the occupants.
(3) If the defendant was a professional person providing advice, time began to run when the plaintiff acted to his detriment in reliance on the negligent advice.

In all these cases it was the occurrence of damage that was relevant, rather than discoverability of the existence of damage.

The 1986 Act is based upon the recommendations of the 24th Report of the Law Reform Committee, *Latent Damage.*[23] In this report the Committee identified three principles as being of critical importance in this area of law:

(1) plaintiffs must have a fair and sufficient opportunity of pursuing their remedy;
(2) defendants are entitled to be protected against stale claims; and
(3) uncertainty in the law is to be avoided wherever possible.

The Committee's recommendations attempt to give effect to these principles by striking a balance between the hardship of the *Sparham-Souter* test to defendants and their insurers, on the one hand, and the problems posed to plaintiffs by the *Pirelli* test, on the other hand.

Section 1 of the 1986 Act inserts new sections 14A and section 14B into the Limitation Act 1980.

The scope of the Latent Damage Act 1986

Section 14A of the 1980 Act applies to any action for damages for negligence, other than an action for personal injuries or death. It was established in *Iron Trades Mutual Insurance and Others* v. *J.K. Buckenham*[24] that section 14A has no application to an action in contract. The importance of this decision has been much reduced by the decision of the House of Lords in *Henderson* v. *Merrett Syndicates Ltd*[25] which confirmed that there can be concurrent actions in contract and tort arising out of the same facts. Thus a victim of a negligent breach of contract may bring an action in the tort of negligence and consequently claim the benefit of the Latent Damage Act.

Section 14A may be contrasted with section 11 of the 1980 Act in that it refers only to 'negligence', whereas section 11 refers to 'negligence, nuisance or breach of duty'.

Limitation periods under section 14A

Section 14A provides that an action for damage not involving personal injuries cannot be brought after the expiration of either –

(a) six years from the date on which the cause of action accrued; or
(b) three years from the starting date, if that period expires later than the period in (a) above.

Section 14A(5) states that the starting date for reckoning the period of limitation is the earliest date on which the plaintiff both had the knowledge required for bringing an action for damages in respect of the relevant damage and a right to bring such an action.

Knowledge

Under the provisions of sections 14A(6), (7) and (8), knowledge means knowledge both:

(a) of the material facts about the damage which a reasonable person would consider sufficiently serious to justify instituting proceedings; and

(b) of the following facts:
    (1) that the damage was attributable in whole or in part to the act or omission which is alleged to constitute negligence; and
    (2) the identity of the defendant; and
    (3) if it is alleged that the act or omission was that of a person other than the defendant, the identity of that person and the additional facts supporting the bringing of an action against the defendant.

Under the provisions of section 14A(9), knowledge that the particular acts or omissions did or did not, as a matter of law, involve negligence is irrelevant. Under the provisions of section 14A(10), knowledge includes constructive knowledge as well as actual knowledge.

The statutory long-stop

Section 14B contains an overriding time-limit, known as a long-stop, for negligence actions not involving personal injuries. It provides that an action for damages for negligence cannot be brought after the expiration of 15 years from the date on which any act or omission alleged to constitute negligence occurred. The fact that the plaintiff still does not know of his cause of action at the end of this 15 year period is irrelevant; once the 15 year period has expired, the plaintiff's cause of action is barred.

The overall effect of sections 14A and 14B

The result of these provisions is that there are now *three* limitation periods in actions for negligence which do not involve personal injury:

(1) a *primary* limitation period of six years starting from the date on which the cause of action accrued;
(2) a *secondary* limitation period of three years starting from the date when the damage was discovered or should have been discovered; and
(3) a long-stop of fifteen years starting from the date on which the act or omission alleged to constitute the negligence occurred.

These periods operate as follows. Where no latent damage is present time will run, as before, for six years from the date on which the cause of action accrued. This will also be the case where the three-year secondary period expires before the six-year primary period. If, however, damage occurs in, say, year one, and becomes discoverable in say, year five, then the primary period is overridden by the secondary period, i.e. time will run out eight years after the date on which the cause of action accrued. This is subject to the fifteen-year long-stop; in other words, in an action for damages for negligence not involving personal injuries time does not run out until fifteen years from the date on which the cause of action accrued.

Subsequent developments

The most important development to have occurred to the law on limitation periods since the passing of the Latent Damage Act is the decision of the House of Lords in *Murphy* and its effect on the rule in *Pirelli*. *Murphy*, it will be remembered, defined economic loss comprehensively to include damage to the product or the premises itself. Thus claims for structural defects in buildings are claims for economic loss and therefore do not sound generally in tort. As a consequence, most cases concerning latent damage to buildings will not give rise to any cause of action in tort and the 1986 Act will not operate in such cases.

However, the 1986 Act may still be of relevance where the plaintiff can base his claim on the *Hedley Byrne* v. *Heller* principle. On the basis of the definition of economic loss in *Murphy*, *Pirelli* is essentially a case concerning such loss – the relevant damage was to the chimney itself. The House of Lords in *Murphy*, however, did not overrule *Pirelli*; rather they sought to explain it in terms of the reliance principle laid down in *Hedley Byrne* v. *Heller*. Thus Lord Keith said:

> It would seem that in a case such as the Pirelli General Cable Works case where the tortious liability arose out of a contractual relationship with professional people, the duty extended to take reasonable care not to cause economic loss to the client by the advice given. The plaintiffs built the chimney as they did in reliance on that advice. The case would accordingly fall within the principle of *Hedley Byrne & Co. Ltd* v. *Heller & Partners Ltd*.[26]

The problem with classifying *Pirelli* as a reliance case is that on this basis the cause of action accrued not when the physical damage occurred in 1970 but when the plaintiffs relied on the defendant's advice which was in 1969 when the chimney was built.

An application of the principle in *Pirelli* to physical damage occurred in *Nitrigen Eireann Teoranta* v. *Inco Alloys Ltd*.[27] Nitrigen were an Irish firm of chemical manufacturers who owned and operated a plant in Ireland. They contracted with Inco in 1981 for the supply of replacement tubes for their plant. One of these tubes cracked in July 1983. It was repaired but in June 1984 cracked again, causing damage to the structure of the plant. Nitrigen accepted that any claim in contract was statute-barred and they sued in tort. The main issue, therefore, was when the cause of action in tort arose, 1983 or 1984? If 1983 then that cause of action too was statute-barred.

May J held that the cause of action in negligence arose in 1984. The cracking of the pipe in 1983 was damage to the thing itself, constituting a defect in quality resulting in economic loss, and was therefore irrecoverable in negligence. In 1984 physical damage to other property had occurred and the judge held that this did establish a cause of action. The plaintiffs were therefore not statute-barred. In coming to this conclusion the judge reviewed the law of negligence and economic loss and its relationship to the limitation of actions. He distinguished this case from *Pirelli* by applying Lord Keith's *dictum* in *Murphy* that *Pirelli* fell within the reliance principle. The defendants in *Pirelli* were a firm of consulting engineers; Inco, however, although specialist manufacturers, were not engaged in any professional capacity and the judge said that the relationship between Inco and Nitrigen did not come within the scope of the reliance principle.

Following *Murphy*, loss arising from defects in property is regarded as pure economic loss rather than physical loss. The problematical issue in this respect for the law of limitation periods is when such loss occurs. One view is that it occurs as soon as the defect exists, because from that moment the property is worth less than it should be, i.e. the plaintiff has paid more for it than its true value. The alternative view is that pure economic loss occurs at the date when the defect was reasonably discoverable, because until that time the property can be sold for its full value or the price which the plaintiff paid for it.

The House of Lords in *Pirelli* based their decision on the first of these two views. However, in *Invercargill City Council* v. *Hamlin*,[28] the Privy Council supported the alternative view. *Invercargill* was an appeal from a decision of the New Zealand Court of Appeal. The case concerned economic loss resulting from defective building foundations. The plaintiff's house was constructed in 1972. The council inspected the foundations during the course of construction and approved them as complying with the building regulations. They clearly did not comply with the building regulations. Over the years a number of cracks and minor defects appeared, but it was not until 1989, when the plaintiff commissioned another builder to examine the property, that the inadequate foundations were discovered. If the rule in *Pirelli* had been applied to these facts then the plaintiff would have been out of time, since the damage would have been held to have occurred in 1972 when the negligent inspection was conducted. The New Zealand Court of Appeal, however, held that the cause of action did not accrue until a reasonably prudent homeowner would have discovered the latent defect, i.e. 1989. Applying *Murphy*, the court said that the plaintiff's loss was purely economic and that such loss occurred when the market value of the house depreciated, which was when the damage was discovered and when the defects were obvious to a potential buyer.

The Privy Council upheld the decision of the New Zealand Court of Appeal. Lord Lloyd giving the judgement of the Privy Council, said:

> [T]he cause of action accrues when the cracks become so bad or the
> defects so obvious that any reasonable homeowner would call in an
> expert. Since the defects would then be obvious to a potential buyer, or
> his expert, that marks the moment when the market value of the build-

ing is depreciated, and therefore the moment when the economic loss occurs.[29]

The Privy Council were anxious not to disturb the decisions of the New Zealand courts and they said that *Pirelli* cannot be regarded as good law in that country. However, they declined to say whether *Pirelli* should still be regarded as good law in England and Wales. Clearly there are still unresolved problems in this area of law.[30]

FRAUD, CONCEALMENT AND MISTAKE

Under section 32(1) of the Limitation Act 1980, where in the case of any action for which a period of limitation is prescribed by the Act, either –

(a) the action is based upon the fraud of the defendant; or
(b) any fact relevant to the plaintiff's right of action has been deliberately concealed from him by the defendant; or
(c) the action is for relief from the consequences of a mistake;

the period of limitation does not begin to run until the plaintiff has discovered the fraud, concealment or mistake or could with reasonable diligence have discovered it.

Section 32(1)(b) is plainly of great relevance to cases of defective buildings where the defect is often covered up during the construction process. Where a builder has carried out defective work at the start of a project of which he is aware, then if he does not advise the architect or the employer of the defect but continues building work which conceals the defect, this will provide evidence of deliberate concealment.[31]

The operation of this provision is illustrated by *Applegate* v. *Moss*,[32] a case involving defective foundations. By a contract made in February 1957 the defendant agreed to build two houses for the plaintiffs and to support them on a raft foundation reinforced with a specified steel network. The houses were completed towards the end of 1957. In 1965 wide cracks appeared beneath the houses and the plaintiffs discovered that the foundations had been defectively laid: there was no raft and the reinforcement was grossly inferior to that specified. The plaintiffs claimed damages for breach. The Court of Appeal held that although their action was brought more than six years after the breach of contract they were not time-barred because there had been concealment within the meaning of what is now section 32 of the 1980 Act.

In *Sheldon* v. *RHM Outhwaite (Underwriting Agencies) Ltd*,[33] the House of Lords held that section 32(1)(b) applies to deliberate concealment after the cause of action accrued (i.e. subsequent concealment). In these circumstances, the limitation period is restarted so that time begins to rerun after the concealment has been discovered.

SUMMARY

1. The subject of limitation of actions is concerned with the time-period within which a plaintiff must commence his action.
2. The purpose of this area of law is to strike a balance between allowing a plaintiff sufficient time in which to bring an action and yet not disadvantaging a defendant by allowing stale claims to be brought against him.
3. An action for breach of a simple contract cannot be brought after the expiration of six years from the date of the breach. This period is extended to twelve years in the case of a contract made under seal.
4. An action in the tort of negligence for death or personal injury must be commenced within three years from the date on which the cause of action accrued or the date (if later) of the plaintiff's knowledge of his injuries.
5. The court has a statutory discretion to disapply this three year time-limit if it appears to be equitable to do so.
6. An action for damages for negligence not involving death or personal injury must be brought within either
   (a) six years from the date on which the cause of action accrued (the primary limitation period); or
   (b) three years from the date when the plaintiff discovered, or should have discovered, the damage (the secondary limitation period).
7. No action for damages for negligence not involving death or personal injury can be brought after the expiration of 15 years from the date of the negligence (the statutory long-stop).
8. In an action for negligent mis-statement, the limitation period is six years from the date when the plaintiff acted to his detriment in reliance on the negligent advice.
9. Where the action is based upon the defendant's fraud or the plaintiff's right of action is deliberately concealed from him by the defendant or the action is for relief from the consequences of a mistake, the period of limitation does not begin to run until the plaintiff has discovered, or should have discovered, the fraud, concealment or mistake.

NOTES

1. [1977] AC 547, p.575 and quoted in Derek Morgan, *Limitation Act 1980*, Current Law Statutes Annotated, Volume 2, chapter 58, Sweet & Maxwell, 1980.
2. DTI/DoE, *Professional Liability – Report of the Study Teams*, HMSO, 1989.
3. [1990] 2 All ER 908.
4. For further discussion of the date of knowledge, see The Law Commission Consultation Paper, *Limitation of Actions* (1998), paras 338–365.
5. [1963] AC 758.
6. [1972] 1 QB 373, p.396.

7. [1976] QB 858.
8. *Ibid*, n.7, p.868.
9. [1978] AC 728.
10. *Ibid*, n.9, p.760.
11. [1986] CLY 210; (1986) 279 EG 218.
12. (1980) 259 EG 491.
13. [1976] QB 801.
14. [1964] AC 465.
15. [1978] QB 554.
16. [1979] Ch. 384.
17. [1983] 2 AC 1.
18. *Ibid*., n.17, p.16.
19. [1985] 1 All ER 352.
20. [1986] 1 WLR 1141.
21. [1982] 2 All ER 753.
22. [1986] 2 All ER 69.
23. Cmnd 9390, 1984.
24. [1990] 1 All ER 808.
25. [1995] 2 AC 145.
26. *Supra*, n.3, p.919.
27. [1992] 1 All ER 854.
28. [1996] AC 624.
29. *Ibid*, n.28, p.648.
30. For proposals for reform, see Law Commission Consultation Paper No. 151, *op. cit.*, n.4. These proposals are discussed in Chapter 12.
31. *Gray* v. *T.P. Bennett & Sons* (1987) 43 BLR 63, cited in Law Commission Consultation Paper No. 151, p.148.
32. [1971] 2 All ER 747.
33. [1996] AC 102.

11

Construction Products – General Liability Issues

INTRODUCTION

The purpose of this chapter is to discuss three legislative measures which originate from the European Community (EC) and which affect liability for construction products:

(1) Part I of the Consumer Protection Act 1987, which is based on the Product Liability Directive 1985;[1]
(2) the Construction Products Regulations 1991 (as amended),[2] which implement into United Kingdom (UK) law the Construction Products Directive 1988;[3] and
(3) the General Product Safety Regulations 1994,[4] which implement into UK law the General Product Safety Directive 1992.[5]

These measures have two purposes. Their principal purpose is to harmonise the laws of the Members States in relation to product safety and thereby remove distortions in competition within the EC. They are part of the Commission's programme for the completion of a Single European Market. Their secondary purpose is the provision of consumer protection, i.e. to ensure that every consumer within the EC has the same high degree of protection in relation to injury or damage caused by defective products. In this second respect, they form part of a comprehensive Community code governing the obligations of producers and suppliers in respect of the safety of the goods and services which they sell.

PART I OF THE CONSUMER PROTECTION ACT 1987

The purpose of this section is to outline the provisions of Part I of the Consumer Protection Act 1987 (CPA) and to examine how far they implement into UK law the provisions of the Product Liability Directive. A detailed critique of this legislation is beyond the scope of this work, though particular attention is paid to those provisions which are of particular relevance to liabilities in the construction industry.[6]

264

The basic principle

The basic principle on which the Directive is based is contained in Article 1, which states:

> The producer shall be liable for damage caused by a defect in his product.

This provision is implemented by section 2(1) of the CPA, which states:

> Subject to the following provisions of this Part, where any damage is caused wholly or partly by a defect in a product, every person to whom subsection (2) below applies shall be liable for the damage.

There are two important features of these provisions to be noted. In the first place, their significance lies in what they do *not* state. They do not state that there is any need to establish fault, and from this it can be deduced that the basis of liability under section 2(1) is strict. The second important feature of section 2(1) is that a claim under it does not depend upon the victim of a defective product having a contract with the producer of that product. In other words, the problem of privity of contract is avoided.

Until the implementation of this Directive, the legal position of a person injured by a defective product varied under the legal systems of the Member States. Some systems required the victim to establish negligence on the part of the producer, while other systems imposed strict liability on the producer. In a system of strict liability for defective products, the damage suffered by the victim is more likely to be passed on to the producer and to form part of the general cost of production than in a negligence system of product liability, where the victim often has difficulty in proving that the producer is at fault. Thus, costs of production are generally higher in a strict liability system of product liability than in a negligence system of product liability. Such differences in costs would distort competition between the Member States and prevent the completion of the Single Market. The implementation of a strict liability system throughout the Community removes these distortions and at the same time provides consumers in the EC with the same degree of protection.

Two points need highlighting in this context. In the first place, the implementation of the Directive does not replace the pre-existing product liability laws of the Member States; rather it is in addition to those laws. Thus, in the UK, Part I of the CPA does not replace the pre-existing fault-based system of liability originating from *Donoghue* v. *Stevenson*.[7] Secondly, the new law is not free of difficulties for the victim: the burden of proof is still on him to show that he suffered damage, that the product was defective and that the defect caused the damage. These requirements may prove stumbling blocks in controversial areas such as defective drugs.

What is a product?

A product is defined in Article 2 of the Directive to include:

> ... all movables, with the exception of primary agricultural products and game, even though incorporated into another movable or into an immovable. 'Primary agricultural products' means the products of the soil, of stock-farming and of fisheries, excluding products which have undergone initial processing. 'Product' includes electricity.

It will be noted, for the purposes of Construction Law, that this definition extends to a movable which has been 'incorporated into an immovable'. The definition of product extends therefore to building components, but not to the building itself.

The definition of 'product' contained in the CPA is based on that contained in the Directive. By section 1(2), a product is defined as:

> ... any goods or electricity and ... includes a product which is comprised in another product, whether by virtue of being a component part or raw material or otherwise.

'Goods' are defined widely in section 45 to include substances, growing crops and things comprised in land by virtue of being attached to it, and any ship, aircraft or vehicle.

In the case of buildings and building components the relevant sections of the CPA are 46(3) and (4). Section 46(3) provides that:

> ... subject to subsection (4) below, the performance of any contract by the erection of any building or structure on any land or by the carrying out of any other building works shall be treated for the purposes of this Act as a supply of goods in so far as, but only in so far as, it involves the provision of any goods to any person by means of their incorporation into the building, structure or works.

Section 46(4) provides, so far as is material, that:

> ... references in this Act to supplying goods shall not include references to supplying goods comprised in land where the supply is effected by the creation or disposal of an interest in the land.

The cumulative effect of these provisions is that if a builder is employed to erect a building on land owned by the employer, the employer will have the protection of the CPA in respect of defective products supplied or produced by the builder and incorporated into the building.[8] Thus, if a builder installs a defective piece of electrical equipment in a building which causes personal injury, then liability will attach to the builder as supplier of that equipment. The builder in this case will not be liable under the provisions of the CPA if the building itself is defective.[9] In the case of a builder who erects a building on his own land and then disposes of that building by way of a contract for the sale or lease of the land, he will not be liable under the provisions of the CPA in respect of any defective products incorporated into the building. It is not clear whether, in this second case, the builder may be liable as producer under the provisions of the CPA in the event of the completed building being defective.[10]

Who is liable?

Under the provisions of Article 3 of the Directive, which are implemented by section 2(2) of the CPA, liability is imposed upon:

(a) the producer of the product;
(b) any person who, by putting his name on the product or by using a trade mark or other distinguishing mark in relation to the product, has held himself out to be the producer of the product;
(c) any person who has imported the product into a Member State from a place outside the Member States in order, in the course of any business of his, to supply it to another.

A producer in relation to a product is defined widely by section 1(2) of the CPA to include:

(a) the person who manufactured it;
(b) in the case of a substance which has not been manufactured but has been won or abstracted, the person who won or abstracted it;
(c) in the case of a product which has not been manufactured, won or abstracted but essential characteristics of which are attributable to an individual or other process having been carried out (for example, in relation to agricultural produce), the person who carried out that process.

Beyond the above three groups, section 2(3) of the CPA provides that any other supplier may be liable, regardless of whether or not he produced the product or the constituent components giving rise to the damage. He must have been asked by a person who has suffered damage wholly or partly as a result of a defect in the product to identify one or more persons who fall within any of the above groups. The request must have been made within a reasonable time after the damage occurred and at a time when it was not reasonably practicable for the person making the request to identify all the persons in these groups. A supplier who fails to give information in response to such a request becomes liable and appears to remain liable even though the information is later discovered by some other means. Clearly, a builder will be liable under the CPA if he supplies defective building materials and cannot identify the person who supplied him with those materials. Further, he will be liable as a 'producer' if he has carried out an industrial process on the materials supplied, e.g. mixing concrete or cement.

What is a defect?

The cornerstone of both the Directive and Part I of the CPA is, of course, the concept of defectiveness. Under the provisions of Article 6 of the Directive and section 3(1) of the CPA, a product is defective when it does not provide the safety which persons generally are entitled to expect, taking into account all the circumstances. A great deal has been written about this concept,[11] and only a few brief comments will be offered here on it. In the first place, it should be noted that defectiveness is limited to the safety of the product. Products which are unmerchantable or unfit for their purpose, but otherwise safe, fall outside the scope of this definition.Secondly, the test of safety is based on consumer expectations. Thus, products which are inherently dangerous or which become dangerous if misused are not necessarily defective.

Section 3(2) of the CPA, implementing and expanding upon the provisions of Article 6 of the Directive, states that in assessing defectiveness all the circumstances must be taken into account, including:

(a) the manner in which, and purposes for which, the product has been marketed, its get-up, the use of any mark in relation to the product and any instructions for, or warnings with respect to, doing or refraining from doing anything with or in relation to the product;

(b) what might reasonably be expected to be done with or in relation to the product; and

(c) the time when the product was supplied by its producer to another.

Paragraph (a) makes it clear that a product may be 'defective', even though it fulfils its design function in precisely the manner in which the manufacturer intends, if hazards associated with its use are not sufficiently brought to the consumer's attention.Paragraph (b) requires the producer to be able to foresee predictable misuse and eliminate any hazards. If this is not possible or feasible, then adequate warnings or instructions must be provided. Under the provisions of paragraph (c) a product will not be considered defective simply because a safer product is subsequently put into circulation.A car with a rigid steering column and no seat belts would be considered defective if so designed today, but fifty years ago such features were acceptable. Section 3(2) of the CPA provides for this by adding:

> ... and nothing in this section shall require a defect to be inferred from the fact alone that the safety of a product which is supplied after that time is greater than the safety of the product in question.

Without this provision, producers would constantly have to recall or modify older products every time they introduced a safety improvement.

What damages are recoverable?

Under the provisions of Article 9 of the Directive, 'damage' means:

(a) damage caused by death or by personal injuries;
(b) damage to, or destruction of, any item of property other than the defective product itself, with a lower threshold of 500 ECU provided that the item of property:
  (i) is of a type ordinarily intended for private use or consumption, and
  (ii) was used by the injured person mainly for his own private use or consumption.

These provisions are implemented by section 5 of the CPA, where subsection (4) puts the lower threshold at £275.

A number of further points need to be noted in relation to these provisions. Firstly, there is no liability for damage to the product itself. This is, of course, the same as the position under the common law of negligence. The manufacturer of a defective, though not dangerous, building will thus not be liable, either in negligence or under the CPA. In each case, a claim is regarded as one for pure economic loss because it involves putting onto the market a product or building of less value than it was supposed to be under the contract.[12] The only possible exception to this rule would be if the plaintiff could show that the damage was caused by 'other property'. In relation to buildings this concept has been given a narrow interpretation following the decision of the House of Lords in *Murphy* v. *Brentwood DC*.[13] Thus, a defect in an integral part of the structure of a building which causes damage to the rest of the building will not be recoverable. On the other hand, a distinct item, such as a central heating boiler, which is incorporated into the building and which is defective, thereby causing damage to the building itself, may well give rise to a claim for damages. Secondly, there is no liability for damage to business property.[14] Thus, if a defective central heating boiler damages a private house, then that will give rise to a claim for damages, but not if the boiler were to cause damage to, say, an office block.

What defences are available?

The Directive and Part I of the CPA provide for a number of defences. The most important of these defences is the development risks defence, which is expressed in the Act in the following terms:

> ... that the state of scientific and technical knowledge at the relevant time was not such that a producer of products of the same description as the product in question might be expected to have discovered the defect if it had existed in his products while they were under his control.[15]

This version of the defence differs significantly from the form which it takes in the Directive:

> ... that the state of scientific and technical knowledge at the time when he put the product into circulation was not such as to enable the existence of the defect to be discovered.[16]

Thus, the test under Part I of the Act is whether a producer of similar products might have been expected to have discovered the defect; under the Directive the test is whether the knowledge existed to discover the defect.

The limitation period

Under the provisions of Articles 10 and 11 of the Directive, which are implemented by Schedule 1 to the CPA, there is a limitation period of three years for the recovery of damages. This period commences on the date that the plaintiff knew of the damage, the defect and the producer's identity. There is a ten year 'long-stop' limitation period from the date that the producer put the product into circulation.

It is difficult thus far to attempt an overall assessment of this legislation for the construction industry, or any other industry, for that matter. The Act has yet to come before the courts and so the full extent of liability under its provisions cannot be accurately gauged. In essence, liability may attach to a building contractor under the provisions of Part I of the Act if defects in goods supplied as part of construction works cause death, personal injury or damage to private property other than the defective works themselves. In view of the definition of defective in the Act and of the existence of a development risks defence, many commentators believe that the scheme of strict liability it introduces adds little to the existing common law of negligence save reversing the burden of proof. This may prove a little too pessimistic. Much will depend on how the courts interpret the development risks defence.

CONSTRUCTION PRODUCTS REGULATIONS 1991

In addition to the general provisions of Part I of the CPA provisions specific to the construction industry are to be found in the Construction Products Regulations 1991, which implement into UK law the provisions of the Construction Products Directive. The Regulations were passed under section 2(2) of the European Community Act 1972 and by Regulation 1 they came into force on 27 December 1991, but do not apply to any construction product which was supplied for the first time in the Community before that date.

The Construction Products Directive was adopted by the European Commission on 27 December 1988. Its general purpose is the achievement of uniform minima of consumer protection in relation to construction products in the Member States. Thus, in the preamble to the Directive it states:

> Member States are responsible for ensuring that building and civil engineering works on their territory are designed and executed in a way that does not endanger the safety of persons, domestic animals and property, while respecting other essential requirements in the interests of general well being.

The preamble notes the disparity throughout the EC in the way in which the Member States regulate the construction of buildings. It is thought that this disparity distorted competition in the EC and that the achievement of uniformity in this area of the law – in particular, the standards to be reached by construction products – would be a significant factor in creating a level playing field in the construction industry in the EC.

What is a construction product?

This is defined by Regulation 2(1) as any product, other than a minor part product, which is produced for incorporation in a permanent manner in works. A minor part product is defined as a construction product which is included in a list of products which play a minor part with respect to health and safety drawn up, managed and revised periodically by the European Commission.[17]

The basic principle of fitness for use

The essential principle on which the Regulations are based is that of fitness for use. Regulation 3(1) provides that construction products must meet certain standards in relation to the fitness for use of the *building works in which they are incorporated*. Fitness for use is defined in terms of satisfying certain essential requirements in so far as these requirements apply to the works. Schedule 2 to the Regulations states that these requirements must be satisfied for the 'economically reasonable working life' of a construction product subject to normal maintenance and forseeable working loads and requirements. They are expressed in terms of six general objectives, namely:

(1) mechanical resistance and stability;
(2) safety in case of fire;
(3) hygience, health and the environment;
(4) safety in use;
(5) protection against noise; and
(6) energy economy and heat retention.

These objectives are set out in detail in interpretative documents published in the 'C' series of the *Official Journal of the European Communities* and they in turn lead to the formulation of harmonised standards for construction products which are transposed into 'relevant national standards'.

The CE marking

One of the key concepts in the Directive and the UK Regulations is the CE marking. This is a mark of quality; under the provisions of Regulation 4(1) any construction product which bears this mark is presumed to satisfy the standards of fitness for use with respect to the essential requirements in Regulation 3 and is therefore entitled to free circulation within the EC, unless there are reasonable grounds for suspecting that the product does not satisfy that requirement or that the CE marking has not been affixed in accordance with Regulation 5. It is important to note that the use of the CE marking is voluntary, so that non-CE marked products which meet the essential requirements are legal.

Regulation 5(1) provides that the CE marking can be fixed to a product provided that four conditions are satisfied. These are:

(i)   the product complies with an appropriate technical specification;
(ii) the appropriate attestation procedure has been followed;
(iii) an EC certificate of conformity or declaration of conformity has been used or made in respect of the product; and
(iv) the product complies with any requirements of other legislation implementing relevant EC directives applying to it.

Under the provisions of Regulation 5(2), the CE marking must be accompanied by sufficient information to enable the manufacturer of the product to be easily identified. In addition certain other information must accompany the mark where appropriate:

(a) indications to identify the characteristics of the product, by reference to relevant technical specifications where they apply;
(b) the last two digits of the year of manufacture;
(c) identification of the approval body involved;
(d) the number of EC certificate of conformity.

The CE marking can be:

- on the product itself; or
- on the label attached to the product; or
- on the packaging; or
- on the accompanying commercial documentation.

The commonest ways in which products are likely to qualify for the CE marking are by conforming to a harmonized European standard or being awarded a European Technical Approval (ETA) by an approved EC issuing body. The British Board of Agreement has been designated for this role in the UK. The development of harmonised European standards is the responsibility of CEN and CENELEC technical committees. The European Organisation for Technical Approvals (EOTA) is responsible for developing the ETA system.[18]

In the case of products bearing the CE marking, Regulations 6(1) and 6(2) contain a requirement to keep available and produce the CE certificate or a copy of it. This requirement is imposed either (a) on the person who affixes the CE mark to a construction product, or (b) if that person is not established in the UK, on the person who first supplies the product in the UK. Regulation 7 states that if a product is not CE marked then it may still be possible to place it on the market (e.g. in the circumstances where no 'relevant technical specification' has been produced for it). However, the supplier of such a product is required to give to an enforcement authority all the information which he has about it.

Offences

The Regulations create three offences in this area. First, it is an offence to make a CE declaration of conformity in respect of, or to affix the CE marking to a construction product otherwise than in accordance with the Regulations. Secondly, by Regulation 5(3), marking has been affixed otherwise than in accordance with the Regulations, it is an offence to supply a construction product on the first occasion when it is supplied in the community. Thirdly, by Regulation 8(1), it is an offence to supply a construction product which does not satisfy the essential requirements of the Regulations.

Removal of construction products from the market

The regulations enable action to be taken to remove from the market construction products which do not satisfy the requirements of the Regulations. Under the provisions of Regulation 9(1), the Secretary of State may serve a prohibition notice prohibiting a person from supplying a product, or a notice to warn requiring him to publish a warning about products supplied. Regulation 9(4) provides that it is an offence to contravene a prohibition notice or a notice to warn. An enforcement authority may serve a suspension notice prohibiting a person from supplying a product for a period of six months from the date of the notice and again, it is an offence to contravene such a notice (Regulations 10(1) and 10(6). It may also apply to the court for an order that a product be forfeited (Regulation 12(1)).

Enforcement of the Regulations

The success of the Regulations, as with all legislation which creates regulatory offences, will depend ultimately on how effectively they are enforced. Like other recent legislation of this kind, they grant impressive, if not draconian, powers to the enforcement authorities. But how widely these powers will be used will depend on the resources available to the enforcement authorities. The Regulations themselves and their Explanatory Notes are silent on this point. Under the provisions of Regulation 15, responsibility for enforcement is placed on trading standards authorities in Great Britain and District Councils in Northern Ireland.[19]

The enforcement mechanism contained in the Regulations is closely modelled on Parts IV and V of the Consumer Protection Act 1987. Powers are conferred on the enforcement authorities to make test purchases, search premises and examine, seize and detain products and records, and customs officers are permitted to seize and detain imported products (Regulations 16–19). Obstructing an officer employed by an enforcement authority is an offence (Regulation 20).

Under the provisions of Regulation 22, compensation is payable to any person for any loss or damage resulting from the exercise of the above powers if:

(a) there has not been a contravention of the Regulations; and
(b) the exercise of these powers does not result from any neglect or default on the part of the person to be compensated.

Defences

The Regulations contain the usual defence of due diligence contained in criminal consumer protection statutes. That is, in proceedings against a person for an offence under the Regulations it shall be a defence for that person to show that he took all reasonable steps and exercised all due diligence to avoid committing the offence (Regulation 26(1)). In addition, where the commission by any person of an offence under the Regulations is due to an act or default committed by another person in the course of his business, then proceedings can be taken against that person in addition to the first-mentioned person (Regulation 27(1)).

Liability issues arising from the Construction Products Regulations

These Regulations impose *criminal* liability upon the *supplier* of a construction product which does not meet the essential requirements; they are not about *civil* liability as such, but arguably they do impinge on the civil liability of design professionals and builders.

Design professions (i.e. architects and engineers) will generally be under a duty to provide reasonable supervision of the building or engineering works. If it turns out that some or all of the materials used in the construction of the works do not meet the essential requirements laid down by the Regulations then arguably the architect or engineer will not have discharged that duty.

Another task which may fall to the architect or engineer is the recommendation of the materials to be used by the contractor. In carrying out this task, these design professionals are under a duty to use reasonable care and skill, but they do not normally guarantee that any recommended product will be fit for a particular purpose. However, it seems that this aspect of the architect's or engineer's duty or care will now extend to ensuring that a product meets the essential requirements before recommending it. If a product which is not CE marked and which does not meet the essential requirements is recommended then, arguably, the duty of reasonable care and skill will not have been satisfied. Further, it must be remembered that the architect or engineer is under a duty to ensure that any products he recommends meet any specifications laid down by the employer. If those specifications go further than the essential requirements laid down by the Regulations then for the architect or engineer simply to satisfy those requirements and no more will not be enough to discharge his legal duty to the employer. In the event of the builder using a product which does not meet the essential requirements but which was *not* recommended by the architect or engineer then presumably the duty of these professionals will be to warn the employer of this fact.

The builder is under implied obligations to supply materials which are of satisfactory quality and fit for their purpose.[20] Arguably, these obligations will now extend to ensuring that the materials he uses meet the essential requirements. Unlike the duty owed by the architect or engineer in this respect this duty is strict, i.e. the builder will still be liable for the use of products which do not meet the essential requirements even though he may have exercised reasonable care and skill in selecting them, e.g. by consulting with the supplier and/or an expert.

Finally in this section, it should be noted that presumably *civil* liability will also be imposed on the supplier of a construction product which does not meet the essential requirements; in these circumstances, arguably he will be in breach of his implied obligations of satisfactory quality and fitness for purpose in the contract of sale with the builder.[21] Again, this liability will be strict. Indeed, it is the fact that the builder in these circumstances has what amounts to an indemnity action against the supplier which the courts have used to justify imposing strict liability with respect to materials on the builder.[22]

To summarise, recent years have seen an increasing emphasis on product safety, both in the civil law and the criminal law, and the Construction Products Regulations are a continuation of that trend. Safety in buildings traditionally has been largely a matter of safety in the *construction* of buildings – the law has required builders to comply with the provisions of the Building Regulations in the construction of buildings. There were no safety requirements relating to *materials* used in the construction of buildings other than the general implied terms in a contract for work and materials that the materials be of satisfactory quality and fit for their purpose. By introducing specific standards of fitness for use for construction products the Regulations are a radical development in this area of law.

THE GENERAL PRODUCT SAFETY REGULATIONS 1994

The General Product Safety Regulations 1994 implement the General Product Safety Directive which was adopted by the European Council on 29 June 1992. Like the other two directives discussed in this chapter, this Directive is part of the Commission's programme for the establishment of the Single Market. Recital 2 of the Directive states that legislation on product safety in the Member States differs in the level of protection it affords to persons, and that these disparities are likely to create barriers to trade and distortions of competition within the EC. The principal purpose of the Directive is to remove these disparities by harmonising the laws of the Member States relating to product safety. The secondary purpose of the Directive is to provide a broadly based legislative framework with a view to ensuring a high level of safety and health of perons, as required by Article 100a(3) of the Treaty of Rome.

The main provisions of the Regulations will now be examined.

The general safety requirement

The key provision in the Regulations is the general safety requirement. This provision is contained in Regulation 7, which states that 'No producer shall place a product on the market unless the product is a safe product'. Regulations 8 and 9 impose certain duties on producers and distributors as part of the general safety requirement. Regulation 8 imposes a requirement as to information and monitoring on producers. Regulation 8(1) states that within the limits of their respective activities, a producer must:

(a) provide consumers with the relevant information to enable them to assess the risks inherent in a product throughout the normal or reasonably foreseeable period of its use, where such risks are not immediately obvious without adequate warnings, and to take precautions against those risks; and

(b) adopt measures commensurate with the characteristics of the products which he supplies, to enable him to be informed of the risks which these products might present and to take appropriate action including, if necessary, withdrawing the product in question from the market to avoid these risks.

Regulation 8(2) provides that the above measures may include, whenever appropriate –

(i) marking of the products or product batches in such a way that they can be identified;
(ii) sample testing of marketed products;
(iii) investigating complaints; and
(iv) keeping distributors informed of such monitoring.

The requirements of distributors in respect of the general safety requirement are contained in Regulation 9. This provides that a distributor shall act with due care in order to help ensure compliance with the general safety requirement and, in particular, without limiting this general duty –

(a) a distributor must not supply products to any person which he knows, or should have presumed, on the basis of the information in his possession and as a professional, are dangerous products; and
(b) within the limits of his activities, a distributor must participate in monitoring the safety of products placed on the market, in particular by passing on information on the product risks and co-operating in the action taken to avoid those risks.

Who is a 'producer'?

Under the provisions of Regulation 2(1), a 'producer' means:

(a) the manufacturer of the product, when he is established in the Community, and includes any person presenting himself as the manufacturer by affixing to the product his name, trade mark or other distinctive mark, or the person who reconditions the product;
(b) when the manufacturer is not established in the Community,
   (i) if the manufacturer does not have a representative established in the Community, the importer of the product;
   (ii) in all other cases, the manufacturer's representative; and
(c) other professionals in the supply chain, insofar as their activities may affect the safety properties of a product placed on the market.

Who is a consumer?

Regulation 2(1) states that '"consumer" means a consumer acting otherwise than in the course of a commercial activity'.

What is a product?

Regulation 2(1) defines a product as:

> any product intended for consumers or likely to be used by consumers, supplied whether for consideration or not in the course of a commercial activity and whether new, used or reconditioned; provided, however, a product which is used exclusively in the context of a commercial activity even if it is used for or by a consumer shall not be regarded as a product for the purposes of these Regulations provided always and for the avoidance of doubt this exception shall not extend to the supply of such a product to a consumer.

Thus, if a builder incorporates into a building owned or used by a person not engaged in a commercial activity an unsafe component, such as a faulty central heating boiler, then that building owner or user will be able to claim the protection of the Regulations.

What is a 'safe product'?

Under the provisions of Regulation 2(1), a 'safe product' means any product which, under normal or reasonably foreseeable conditions of use, including duration, does not present any risk or only the minimum risks compatible with the product's use, considered as acceptable and consistent with a high level of protection for the safety and health of persons. Regulation 2(1) goes on to state that in assessing the safety of a product several factors must be taken into account –

(a) the characteristics of the product, including its composition, packaging, instructions for assembly and maintenance;
(b) the effect on other products, where it is reasonably foreseeable that it will be used with other products;
(c) the presentation of the product, the labelling, any instructions for its use and disposal and any other indication or information provided by the producer; and
(d) the categories of consumers at serious risk when using the product, in particular children.

The fact that higher levels of safety may be obtained or other products presenting a lesser degree of risk may be available shall not of itself cause the product to be considered unsafe.

When is a product safe?

The provisions for determining when a product is safe are contained in Regulation 10. Regulation 10(1) provides that where a product conforms to the specific rules of the law of the United Kingdom laying down the health and safety requirements which the product must satisfy in order to be marketed, there shall be a presumption that, until the contrary is proved, the product is a safe product.

Under the provisions of Regulation 10(2), where no such specific rules exist, the conformity of a product to the general safety requirement must be assessed by taking into account the following matters –

(i) voluntary national standards of the United Kingdom giving effect to a European standard; or
(ii) Community technical specifications; or
(iii) if there are no such voluntary UK standards or Community technical specifications –
    (a) standards drawn up in the United Kingdom; or
    (b) the codes of good practice in respect of health and safety in the product sector concerned; or
    (c) the state of the art and technology and the safety which consumers may reasonably expect.

Offences

Regulation 12 provides that 'Any person who contravenes Regulation 7 or 9(a) shall be guilty of an offence'. There are two (contrasting) offences created by this provision. Breach of Regulation 7 is a strict liability offence, whereas breach of Regulation 9(a) is essentially fault-based in that the distributor knows, or should know, that the product concerned is dangerous.

Defences

In common with other consumer protection legislation, the Regulations provide for a due diligence defence. This defence is contained in Regulation 14(1), which provides that 'in proceedings against any person for an offence under these Regulations it shall be a defence for that person to show that he took all reasonable steps and exercised all due diligence to avoid committing the offence'. The essence of this defence is that in order to avoid committing an offence under the Regulations, a manufacturer or distributor must be able to show that he has set up a safety system which is designed to prevent unsafe goods from being placed on the market and that he has acted diligently in putting that system into operation. Where the person charged with an offence under the Regulations alleges that the commission of the offence was due (a) to the act or default of another, or (b) to reliance on information given by another, then, under the provisions of Regulation 14(3), he must serve a notice on the person bringing the proceedings identifying that other person. Regulation 14(4) provides that a person is not entitled to rely on the due diligence defence by reason of relying on information supplied by another unless he shows that it was reasonable in all the circumstances for him to have relied on the information, having regard in particular –

(a) to the steps which he took, and those which might reasonably have been taken, for the purpose of verifying the information; and
(b) to whether he had any reason to disbelieve the information.

Enforcement

The enforcement provisions are contained in Regulation 11. The main features of Regulation 11 are that it extends section 13 of the CPA 1987 (prohibition notices and notices to warn) to the Regulation and that the requirements of the Regulations constitute safety provisions for the purposes of sections 14–18 of the 1987 Act (suspension notices, forfeiture and powers to obtain information).

The relationship between the 1994 Regulations and the Construction Products Regulations

The question arises as to what is to be the relationship of this general safety duty to the detailed requirements of the Construction Products Regulations. It seems that where specific safety legislation is in existence then that will take precedence over the general duty, but where gaps exist or where the general duty would impose additional requirements then the general duty will apply.[23]

Liability issues arising from the General Product Safety Regulations

The essence of the 1994 Regulations is to impose *criminal* liability upon the manufacturer or distributor of a product which does not meet the general safety requirement. But, as in the case of the Construction Products Regulations, the General Product Safety Regulations will almost certainly have implications for the *civil* liability of design professionals and contractors. Thus architects and engineers will be under a duty to take reasonable care to see that any materials they recommend comply with the general safety requirement if such products are not covered by the provisions of the Construction Products Regulations. A contractor who supplies materials which do not meet the general safety requirement presumably will be in breach of his obligation to supply materials of satisfactory quality and fit for their purpose.

One point on which the 1994 Regulations are silent is whether or not they create an action for breach of statutory duty in the event of an individual suffering damage as a result of a producer or distributor being in breach of his duty under the Regulations. Under the provisions of section 41 of the

CPA, a breach of the general safety duty in Part II of that Act would enable the victim to sue for breach of statutory duty.

SUMMARY

1. Three measures emanating from the European Community bear on liability for defective construction products: Part I of the Consumer Protection Act 1987 (CPA), the Construction Products Regulations 1991 and the General Product Safety Regulations 1994.

Part I of the CPA

2. Under the provisions of the CPA, a producer is strictly liable for damage caused by a defect in his product.
3. For the purposes of the CPA, a producer includes a supplier regardless of whether or not he manufactured the product or the constituent components giving rise to the damage. Clearly, therefore, a contractor or design profesisonal who supplies materials is caught by the Act.
4. A product is defined by the Act as any goods or electricity and includes component parts. Goods incorporated into a building come within the scope of this definition, unless the builder is disposing of an interest in the land.
5. The CPA provides that a product is defective when it does not provide the safety which persons generally are entitled to expect.
6. A producer can be liable under the CPA only if his defective product results in death or personal injury or damage to other property, not for damage to the product itself.
7. The CPA contains a number of defences, the most important of which is the development risks defence. Under this defence, a producer will not be liable under the provisions of Part I of the CPA if he can show that the state of scientific and technical knowledge at the relevant time was not such that a producer of similar products mights have been expected to have discovered the defect.

The Construction Products Regulations 1991

8. Under the Construction Products Regulations 1991 construction products must be fit for use in the building works in which they are incorporated by meeting certain essential requirements.
9. These essential requirements are set out in detail in the 'C' series of the *Official Journal of the European Communities* and are transposed into relevant national standards.

10. A construction product will be presumed to satisfy the essential requirements if it bears a CE marking.
11. It is an offence to supply a construction product where the CE marking has been affixed otherwise than in accordance with the Regulations.
12. It is not an offence to place on the market a construction product which is not CE marked, but the supplier of such a product must be able to show to an enforcement authority that it meets the essential requirements.
13. Responsibility for enforcement is placed on trading standards authorities and they have powers to make test purchases, search premises and seize and detain products and records.
14. It is a defence for any person charged with an offence under the 1991 Regulations to show that he exercised all due diligence to avoid committing the offence.
15. A design professional who recommends materials that do not meet the essential requirements will arguably be in breach of his duty of reasonable care and skill owed to the employer.
16. A contractor's duty to use only materials that are of satisfactory quality and fit for their purpose will presumably extend to ensuring that the materials meet the essential requirements.

The General Product Safety Regulations 1994

17. The key provision in the General Product Safety Regulations 1994 is the general safety requirement that 'No producer shall place a product on the market unless the product is a safe product'.
18. Producers have a monitoring and information duty under the Regulations. They must monitor their products in order to be aware of any risks attaching to them and they must provide consumers with the necessary information to enable an assessment to be made of the risks inherent in a product throughout its period of use.
19. Distributors also are under a duty to ensure compliance with the general safety requirement.
20. A producer means not only the manufacturer of the product but also other professionals in the supply chain.
21. The 1994 Regulations are concerned only with products intended for consumers, i.e. persons not acting in the course of a commercial activity.
22. A product will be a safe product if it complies with specific health and safety requirements of UK law or, if no such requirements exist, with voluntary UK standards, codes of practice, EC specifications or the state of the art and technology.
23. It is an offence for a producer or a distributor to place on the market a product which contravenes the general safety requirement.

24. A producer or distributor charged with this offence will have a defence if he can show that he exercised all due diligence to avoid committing it.
25. If the defendant alleges that the commission of the offence was due to the act or default of another or to reliance on information supplied by another, then he must identify that other person. Further, in the case of reliance on information supplied by another, he must be able to show that he took reasonable steps to verify that information.
26. Wide powers (prohibition notices and notices to warn, suspension notices, forfeiture and powers to obtain information) are given to the enforcement authorities.
27. Design professionals will arguably be under a duty to take reasonable care to see that any materials they recommend comply with the general safety requirement, if such products are not within the scope of the 1991 Regulations.
28. A contractor who supplies materials which do not meet the general safety requirement will arguably be in breach of his obligation to supply materials of satisfactory quality and fit for their purpose.

NOTES

1. 85/374/EEC, OJ No. L210/29.
2. SI 1991 No. 1620, as amended by the Construction Products, (Amendment) Regulations 1994, SI 1994 No. 3051.
3. 89/106/EEC, OJ No. L40/12.
4. SI 1994 No. 2328.
5. 92/59/EEC, OJ No. L228/24.
6. For more detailed treatment of this area of law, the reader is referred, in particular, to Bradgate, J.R. and Savage, N. (1987) NLJ 929, 953, 1025, 1049; Merkin, R., *A Guide to the Consumer Protection Act 1987*, Financial Training Publications Ltd, 1987; Clark, A, *Product Liability*, Sweet & Maxwell, 1988; Wright, C.J, *Product Liability*, Blackstones, 1992; and Geddes, A., *Product and Service Liability in the EEC*, Sweet & Maxwell, 1992.
7. [1932] AC 562.
8. The builder will also be under a duty to supply materials which are of satisfactory quality and fit for their purpose under the provisions of Part I of the Supply of Goods and Services Act 1982 (as amended).
9. He will, however, owe a duty of care to the employer for the completed building under the provisions of the Defective Premises Act 1972.
10. The provisions of Part I of the Supply of Goods and Services Act 1982 do not apply to this case; however, the builder does owe a duty to the purchaser under the provisions of the Defective Premises Act 1972.
11. Clark, A., *supra*, n.6, Ch. 2.
12. See, in particular, *D & F Estates Ltd* v. *Church Commissioners for England* [1988] 2 All ER 992 and *Murphy* v. *Brentwood DC* [1990] 2 All ER 908.
13. *Ibid*, n.12, per Lord Oliver.
14. C.P.A., section 5(3).

15. C.P.A., section 4(1)(e).
16. Article 7(e).
17. Such lists are published in the 'C' series of the *Official Journal of the European Communities*.
18. See DoE (1992) *Euronews Construction*, May, p.3.
19. Guidance on the responsibilities of these bodies in enforcing the Regulations is provided by DoE Circular 13/91.
20. Supply of Goods and Services Act 1982, sections 4(2)–(6).
21. Sale of Goods Act 1979, section 14(2).
22. See *Young and Marten* v. *McManus Childs* (per Lord Reid) [1968]2 All ER 1169, 1172.
23. See DTI introduction to the Draft Directive on General Product Safety, Com. (89) 162.

12

Reform of Construction Law

INTRODUCTION

Construction Law at present can hardly be said to be in a satisfactory state and a number of proposals have been put forward for its reform. It is the object of this chapter to examine these proposals.

The need for reform and the adequacy of proposals for reform can be properly understood only if the structure and principles of the existing law are grasped. It is worthwhile, therefore, summarising the present law governing liability for the construction of defective buildings and recounting briefly the recent fluctuations in these liabilities. The law at present governing this area can be summed up as follows:

1. A contract for the sale of a dwelling is subject to the maxim of *caveat emptor*, unless the seller had provided the buyer with a warranty as to the quality of the dwelling. This is very unlikely as in most cases the buyer will be expected to survey the property to see if it has any defects. Generally speaking, the only basis on which the seller of a dwelling may be liable to the purchaser for defects in it will be a misrepresentation on which the buyer relies, e.g. a false statement that the dwelling has been rewired recently.

2. Where the seller is a vendor/builder or where the owner or occupier of a dwelling has employed a builder to carry out improvement works on the dwelling then the buyer or the owner or occupier will have the protection of the implied obligations of workmanship and quality and fitness of materials.[1]

3. A subsequent purchaser or tenant of the building will have no action in tort against the builder unless either (i) he can show that he relied on the builder in the sense in which reliance is now defined by the courts, or (ii) the defective building work can be brought within the complex structure theory as now defined by the House of Lords.[2]

4. When a local authority carries out its building control function it is not liable in negligence to the owner or occupier of a building for the cost of remedying a dangerous defect in the building which is discovered before such owner or occupier suffers personal injury or damage to other property. The question of whether a local authority is liable in negligence to

285

an owner or occupier of a building who does suffer personal injury or damage to other property as a result of a latent defect in the building is undecided.[3]

5.   A design professional owes a duty to the employer to carry out the design of the building works with reasonable care and skill.[4]

6.   In the case of a dwelling the builder, designer or developer will be liable for breach of the obligations contained in section 1(1) of the Defective Premises Act 1972. Such liability will be owed to the first buyer and to subsequent buyers, subject to the limitation period laid down in the Act.

7.   Where a dwelling is subject to the NHBC scheme then the builder will be liable for breach of the warranties contained in that scheme. Again, liability will be owed to the first buyer and to subsequent buyers. The warranties cover a period of ten years from the date of completion of the dwelling.

8.   A surveyor employed by a mortgagee to carry out a mortgage valuation survey of a low or moderately priced dwelling-house owes a duty of care not only in contract to the mortgagee, but also in tort to the mortgagor.[5]

9.   A professional person in providing advice and/or services to his client will owe him a duty of care under the general law of tort as well as under the contract.[6]

10.   The benefit of the contractual obligations of the contractor and the design professional to the employer do not extend to third parties unless such parties are provided with collateral warranties to that effect or are named in the original contract.

11.   An action for damages for defective building work resulting from negligence must be brought within either six years from the date of the negligence or within three years from the date when the plaintiff discovered, or should have discovered, the damage. These periods are subject to the rule that no action can be brought after the expiration of 15 years from the date of the negligence.

Two legal concepts underlie these propositions: first, the doctrine of privity of contract, that a person cannot enforce rights under a contract to which he is not a party, and secondly, the rule that the cost of repairing a defect in a building to prevent personal injury or damage to other property is economic loss and as such is not recoverable in tort by a third party.

The immense importance of these legal propositions for liabilities in the construction industry must be seen against the complex structure of legal relationships which arise in any construction projects. As we have seen in Chapter 1, construction projects typically involve a number of different contracts between the developer, the main contractor, subcontractors, the architect or engineer and financiers. In view of the doctrine of privity of contract, those not privy to a particular contract cannot rely on its provisions to found a contractual action. Further, following the decisions in *D & F Estates Ltd* v.

Church Commissioners for England[7] and *Murphy* v. *Brentwood District Council*, a builder will not be liable in tort to a subsequent purchaser in respect of the cost of repair of defects in the quality of the building unless it can be shown that there is a special relationship between the parties. So far in the area of Construction Law, only surveyors have been brought within the scope of the concept of the special relationship.[8] The result of these developments has been that developers, subsequent purchasers and tenants frequently seek to protect themselves by means of collateral warranties made with the developer, the main contractor, subcontractors and the architect or engineer. This trend introduced considerable complexity into the legal structure of the construction process. It has been estimated that in the case of an average shopping centre, a design professional may be expected to enter into separate collateral warranties with the financiers, the purchasers and 50 or more tenants.[9]

As we have seen in Chapter 9, an important exception to the doctrine of privity of contract is created by the Contracts (Rights of Third Parties) Act 1999. The provisions of that Act will permit a third party to enforce a term of the contract if the contract expressly confers a legally enforceable obligation on him. Thus, subsequent purchasers, tenants and funding institutions can be granted a right to enforce the contractual obligations of the building contractor or of the design professional without the need for a large number of collateral warranties.

In the law of tort, a number of developments have occurred since the decision in *Murphy* to suggest that, although still important, the exclusionary rule no longer occupies as central a place in the English law of obligations as it did when the decision was handed down. Crucially in this context, it did not disturb the principle of reliance laid down in *Hedley Byrne & Co.* v. *Heller & Partners*[10], and a number of decisions indicate a willingness on the part of the appellate courts to deploy the reliance principle in order to permit the recovery of economic loss. The most important of those decisions is *Henderson* v. *Merrett*,[11] where the House of Lords held that the *Hedley Byrne* principle may give to a tortious duty of care in the context of negligent advice irrespective of whether there is a contractual relationship between the parties. In *White* v. *Jones*,[12] the House of Lords extended the *Hedley Byrne* principle by holding that the assumption of responsibility by a solicitor towards his client when preparing his client's will extended to a beneficiary under the will. The beneficiary, in these circumstances, could not be said to have relied on the solicitor, but the solicitor could reasonably foresee that, in the event of his negligence, the beneficiary would be deprived of his legacy under the will. Moreover, preparing a will is not making statement but performing a task.

These post-*Murphy* decisions are significant in two respects. In the first place, the *Hedley Byrne* principle as an exception to the exclusionary rule depends upon the assumption that it is possible to distinguish between negligent acts or omissions and negligent misstatements. However, Lord Devlin in *Hedley Byrne* questioned the validity of this distinction.[13] Further, Lord Goff in *Henderson* v. *Merrett* said that the *Hedley Byrne* principle extended to services[14] and in *White* v. *Jones* the principle seems to have been extended to an act or, more accurately, an omission. If the distinction between negligent acts or omissions and negligent mis-statements is no longer valid then *Hedley Byrne* cannot be regarded as an exception to the exclusionary rule and either that case or *Murphy* is wrongly decided. The second important feature of the post-*Murphy* decisions on negligence is that they do not rest upon a sharp distinction between situations involving liability in tort and situations involving liability in contract. The decision in *Murphy* rested upon a dichotomy between the law of contract and the law of tort.

In contrast to the post-*Murphy* decisions of the House of Lords, the appeal courts of New Zealand, Australia and Canada have departed completely from the exclusionary rule.[15] Thus, the majority of the Australian Court of Appeal in *Bryan* v. *Maloney* said that the view of the House of Lords in *Murphy* rested 'upon a narrower view of the scope of the modern law of negligence and a more rigid compartmentalisation of contract and tort than is acceptable under the law of this country'.[16] These Commonwealth decisions differ in scope but, in general, they may be said to permit recovery in the tort of negligence for loss resulting from a defective building.

These post-*Murphy* developments must be read with caution, however. In the first place, Commonwealth decisions are not binding on the English Courts; they are merely of persuasive authority and there is no evidence that the Commonwealth decisions relating to negligence and defective buildings have persuaded the English Courts to depart from the exclusionary rule. Secondly, the decisions of the English courts extending the reliance principle have not affected third party liabilities in the construction industry. Indeed, Lord Goff in *Henderson* v. *Merrett* was at pains to stress that the rule there laid down did not in any way by-pass the chain of contracts to be found in most construction projects.

The lasting importance of the exclusionary rule can be seen by examining its implications for third party liabilities. In this context, a distinction must be made between commercial buildings and dwellings. The former are not usually subject to any guarantees, but third parties may have a remedy against the contractor or design professional in the event of their being the recipient of an appropriate collateral warranty or of their being named as a beneficiary to the contract made between employer and contractor or between employer and design professional. However, an action for breach of contract must be brought within six years from the date of the breach and many defects in buildings occur outside that period. Virtually all new dwellings are covered by the NHBC ten year guarantee scheme and it may be wondered, therefore, why the decisions in *D & F Estates* and *Murphy* are considered so critical from a consumer protection standpoint. There are two specific reasons. First, the NHBC scheme is of no use where the defects come to light more than ten years after the dwelling is completed. In the case of defects caused by inadequate foundations that is usually the case; thus in *Murphy* the cracks did not appear until some twelve years after the house was built. Secondly, loss or damage resulting from defects caused by subsidence and inadequate foundations are not generally covered by domestic first party insurance. It is open to a house purchaser to sue his surveyor in these circumstances but failure on his part to discover a latent defect such as too shallow foundations is unlikely to constitute negligence, even if he has carried out a structural survey.

Finally, it must be remembered that the decisions in *D & F Estates* and *Murphy* may have rendered virtually redundant the reforms introduced into the law of limitation of actions by the Latent Damage Act 1986. The purpose of these reforms was to give plaintiffs in defective buildings cases a longer period in which to commence an action than they had under the Pirelli rule. However, such extension of the limitation period is of little use if the plaintiff has no cause of action.

There have been a number of proposals for the reform of Construction Law and areas of law which bear heavily on Construction Law. They are:

(1) a study set up by the DTI and the DoE – the resulting report of which is known as the Likierman Report;[17]
(2) proposals by the Law Commission for the reform of the doctrine of privity of contract,[18] which are implemented by the Contracts (Rights of Third Parties) Act 1999;[19]
(3) the report of the Latham Committee[20] and the subsequent report of Working Group 10 of the Construction Industry Board;[21]
(4) a consultation paper by the Common Law Team of the Law Commission on joint and several liability;[22]
(5) the Limited Liability Partnerships Act 2000;
(6) a Law Commission consultation paper on limitation of actions;[23] and
(7) proposals for the harmonisation of Construction Law throughout the member states of the European Union.[24]

THE LIKIERMAN PROPOSALS

The Likierman Report is in effect three reports produced by independent Study Teams: the Auditors' Study Team, the Surveyors' Study Team and the Construction Professionals' Study Team. The report of the Construction Professionals' Study Team is the longest of the three reports; in addition there are a number of annexes not included in the published report.[25] In this section the proposals made by the Construction Professionals' and Surveyors' Study Teams are examined.

Before examining the details of the Likierman recommendations it is important to remember the legal background against which the Study Teams were set up. The dominant feature of this background was an expanding law of negligence and in particular an expansion in the scope of the duty of care owed by a professional person to third parties. Although this expansion had come to an end by the time the report was published (1989), it greatly influenced the report's philosophy. That philosophy was concerned mainly with the interests of professional defendants and their fear of virtually unlimited liability and very high, if not prohibitively high, PII premiums. The report of the Construction Professionals' Study Team pointed out that an expanding law of tort in the period from the mid-1960s to the mid-1980s was accompanied by two further developments with implications for PII. First, there was a significant growth in the volume of defects that were discovered in recently completed buildings, partly as a result of the novel designs and new building materials which were introduced into the construction industry in the 1960s. Secondly, there was an increasing readiness on the part of building owners to seek legal redress, no doubt encouraged by developments in the law of tort.

The recommendations of the Construction Professionals' Study Team

The Study Team considered a number of proposals that were made to them for reforming the law of professional liability. Those proposals were of three kinds:

(i)   radical reform of risks and liabilities in the industry;
(ii)   consolidation of the existing law into a Construction Industry Bill; and
(iii)   amendments to legislation together with other measures to reduce uncertainty.

In effect the Study Team opted for the third set of proposals. The details of these proposals are as follows:

(1)   Limited liability

Construction professionals, along with other professionals have under the present law unlimited liability for the consequences of any negligence on their part. Although the Study Team concluded that it would not be possible to justify legislation to limit the liability of construction industry professionals without also considering limiting the liability of other professionals, they were in sympathy with the arguments that are often put forward in favour of such a proposal. These arguments include, in the first place, the consideration that the great majority of the industry's clients are limited liability companies or public corporations whereas consultants are frequently employed in partnerships with each partner being jointly and severally liable for the negligent acts of all the partners. Secondly, it is argued that the liability incurred should bear some relationship to the fee charged so that a service provided for a small fee should not give rise to unlimited liability.

Neither of these arguments seems particularly convincing, though the first point may seem to have a sort of rough and ready equity to it. The second argument ignores a fundamental principle of the law, which is that liability for negligence must be seen from the standpoint of its consequences; indeed it is damage consequent upon a careless act or omission which turns that act or omission into negligence in the eyes of the law. The fee charged for a particular job has no bearing either on this question or on the degree of care and skill which the law requires of the professional in carrying out the job.

The fact that many construction professionals have only limited resources with which to meet the damages awarded against them in negligence action may well point to any limitation clause in their contract of engagement as being reasonable under the provisions of section 11(4) of the Unfair Contract Terms Act 1977.[26] It seems better to deal with the problem of limited professional resources in this way. Both of the above factors can be taken into account in assessing the reasonableness of the limitation clause and, moreover, the statutory concept of reasonableness is more flexible than capping, as it is known, enabling each case to be judged on its merits.

(2)   Mandatory PII

This proposal was rejected by the Study Team principally on the ground of the cost of cover required. This argument seems to ingore the primary principle of insurance, that it is a means of spreading the losses resulting from negligence over the whole construction industry instead of those losses being allowed to lie where they fell. Moreover, some professional bodies, notably the Law Society and the RICS require their members to take out PII.

(3)   Strict liability

Not surprisingly the Study Team rejected any proposal for strict liability in the construction industry. Such a scheme would be a major departure from the duty of reasonable care and skill imposed upon construction professionals, except where they agree to design a building for a purpose made known to them in advance.

(4)   A reduction in the limitation period

As we have seen in Chapter 10, the purpose of the law of limitation of actions is to strike a balance between on the one hand, plaintiffs, who should be allowed adequate time in which to commence an action, and on the other hand, defendants, who need to know with certainty that beyond a certain time scale claims cannot be pursued against them. The problem of striking this balance is particularly acute in the construction industry because of the problem of latent defects, i.e. defects which may not be discoverable for many years after the completion of a building. The Study Team were of the view that the present law allowed too long a limitation period and they recommended:

(i)   that there should be a limitation period for negligent actions in tort and in contract (whether or not under seal) of ten years from the date of practical completion or effective occupation; and

(ii) that this ten years limitation period should act as a long-stop extinguishing these rights.

The aim of the Report's proposals in this respect was two-fold: (i) to provide a limitation period that was common to contract and tort and that commenced at the date of completion so that there would be no need to determine either the date when the damage occurred or when it was reasonably discoverable; and (ii) to bring the law of building into line with product liability, where, under the provisions of the Consumer Protection Act 1987, there is an absolute long-stop of ten years.

The proposal for a common limitation period seems a commendable one since it would infuse some much needed simplicity into this area of the law, but the aim of equating building law with product liability in this respect is much more debatable. Defects in buildings are much more likely to take longer to manifest themselves than defects in products and that would seem to justify a longer limitation period for them if the interests of plaintiffs and defendants are to be correctly balanced.

(5)   Joint liability

Under the present law, which is contained in section 1(1) of the Civil Liability (Contribution) Act 1978, where two or more persons are responsible for the plaintiff's losses or injuries then if the plaintiff so chooses he can take proceedings against only one of those persons, and, if he is successful, that defendant will be liable for the whole of his loss. This rule struck the Study Team as operating particularly unfairly in the construction industry where many clients are large scale companies with the necessary means of verifying that all parties have adequate financial backing. They recommended that construction professionals should no longer owe 100 per cent liability to the plaintiffs where they were only partially at fault. They did, however, go on to say that there should be an exception to this rule in the case of claims of less than £50,000 made by domestic clients.

To sum up, the Study Team's principal recommendations for reform of the law were two-fold:

(1) an amendment to the Limitation Act 1980 and the Latent Damage Act 1986 in order to achieve a limitation period of ten years from the date of

completion of the building, both for actions in contract and actions in tort;

(2) the abolition of joint liability in commercial transactions not involving personal injury where the plaintiff's claim exceeds £50,000 and where the defendant's actions were partly the cause of the plaintiff's damage and were not carried out jointly with another defendant.

The recommendations of the Surveyors' Study Team

1. Limiting liability

The report made two proposals for avoiding the uncertainties of the reasonableness test in the Unfair Contract Terms Act: (i) model clause 'certification'; and (ii) capping.

(i) Model clause 'certification'

This would be a scheme whereby a statutory body such as the Office of Fair Trading would approve standard clauses submitted by professional organisations and certify that such clauses were reasonable for incorporation into a contract between a professional and a consumer. Under such a scheme the Unfair Contract Terms Act would be amended so that it would not apply to such clauses. This suggestion is unlikely to see the light of day in view of the implementation of the EC Directive on unfair terms in consumer contracts[27] by the Unfair Terms in Consumer Contracts Regulations 1999.[28]

(ii) Capping

The Study Team examined the possibility of capping, i.e. introducing legislation to limit liability for damages resulting from negligence. However, they rejected the idea, for a variety of reasons, principally because they felt that it would be difficult to construct an equitable scheme. In any event, as we have just seen in the section on construction professionals, such a scheme seems to be unnecessary in view of the fact that under the provisions of section 11(4) of the Unfair Contract Terms Act it is possible for a small firm with limited financial resources to limit its liability for damages resulting from its negligence.

2. Compulsory PII

Since 1 January 1986 it has been compulsory for all chartered surveyors in private practice who are members of the RICS to take out PII. The Study Team recommended that insurance cover be compulsory stating that it would encourage standards to rise, promote risk management procedures, give added protection to the consumer, and put all practitioners on an equal footing in the market place. This seems a good recommendation based on sound reasoning. One could also add that insurance is a means of loss-spreading, i.e. it is better that the losses resulting from the negligence of surveyors be spread over the whole body of consumers of surveying services, rather than be allowed to lie on the unfortunate few. It has, however, resulted in a large increase in the number of claims and a huge rise in the cost of premiums.

3.   Strict liability

The introduction of no-fault liability for surveying services was, not surprisingly, rejected by the Study Team, principally because of the increase in PII premiums which, they felt, would inevitably result from such a reform. The introduction of strict liability into the law concerning the supply of services would, of course, be a major departure from the law as it stands, because it would involve an implied warranty as to results on the part of the supplier, something firmly rejected by the courts.[29]

THE LATHAM PROPOSALS

The Latham proposals are the result of a review which was undertaken into (a) the procurement and contractual arrangements of the UK construction industry, and (b) the current roles, responsibilities and performance of the participants in the construction process. That review was carried out by representatives of the Department of the Environment, the industry funding organisations,[30] the British Property Federation and the Chartered Institute of Purchasing and Supply. Eleven working groups were set up to implement the Latham proposals. Working Group 10 (WG10) was formed to develop the recommendations of the Latham Report concerning liability and latent defects insurance.

The Latham Report covers a wide range of procedural arrangements in the UK construction industry, including dispute resolution, as well as construction liability issues. This section of the chapter concentrates solely on the liability issues and proposals for their reform by Latham and WG10.[31] These proposals concern principally the following matters:

(1)   joint liability;
(2)   limitation periods;
(3)   transfer of clients' rights; and
(4)   latent defects insurance.

(1)   Joint liability

The Latham Report recommended that in construction cases (other than in relation to personal injury) defendants should have their liability limited to a fair proportion of the plaintiff's loss having regard to the relative degree of blame. All of the bodies represented on WG10 supported this proposal, which is almost identical to the proposal concerning joint liability in the

Likierman report. It is important to note, however, that the Likierman report recommended that there should be an exception to this rule for claims of less than £50,000 made by domestic clients.

In the view of WG10 a move away from joint liability would have two advantages for the construction industry. First, clients would have an incentive to define responsibility more clearly to avoid any possibility of joint liability. Secondly, it could overcome the defensiveness and lack of co-operation which is often the result of the current regime.

The present law is clearly of great concern to construction professionals and consultants, who may have only limited resources in which to meet a claim. True they can claim an indemnity against any other party who is also responsible for the plaintiff's loss, but that other party may have gone into liquidation. What both the Likierman and the Latham reports fail to point out, however, is that this problem can be dealt with by the use of a limitation clause in the professional/client contract, under which the professional would limit his liability to the client. Such a clause would be subject to the provisions of section 11(4) of the Unfair Contract Terms Act 1977.[32]

(2) Limitation periods

The Latham Report and WG10 recommend that these should be a single ten-year limitation period applying to all actions for defective building works, whether founded on breach of contract or in negligence. The limitation period should start to run from the date of practical completion or occupation of the whole building. This proposal is identical to that of the Likierman report.

The Likierman and Latham reports recommend that the ten-year limitation period should act as a long-stop and that its expiry should therefore extinguish the plaintiff's right rather than merely bar his remedy. WG10, however, recommend that the remedy merely be barred, in order to preserve rights of contribution and to ensure that indemnities should continue to operate outside the ten-year period.[33]

Section 32 of the Limitation Act 1980 provides for an extension to the limitation period in the event of deliberate concealment of facts relevant to the plaintiff's case by the defendant. The section makes no reference to any intention to deceive on the part of the defendant and deliberate concealment could therefore extend to the covering up of work in the course of the normal construction process. In order to avoid this interpretation of section 32, WG10 propose that deliberate concealment should extend the ten-year period only if it was carried out with an intent to deceive.

(3) Transfer of clients' rights

The Latham Report recommends that if a building is legally transferred to a subsequent owner or if it is leased under a full repairing and insuring lease then the client's contractual rights should be made available automatically to such successive owner or tenant. Any loss recoverable under this proposal should be limited to the cost of repair and reinstatement of the project. The following categories of loss should not be recoverable:

(a) damage to movable 'other' property;
(b) damage to the personal property of the occupants; and
(c) consequential and economic loss, except where it relates directly to the repair and reinstatement of the building to its originally intended condition.

This principle is supported by WG10.

In effect, the implementation of this proposal would put non-domestic buildings on the same footing as dwellings are under the provisions of the Defective Premises Act 1972 (though with a longer limitation period – ten years as opposed to six under the provisions of the 1972 Act). Under the provisions of the Contracts (Rights of Third Parties) Act 1999, subsequent owners and tenants are permitted a remedy against the contractor or design professional, if they are named in the contract between the client and contractor or design professional. The Latham/WG10 proposal goes much further than this; under it, subsequent owners and tenants of defective buildings would be able to obtain a remedy against the responsible party automatically, without the need to be named as a third party beneficiary in the contract between client and contractor or design professional. The Latham/WG10 proposal is a proposal for a statutory transmissible warranty of quality for non-domestic buildings.

(4)   Latent defects insurance

Latent defects insurance is a form of first party insurance whereby payment is made to the insured when certain specified kinds of damage appear in the building concerned. The Latham Report recommends that legislation should be introduced to provide for compulsory latent defects insurance for a period of ten years from the date of practical completion for all new commercial, retail and industrial building work.[34] This insurance, the Report states, should be based on BUILD insurance.[35] BUILD insurance was first proposed by the NEDC in 1988. Its essence is to provide non-cancellable material damage and insurance to cover the structure (including the foundations) and the weather shield envelope of the building for a period of ten years from the date of practical completion. Engineering services are not covered by BUILD.[36]

The Latham Report sees a number of advantages to introducing a statutory requirement to take out latent defects insurance. It would mean that insurance companies would become involved in construction quality and standards and, the report argues, they would insist on supervising such matters.[37] Further, the report states, the involvement of the insurance companies in construction quality would extend knowledge of defects and how to rectify them.[38]

The report of WG10 examines in more detail how such a statutory requirement would operate.[39] One of the most important questions concerning such a scheme is: who would be under a statutory duty to take out the insurance? There was a division of view within WG10 on this issue. One view was that the statutory obligation should be imposed on the main contractor, on the grounds that he was likely to be more experienced than the client in the purchase of such insurance due to being a regular buyer. If he was a bulk buyer then he might be able to buy it more cheaply than the client. The other view was the client should be required to take out the insurance as he was the primary beneficiary under the policy.

Latent defects insurance is generally arranged in the early stages of the design of the building, when the client submits a proposal form. The insurer would then grant cover subject to a satisfactory technical audit. WG10 was concerned that insurers should not make unreasonable demands before granting cover and they considered that the issue of what constitutes a satisfactory technical audit should be discussed further with insurers, client and the industry before any statutory scheme is drafted.

What would be the sanction for failing to take out the insurance? WG10 concluded that a failure to obtain suitable latent defects insurance should be treated in the same manner as a breach of the Building Regulations and should, therefore, be a criminal offence.

FEASIBILITY INVESTIGATION OF JOINT AND SEVERAL LIABILITY

In 1996 the Common Law Team of the Law Commission conducted a feasibility study of joint and several liability following attacks on this principle in a construction industry/ Department of the Environment (CI/DoE) Consultation Paper[40] and in a paper by The Institute of Chartered Accountants.[41]

The CI/DoE paper states that joint and several liability arises when more than one defendant is held to be liable for a particular action or activity, though the defendants have acted independently. The consultation paper puts forward a number of arguments for replacing this principle by proportionate liability. These arguments are as follows:

(1) In many cases a defendant who has met the whole of a plaintiff's claim will be able to claim a contribution from the other defendants, but he will not be able to do so where another defendant has become insolvent.

(2) The nature of construction projects makes the problems associated with joint and several liability more acute, because of the network of contracts and collateral warranties. The DoE paper states that in a worst

case scenario this could result in a defendant with, say, ten per cent liability meeting 100 per cent of the damages and the litigation costs.

(3)   A construction project often includes parties with a range of financial
      assets – consultants with comprehensive professional indemnity insur-
      ance, large companies with a solid financial base and smaller compa-
      nies with limited assets. In this situation, action tends to be taken
      against the 'deepest pocket', regardless of the extent of liability.

The CI/DoE consultation paper recommends that in construction cases not
involving personal injury, liability arising from latent defects should be sole
liability based on the apportionment of fault. The paper goes on to emphasise that in cases where there are concurrent liabilities defendants should
have their liability limited to a fair proportion of the plaintiff's loss, having
regard to the relative degree of blame.

The Common Law Team of the Law Commission in their feasibility study
explain this principle of proportionate liability as follows:

> Under a system of proportionate liability a concurrent wrongdoer's lia-
> bility to a plaintiff is limited to the extent of its [*sic.*] proportionate lia-
> bility. Thus, if P has suffered a £100,000 loss as a result of the
> wrongdoing of D1 and D2, each of whom is equally to blame, then the
> liability of each will be limited to £50,000 and there will be no right of
> contribution between them.[42]

The Common Law Team go on to point out that under such a system the loss
could be divided either between the parties to the action or between all the
wrongdoers.

The Common Law Team were not in favour of replacing joint and several
liability by full proportionate liability and they set out in their feasibility
study a number of arguments of principle for coming to this conclusion.[43]
The most important of these arguments are as follows. First, full proportionate liability is unfair to plaintiffs because it means that the risk of one defendant's insolvency is borne not by the other defendants as under the system
of joint and several liability, but by the plaintiff. Secondly, it is misleading
to say that defendants may have to pay 100 per cent of damages even though
they are, say ten per cent at fault. As a matter of causation and blameworthi-
ness relative to the plaintiff, joint and several liability follows from each
defendant being 100 per cent responsible for the whole of the plaintiff's loss.
The Common Law Team were also of the view that a modified scheme of
proportionate liability, where the plaintiff has been contributorily negligent,
was not justified.[44] Their overall conclusion was that a full Law Commission
project on joint and several liability should not be undertaken.

The Common Law Team, however, did discuss in their consultation paper
some possible alternative solutions to the problem of defendants with 'deep

pockets' and/or professional indemnity insurance.[45] The first of their alternatives is compulsory insurance schemes for all defendants. This would mean that if a plaintiff obtained judgement against one defendant, that defendant could be assured that his contribution claim against the other defendants would be met in full. The second of their alternatives is an examination of the operation of the requirement of reasonableness in the Unfair Contract Terms Act 1977 to the exclusion or limitation of professional liability for economic loss. Despite the provisions of section 11(4) of that Act, the Common Law Team felt that more detailed guidance is needed on exemption or limitation clauses.[46] Their third alternative is for a capping of professional liability by statute though the Common Law Team noted that this would be a departure from the principle of full compensation for plaintiffs and they conclude that 'it simply benefits defendants at the expense of plaintiffs.'[47]

THE LIMITED LIABILITY PARTNERSHIPS ACT 2000

The Limited Liability Partnerships Act 2000 creates a new form of legal entity, the limited liability partnership (LLP). The essential feature of an LLP is that it is a body corporate and is a legal person separate from its members. The idea for the introduction of this form of business organisation in Great Britain arose from the DTI's feasibility investigation of joint and several liability, discussed in the previous section of this chapter, and its subsequent consultation on whether the concept of the LLP should become part of English and Scottish law. In February 1997 the Department published a consultation paper, 'Limited Liability Partnerships: A New Form of Business Association for Professions'. The response was favourable to the introduction of the LLP.

The LLP goes some way to meeting the concerns expressed in the Likierman and Latham reports about unlimited liability for partners in the light of a general increase in professional negligence claims and in the size of those claims. The LLP's existence as a corporate entity means that it is more akin to a company than to a partnership: a third party will usually contract with the LLP itself rather than with an individual partner. Should a partner be negligent in the work that he carries out for a client, the client's action *in contract* will lie against the LLP.

However, the introduction of the LLP does not meet all of the concerns of professional persons about unlimited liability. Although an action *in contract* for negligent work by a member of an LLP will generally be brought against the LLP, a *tort* action is still available against the partner himself.

LAW COMMISSION'S PROPOSALS FOR REFORM OF THE LAW OF LIMITATION OF ACTIONS

In 1984 the Law Reform Committee stated that the law of limitation of actions should be governed by three principles:

(i)   plaintiffs must have a fair and sufficient opportunity of pursuing their remedy;

(ii) defendants are entitled to be protected against stale claims; and

(iii) uncertainty in the law is to be avoided wherever possible.[48]

The Law Commission, in their consultation paper on the law of limitation of actions, lay great stress on the uncertainty and complexity of the present law, in terms of the different limitation periods, as a pressing argument for reform. They also point to the unfairness that can result from the inconsistencies produced by so many regimes.[49]

In place of the present law, the Law Commission propose a core regime applicable to most causes of action in contract and tort. The central features of the core regime would be as follows:

(1)   There would be an initial limitation period of three years that would run from the date when the plaintiff knows, or ought reasonably to know, that he has a cause of action.

(2)   There would be a long-stop limitation period of ten years, or in personal injury claims of 30 years, that would run from the date of the act or omission which gives rise to the claim.

(3)   Deliberate concealment (initial and subsequent) would extend the long-stop. Acknowledgements and part payments would start time running again but not once the initial or long-stop limitation period has expired.

(4)   There would be no judicial discretion to disapply a limitation period.[50]

These proposals apply to the general law of obligations. Their particular significance for Construction Law is the recommendation for a ten-year long-stop, which would replace the existing 15-year long-stop. We have seen that the Likierman and Latham reports recommend a ten-year long-stop for claims for defective building works. It is important to note a crucial difference between the Likierman/Latham proposal and the Law Commission proposal. Likierman and Latham propose that the ten-year long-stop should start to run on the date of practical completion of the building; the Law Commission propose that the ten-year long-stop should commence when the plaintiff discovers, or should discover, that he has a claim. The Law Commission proposal is more favourable to the plaintiff for the date of discoverability may be long after the date of practical completion of the building.

PROPOSED HARMONISATION OF CONSTRUCTION LIABILITY IN THE EUROPEAN UNION

In October 1988 the European Parliament adopted a resolution calling for the standardisation of contract clauses, the harmonisation of responsibilities and the promotion of housing insurance in the construction industry. In response, the European Commission sponsored a study into these issues under the chairmanship of Claude Mathurin, the French General Engineer of Bridges and Roads. His report, known as the Mathurin Report, was published in February 1990.[51] It has largely been superseded by the work of a number of pan European construction industry groups which have been set up by the Commission to consider the issues raised by harmonising construction liability. These groups are known as the GAIPEC working groups.[52] It is their proposals which will form the basis of any draft directive on this subject, and not those of the Mathurin Report. Nonetheless the Mathurin Report is an important landmark in the development of this subject and it is instructive to examine its proposals.

The Mathurin Report

The Mathurin Report was the result of a survey of the general characteristics of construction liability in the legal systems of the Member States. It set out the case for harmonisation of construction liability in terms of the now familiar aims of the New Approach Directives, namely contributing to the creation of a single market by removing legal obstacles to free trade between the Member States and protecting the consumer. It recommended three directives to achieve harmonisation:

  (i)   a directive defining the role of the main parties in the construction process – client, designer, contractor, building control officer etc;
 (ii)   a directive on the responsibilities of architects and engineers in the construction process; and
(iii)   a directive devoted to liability, guarantees and insurance.

  It was the third of these proposed directives that was the most important of the Report's recommendations. The main elements of this proposal are as follows:

  (i)   There should be a standardised specific liability of the builder. In particular, the Report recommended that the liability of the builder should be invoked in the event of a breach of any of the six essential requirements contained in the Construction Products Directive. This specific liability should be for a ten-year period except in two cases, where liability would be for a 30-year period:
        (a) a collapse of the structure; and

(b) a deterioration of the structure to the extent that it becomes impossible, functionally and economically, to use it as originally planned.

(ii) For every new structure and every renovated structure constructed by a builder or sold within five years of its approval, there should be a guarantee as to soundness of structure backed by a third party. This guarantee was to be known as 'a European guarantee', and it would have signified that the structure met certain harmonised standards, in particular the six essential requirements of the Construction Products Directive. In the case of housing, the Report recommended that the European guarantee should, in addition, contain a guarantee of satisfactory delivery of the structure in the event of the builder's failure to perform. The Report recommended that the absence of a guarantee should be a criminal offence.

(iii) The liability of the developer and builder should be strict, but the specific liabilities of the other parties should depend upon the existence of proof of a causal link between the damage suffered and the service supplied, and also of proof of a party's negligence.

The Report was clearly much influenced by the UK's NHBC scheme and the recommended third directive is, in effect, an extension of the principle underlying that scheme to non-residential buildings.

The GAIPEC proposals

It is the proposals of the GAIPEC working groups which are likely to form the basis of any future directive on construction liability. These proposals were published in an annex to a Commission staff discussion paper.[53] This paper reaches no conclusions and contains no recommendations. Rather, it raises a number of questions for discussion on any future harmonisation of construction law in light of the principle of subsidiarity set out in Article 3b of the Maastricht Treaty. In particular, the paper invites comments on a number of specific matters:

- scope;
- acceptance;
- liability;
- financial guarantee; and
- quality control.

The limits of space means that the range of influences which impinge on these matters cannot all be examined in this text. Nonetheless, reference to the key issues is essential. In the first place, there are two aspects to scope: material scope and legal scope. The main question which the discussion paper sees in relation to the material scope of any future actions is whether it should be limited to consumer protection and include only dwellings or extend to include construction works other than housing. In relation to legal scope, the discussion paper sees the main issue as whether any community measure should apply to all liabilities borne by participants in the construction process or whether it should be confined to contractual liability. The second key issue is the conditions which should govern the liability of participants: should the liability of the participants be based on proven fault (which is the rule at present applying in most Member States) or should there be a presumption of fault, whereby the plaintiff would have to prove only the existence of damage or a causal link between this damage and the activity of the defendant. The discussion paper states that whatever definition of fault is finally adopted, it must take account of the six essential requirements of the Construction Products Directive.[54] The discussion paper goes on to point out that the GAIPEC working groups are in favour of the introduction of a financial guarantee, but it states that the principle of subsidiarity may allow the Member States to deal with the practical implementation of such a measure. Finally, the discussion paper emphasises that the aim of liability and guarantee measures is to improve the quality of construction works. In this connection, it raises the question of whether there should be a Community quality control system, with the implementation of such a system again in the hands of the Member States.

CONCLUSION

The question at the heart of any discussion on the reform of construction law is how wide the ambit of third party liability should be drawn.Readers of this work will be aware that the recent dramatic swings in the tort of negligence have mostly involved building and construction cases. It is for this reason that Construction Law is so illuminating an area of study; it highlights the problematical areas of economic loss and negligence and the relationship between contract and tort. None of the proposals for reform discussed so far in this chapter really address these issues. The Likierman Study Teams were set up at a time when the law of negligence had become plaintiff-orientated and they were concerned to redress the balance of the law in favour of the defendant. The Latham/WG10 proposals for reform of limitation periods again favour defendants; their proposal for compulsory latent defects insurance leave unresolved a number of crucial issues, not least the extent of the loss to be covered by such insurance. The Law Commission's proposals for reform of limitation periods strike a fairer balance between the interests of plaintiffs and defendants than do those of Likierman and Latham on this subject, but a fair limitation period is of no avail to a plaintiff who has no cause of action.

The decisions of the House of Lords in *D & F Estates* and *Murphy* brought to an end the expansionist phase of negligence. Since those decisions were handed down, there has been a re-emergence of negligence in the form of concurrent liability in contract and tort of professional persons following the decision of the House of Lords in *Henderson* v. *Merrett Syndicates Ltd* and the expansion of *Hedley Byrne* v. *Heller* liability following the decisions of the House of Lords in *White* v. *Jones* and *Spring* v. *Guardian Assurance plc*. There is no evidence, however, that these developments have disturbed the exclusionary rule in relation to third party liability in negligence and the passage in Lord Goff's speech in *Henderson* stressing the continuing sanctity of the matrix of contracts in a construction project should never be forgotten by a construction lawyer.

The passing of the Contracts (Rights of Third Parties) Act 1999 is one of the most significant reforms to have occurred since the publication of the first edition of this work. It must be remembered, however, that the benefit of a contract will extend to a third party only if he is named in the contract or if on a proper construction of the contract it appears that the parties intended it to be enforceable by him. Thus, if the parties to a construction contract do not name a third party as a beneficiary and it cannot be said that on a proper construction of the contract they intended it to be enforceable by him, then that third party will be without a remedy under the Act in the event of the building proving defective. Moreover, if a building is transferred to a third party after the building contract was concluded it cannot be said that the contracting parties intended to confer a benefit on the third party.

The conclusion which must be drawn from this analysis is that only a reform of tort law in the area of premises liability can substantially improve the legal position of third parties in the construction process. In devising such reform there is clearly a balance of interests to be struck. On the one hand, there is the interest of plaintiffs. If they are subsequent purchasers or tenants of a commercial building which proves defective they will now be without a remedy against the builder or designer of the building. A subsequent purchaser or lessee of a dwelling subject to an NHBC guarantee will be in a stronger position but only if the defects reveal themselves before the expiry of ten years following completion of the building. Many such plaintiffs will not have first party insurance to cover defects such as subsidence or heave. On the other hand, there is the interest of defendants with their (arguably quite legitimate) fear of virtually unlimited liability and very high PII premiums.[55] Arguably tort law is the proper vehicle for achieving a satisfactory balance of these conflicting interests. Contract law is designed to give effect to the intention of the parties to the contract in question and despite statutory intervention it is largely *laissez-faire* in its philosophy. It is not essentially a regulatory mechanism for re-allocating losses. Tortious liabilities, in contrast, are imposed by the law and it is just that characteristic of tort law that makes it so suitable for carrying out a regulatory role.

A new Defective Premises Act?

The English appellate courts have set their face against a regulatory or welfarist philosophy of the common law of tort. The Law Lords in *D & F Estates* and *Murphy* were adamant that it is the task of the legislature to carry out any reform of product and premises liability. Statute law reform seems to be the only way forward in this area and a new Defective Premises Act has been suggested as one solution.[56] The purpose of this statutory reform would be to replace existing duties contained in section 1 of the Defective Premises Act 1972 with a new strict liability duty for the quality of buildings. Such an Act should apply to all buildings, not just dwellings. Sections 1 and 2 of the 1972 Act would be repealed.

The key problem for such new legislation would be to define the content of the new duty. It is essential that it address the issue of economic loss and liability for defective buildings, and clarify exactly the nature of the loss to be covered, thus avoiding the ambiguity of the duty in the 1972 Act.[57] It should allow recovery for economic loss not just by the other contracting party, but also by all third parties in the construction process. Such liability would be imposed on the main contractor, subcontractor, design professionals, developers and local authorities.

The enactment of such a duty would repeal the common law rule on negligence and economic loss in relation to buildings laid down in *D & F Estates* and *Murphy*. The Law Lords in those cases saw recovery for economic loss as solely the province of the law of contract and they considered that creating tortious liability for defective buildings would lead to the introduction into English law of a transmissible warranty of quality for products. The origins of those arguments lie in the dissenting speech of Lord Brandon in *Junior Books* v. *Veitchi*.[58] He asked: if there were a warranty of quality in tort by what standard would such warranty be judged? He clearly saw this as an insurmountable obstacle to any liability in tort to third parties for a defective building or for a defective chattel. It has not proved to be an insurmountable problem in other jurisdictions. Thus in New Zealand the Consumer Guarantees Act 1993, which came into effect on 1 April 1994, introduced liability on the part of the manufacturer of a defective chattel towards the ultimate purchaser for the cost of repairing it, where such purchaser is a consumer. The Act sets out a number of guarantees which are implied where goods or services are supplied to a consumer.[59] The consumer will have an action against the manufacturer where the goods fail to comply with the guarantee as to acceptable quality and with the guarantee as to correspondence with description where the description was applied by on behalf of the manufacturer. In short it allows the consumer to enforce the familiar implied terms in the Sale of Goods Act[60] against the manufacturer as well as the retailer. This is clearly a consumer protection measure in the field of personal estate. However, it is suggested that its provisions could form a basis for a new English Defective Premises Act, where such guarantees of quality could apply to real estate and to commercial buildings as well as dwellings.

A new Defective Premises Act of this kind is unlikely to conflict with the provisions of any future EU directive on construction liability. Until such a reform is put in place that elusive balance between the interests of plaintiffs and defendants in the construction process is unlikely to be achieved.

SUMMARY

1. Two legal concepts have dominated Construction Law: the doctrine of privity of contract and the exclusionary rule relating to negligence and economic loss.

2. An important exception to the doctrine of privity was created by the Contracts (Rights of Third Parties) Act 1999, which permits a third party to enforce a term of a contract if he is named in the contract as having a legally enforceable right under the contract or if, on a proper construction of the contract, the term purports to confer such obligation on him.

3. If neither of these statutory requirements is met then the third party will have no remedy under the 1999 Act.

4. Under the exclusionary rule, a building contractor will not be liable to tenants or subsequent purchasers of the building in tort for economic losses sustained by those parties as a result of defects in the buildings. The development of concurrent liability in tort, following the decision of the House of Lords in *Henderson* v. *Merrett Syndicates* has not affected the exclusionary rule.

5. There have been a number of proposals for the reform of Construction Law and of the common law in general which would affect construction liability.

6. The Latham report and a CI/DoE report proposed the replacement of joint and several liability by proportionate liability for cases not involving personal injury but this proposal was rejected firmly by the Common Law Team of the Law Commission.

7. The Likierman and Latham reports recommended a single ten-year limitation period applying to all actions for defective building works. This period should start to run from the date of practical completion of the works.

8. The Law Commission propose two limitation periods: an initial limitation period of three years, to run from the date when the plaintiff knows, or should know, that he has a cause of action, and a long-stop limitation

period of ten years (or 30 years in personal injury cases) to run from the date of the act or omission giving rise to the claim.

9. A European Commission paper has made a number of propsals for the harmonisation of construction liability throughout the European Union.
10. None of these proposals for reform affect the exclusionary rule in relation to third party liability in negligence for defective building works.

NOTES

1. *Hancock* v. *Brazier* [1966] 2 All ER 901 and sections 4 and 13 of the Supply of Goods and Services Act 1982.
2. *Murphy* v. *Brentwood District Council* [1990] 2 All ER 908, p.919 (*per* Lord Keith), p.928 (*per* Lord Bridge) and p.932 (per Lord Oliver).
3. *Murphy* v. *Brentwood District Council*, *ibid*, n.2.
4. *Greaves & Co. (Contractors) Ltd* v. *Baynham Meikle* [1975] 3 All ER 99.
5. *Smith* v. *Bush*; *Harris* v. *Wyre Forest District Council* [1989] 2 All ER 514.
6. *Henderson* v. *Merrett Syndicates* [1995] 2 AC 145.
7. [1988] 2 All ER 992.
8. *Op. cit.*, n.5.
9. *Bates* [1990] EG 57, referred to in Law Commission Consultation Paper 121 (1991) p.78.
10. [1964] AC 465.
11. *Op. cit.*, n.6.
12. [1995] 2 AC 267.
13. *Supra*, n.10, p.516.
14. *Supra*, n.6, p.181.
15. See Chapter 3.
16. (1995) 74 BLR 35, p.52.
17. *Professional Liability – Report of the Study Teams*, HMSO, 1989.
18. *Privity of Contract: Contracts for the Benefit of Third Parties*, Law Com. No. 242 (1996).
19. Discussed in Chapter 9.
20. Sir Michael Latham, *Constructing the Team*, HMSO, 1994.
21. The Construction Industry Board, *Liability Law and Latent Defects Insurance*, 1997.
22. Department of Trade and Industry, *Feasibility Investigation of Joint and Several Liability*, HMSO, 1996.
23. Law Commission Consultation Paper No. 151 (1998).
24. See the Mathurin Report (1990) and the GAIPEC proposals (1993).
25. These can be obtained from the Construction Directorate of the Department of the Environment.
26. Section 11(4) provides that where a person seeks to restrict his liability in this way, the court shall have regard to (a) the resources which he would expect to be available to him for the purpose of meeting the liability; and (b) how far it was open to him to cover himself by insurance.
27. 93/13/EEC, OJ 1993 L.95/29.
28. SI 1999 No. 2083. See Chapter 3.
29. See *Greaves & Co (Contractors) Ltd* v. *Baynham Meikle* [1975] 3 All ER 99 and *Thake* v. *Maurice* [1986] QB 644.
30. Details of these organisations are contained in Appendix 1 of the Latham Report.

31. Liability issues are discussed principally in Chapters 8 and 11 of the Latham Report. The Latham proposals in this area are based on the majority report of a working party set up by the DoE in 1993 to discuss post completion liability for defective buildings.
32. *Op. cit.*, n.26.
33. See pp.11–12 of the WG10 report.
34. Para. 11.24.
35. Para. 11.23.
36. BUILD is described in more detail in Chapter 9.
37. Para. 11.19.
38. Para. 11.20.
39. See Chapter 4 of the WG10 report.
40. *Latent Defects Liability and Build' Insurance*, 1995.
41. *Auditors' Liability: The Public Interest Perspective*, 1995.
42. *Supra*, n.22, para. 3.5.
43. *Supra*, n.22, paras 3.12–3.16.
44. *Supra*, n.22, Part IV.
45. *Supra*, n.22, Part V.
46. *Supra*, n.22, para. 5.19.
47. *Supra*, n.22, para. 5.37.
48. *Twenty-fourth Report: Latent Damage* (Cmnd. 9390, 1984), para. 4.1.
49. Law Commission Consultation Paper No. 151, paras 1.23–1.28. See also Burrows, Andrew, *Understanding the Law of Obligations*, Hart Publishing, Oxford, 1998, pp.179–181.
50. The statutory discretion in section 33 of the Limitation Act 1980 has led to over 115 appellate decisions: Burrows, *op. cit.*, n.41, p.181.
51. It is available free of charge from Agence Qualité' Construction, 30 Place de la Madeleine, Paris 75008.
52. Groupe des Associations Industrielles et Professionnelles Européenes de la Construction.
53. Commission of the European Communities, *Commission staff discussion paper concerning possible community action with regard to liabilities and guarantees in the construction sector* (1993).
54. 89/106/EEC, OJ No. L40/12. Implemented in the UK by the Construction Products Regulations 1991 (SI 1991 No. 1620). See Chapter 11.
55. The problems facing owners of defective dwellings are highlighted in the report of the National Consumer Council, *Murphy's Law* (1991); the problems facing owners and occupiers of commercial buildings under the law as it now stands are described in the NEDO BUILD report; for a forceful presentation of the difficulties facing defendants see the Inaugural Lecture of the Centre for Professional Law and Practice, University of Leicester given by Lord Oliver and published in (1988) 4 PN 173.
56. See Nicholas Brown (1990) 6 PN 150.
57. See *Thompson* v. *Alexander* (1992) 59 BLR 77.
58. [1983] 1 AC 520.
59. For a more detailed account of the provisions of the Act, see Todd (1993) 9 PN 54.
60. In this case, the New Zealand Sale of Goods Act 1908.

Bibliography

Primary sources

The primary sources of Construction Law are, as in any other area of law, case-law, UK statutes and European legislation. They are to be found in the tables at the beginning of this work.

Secondary sources

The following are the texts in Construction Law and related areas to which I have principally referred in the preparation of this work. Other texts and journal articles are referred to in the notes.

Allen, D.K., *Latent Damage Act 1986,* Current Law Statutes Annotated, Ch. 37, Sweet & Maxwell, 1986.

Bickford-Smith, S., Palmer, N. and Redman-Cooper, R., *Butterworths Construction Law Manual*, Butterworths, 1993.

Burns, A., *The Legal Obligations of the Architect,* Butterworths, 1994.

Burrows, A., *Understanding the Law of Obligations,* Hart Publishing, Oxford, 1998, pp.179–181.

Construction Industry Board, *Liability Law and Latent Defects Insurance*, 1997.

Consumer Council, *Murphy's Law,* 1991.

Cornes, D.L., *Design Liability in the Construction Industry,* 3rd edn, Blackwell Scientific Publications, 1989.

DTI/DoE, *Professional Liability – Report of the Study Teams* (The Likierman Report), HMSO, London 1989.

DTI, *Feasibility Investigation of Joint and Several Liability by the Common Law Team of the Law Commission*, HMSO, 1996.

Emden's Construction Law, 8th edn, Butterworths, 1990, Binder 1.

Furmston, M.P., *Cheshire, Fifoot & Furmston's Law of Contract,* 13th edn, Butterworths, 1996.

Furmston, M., *Powell-Smith & Furmston's Building Contract Casebook*, 3rd edn, Blackwell Scientific Publications, 2000, Chs 6, 19, 22 and 23.

Furst, S. and Ramsey, V., *Keating on Building Contracts*, 7th edn, Sweet & Maxwell, 2001.

Geddes, A., *Product and Services Liability in the EEC,* Sweet & Maxwell, 1992.

Hepple, B.A. and Mathews, M.H., *Tort: Cases and Materials,* 5th edn, Butterworths, 2000.

Holyoak, J.H., *Negligence in Building,* Blackwell Scientific Publications, 1992.

Holyoak, J.H. and Allen, D.K., *Civil Liability for Defective Premises,* Butterworths, 1982.

Jackson, R.M. and Powell, J.L., *Jackson & Powell on Professional Negligence,* 4th edn, Sweet & Maxwell, 1997.

Jones, Neil F. & Co., *Professional Negligence in the Construction Industry,* LLP Reference Publishing, 1998.

Latham, Sir Michael, *Constructing the Team,* HMSO, 1994.

Law Commission, *Privity of Contract: Contracts for the Benefit of Third Parties,* Law Com. No. 242, London, HMSO, 1996.

Law Commission, *Limitation of Actions,* Consultation Paper No. 151, London, HMSO, 1998.

Morgan, D., *Limitation Act 1980,* Current Law Statutes Annotated, Ch. 58, Sweet & Maxwell, 1980.

Rogers, W.V.H., *Winfield & Jolowicz on Tort,* 15th edn, Sweet & Maxwell, 1998.

Speaight, A. and Stone, G., *The Law of Defective Premises,* Butterworths, 1982.

Speaight, A. and Stone, G. (Eds), *AJ Legal Handbook,* 6th edn, The Architectural Press, 1996.

Uff, J., *Construction Law,* 7th edn, Sweet & Maxwell, 1999.

Weir, T., *A Casebook on Tort,* 9th edn, Sweet & Maxwell, 2000.

Winward Fearan & Co., *Collateral Warranties,* Blackwell Scientific Publications, 1990.

Index